The Lewis Walpole Series in Eighteenth-Century Culture and History

The Lewis Walpole Series, published by Yale University Press with the aid of the Annie Burr Lewis Fund, is dedicated to the culture and history of the long eighteenth century (from the Glorious Revolution to the accession of Queen Victoria). It welcomes work in a variety of fields, including literature and history, the visual arts, political philosophy, music, legal history, and the history of science. In addition to original scholarly work, the series publishes new editions and translations of writing from the period, as well as reprints of major books that are currently unavailable. Though the majority of books in the series will probably concentrate on Great Britain and the Continent, the range of our geographical interests is as wide as Horace Walpole's.

DEMOCRACY IN DARKNESS

Secrecy and Transparency in the Age of Revolutions

KATLYN MARIE CARTER

Yale
UNIVERSITY PRESS
New Haven and London

Published with assistance from the Annie Burr Lewis Fund and from the foundation established in memory of Philip Hamilton McMillan of the Class of 1894, Yale College.

Yale University Press books may be purchased in quantity for educational, business, or promotional use. For information, please email sales.press@yale.edu (U.S. office) or sales@yaleup.co.uk (U.K. office).

Set in Janson type by IDS Infotech, Ltd.
Printed in the United States of America.

Library of Congress Control Number: 2023931892
ISBN 978-0-300-24692-6 (hardcover : alk. paper)

A catalogue record for this book is available from the British Library.

This paper meets the requirements of ANSI/NISO Z39.48-1992 (Permanence of Paper).

10 9 8 7 6 5 4 3 2 1

To my parents

Contents

Acknowledgments ix

Introduction 1

PART I SUSPECTING SECRECY

1. Piercing the Impenetrable Darkness 23
2. Cracking the *Secret du Roi* 57

PART II PERFORMING PUBLICITY

3. Behind the Veil of Secrecy 75
4. Building a House of Glass 104
5. Mere Spectators of Events 136
6. Politics Behind the Curtain 167

PART III SPECTATORSHIP

7. Surrounded by Spectators 205
8. The Disastrous Effects of Publicity 237

Epilogue: Democracy Dies in Darkness? 267

Notes 279

Index 369

Acknowledgments

As with everything in life, this book is the product of generosity and encouragement from family, friends, mentors, colleagues, interlocutors, and institutions. It would be impossible for me to adequately express my sincere gratitude to all of them.

The origins of this project date back to my time studying history as an undergraduate at the University of California, Berkeley. There, I had the privilege to learn from many inspiring graduate students and faculty, especially Carla Hesse, who took me under her wing as a research assistant and gave me the confidence to do historical research. I also worked as a reporter and editor at the *Daily Californian*, which taught me more than any class ever could about the press. Before Berkeley, I was fortunate that my first introduction to what it means to study history came early, at Beaverton High School. There, with the guidance of Peter Edwards especially, I developed a love for reading and writing history. My interest in French history in particular is owed to my time at the French American International School, where my teachers gave me the gift of foreign language and appreciation for another culture.

I generated the questions that motivate this book and undertook the research that undergirds it at Princeton University. The mentorship of the faculty there was a gift of inestimable value. My advisor, David A. Bell, encouraged me to ask big questions and prepared me to execute the necessary research. I cannot thank him enough for his thoughtful engagement with every piece of my written work, from my first-year seminar papers to this completed book. He has been my relentless champion and his balance of encouragement and rigorous criticism made this manuscript better at every stage. Sean Wilentz was generous enough to take me on as a student who came to him as a scholar of France wanting to explore the American Revolution. He guided me through my initial foray into American history and constantly pushed me to think bigger. Linda Colley's work has long been an inspiration to me and her confidence in my ability has significantly shaped this project and my scholarly trajectory. I am deeply indebted to Wendy Warren, whose seminar on colonial American history led me to pursue transnational research. She has provided me honest advice and a model of scholarship I strive to emulate. Sophia Rosenfeld's scholarship inspired my attempt to write a history that was not bounded by national borders and her engagement with my work has significantly shaped this book. Beyond my committee, I was fortunate to learn from many great minds at Princeton, especially Anthony Grafton, Philip Nord, Yair Mintzker, Alec Dun, Michael Gordin, Ekaterina Pravilova, Eleanor Hubbard, Adam Beaver, and Janet Chen.

Princeton was more than an intellectual community to me; it became a home. The French historians in the department—Nimisha Barton, David Moak, Zoe Buonaiuto, Benjamin Bernard, Matthew McDonald, and especially Patrick De Oliveira (who weathered the archival experience alongside me in Paris)—all enriched my work and became good friends. Graduate school was fun and writing invigorating thanks to the friendships that grew in Dickinson Hall and Firestone Library. I am especially thankful to Richard Anderson, Dan Barish, Olivier Burtin, James Casey, Christian Flow, Josh Garrett-Davis, Joppan George, Saarah Jappie, Tommi Lankila, Jane Manners, Diana Andrade, Lee Mordechai, Morgan Robinson, Fidel Tavarez, Sean Vanatta, Matthew Chan, Teresa Davis, Heidi Hausse, Molly Lester, Chris Florio, Alex Chase-Levenson, Meg Leja, Andrew Edwards, Emily Kern, Emily Prifogle, Kalyani Ramnath, Devika Shankar, Joel Suarez, Paula Vedoveli, José Argueta Funes, and Anne Kerth. I was also fortunate enough to make friends outside the history department, who continue to provide very welcome refuge from purely scholarly talk: Sara Vanatta, Veronica Valentin, Elise Wang, Jasmin Mujanovic, and Rohit Lamba.

Writing this book took me around the world. In Paris, I spent many days in the Archives Nationales and I am thankful for the patience of the archivists and staff at the Marais and Pierrefitte sites. I also spent many afternoons in the Bibliothèque Historique de la Ville de Paris and the Bibliothèque nationale de France, where I am grateful to the librarians and staff who helped me access the materials I sought. In the United States, I undertook research at multiple institutions with generous grants from each one. At the Historical Society of Pennsylvania and Library Company of Philadelphia, I benefited from conversations with Jim Green and Connie King. There, I became friends with Nora Slonimsky and Mark Boonshoft; my conversations with them since have been enormously fruitful. I am grateful to Kate Viens and Conrad Wright for their suggestions and help navigating the collections at the Massachusetts Historical Society and to the staff at the Virginia Historical Society. While in Boston, I was welcomed by Corinna, Jan, and Tommy Matlis, who made my stay enjoyable. I also spent a memorable month at the Fred W. Smith National Library for the Study of George Washington at Mount Vernon. There, I discussed my ideas with Lindsay Chervinsky, Erin Holmes, and Douglas Bradburn. Their curiosity and knowledge helped me see my work from new angles.

All of this research was made possible by financial support I received from the Princeton History Department, Princeton Institute for International and Regional Studies, the American Society for Eighteenth-Century Studies, the Council for European Studies, the Omohundro Institute of Early American History & Culture, the Laurance S. Rockefeller Graduate Prize Fellowship at the University Center for Human Values at Princeton, and the Friends of the APS Fellowship in Early American History at the American Philosophical Society.

I finished my dissertation there, in an office overlooking Independence Hall. My thinking benefited greatly from discussions with Patrick Spero, Dave Gary, Estelle Markel-Joyet, and Abby Shelton, who pointed me in the direction of many sources. This project was also enriched by conversations with other fellows at the APS, particularly Alexandra Montgomery, Brandon Layton, Amy Ellison, and Diana Marsh. I began to turn my dissertation into a book as a postdoctoral fellow at the University of Michigan's Weiser Center for Emerging Democracies in Ann Arbor. There, I gained interdisciplinary insight and camaraderie from my peers—Margaret Hanson, Jean Lachapelle, Fiona Shen-Bayh, and Natalia Forrat—and mentors, Allen Hicken, Dan Slater, Gregory Dowd, Joshua Cole, Susan Juster, Deena Goodman, Matthew Spooner, and Lisa Disch. The Weiser Center facilitated a manuscript workshop in which Paul Friedland, Seth Cotlar, Nathan Perl-Rosenthal, and Gregory Dowd generously participated. Their thoughtful engagement with my manuscript made the book considerably stronger.

I completed this book at the University of Notre Dame, where I was welcomed in the department of history and supported especially by

Elisabeth Köll and Jon Coleman as department chairs and by John McGreevy and Kathleen Sprows Cummings as mentors. Patrick Griffin's rigorous reading of my manuscript and his advice have been invaluable. I have also benefited from the guidance and insight of Alexander Martin, Karen Graubart, Darren Dochuck, Brad Gregory, Ted Beatty, John Deak, Daniel Graff, Margaret Meserve, Julia Adeney Thomas, Thomas Tweed, and Mariana Candido. I spent a memorable year as a fellow at the Notre Dame Institute for Advanced Study, where Meghan Sullivan's support bolstered me a great deal. Throughout, my students have kept me thinking about this project in new ways—especially Brigid Harrington, who worked as my research assistant, checking facts and gathering references for this book. South Bend has become my home thanks to friends like Sarah Shortall, Joshua Specht, Emily Remus, Randy Goldstein, Rebecca McKenna, James Lundberg, Katie Jarvis, Ian Johnson, Liang Cai, Korey Garibaldi, Francisco Robles, Pedro Aguilera-Mellado, Kate Uitti, Abi Ocobock, and Paul Ocobock—who went above and beyond reading this book's introduction at the last hour.

I thank Yale University Press, the anonymous reviewers, and my editor, Adina Popescu Berk, for steering the book through the publication process. Portions of chapters 3 and 6 appeared in an article published in the *Journal of the Early Republic*, which Andrew Shankman and the anonymous reviewers strengthened significantly. I also owe thanks to Joanna Hope Toohey, who took pictures for this book in the Archives Nationales, and to Emily McKnight and Elizabeth Casey for their careful copyediting. I am grateful for support from the Institute for Scholarship in the Liberal Arts, College of Arts and Letters, at the University of Notre Dame. While I cannot personally thank every interlocutor who has shaped my thinking along the way, I can confidently attest that exchanges in every conference, workshop, and seminar at which I presented were formative.

To my friends and family who have known me since before I began this project—especially Cristina Bautista, Bryan Thomas, Katherine Young, Lia Johnston, Megan Cook, and Reed VanBeveren—I can't thank you enough for listening to me ramble about the eighteenth century and vent about the writing process. A special thank you goes to Donna Canada-Smith, who spent a summer alongside me in the archives and very kindly read my full manuscript with a keen eye for detail.

Above all, I thank my family. My grandparents, Barbara and Milo Wood and Harry and Carol Carter, lived remarkable lives and I think of them often. My cousins Barbara Goodwin and Harvey Pye and my uncle

Tom Wood have been my cheerleaders for as long as I can remember. I have inspiring siblings in Carolyn, Jackson, and Logan Carter. They have been my constant companions and sources of inspiration as I watch them pursue their own dreams. And to my parents, David and Melinda Carter, who have given me every opportunity, believed in me always, and never questioned my path: this book is dedicated to them.

Not only this book but my entire life would not be what it is without Nikhil Menon. He read and improved every page of this manuscript, endured countless hours discussing democracy, and built me up through every episode of doubt. He has made my work better, my life more meaningful, and my world joyful. I cannot possibly thank him enough for his unflagging support and love. As I finished this book, we welcomed our daughter, Anjali Olivia, to the world. She is a bundle of energy and ray of light—she is everything.

DEMOCRACY IN DARKNESS

Introduction

WHEN PROMINENT MEN FROM across the newly independent American states gathered in Philadelphia over the summer of 1787, few outside knew exactly what they were doing within the walls of the Pennsylvania State House on Chestnut Street. Meeting behind closed doors, with guards planted outside, the delegates drew curtains and nailed windows shut to thwart potential eavesdroppers. The members of the Constitutional Convention hashed out a new political framework for the United States in secret.

One morning that sweltering summer, a delegate accidentally dropped his notes outside. They were picked up and delivered into the hands of the famous general George Washington, who had been recognized as the president of the convention. After the deliberations ended that afternoon, Washington stood up and threw the papers down on a table, declaring: "I am sorry to find that some one Member of this Body, has been so neglectful of the secrets of the Convention as to drop in the State House a copy of their proceedings." The legendary commander's frustration was reportedly so intense that he "quitted the room with a dignity so severe that every Person seemed alarmed." William Pierce, a delegate from Georgia, recounted approaching the table with anguish after he had reached in his pocket to find his own copy of the proceedings missing. Only when he saw that the notes were in another's handwriting and then found his copy in a coat pocket that night did he breathe a sigh of relief. No one, according to Pierce's recollection, ever claimed the dropped papers.[1]

Across the Atlantic, almost exactly two years later, more than a thousand delegates gathered in a vast converted storage hall outside the gates of the opulent palace of Versailles. Convened at the invitation of King Louis XVI, the men struggled to accomplish their task: reforming the (as yet unwritten) French constitution. Amidst hundreds of onlookers who milled among them, one deputy suggested they expel "strangers," as members of the public were called, and close the doors. He was met with an avalanche of disdain. "Strangers! Are there any among us?" Constantin-François Chasseboeuf de Volney thundered. "Do they not have the greatest interest in having their eyes fixed upon you? Have you forgotten that you are all but their representatives, their proxies?" Volney, a deputy from the Third Estate—delegates who were not nobility or clergy—believed that meeting in secret would be a violation of their role as representatives of the French people. Could they suppress the gaze of the people, Volney asked, when they owed them an account of all their work, of all their thoughts even? "I cannot respect he who seeks to hide himself in the shadows," he declared; "the grand day is made to shed light on the truth, and I am proud to think like the philosopher who said that all his actions never had anything secret and that he wished that his house was made of glass."[2]

Why was Washington so concerned with maintaining secrecy in the Constitutional Convention, while Volney found deliberating in anything less than a glass house to be a violation of his duty as a deputy in the Estates General? What can these attitudes tell us about how these men and their colleagues understood whom they were representing and how they should do it? Perhaps most importantly, what was the effect of the framers meeting behind closed doors to devise a constitution in the name of the people? And of the French revolutionaries convening in front of a boisterous audience as they drafted a constitution for the first time? The answers to these questions shed light on the origins of modern democracy, the nature of its legitimacy as a government by and for the people, and on transparency as a democratic value.

Almost all histories of the Constitutional Convention note that it was held behind closed doors, just as most histories of the French Revolution highlight the presence of crowds in the Estates General and subsequent assemblies. But the significance of these facts has yet to be fully recognized, down to their impact on the reliability of the very records we use to ascertain what these men said in those spaces. These records hold lasting power in polities governed by the principles professed and, in the case of the United States, even political structures crafted in these meetings. Claiming sovereign authority as representatives of the people was more than a rhetorical act; it required procedures to structure the work of representatives as they made the claim day after day. Democracy is not just an idea but a set of practices that accrue definitional power over time.[3] Remarks like those of Washington and Volney, and the procedural decisions they justified, had profound implications for the nature of representative democracy at its founding.

Representative democracy. This celebrated form of government is at the heart of our story. Though today we think of representative government and democracy as interchangeable, this was not always so. In fact, as the American framers devised structures like the Electoral College and French deputies pondered significant decisions like the fate of the king, some went so far as to deem political representation and democracy incompatible.

In early 1793, amid debate over whether the French legislature should hold a popular referendum on the judgment of Louis XVI, one deputy said he knew "that in a democracy, it would be the people who would judge the tyrant, because in a purely democratic state, the people do everything themselves; but what we are here [in] France is not a democracy."[4] Indeed, France was not a democracy by eighteenth-century standards. Democracy, at that point, mainly referred to a form of government exercised in ancient republics where the citizenry directly participated in governance. It was widely considered inapplicable in modern societies because, for one, they were too large—both in population and geography.[5] James Madison, known today as the chief architect of the American Constitution, made a similar distinction five years earlier in *The Federalist Papers* when he distinguished between a democracy as government by the people directly and a republic as "a Government in which the scheme of representation takes place."[6] Yet by 1794, Maximilien Robespierre, the reputedly incorruptible French revolutionary, declared that the Revolution should aim to establish "a democratic or republican government: these two words are synonyms." Democracy, he contended, was not "a state wherein the people continually assembled, manage all public affairs by themselves," or even met in groups to decide the direction of society. "Democracy is a state wherein the sovereign people, guided by laws of their own making, does all that it can properly do on its own, and does by delegates all that it cannot do itself."[7] In making such a declaration, Robespierre redefined democracy to include a previously distinct form of political organization: representative government. The fusing of these terms—representative government and democracy—has since become so naturalized that today we often fail to recognize representative democracy as an invention that can be traced to a particular historical moment.[8] This book tells the story of that synthesis and identifies the use of secrecy as a key to the uneasy blending of these concepts.

It is a story of disjuncture. Disjuncture between how rhetorically central transparency was to representative democracy at its founding and how prominent secrecy was in its practical application. Transparency came to be considered fundamental to representative government in the Age of Revolutions, a period of political tumult starting in the late eighteenth century.[9] In practice though, this belief was at odds with reality. Despite the loudly professed emphasis on transparency, or publicity as contemporaries called it, it was the use of secrecy that secured the legitimacy of newly created representative democracies across the Atlantic World.[10] Ironically, commitments to transparency in the governments born of revolution in America and France often resulted in losses of public trust and instability. When elected officials in the early United States and revolutionary France made claims to speak for the people, the use of secrecy actually strengthened those claims by deferring popular disagreement to after the promulgation of constitutions and the passage of laws rather than during the deliberative process.[11] The very meaning of democracy was changed in the process. The term was vacated of its more participatory connotations to assume its modern definition as a system of representation. By the end of the Age of Revolutions, democracy meant something new: it was widely understood as a means by which the people ruled themselves through elected representatives, rather than a government necessarily characterized by the degree of popular participation in it.

Arguments about the place of secrecy and transparency in government were one of the primary ways in which representative democracy was articulated as a concept. Underlying procedural decisions went a long way to determining how it took shape in practice. This book uncovers a paradox at the heart of modern representative democracy: at its origin, its legitimacy and stability depended upon a degree of secrecy that was simultaneously deemed anathema to this form of government. To understand this paradox is to untangle the concept of representative democracy itself.

Revolutionaries in the United States and France confronted a common question: how could they make representative government legitimate as a government by and for the people? In setting up such regimes, they also created a shared problem: where did secrecy fit in a context where gaining public trust seemed to demand transparency? In navigating the tension between an ideological imperative to eradicate secrets from the state and a practical need to limit the extent of transparency in government, politicians determined the character and durability of representative regimes and defined "the people" they represented. In both contexts, ultimately, secrecy was strategically deployed and defended to advance a vision of political representation as legitimated solely in the moment of election rather than an ongoing reflection of professed public opinion—what I call an insulated style of representation. However, pushes for transparency in government kept alive an alternate theory of political representation, one demanding ongoing alignment with public opinion in decision-making—what I term a reflective type of representation.[12]

Using debates about secrecy and transparency as a lens to understand the invention of representative democracy also reveals how transparency became a cornerstone of modern democracies and the way in which state secrecy was deemed dangerous. These are ideas we live with today and they are a direct result of a transformation in thinking that took place in the latter half of the eighteenth century. The question of what can justifiably be kept secret in government remains at the heart of contests over the meaning and practice of representative democracy. When these debates intensify, political scientists consistently tie the issue back to ideas about democracy and how it should function. While some have deemed public visibility essential to democracy as a form of government, others have suggested transparency actually threatens democratic government by legitimizing a passive form of citizenship.[13] As a work of history, this book is not aimed at determining whether secrecy promotes or diminishes democracy. Rather, it explains how, why, and with what effect the question of state secrecy was linked to, and shaped, the meaning of representative democracy in the first place. Attitudes about state secrecy and transparency, like understandings of representative democracy, are not ahistorical; they have been shaped in different contexts over time. Today, we largely still live within the institutional frameworks established in the eighteenth century, which should prompt a thorough investigation of their construction. When we make decisions about what the public should and should not see in government, we are making determinations about who should be represented, how representation should work, and what makes it democratic.

Representative Democracy

> The English people think that they are free, they are strongly mistaken; they are free only in the moment in which members of Parliament are elected: once they are elected, the people are slaves, they are nothing. In the brief moments of its liberty, the use of it that the people make warrants it being lost.[14]

In 1762, the Genevan philosopher Jean-Jacques Rousseau—widely read by political thinkers on both sides of the Atlantic—so characterized the oft-lauded system of English political representation. By electing representatives, he suggested, the people enslaved themselves, cutting themselves out of the political process between elections. His declaration proved prescient in two ways. First, his use of slavery as a metaphor for political disempowerment presaged its widespread application in the British imperial conflict and was at the same time tone-deaf to the irony that many of those making such arguments were actually enslaving people. Second, this rethinking of representative government would become a core component of the American revolutionary cause only a decade later and a central undertaking of the French another decade after that.[15]

This was a primary—perhaps *the* primary—challenge of the Age of Revolutions: how to establish representative governments as instruments of popular sovereignty. After all, these were still governments of the few over the many, though now the few were ostensibly the voice of the many.[16] How to make these few legitimate as the voice of the many—to define who constituted the many and foster trust that they were being represented—was at the center of political experiments in the late eighteenth century. Disagreements over how to do this involved a contest between two understandings of how political representation should work.

On the one hand, there were those who saw representative government as a necessary evil, an imperfect replacement for direct democracy. Thomas Paine, who made a name for himself as an arch revolutionary as he moved around the Atlantic World, exemplified this vision. Paine's ideal form of government, which he laid out on the eve of the American Revolution in the widely distributed *Common Sense*, was a tree, "under the branches of which, the whole colony may assemble to deliberate on public matters."[17] Once a polity became too big for this to be feasible, representatives should "act in the same manner as the whole body would act were they present."[18] This vision of representation—which political theorists refer to as "agent" or "mandate"—presumed the existence of a popular will outside the government and posited that it was the duty of representatives to solicit and constantly reflect that will in making decisions.[19] To make representatives legitimate as voices of the people required, first, locating concrete manifestations of "the people," and, second, finding ways to make the representative process reflective of their wishes. This ideal of reflective representation guided American revolutionaries rebelling against the British in the face of the imperial reforms launched after the Seven Years' War and critics of the absolute monarchy in France who desired representative institutions.[20]

When Anglo-American colonists severed ties with the British in 1776, declaring independence and launching a years-long war for which they were ill-prepared, the American states set up governments with representative legislatures at their core. Many expected these legislatures to be directly responsive to constituents, to the growing consternation of skeptics.[21] In the American case, like the British, locality was considered the basic unit of representation; British Whigs and American Patriots generally believed the ideal legislature was to replicate the community in miniature and each representative should be beholden to his community's specific interests.[22] While these American experiments with a new style of political representation were playing out, the French monarchy was contending with a series of political crises that generated ever greater criticism of the royal regime's lack of accountability to the population. Challenges to the king's status as representative arose alongside calls for more direct forms of deputized decision-making.[23] What these forms would be remained unsettled up to the 1789 convening of the Estates General. This was a body assembled at the king's pleasure and composed of deputies from the clergy, nobility, and the Third Estate (essentially everyone else, comprising the vast majority of the population).[24] Though the situations were different, there was an underlying commonality in the American and French contexts: an emergent belief that representative government could and should be a tool of popular sovereignty, a way for the people to govern themselves.[25] Transparency, we will see, was envisioned as a way to achieve this.

But not everyone agreed that making representative government legitimate as a form of popular sovereignty was about finding a way to make representatives reflect specific people and their will. Representative government was not just a practical necessity: it had the potential to improve upon direct democracy because it was possible, as Madison put it, "to refine and enlarge the public views, by passing them through the medium of a chosen body of citizens, whose wisdom may best discern the true interest of their country."[26] The public will, the elusive common good, did not exist outside the government. Rather, it was created among representatives through the deliberative process. "It may well happen that the public voice pronounced by the representatives of the people, will be more consonant to the public good, than if pronounced by the people themselves convened for the purpose," Madison went on.[27] This type of representation, which political theorists refer to as "trustee" or "independence," was fundamentally insulated from the influence of the unelected, rendering "the people" abstract.[28] As the English politician and writer Edmund Burke declared in 1774: "Your representative owes you, not his industry only, but his judgment; and he betrays, instead of serving you, if he sacrifices it to your opinion."[29] To perform this function, that representative needed to be protected from outside pressure. At times, the representative under this model would not only need to be insulated but could actually take on a directive role. Rather than reflect public opinion, his duty was to shape it; rather than decipher the common will, his job was to create it. Making the few the legitimate voice of the many under this ideal of insulated representation was a different prospect; secrecy, not transparency, was crucial.

As they went about constructing new governments, many of the men who met in Philadelphia and Versailles in 1787 and 1789, respectively, began to articulate this insulated vision of political representation. Representatives were going to work far away from their constituents in national capitals; not everyone would vote for them; and constituent instructions were done away with. Treating these moments together should not erase the significant differences between the Constitutional Convention and the Estates General, nor between the political situations in which they arose. The American convention was a gathering of delegates elected by state legislatures—themselves already representative institutions—and sanctioned by the Continental Congress, which was akin to a coalition government. In the French context, the Estates General was convened by the king, broken into socio-legal castes, and selected by primary assemblies of those groups to convey grievances to the monarch. The representative nature of each body varied in terms of who or what they were representing and how they were elected; their degrees of authority were different; and, perhaps most importantly, the political cultures from which they emerged were distinct. Nonetheless, these gatherings share significant similarities. Though the American convention essentially gathered of its own will and the Estates General assembled by invitation of the crown, both bodies were formed with specific mandates to propose reforms. Both surpassed these mandates, dedicating themselves to writing new constitutions for the polities they were in the process of creating. In doing so, both sets of delegates made the decision to abandon instructions—sometimes binding—from those who had sent them to deliberate. Most significantly, both bodies adopted the voice of the people and staked their legitimacy on it.

In North America, Madison and like-minded delegates came to the Constitutional Convention with concerns about an "excess of democracy" in the state legislatures, which they feared were too responsive to popular pressure.[30] In their ideal republic, the legitimacy of representatives as voices of the people was to come from the moment of their election (insulated representation), not from mirroring an externally formed public opinion at every stage in political decision-making (reflective representation). Public opinion could be refined and improved through representatives' deliberations.[31] In France, also, the legitimacy of political representation was abruptly redefined as deputies to the Estates General discarded the binding instructions they carried from their constituents. Instead, the outspoken constitutional thinker Emmanuel-Joseph Sieyès, and many who agreed with him, began to articulate a theory of political representation wherein each deputy was to deliberate in the interest of the nation as a whole rather than echo specific slivers of it. The result was a rhetorical investment of sovereignty in "the people" while simultaneously sidelining tangible expressions of their will.[32] The ideal of reflective representation that had undergirded demands for reforms and new institutions in both North America and France throughout the 1770s and 1780s was replaced with insulated representation. Despite an awareness in both countries of the uniqueness of a founding moment, these notions extended beyond, laying the base for the frameworks being created in the meetings where Madison and Sieyès found themselves.

While the ideology and rhetoric that constituted this new conception of representative government have been heavily scrutinized, it remains strikingly unclear how this model was translated into practice.[33]

It remains murky how, why, and even whether people came to accept this new style of representative government as a form of popular sovereignty. Looking at the decisions and debates over the place of secrecy in government builds on scholarship that has examined political culture to illuminate the process whereby this vision was challenged and solidified through practices.[34] In deciding who could bear witness to which parts of the political process, politicians were indirectly defining "the people" and shaping the very meaning of representative politics. Those who advocated greater transparency in the process were often doing so to push for the enactment of reflective representation in the sense of it being directly aligned with expressed public opinion.[35] Proponents of secrecy in the representative process, on the other hand, characterized it as a way to divorce the legitimacy of new regimes from the pressure to constantly align their actions with the shifting sentiments of an ill-defined "people." Strategic considerations, pressures of circumstance, and the material interests of those involved undoubtedly motivated procedural decisions and shaped stances on the use of secrecy as much, if not more than, theoretical commitments. Decisions about the place of secrecy were not always ideologically consistent, but they were meaningful in the sense that practices either challenged or reinforced ideas in a feedback loop.[36]

In the young United States, political figures like Washington—Federalists, as supporters of the Constitution were known—developed a theory of secrecy's utility to representative government. They strategically deployed secrecy to shield portions of the political process from public view in a bid to counter the expectation that representatives were to constantly reflect public opinion. The concepts of public opinion, as well as those of "the people," "public," or "nation," were unstable and proved problematic in the early republic.[37] In fact, a contingent of the population was trying to constitute public opinion, asserting an active role for citizens in holding representatives accountable to their wishes between elections and pushing for publicity in government as the way to facilitate public vigilance.[38] Federalists were not unaware or unconcerned with public opinion; they may have relied on the impossibility of identifying or manifesting it in a fragmented national public sphere.[39] The legitimizing of representative government as democratic was predicated on, and advanced by, the strategic use of secrecy to limit the political power of public opinion, thus voiding democracy of its more participatory connotations. By the time more doors to government were opened as Democratic-Republicans took power in 1801, representative democracy had been tamed, defanging the impact of transparency in government as a result.

Revolutionary France initially moved in the opposite direction. Representatives attempted to legitimize political representation by proclaiming, like Volney, the value of transparency in the deliberative process and establishing practices designed to promote it. But it was not clear what this ideal meant. A contest between politicians and radical Parisians to define it as a passive broadcast versus an active vigilance proved central to negotiating the function of representative government. In repeatedly proclaiming the value of publicity to representative politics and adhering to practices designed to ensure it, revolutionaries worked at cross-purposes with the insulated theory of political representation they were attempting to translate into practice.[40] As the notion of active vigilance and surveillance over elected officials took hold, deputies gradually began to close doors and shield more of the political process from public view in an attempt to solidify their legitimacy. Despite continuing to proclaim the value of publicity, Jacobin leaders deployed secrecy in government, justifying it as temporarily necessary to represent a people they were simultaneously trying to bring into being. This gap between rhetoric and practice led to a reintroduction of secrecy in the late 1790s and facilitated the transformation of publicity's meaning into a controlled broadcast. The redefined concept was, in turn, crucial to Napoleon Bonaparte's rise as a representative in the most insulated sense possible.

Historians and political theorists tend to treat reflective representation as more democratic than insulated representation.[41] This judgment is based on the degree to which each type maintains an active role for citizens as participants in political decision-making and the extent to which the government is designed to be responsive to the population's desires and demands. On this basis, many scholars ask whether these revolutions, and the constitutions and governments born of them, were democratic. Focusing on the evolution from a reflective to an insulated style of representation, many conclude, as Bernard Manin put it, that "contemporary democratic governments have evolved from a political system that was conceived by its founders as opposed to democracy."[42] But this conclusion misses the mark for two reasons.

The designation of these types of representation as more and less democratic is not so simple, firstly, due to a challenge at the heart of the fiction of popular sovereignty—the government of the few as the voice of the many.[43] The fundamental impossibility of convening the many or definitively deciphering their will presents two potential dangers: too much power in the hands of the few to claim that voice of the many; or deference to whichever segment of the many can most convincingly claim to voice its views.[44] Looking at the way political representation was practiced in both France and the early United States illustrates the undemocratic potential in each extreme. French commitments to transparency, for example, did facilitate the persistence of a form of reflective representation that had the potential to foster popular participation and inclusiveness of citizens without a formal political voice (like women) affording them agency and the ability to claim membership in "the people" being represented.[45] However, it also empowered those who were proximate to political assemblies to claim the voice of the people despite merely being a loud, present segment of them.

This eventuality was largely avoided in the United States, in part through limiting transparency in order to establish an insulated form of political representation, which guarded against usurpations of the people's voice by any particular group. This type of representation, facilitated by the strategic use of secrecy, had its merits—as Madison recognized early in his career when he aimed to cure the "mischiefs of faction" and potential for majority oppression of minorities, advocating insulated government to promote wise decision-making carried out by enlightened officials.[46] Indeed, it made government by the people sustainable. And yet it was a limited "people," excluding from the "public" being represented those—the enslaved, free Black men, women, and even many poorer white men—whose voices were not recognized with the right to vote. The development of the Terror in France, characterized by a government structure Jacobin leaders built largely in secret and in the same spirit of insulated representation, shows the exclusionary extreme of this style of representative government.[47] Later, as he worked within the new federal government, Madison in fact seemed to change his mind. He came to see the potential empowerment of the few in government to claim the voice of the people as the greater threat, switching his position to promote publicity and reflective representation as the best, though imperfect, way to represent the interest of the people.

The curious convergence of Federalist and Jacobin practices of political representation highlights an uncomfortable mismatch between what we might think of as undemocratic procedures in the pursuit of democratic policies. Jacobins at the time and since tend to be labeled radical democrats, but that is due to the policies they pursued, not their style of governing.[48] Even today, what we might deem democratic outcomes of promoting rights, equality, or justice are not infrequently achieved through undemocratic means that bypass hostile majorities. This is the second problem with asking whether these revolutions were democratic. When historians and political theorists pose this question, the very premise is undermined by a lack of clarity on what democracy means. If considered in terms of promoting freedom and equality, the Haitian Revolution might well be considered the most democratic of the era. Yet it did not result in the construction of a representative government, making it one of the least procedurally democratic.[49] As democracies have evolved over time, our focus has necessarily widened to integrate questions of race, gender, wealth, and empire into investigations of their history. This has called into question how truly democratic modern democracies are, or have ever been, at precisely the moment many seem to be wavering.[50] While it is worth asking whether these revolutions or the constitutions they generated were democratic, there is a more fundamental issue that needs to be settled first: how the very meaning of the word "democracy" came to encompass political representation and was changed in the process.

This book is animated by a quest to uncover the way in which the modern meaning of democracy was worked out, partly through procedural decisions and the ways in which they were justified.[51] Though the tension between these two types of representation—reflective and insulated—remains, both conceptions have been subsumed under the mantle of democracy. By recovering the contest between these two models, and the way it was negotiated through decisions and debates over the role of secrecy in government, we can identify a mismatch. Transparency won out as a key to democracy, but insulated representation came to define what democracy meant. As a result, the meaning of transparency was also changed from a notion implying an active dialogue between the public and elected officials to one entailing broadcast to a passive audience.

Secrecy and Transparency

> That a secret policy saves itself from some inconveniences I will not deny; but I believe, that in the long run it creates more than it avoids; and that of two governments, one of which should be conducted secretly and the other openly, the latter would possess

> a strength, a hardihood, and a reputation which would render it superior to all the dissimulations of the other.[52]

Months before the French Estates General convened in 1789, across the English Channel, jurist-philosopher Jeremy Bentham pointed to the toxicity of secrecy in representative government. His was a clear expression of what had by then become a widespread belief. By the last quarter of the eighteenth century, politicians, philosophers, and journalists had all begun to wonder why governments kept secrets and whether this was justified, particularly under regimes that claimed to represent the people. Questions about how political representation ought to work and what could legitimately be kept secret by the government were intimately connected for those who pondered them. Mounting calls for parliamentary reform across the British Empire and intensifying demands for representative institutions in France were directly linked to a rising disdain for state secrecy. If the people were being deprived of their liberty—as Rousseau suggested—many in Britain, British North America, and France were beginning to argue that state secrecy was one of the main tools being used to accomplish this deprivation.

Secrecy had been broadly understood as central to the operations of most early modern European states, from Italian republics in the Renaissance to the centralizing absolutist monarchies of Spain and France in the seventeenth century. It was largely accepted as a necessary part of governance and statecraft, though not entirely unquestioned.[53] Only in the eighteenth century did state secrecy begin to take on a marked negative connotation.[54] On the eve of the revolutions that would first experiment with modern representative democracy, lifting the proverbial veil off the machinations of state power was a common trope in political discourse. Enlightenment was not just about individual, scientific, or economic discovery; it was often about shining light on political processes. New notions of popular sovereignty and, in particular, the rise of accountability as a concept called state secrecy into question.[55]

Anxiety about secrecy was also linked to broader cultural and intellectual currents shaping the late eighteenth century. Certainly, the complex intellectual movement known as the Enlightenment, with its emphasis on the eradication of ignorance through the illumination and application of knowledge, was connected to the increasingly nefarious associations surrounding secrecy.[56] This same intellectual movement was accompanied by a rapid expansion of the press in much of Western Europe and North America, coinciding with rising literacy rates and the commercialization of printing.[57] The growth of this realm of public discussion and the emergent political salience of "public opinion" (an entity that remained problematically ill-defined throughout the period) also contributed to the sense that politics was something to be publicly considered rather than privately managed.[58] Secrecy was also rendered increasingly suspect as state bureaucracies grew more complex and anonymous, leading to conspiracy theories.[59] Attitudes about religion likely also played a role. The Catholic Church, often associated with secrecy by contemporaries—due to beliefs and practices like transubstantiation and confession—was embattled in this period in France and had long been suspect in Protestant-dominated British and British-American culture.[60] Among intellectuals, secrecy became a barometer for evaluating and characterizing the nature of a government in the emergent science of politics, particularly comparative politics. This confluence of factors proved combustible, calling the acceptability of state secrecy into question and posing the possibility of transparency as an ideal.

Before we proceed, a note on terminology is warranted. Though "secret" can be used to refer to the unknown, in the sense of something mysterious, I adopt a narrower definition of the term as something that is knowable but intentionally hidden.[61] To be more precise, the story that follows is focused on collective secrecy, in the form of secrets kept by the state. It traces procedures and the debates they engendered particularly in constituent and legislative institutions, to some extent in executive bodies, and less so in judicial organs. This generally reflects the focus of people at the time, although the introduction of publicity into judicial procedures was a crucial part of the process as well.[62] Further, my analysis focuses principally on what Rahul Sagar calls "civil forms of secrecy," which connotes forms of confidentiality used to enhance values such as candor, effective deliberation, efficiency, or fairness.[63] But I do not start with stable conceptual definitions and work outward. Instead, I examine how these concepts evolved by analyzing their application and changing meanings in the specific and momentous context of the late eighteenth century.

The term "publicity" serves as an especially poignant example. Though still applied by political theorists to mean open or transparent, in common discourse—especially in French—the term implies advertising, promotion, or spectacle. It is precisely the instability of this concept, and the political implications of that instability, that I argue was formative to modern understandings of representative democracy. In fact, "transparency" was not a term used much in French or English in the eighteenth century to describe what we now understand it to mean in a political context: visible political deliberation, publicly identifiable officials, and a minimally restricted press.[64] In both English and French, the terms "transparent" and "transparency" were defined in mainly technical terms to signify something that was diaphanous and translucent. Publicity, or *publicité* in French, was the term writers most often applied when talking about openness, visibility, and the opposite of secrecy in relation to the government.[65] Though the term "publicité" was defined in the 1764 *Dictionnaire critique de la langue française* as signifying "notoriety," it was related to the term "public," which carried as one definition: "In public. Way of speaking adverbially which signifies, In the presence of everyone, in view of everyone, appearing in public, showing one's self in public, speaking in public."[66] In English, "publicity" was in the family of terms related to "public," defined in Samuel Johnson's 1755 *Dictionary of the English language* as: "1. Belonging to a state or nation; not private; 2. Open, notorious, generally known; 3. General, known by many; 4. Regarding not private interest, but the good of the community."[67] By the early nineteenth century, Noah Webster's *Dictionary*, first published in 1828, defined the term "publicity" as "The state of being public or open to the knowledge of a community; notoriety."[68] The meaning of this term at the time was malleable, and it was partly through its application to representative politics that its meaning was refined.

In fact, one challenge contemporaries faced was that the concept of transparency contained values that could and often did conflict. The performance of political processes did not always seem to align with the goal of promoting authenticity, another prominent value advanced in opposition to the perception of shadowy forces and the inherent deception involved in court politics.[69] Politics behind the curtain, so to speak, sparked constant concern and speculation about what people could not see. Secrecy was gendered female and the ideals of transparency and authenticity took on tones of masculinity.[70] Revolutions and the republics they eventually established were founded on a rejection of this conspiratorial, secretive, and feminized style of politics. From then on, politics and the public sphere were to be characterized by publicity and authenticity.[71] Both fell under the conceptual umbrella of transparency, though they could often be in tension.[72] The way in which these values were enacted also shaped their meanings and could have conflicting effects. Having an audience present in legislative deliberations was distinct from reporters recording deliberations and disseminating them to distant readers.

Finally, as anyone who follows politics today can attest, secrecy and transparency are not necessarily inverse sides of a coin or opposing poles on a continuum. This was true in the eighteenth century as well. Opening doors can, and often does, have the effect of pushing meaningful activity from those spaces to other closed areas. Similarly, making material public can actually be a tactic to hide information by inundating people with too much to comprehend. Transparency, in short, can often be more for show than an actual revelation of substance. On the other hand, secrecy can also sometimes be a performance rather than an effective lockdown on information. As this book will chronicle, there were many cases in the eighteenth century where supposedly secret information circulated widely because holders of the information did not consider sharing it with their wives, for example, to be a violation of confidentiality. We must proceed with these caveats constantly in mind. The meanings of these concepts were worked out in practice and many complications arose as part of that process. The performance of transparency and secrecy was often at the heart of discussions and disagreements in the revolutionary era, even more so than the actual enactment of either. Yet the very act of revelation, the mere implication of a gap between public and private, could be of great political consequence.

Democracy in Darkness

The book proceeds in three parts, tracing the arc of how democracy was at once made safe for transparency and transparency was made safe for democracy. Part I is comprised of two chapters that cover the mounting suspicion of secrecy in government during the eighteenth century, particularly during the Enlightenment. Spanning the 1770s and 1780s, chapters 1 and 2 address why state secrecy came to be considered despotic and how calls for publicity were linked to efforts to reform or implement representative government. Covering the American War of Independence, chapter 1 focuses on the evolution of political representation through the practices of American institutions with regard to secrecy and transparency. As newly independent states began to promulgate constitutions, many included provisions for publicity in legislatures. Yet the Continental Congress relied on secrecy in its work. The chapter traces an emerging critique of secrecy during the war and afterward. Many began to argue that the Congress needed to work in public if it was to become a permanent representative body. Chapter 2 crosses the Atlantic to France, where the Bourbon monarchy was struggling to make ends meet in the wake of the American war. It traces how calls for reform under Louis XVI began to emphasize secrecy as a cancer on the monarchy and how publicity became central to calls for reform and the implementation of representative institutions.

Part II moves the story forward to the founding of the United States and the outbreak of revolution in France. It explains how determining the balance of secrecy and transparency in new governments became central to shaping the type of political representation they practiced. Four chapters cover the period from 1787 to 1795 in the United States and France to show how new governments were set up and how the meaning of representative democracy was contested and cemented in the process. In doing so, the chapters identify a curious convergence between Federalists in America and Jacobins in France (their avowed ideological enemies) in terms of how leaders in both factions conceived of political representation as insulated and their use of secrecy in attempting to enact that vision. Chapter 3 is centered on the Federal Convention that met in Philadelphia over the summer of 1787 to craft the American Constitution. As the Constitution was ratified and the new government set up, the question of what would be done in the open versus what could legitimately be kept secret was far from resolved. While Federalists theorized a utility for secrecy in the new government, their opponents pushed for more publicity to guarantee a more reflective form of representation.

Crossing back to France, chapter 4 covers the emergence of the National Assembly in 1789. Despite articulating an insulated theory of political representation similar to that held by American Federalists, the deputies repeatedly committed themselves to the principle of publicity as a cornerstone of their legitimacy. However, their dedication to allowing an audience, facilitating reporting on their deliberations, and communicating constantly with constituents posed challenges to their legitimacy rather than securing it. Chapter 5 focuses on how Jacobin deputies (who had been the most radical) responded to these challenges by reinstating secrecy in government and redefining publicity as a passive broadcast rather than an active dialogue with the public. Attempting to bring practices more in line with an insulated style of political representation, the

National Convention began to move important work to secret committees and assert its ability to speak on behalf of the people as legitimate because the public was able to passively watch them.

Chapter 6 jumps back across the Atlantic to show how the question of secrecy was central to the emergence of party politics in the new American republic. The central event is the ratification of a commercial treaty with the British in 1795, which was widely perceived to be against the will of the people. Newly formed popular societies pointed to secrecy as a pernicious force in government, one used to undermine the people's wishes in the process of political representation. Federalists began to relent, seeing secrecy as undermining their causes and deciding they would enter the fight to shape public opinion. The Senate opened its doors and the pressure for greater transparency appeared to have made significant strides. Yet the chapter suggests that the opening of doors pushed meaningful activity off the floor of Congress and led to a focus on regulating the press, an issue which would become a battleground between Federalists and Democratic-Republicans in the final years of the decade.

Part III covers the end of the revolutionary period, bringing the story up to 1800 in the United States and France. The two chapters show how a revised version of publicity as a passive value was entrenched as central to the legitimacy of representative government. Chapter 7 takes the story through the administration of President John Adams, foregrounding the ongoing struggle between Federalists and Democratic-Republicans over the type of political representation that would be practiced in the new republic. It traces debates over foreign policy and the imposition of the Alien and Sedition Acts up through Thomas Jefferson's election as president, which marked a shift to a policy of greater transparency and more ostensibly reflective representation. However, the chapter probes the sincerity of Jefferson's commitment to publicity, suggesting that he completed a transformation of the term from an active to passive process and thereby contributed to voiding representative democracy of its participatory potential. Chapter 8 examines the way in which the French National Convention went about dismantling the apparatus of the Terror, with a focus on how blame was ultimately placed on an excess of publicity. Deputies began to openly theorize a use for secrecy in representative government and redoubled efforts to introduce it into administration. With the rise of Napoleon Bonaparte and the establishment of the Constitution of the Year VIII in 1799, representative government became not only insulated but entirely symbolic and devoid of its democratic elements. On the eve of 1800, the new constitution proclaimed the Revolution over. A new form of publicity was central to the Napoleonic regime, but its focus shifted from legislative bodies to Napoleon's person; it became entirely performance. In reality, the regime operated nearly entirely behind closed doors.

It is a truism rarely scrutinized in modern democracies that secrecy poses a threat to government by and for the people. Today, the masthead of the *Washington Post* proclaims that "Democracy Dies in Darkness." But this widespread sentiment obscures the odd truth that American democracy was in fact born in darkness. How do we reconcile this? Attempting to do so forces us to interrogate the way in which representative democracy took on its modern meaning in the Age of Revolutions. Reckoning with this fundamental paradox can shed new light on the nature of the governments under which many of us continue to live.

PART I

Suspecting Secrecy

CHAPTER ONE

Piercing the Impenetrable Darkness

In June 1773, a pamphlet appeared in Boston claiming to contain several private letters written by Thomas Hutchinson, the embattled royal governor of Massachusetts. The letters dated from the late 1760s and were addressed primarily to Thomas Whately, a secretary to the Treasury during the drafting of the widely hated Stamp Act. Though they did not contain any stances the governor had not more or less taken publicly, their publication proved the death knell of Hutchinson's career. Behind the leak was Benjamin Franklin. Then working as an operative of the Massachusetts Assembly in London, he had obtained the letters under circumstances that remain mysterious. After the fact, Franklin wrote that it was his "duty to give my constituents intelligence of such importance to their affairs," and he recounted having obtained permission to send them to Boston "on these express conditions: that they should not be printed, that no copies should be taken of them, that they should be shown only to a few of the leading people of the government, and that they should be carefully returned."[1] A limited circulation of the letters, Franklin seemed to hope, would prove to angry colonists that their grievances did not rightly lie with the British ministry and that their troubles were instead the result of individuals who misrepresented colonial concerns and could be removed.[2]

Upon the letters' arrival in Boston, pressure quickly mounted to publish them. On June 2, Samuel Adams, the assembly clerk and popular leader of colonial opposition to imperial policies, read them aloud in the Massachusetts Assembly. The next day, the *Massachusetts Spy* reported on their existence, speculating that the letters would bring "many *dark* things to *light*."[3] Roughly two weeks later, the letters were printed and the assembly voted to petition the king for Hutchinson's removal from office. The correspondence took the colonies by storm; the pamphlet containing them went through ten printings on both sides of the Atlantic over the ensuing year, and the letters were serialized in newspapers up and down the coastline.[4] Hutchinson became the bête noire of American agitators and British-American relations continued to deteriorate. As the Reverend Samuel Cooper, influential minister of the Brattle Street Church in Boston, wrote to Franklin on the eve of the letters' first publication: "they strip the mask from the writers who, under the professions of friendship to their country, now plainly appear to have been endeavoring to build up themselves and their families upon its ruins."[5] In publicizing Hutchinson's private correspondence, colonial agitators claimed to have exposed him, unmasking him and seemingly proving the existence of a conspiracy against them. The governor's defenders maintained that publishing the letters was a violation of privacy, while Franklin defended the publication on the basis that the letters were exchanged between public officials about public affairs.[6] The controversy exemplified changing expectations about public officials and whether what they wrote ought to be, well, public.[7]

This incident is instructive for ascertaining the mindset of frustrated Anglo-American colonists on the eve of the Revolution's outbreak. Royal officials could not be trusted; the distance between the colonies and the seat of government allowed for misrepresentation and dissembling; and the time had come to start exposing two-faced liars.[8] The mentality echoed ongoing debates in Great Britain itself as struggles over parliamentary reform had recently reached a crescendo in a conflict over public access to deliberations in the House of Commons. Hutchinson's downfall was yet another manifestation of suspicion in the supposed secret maneuverings of state officials. It was also indicative of the performative power of unveiling private material for the public. Though the letters were not necessarily revelatory in substance, the very act of revealing them seemed to confirm suspicions that something was previously hidden and that exposing it could bring about accountability.

These angry colonists, like their radical Whig counterparts in Britain, were convinced that secrecy was a scourge preventing reflective political representation. Their solution was exposure, revelation, and greater publicity in politics.

Conflicts over the use of secrecy in government were a pervasive and crucial aspect of the political culture of the American Revolution, on both sides of the Atlantic. Americans were not alone in their worry about the secret machinations of ministerial officials.[9] In the years preceding the outbreak of war, rumblings of discontent and demands for more publicity in Parliament arose in the metropole as well. Reform-minded colonists were aware of efforts to open the House of Commons to reporters and felt themselves part of the struggle to pull the veil from the operations of government. Secrecy was one lens through which they understood their conflict with Britain, and it became a practical challenge for newly formed political institutions at the continental and state levels.

The widespread anxiety over secrecy clarifies a central revolutionary project: redefining representative government as tool a of popular sovereignty.[10] Although those active in the Patriot movement identified secrecy as an obstacle to being properly represented in London, many soon wavered over how much publicity they demanded from the newly created institutions they set up to govern themselves. The decisions they made, and the way in which those determinations were challenged, illuminate how various groups of Americans thought about the new institutions they built, whom these institutions represented, and what they expected of them.[11] Focusing on discussions about secrecy in government sheds new light on the questions of what was at stake in determining home rule and who should rule at home, as Carl Becker put it.[12]

As war broke out, local political organs and the newly formed Continental Congress worked mainly in secret. Military conflict and diplomatic necessity served as justifications for secrecy. Publicity was directed outward, valued more as a tool for exposing enemies among the population than for performing government activity. But as the conflict wore on and emergent political institutions became more permanent—from new state constitutions to the entrenchment of Congress as a continental government—the use of secrecy generated suspicion. Many began to argue that, if these bodies were to be considered representative, the people needed to see what they were doing. Even before the war ended, calls to open the doors to Congress appeared in the press, based on the premise that it was a representative body, accountable to the people—an entity yet to be clearly defined—in its operations.[13] In some states, constitutional framers established publicity as a central tenet of the new legislatures as representative bodies. In Congress, despite a case made from within and without for opening the doors, delegates remained committed to secrecy even after the war had ended, reinforcing a conviction that the body was not representative of the people but was instead more akin to an assemblage of state ambassadors. Determinations of which nascent political bodies should work in public view, and why, map onto evolving conceptions of representative politics, both who was being represented and how it should work, during this formative phase of American political institutions and thought.[14]

Tracing the deployment of secrecy, both practically and rhetorically, and the thinking about its proper place in government highlights the way in which ideas could shape and simultaneously be shaped by the attempt to translate them into institutions. Revolutionary leaders were not always consistent; it was in the gaps between thought and action that they forged a new political culture during the war. Indeed, war left an indelible mark on representative institutions in the American republics and the emergent national political sphere before 1787. From a widespread ferocity for exposing secrets to a general penchant for keeping them, those Americans fighting over constructing republican governments wrestled with the implications of their decisions for the way representation worked.

England was the primary frame of reference for American colonists—and for writers across the Atlantic World for that matter.[15] There, secrecy was a fundamental part of the political process, despite mounting pressure to establish more publicity in the decades prior to the outbreak of the American War of Independence. The roughly ten years preceding the dawn of the 1770s marked a dissolution of political stability, the introduction of ideologically driven oppositional politics, and the emergence of a popular political culture.[16] Historians often point to the 1770s and 1780s as the point at which this genuinely public political sphere emerged in Britain, necessitating a renegotiation of the relationship between an empowered notion of public opinion and the government.[17] Critiques of the royal ministry and Parliament—composed of the House of Lords and the House of Commons—began to intensify, and calls for reform mounted over the latter half of the century. Debates about secrecy and publicity in the political process were at the crux of this upheaval.

Two events in the 1760s set the stage for a re-conceptualizing of political representation, raising new questions about the nature of Parliament's legitimacy. The first was the Stamp Act crisis of 1765. Establishing a direct tax on American colonists in the form of stamps on legal and commercial paper, the Stamp Act spurred outcry along the eastern seaboard. American claims that colonists were not represented in Parliament because they did not vote for members, nor did members come from their communities and share their interests, echoed in the London press. Britons back across the Atlantic began to extend the logic to the heart of the empire: if one did not vote for a member, was one actually represented in Parliament? Increasingly, this question was answered in the negative by a significant segment of the engaged population.[18]

Parliament's response to the uproar was to repeal the taxes imposed on the colonists, but also issue an emphatic declaration that political representation did not require direct participation: laws passed in London bound inhabitants of the colonies whether or not they elected members. Considered this way, the House of Commons was a legitimate representative body, functioning as it ought. The doctrine of virtual representation implied in the Declaratory Act entailed a theory about accountability and the nature of a member of Parliament's duty and relationship to his constituents and the population writ large.[19] Under this theory, each member of Parliament was meant to represent the interest of the nation—and, at this point, empire—as a whole, rather than serving the particular interests of his segment of constituents. In a 1774 speech rejecting the principle of instruction for members, Edmund Burke—member of the House of Commons from Bristol—laid out this vision of representation, calling Parliament "not a *congress* of ambassadors from different and hostile interests" but rather "a *deliberative* assembly of *one* nation, with *one* interest, that of the whole; where, not local purposes, not local prejudices, ought to guide, but the general good, resulting from the general reason of the whole."[20] George Grenville, the minister famous for the conception of the Stamp Act, once elaborated this theory by explaining that this was why the House was referred to as the "*Commons in Parliament assembled* and not the *Representatives of the Commons*."[21] Many members of Parliament would uphold this insulated conception of political representation through the following two decades of mounting upheaval and well into the nineteenth century.[22]

However, the theoretical quandaries raised by the Stamp Act crisis were compounded in 1768 when John Wilkes, the popular thorn in the side of the ministry, was elected to the House of Commons from Middlesex. Based on accusations of seditious libel, he was promptly expelled, only to be replaced by his opponent who had overwhelmingly lost the election. Outrage ensued, fueled by Wilkes's carefully orchestrated self-promotion from exile in France, characterizing himself as a symbol for "English Liberty."[23] Pamphleteers, political societies, and politicians engaged in a war of words over whether Parliament had a right to eject a popularly elected member in favor of a candidate of its own determination. Once again, the struggle boiled down to the nature of the relationship between elected representatives and the people they were meant to represent: were members meant to reflect the wishes of the public (itself variously defined) or were they to make determinations of the public interest themselves?[24] Was representation to be reflective or insulated?

American colonists and British residents considered these two events—the Stamp Act and Middlesex Election—part of a crisis of corruption that eroded trust in Parliament and raised questions about its representative function.[25] The Boston Sons of Liberty, which began a correspondence with Wilkes in 1768, cast his plight as intricately bound up with their own.[26] Wilkes responded to the club on multiple occasions, always affirming his support for American interests and viewing their protests of taxes to be integral in the struggle to preserve English liberty.[27] This trans-Atlantic struggle to conceptually define political representation and the nature of the relationship between elected government and the body of the people played out in no small part through debates about state secrecy and battles over the visibility of governance. A 1769 pamphlet on the Middlesex Election decision, for example, argued that "in this country, the publick has the right upon all occasions, but most particularly upon such as this, to be fully informed."[28] Such a conviction became central to British political culture. Reformers increasingly advocated visibility, publicity, and vigilance as remedies to ensure representative government was reflective of the interest of the common people.

Throughout the late 1760s and into the next decade, pamphlets contesting Parliament's authority also proliferated in the colonies, proposing theories of what made representation legitimate.[29] Among these theories was the ability of the represented to effectively exercise surveillance over the government. In order to maintain this surveillance, Patriot writers advocated reform of the way representation was apportioned, the binding of representatives to constituents' instructions, the changing of seditious libel laws to free the press to further criticize government, and the withdrawal of government from control over religious practice.[30] The linchpin of the colonists' claim that they were not represented in Parliament was that they did not share the same interests as residents across the Atlantic.[31] But when it came to defining what political representation should look like, colonial writers advanced the idea that "consent was a continuous, everyday process"—reflective representation.[32] Once representative government was necessary because a polity had become too large, Thomas Paine urged the election of a large number of representatives, each conveying the interest of a particular place and facing frequent election to ensure "their fidelity to the public will."[33] This reflective vision of representation implied, along with the notion that instructions were necessary to guarantee accountability, that the people needed to be able to see what their representatives were doing.

It appears this ideal was gaining traction in practice over the course of the eighteenth century in many colonial assemblies. While historians have suggested that colonists practiced a more direct form of representation within their communities, scholarship on colonial assemblies has tended to focus within one colony, making generalizations difficult.[34] Yet a study of changes in assembly procedure over the course of the eighteenth century in Virginia, Massachusetts, and Pennsylvania suggests the colonies had gradually moved in the direction of a more reflective style of representation. Of particular note was a shift over time toward greater publicity. Although none of the three colonial assemblies published journals in 1700, by mid-century all three did.[35] The information contained in the journals would have been limited and difficult to understand, and most assemblies officially banned reporting on their proceedings, but already in the 1730s pamphlets and newspapers sometimes contained descriptions of legislative activity, particularly in the event of disputes with executive authority.[36] While these reports did not offer transcriptions of debates, they did sometimes provide information on who voted which way or spoke in favor of, or against, particular measures. The result was that by the 1760s, legislative journals were much more robust, often containing the names of members who proposed and voted for legislation.[37] By the end of the colonial period, the Pennsylvania Assembly opened its doors to spectators, who "expressed their opinions on particular bills so audibly that they had to be admonished against hissing and clapping."[38]

Back in London, the contest over whether Parliament ought to debate in public and ought particularly to be open to reporters was the point at which the relationship between debates about the government's use of secrecy and the functioning of political representation collided most forcefully. Determining who could sit on the limited number of hard benches in the cramped chamber amounted to nothing less than defining the relationship between political representatives and the people whom they purported to represent. The doorstep of the converted St Stephen's Chapel at Westminster became a symbol for this contest to those who sought to eliminate barriers between the chamber and the streets and pages of periodicals. The ability of printers in particular to cross that threshold and to publish proceedings of the House of Commons became a flashpoint by which the role of secrecy in a representative government was extensively debated. Suggesting a changing understanding of what it meant for Parliament to be representative, printers won a hard-fought battle in 1771 when the House of Commons grudgingly conceded that reporters could publish accounts of their deliberations.[39] The persistence of an official commitment to secrecy, however, suggests that this transformation in thinking about the definition of political representation remained far from fully realized in Britain at the end of the eighteenth century. In fact, throughout the American War of Independence, the House of Commons would often meet in secret session. This was less often the case in newly created legislatures across the Atlantic.

After deciding to break with the British in 1776, revolutionaries set about writing constitutions for their newly independent states. American rebels took on the intertwined tasks of defining political representation and delineating the bounds of secrecy within their own governments. They generally aimed to establish reflective representation, firmly rejecting the idea of virtual representation once and for all. For many, that meant rejecting secrecy in legislatures and committing to greater publicity of political processes. A brief overview of the way secrecy was treated in the state constitutions adopted from 1776 to 1780 makes clear that this question was top of mind for those forming new governments, even if there was not complete consensus in how it was viewed. States broadly fell into three categories: those that did not broach the topic of secrecy or publicity explicitly in the constitutions; those that saw fit to define provisions for maintaining secrecy, particularly in executive organs; and those that sought to guarantee the publicity of legislative proceedings. The way states handled this question spoke to visions of the separation of powers between executive and legislative and, in the case of those that ensured publicity, to the way legislatures were to function as representative. Aside from the few constitutions that did not mention secrecy or publicity—Delaware, New Hampshire, New Jersey, and South Carolina—the rest took a stance on the way secrecy was to be used in the government.[40] The very fact that they addressed the issue suggests the extent to which it was becoming a live question, particularly in setting up republican governments. Generally, states built on colonial practices, with some regional distinctions. Constitutions that either did not mention publicity or maintained guarantees for secrecy were most often southern states, while those committing most explicitly and extensively to publicity tended to be mid-Atlantic states.

Before establishing constitutions, colonies created interim governing entities as colonial authority broke down and violence broke out. These provincial conventions, congresses, councils, and committees were formed starting in the summer of 1774 alongside local organizations at the town and county levels—all of which were dedicated to advancing the American cause of resistance to perceived British persecution. Aside from military preparations, in anticipation of the violence that broke out in the spring of 1775, these committees were concerned with discerning enemies among the populations they sought to govern. They formed a crucial link between localities and the continental effort.[41] In many ways they were the basis of the Continental Congress's authority on both ends: in providing support for its initiatives and then in enforcing its directives at the local level. In fulfilling this role of enforcement, concerns about secrecy turned into systematic vigilance in the form of surveillance and a valorization of publicity in the sense of exposing enemies (specifically those with loyalist sympathies). Publicity was thus first prized in the states as a tool enacted by governments to surveil the population, rather than the other way around.

The collapse of colonial governments occurred at varying points depending upon the colony, leading to an uneven transfer of authority to newly established bodies. At the colony level, legislative bodies—variously called congresses or conventions—were convened and frequently appointed either committees or councils of safety as quasi-executive organs. In some states, these committees or councils tended to be shorter-lived than in others where they became more fixed features of new governments. In Massachusetts, Virginia, and in the Carolinas, for example, committees appointed by the interim provincial congresses in 1774–75 were largely disbanded by 1776.[42] In the mid-Atlantic colonies of New York, New Jersey, and Pennsylvania, state-level committees of safety remained active through 1777 and even into 1778.[43] In still other places, like Connecticut and New Hampshire, state committees of safety continued to operate after the war ended, disbanding only in 1783 and 1784, respectively.[44]

A number of the newly created provincial conventions and congresses met behind closed doors and the committees or councils of safety they appointed were sometimes not required to report their activities to the body that had created them.[45] These state-level committees, which were often formed to stand in as the government when legislatures lacked quorum, were primarily tasked with procuring provisions for the militia, summoning it when merited, coordinating with the army, enforcing the embargo, and monitoring for enemies of the American cause. The committees, which ranged in size from a handful to a few dozen members, were the principal points of contact for continental political and military officials seeking information or delivering directives. Committees were instructed by the interim state legislatures to "keep watch" for possible military attacks but also for threats from within the population. In this capacity, they took on quasi-judicial roles as many of them became a point, or sometimes the final point, of trial for suspected "Tories," or loyalists.[46] Regardless of the way in which they originated, these local committees shared a common motive of exercising vigilance.[47]

As states drafted constitutions to establish more permanent government structures, publicity was the norm and secrecy, it seems, was no longer taken for granted. Those state constitutions that included provisions for secrecy tended to do so in relation to the executive arm of the government they created. In Maryland, for example, the need for secrecy was mentioned in relation to the Council of the Governor—a small body of men selected from and by the state legislature to advise the executive. Noting that the council would be required to keep a record of proceedings, the constitution also allowed it to appoint its own clerk, "who shall take such oath of support and fidelity to this State, as this Convention, or the Legislature, shall direct; and of secrecy, in such matters as he shall be directed by the board to keep secret."[48] The Virginia constitution created an identical council "to assist in the administration of government" and similarly noted "this Council may appoint their own Clerk, who shall . . . take an oath of secrecy, in such matters as he shall be directed by the board to conceal."[49] Using the stronger term "conceal," the Virginia clause nonetheless shared the same intent as that in the Maryland framework. Georgia was the final state to reference a need for secrecy and provisions for maintaining it. "When any affair that requires secrecy shall be laid before the governor and the executive council," it was up to the executive to administer an oath for members of the council and "to the secretary and other officers necessary to carry the business into execution."[50] The oath entailed a pledge, when any secret business came up, to not "in any manner whatever, either by speaking, writing, or otherwise reveal the same to any person, whatever, until leave given by the council, or when called upon by the house of assembly."[51]

These provisions for secrecy helped to distinguish executive from legislative power, partly on the basis of the manner in which they were to operate. Moreover, though the constitutions did not directly address provisions for publicity in the legislature, what these clauses suggest is that some degree of openness may have been assumed. Provisions requiring oaths to be taken either by members, clerks, or both of the executive councils marked the executive as a realm of government requiring a certain degree of confidentiality in its operations. The implied contrast was to the legislative branch, which these constitutions did not address with regard to secrecy. Furthermore, all three of these constitutions took care to note that the oath would be administered with regard only to issues either the council, governor, or both deemed necessary to be kept confidential. The further implication of this decision was that there were areas of state activity where secrecy was not required. Finally, the fact that these constitutions addressed the necessity of secrecy at all suggests that it could not be assumed that these entities could operate in secret and that they could not expect to keep all activity secret. Even in guaranteeing the ability of executive councils to employ secrecy, the provisions were acknowledging the limits of its legitimate use. While these three constitutions implied a degree of publicity in the legislature's work, five other states made explicit guarantees for it. In doing so, they conveyed an understanding of political representation as reflective. Requiring a precise degree of publicity in their proceedings suggested that deputies in these legislatures were liable to scrutiny by those who had elected them as well as the broader public. There was a presumed need for people to know what happened inside state houses for the government to function properly.

Among the most limited of those constitutions was that of North Carolina, which guaranteed free press in the state and also called for the journals of both houses of the General Assembly to be "printed and made public, immediately after their adjournment."[52] The constitution also included a provision allowing for the "yeas and nays, upon any question" to be entered on the journal when a motion was made and seconded to do so.[53] Although North Carolina's constitution fell short of requiring open doors, it nonetheless recognized the value in printing journals regularly and allowing at least a limited window into the activity inside by noting that the votes would be published when called for. In requiring regular and rapid publication of the journals and the notation of votes when demanded, the constitution of North Carolina went some way to defining the nature of political representation in the legislature. Deputies were to be held accountable for their decisions. Even if it was not possible to know everything one's representative said in real time, the constitution seemed to recognize a need for constituents to learn how representatives voted, without much delay. Still, the framework upheld the sense that only completed work was to be exposed to public view, much in the same manner as delegates in the Continental Congress would maintain through the 1780s.

In Massachusetts, where the constitution was not adopted until 1780, the relationship between representative government and working in public view was articulated mainly in the declaration of rights, as opposed to being outlined in the structural sections of the framework. Aside from requiring the recording of ayes and nays when a two-thirds vote of the legislature was taken to override the governor's objection to a proposed law, the constitution abstained from articulating protocols for the ideals laid out in the declaration.[54] Despite the lack of procedural clarity, Article V of the Declaration of Rights stated that all power was lodged in the people and that "the several magistrates and officers of government vested with authority, whether legislative, executive, or judicial, are their substitutes and agents, and are at all times accountable to them."[55] As a result of this relationship, the people "have a right to require of their lawgivers and magistrates an exact and constant observation of them, in the formation and execution of the laws necessary for the good administration of the commonwealth."[56] Though the constitution established this principle, the way in which it was to be carried out in practice was left more open-ended than in North Carolina, which lacked more explicit theoretical definitions underpinning its procedural requirements.

Unlike North Carolina and Massachusetts, the states of New York, Pennsylvania, and Vermont went further in guaranteeing the publicity of legislative work, providing for it throughout the deliberative process rather than just at the end of a session. Working in public view, in fact, was central to fulfilling their roles as representative organs. While these constitutions allowed for exceptions to working with open doors and printing journals in cases "when the welfare of the state shall require their debates to be kept secret," the default was to be open.[57] The importance of these requirements should not be underestimated. While colonial assemblies had been moving toward greater publicity prior to the Revolution, establishing a constitutional requirement to allow a public audience in legislative meetings was radical in that it provided a positive guarantee, rather than a tolerance. While an audience was generally allowed inside the House of Commons by this point, for example, it was merely tolerated, not officially sanctioned; the public and reporters could be, and often were, removed at the request of members.[58] Provisions requiring open doors, then, were a significant way in which these states' constitutions were radical at the time they were promulgated. Moreover, the deliberate translation and circulation of these constitutions in France, carried out by Benjamin Franklin, raises the question of whether such procedures may have been more influential than those of Congress on the thinking of French figures who would convene in Versailles for the Estates General in 1789.[59]

Looking at the language in these constitutions is the first step to grasping their centrality to enacting political representation in a reflective form. The New York state constitution, which was not adopted until April 1777, explicitly made publicity a core tenet of its legislature. Article 15 noted that "the doors, both of the senate and assembly, shall at all times be kept open to all persons, except when the welfare of the state shall require their debates to be kept secret."[60] Not only were the meetings of the upper and lower houses of the legislature to be public, but "the journals of all their proceedings shall be kept in the manner heretofore accustomed by the general assembly of the colony of New York; and except in such parts as they shall, as aforesaid, respectively determine not to make public be from day to day (if the business of the legislature will permit) published."[61] Authors of the New York constitution stated the necessity of exposing the work of its legislature to public scrutiny as it was happening, not just upon its completion. This was tantamount to defining the relationship between elected representatives and the people on whose behalf they were speaking. The constituent had power to observe the representative throughout the process of crafting legislation and to form a judgment of the elected official based on this full picture as opposed to simply agreeing or not with completed decisions.

Some six months prior to the adoption of New York's constitution, the state of Pennsylvania had promulgated its own. Much like that of New York, the constitution declared that "the doors of the house in which the representatives of the freemen of this state shall sit in general assembly, shall be and remain open for the admission of all persons who behave decently, except only when the welfare of this state may require the doors to be shut."[62] Even in this clause, however, the Pennsylvania constitution was more specific than that of New York in referring to the legislature as the "representatives of the freemen of this state," making very clear the connection between working with open doors and being agents of particular people. The constitution in Vermont, which was promulgated in July 1777, contains a nearly direct copy of this clause of the Pennsylvania constitution.[63] But Pennsylvania went further. In addition to requiring the legislature to meet with open doors and print its journals, with vote lists (and the reasons for individual votes if a member desired), on a weekly basis, the public was to be actively brought into the legislative process.

Section 15 of the Pennsylvania constitution stated that "all bills of public nature shall be printed for the consideration of the people, before they are read in general assembly the last time for debate and amendment." This was required "to the end that laws before they are enacted may be more maturely considered, and the inconvenience of hasty determinations as much as possible prevented." And not only were the laws to be printed for public consideration, but "for the more perfect satisfaction of the public, the reasons and motives for making such laws shall be fully and clearly expressed in the preambles."[64] The unelected public was to be brought into the legislative process, informed enough to develop and express opinions on laws under consideration with the implied purpose of influencing their adoption. Moreover, press freedom was declared and its purpose articulated in Pennsylvania: "The printing presses shall be free to every person who undertakes to examine the proceedings of the legislature, or any part of government."[65] Here, the constitution came as close as any ever had come to defining a role for the press as a watchdog in a republican government. While guarantees of press freedom in other state constitutions and rhetoric about its importance to liberty in the Anglo-American tradition certainly implied this role, the Pennsylvania constitution made explicit the relationship between the press and representative government. In such a structure, the unelected public and the press were to be active participants in governing. As elected representatives, members of the state legislature were required to work in public view, explain actions to constituents and welcome their opinions in the law-making process, and submit to scrutiny in all their work.[66]

Pennsylvania became a radical model for how to run an independent republic.[67] The legislature was the training ground for political reporters who would later cover the federal House of Representatives; Mathew Carey and Thomas Lloyd both honed their early shorthand systems while covering the Pennsylvania Assembly during the confederation period. Still, reporting of deliberations in the state assembly was limited; Carey first published a pamphlet containing transcripts of speeches on a single issue and then began selectively printing debates in the *Pennsylvania Evening Herald* in 1785. It was only in 1787 that Lloyd first sought copyrights for his reports of assembly debates, which were often limited summaries without much detail at all.[68] When the framers of the Federal Constitution convened that summer and complained about an "excess of democracy" in the state governments, provisions like those in New York and Pennsylvania were likely among their concerns. In fact, the Pennsylvania Constitution, widely considered to be the most democratic of those implemented during the war and confederation years, provoked ongoing debate from the moment it was adopted. Moreover, when the delegates to the Federal Convention arrived in Philadelphia, Pennsylvania's constitution was in crisis. Much of the subsequent debate over ratification of the Federal Constitution in Pennsylvania was influenced by existing divisions there over the state's own constitution.

But this was all still a decade away. As the state governments found their footing, a continental coalition went about securing its own legitimacy as a voice for the inchoate American people. Among those delegates at the center of this project, a different calculus with regard to secrecy and publicity prevailed. It carried significant consequences for the nature of the government they formed.

As delegates from the American colonies first gathered in Philadelphia in 1774, they immediately vowed to work in strict secrecy. First conceived of as a temporary body, convened to form a petition of grievances and definition of Parliamentary sovereignty, the Congress soon became a fixture of American government. At the beginning, working in secret may have been intended to project unity, both in the sense of protecting individual delegates against British recrimination and allowing for more open debate under the circumstances. That context was a domestic population divided over the path to take, fear of British alliances with enslaved people and Native Americans within and bordering the colonies, and tenuous control over colonial governments.[69] Once the second Continental Congress convened in the spring of 1775, after the outbreak of violence in Massachusetts, the delegates rededicated themselves to working in secret. As the body took on the task of managing a war and negotiating diplomatic relations, secrecy became a dominant feature of its operations, thus indicating a rejection of the notion that they were representatives in a sense at all similar to elected officials in state legislatures. Delegates took oaths to maintain secrecy, secret committees were created, and secret journals kept. Moreover, delegates grew increasingly reticent over time to commit information to writing, fearing their letters would be intercepted. Though they frequently lamented not being able to consult with friends or report back to state officials on proceedings, most concluded that guarding their deliberations was a necessity as they worked amidst British military invasion and tried to secure foreign allies.

By 1779, a series of leaks brought factional divisions to light and the Congress began to face challenges to its legitimacy, specifically as a representative institution. Under mounting pressure to open more of their work to public view, some members of the Congress even began considering potential benefits of greater publicity. They moved to print their journals more regularly in an effort to counteract suspicion, but they stopped short of opening their meetings to reporters or an audience. After having resigned the presidency in December 1778, South Carolina delegate Henry Laurens wrote to New Jersey governor William Livingston lamenting that the Congress did not open its doors amidst the crisis of public confidence.[70] Nevertheless, even when the war drew to a close and after the peace treaty was signed, the Congress continued to adhere to secrecy in its operations. As the focus on constructing new representative republics turned further to the states, opening Congress to public view seemingly became less of a priority. Understanding why delegates to the Continental Congress adhered to secrecy from the beginning presents a puzzle considering they met amidst a culture of vigilance and pervasive desire to unveil secret operations of the British government and the maneuvers of their own neighbors.

The Congress's relative comfort with working in secret should be interpreted both as a result of perceived exigency but also as an indication of the way in which the body conceived of itself. The Continental Congress did not start out as a representative institution like the House of Commons or state legislatures. In actuality, delegates seemed to consider themselves more as ambassadors from their states, and the body served more as an executive organ than a legislative one.[71] Their use of secrecy is both an indicator and a result of this self-conception. Yet Congress's function and source of legitimacy was far from fixed, and tracing changing attitudes about its use of secrecy shows how these evolved over the course of the War of Independence. Pressure to open doors and some delegates' willingness to contemplate adopting more publicity in their proceedings show how the institution came to be considered representative of a nebulously defined people as it became a fixture of American politics. This shift also demonstrates how publicity was becoming central to conceptions of what political representation entailed, specifically an expectation that it be reflective. The maintenance of secrecy also established the precedent for rejecting that vision of reflective representation on the national level.

Though they did not conceive of themselves as representatives of the people, the congressional delegates surely saw themselves as representatives of their states. Most arrived in Philadelphia in September 1774 with instructions and a specific mandate: to convey colonial grievances to the British government.[72] Yet there were factions among them from the outset; the more radical delegates from Massachusetts favored again implementing a non-importation effort, while those from the mid-Atlantic, in particular, were largely against taking such steps.[73] In the wake of what came to be called the Coercive Acts and the beginnings of colonial government breakdown in colonies like Massachusetts, the delegates faced a difficult task. Being technically vested with authority by the assemblies that had sent them on behalf of colonies, the delegates were also vehicles for acting on the more radical resolves of committees forming in local communities.[74] Ultimately, Congress claimed to be the decisive voice of the American colonies to the British king and Parliament at a crisis point. Upon his arrival, Connecticut delegate Silas Deane directed his wife to "inform my friends that we are in high spirits, if it is possible to be really so when the eyes of millions are upon us, and who consider themselves and their posterity interested in our conduct."[75] This sense of being watched, of being scrutinized, became a common refrain in writings of elected delegates on both sides of the Atlantic during the Age of Revolutions. Convening in bodies that would pronounce in the name of a people on subjects considered to be of vital and enduring importance entailed significant pressure.

Yet in a very real sense, the "eyes of millions" were not on the delegates as they worked, or if they were, they could not see very much. Upon convening, the Congress resolved that "the doors be kept shut" and that "the members consider themselves under the strongest obligations of honor to keep the proceedings secret until the majority shall direct them to be made public."[76] Though it appears not all delegates arrived with the expectation that they would meet in secret, they seem to have been quickly convinced of its necessity.[77] Withholding information was meant to be temporary, as the "designs and plans of the Congress must not be communicated until completed," John Adams wrote to his wife, Abigail.[78] In apologizing to their correspondents for not being able to provide information, delegates repeatedly noted the idea that nothing should be published until it was decided.

Many delegates asserted that the reason for keeping work in progress under wraps was to avoid confusion and disturbance. A letter written by Caesar Rodney of Delaware to his brother in mid-September 1774 declared that the withholding of details "until the whole business is done" was designed to "avoid needless disputations out of doors." Though he acknowledged the procedure was "much to the disappointment of the curious," Rodney nonetheless appears to have adhered to its strictures.[79] Delegates even held back from reporting to the governors, legislatures, and local committees that had sent them to the Congress. When they sent a copy of the completed proceedings to the Freeholders of Dutchess County in early November, the New York delegation noted that it was "with regret that we have thus long been obliged to withhold this mark of respect, which we owe our worthy constituents."[80] Despite the delegates' sense of responsibility to report to those who sent them, they continued to keep private the petition addressed to the king, "which cannot in point of decorum be made publick until it has been laid before the throne."[81]

When the delegates did publish their proceedings at the end of October 1774, they contained very little detail. The "Extracts from the votes and proceedings of the American Continental Congress" came in at just under forty pages and contained a preamble and list of resolutions passed, in addition to an address from the Congress to British subjects and one to the inhabitants of the colonies. Prefaced by the declaration that the resolutions were taken "in a full and free representation of these colonies," the resolves were then printed without any record of debates or vote tallies within the Congress. Presented as faits accomplis, the proceedings concluded with an address from the Congress as a whole to the American colonists. In it, delegates explained their reasoning for adopting non-importation, consumption, and exportation to combat British measures, calling their decisions a result of their having "diligently deliberately and calmly enquired into and considered those exertions, both of the legislative and executive power of Great-Britain, which have excited so much uneasiness in America, and have with equal fidelity and attention considered the conduct of the colonies."[82]

The fact that the Congress had worked behind closed doors and published a limited account of its proceedings was not lost on those who opposed their resolutions. Some writers cited the secrecy with which the delegates' work was undertaken as a reason to question the Congress's legitimacy as a voice of the American colonists. After warning readers that their interests had been abandoned in Philadelphia—that non-importation would disproportionately hurt farmers and damage the prospects for restoring peace with the British—loyalist Samuel Seabury, writing as "A Farmer," raised suspicion about the way the deliberations had unfolded. "Much stress has been laid, it seems, upon the *unanimity* of the Delegates, and it has been urged, that *all the inhabitants of the continent* should think themselves in honor obliged to abide *passively* by their decisions, be they what they may, as they were *their Representatives*," he wrote. Not only did the vast majority of the population of New York, where he was writing, have no say in their election, "it is now pretty generally understood and it is an undoubted fact, that not only *most* or *all* of the New York members, but many others . . . warmly opposed their conduct in a MULTITUDE of instances." He went on to note that the public was essentially being tricked as the delegates "had unhappily agreed, before their entrance into any business, that neither *protest* nor *dissent* should appear [in the] *minutes.*" The Congress had employed "*arts and stratagems*" that amounted to "UNFAIR DEALINGS," and colonists should have no faith in the delegates, nor should they obey their directives.[83] Even if congressional delegates did not conceive of themselves as representatives of the people, there were many who saw them this way—and with reason, as the Congress did act in the name of the American people. Moreover, those who did hold this view considered the delegates' adherence to secrecy to be a nefarious trick that undermined their legitimacy as representatives.

Despite this criticism, when the second Continental Congress met in the spring of 1775, the delegates immediately resolved to retain the secrecy rule.[84] What this meant in practice was that the delegates would meet behind closed doors; their journals were split into those revised for publication and those deemed "Secret Journals" (and later, "More Secret Journals"); and secret committees were created to oversee classified financial and diplomatic operations.[85] When Deane wrote back to his wife, he urged her to "believe nothing you hear reported of us, for our doings will not be published but by an authority of the whole."[86] Partly because of the way the journals were kept, there is no record of discussion within Congress regarding the secrecy rules, making reference to delegates' letters of paramount importance in gleaning their justification. As war broke out and the Congress undertook diplomatic negotiations in search of financial support, it is clear from their correspondence that working in secret became crucial. The delicacy of military and diplomatic maneuverings demanded discretion, and the conditions of working in a war zone made this all the more difficult to maintain. Ultimately, the delegates felt little need to make excuses for their secrecy during the initial period of the war, even if they did lament its drawbacks.

Starting as early as that fall of 1775, the delegates were worried their letters might be intercepted and revealed, much like what had happened to Hutchinson before the war's outbreak. John Adams had, at first, frequently fudged the secrecy rule in writing to his confidant, Massachusetts politician James Warren, noting that his letters were "secret and confidential as the saying is" but that "in confidence, I am determined to write freely to you at this time."[87] But in October 1775, he wrote to Warren that "our obligations of secrecy are so braced up that I must deny myself the pleasure of writing particulars."[88] Adams began to think twice about what he committed to writing, even to his wife, Abigail. That same month, he apologized for not being able to convey any substantive news to her and warned her to be careful with anything he had sent. "My letters have been and will be nothing but trifles. I don't choose to trust the post. I am afraid to trust private travelers. They may peep," he wrote. "Accidents may happen; and I would avoid, if I could, even ridicule, but especially mischief. Pray, bundle up every paper, not already hid and conceal them in impenetrable darkness. Nobody knows what may occur."[89] The letter strikes a tone of near paranoia. But over the course of the war, intercepted letters remained a constant specter for many delegates who would cite the fear as reason for not conveying details of

2. 39

Thursday May 11.

agreeable to the order of yesterday the congress was opened with prayers by the revd Mr Duche

After prayers the Congress according to adjournment proceeded to business

The Delegates from the several Colonies produced their credentials, which were read & approved as follows

[illegible]

Upon Motion Resolved that the thanks of the Congress be given to the revd Mr Duche for performing divine service agreeable to the desire of the congress & for the excellent prayer so well adapted to the present occasion

Ordered that Mr Bland Mr Willing & Mr Sullivan be a committee to wait upon Mr Duche & return him the thanks of this congress agreeable to the above resolution

Upon Motion resolved

That the doors be kept shut during the time of business & that the members consider themselves under the strongest obligations of honor to keep the proceedings secret, until the majority shall direct them to be made public

A circular Letter from the agents Wm Bollan, B. Franklin & Arthur Lee, Esqrs directed to the speakers of the several assemblies, with sundry papers therein referred to was laid before the congress & read — the letter is as follows (here insert it)

Mr J. Hancock laid before the congress a Letter from the provincial congress of Massachusetts bay together with sundry resolutions formed by sd Congress, a letter sent by sd congress to their agent in England & an address to the inhabitants of G B on the late engagement between the troops under Genl Gage & the Inhabitants of Massachusetts bay and also a number of depositions duly attested relative to the commencement of hostilities, all which were read and are as follows (here insert them)

Ordered that the Secy have the above depositions & the address to the inhabts of G B published

Resolved Un. That the congress will on monday next resolve itself into a committee of the whole to take into consideration the state of America

Ordered that the Letter from the pro: congress of Massachusetts bay be referred to that Committee

Adjourned till tomorrow at 10 o'Clock

Friday 12th May the Congress met and adjourned till tomorrow at 10 o'Clock

Page from Continental Congress *Rough Journals*, Vol. 1, noting the vote taken on May 11, 1775, to maintain secrecy in the Second Continental Congress. (Source: U.S. National Archives and Records Administration)

deliberations.[90] Letters like these suggest the commitment to secrecy was treated with varying degrees of severity over the course of the war. Early on, for example, Adams wrote to close friends and his wife without much compunction, or maybe even thinking such correspondence did not technically violate the secrecy rule.[91] Yet, with the threat of interception rising, Adams at least took the secrecy rule much more seriously, indicating that a more effective lockdown on information may have taken hold.[92]

Intercepted mail could have repercussions for the military movements of the Continental Army, as well as for the diplomatic and commercial efforts the Congress was undertaking in Europe. It was in this realm that deputies were particularly careful to keep work under wraps. The "secret committees" were first created to deal with overseas affairs and quickly became central nodes of congressional activity. A "Secret Committee" was first created in September 1775 to negotiate the importation of gun powder.[93] Over the following years, the committee came to manage the commercial and financial affairs of the continental effort, and it would eventually face critiques for its shadowy operation. Another committee, the Committee of Correspondence—initially created in November 1775 and renamed the Committee of Secret Correspondence in January the following year—was tasked with "corresponding with our friends in Great Britain Ireland and other parts of the world and that they lay their correspondence before Congress when directed."[94] This committee reached out to trusted colonists who were abroad at the time to seek their regular reporting on the dispositions of foreign governments toward the rebels. As their operations became more formalized, Congress eventually dispatched operatives to France to seek military and financial aid in the conflict.

There, at the court of Louis XVI—which, as we will see, was known for its secrecy—the American envoys quietly attempted to gauge the possibility for support in their struggle to throw off British rule. Given the dangers of interception in the trans-Atlantic journey, correspondence between the committee and its operatives abroad was scarce. Commissioner Arthur Lee reportedly wrote a dispatch into the covers of a pocket dictionary at one point in an effort to smuggle it back to the colonies unseen.[95] News of a negotiated loan from the French was handled with extreme caution. Committee members concluded that they must take measures to keep secret what the French court wanted done quietly, and telling Congress was not the way to do it. "We find, by fatal experience, the Congress consists of too many members to keep secrets," they declared; "this committee ought to keep this secret, if secrecy is required."[96]

Even though they remained broadly committed to maintaining secrecy, the delegates did not uphold the policy without lamenting its shortcomings, and these scruples began to grow stronger over time. Jack Rakove has suggested the delegates initially "felt no compunction" at closing their doors because they were confident in their authority after an outburst of popular support following the battles of Lexington and Concord.[97] At the outset of their work, the delegates had indeed received a slew of petitions from local committees conveying their support for the resolves of the Congress. On their way to meet in the spring of 1775, delegates encountered displays of support and thereby gained some sense of popular sentiment going into their deliberations.[98] But once they were ensconced in Philadelphia—and later chased to Baltimore, Lancaster, Princeton, and Annapolis at various points—some quickly felt isolated. The secrecy requirement only served to heighten this sense of seclusion, leading some to draw a distinction between the free conversations they witnessed outside and the deliberations of Congress. Tasked with speaking on behalf of the colonies, many delegates felt the need to confer, discuss, and take the temperature, so to speak, of the people on whose behalf they were acting. Some perceived the commitment to working in secret as an impediment, though a necessary one, to fulfilling their role. This anxiety indicates an underlying sense that they were ultimately representatives of the people and that they generally understood this role as reflective: they were ideally supposed to reflect public opinion in their decisions. Secrecy was an obstacle to performing this role, a hindrance which most delegates seemed to tolerate due to the extraordinary military circumstances of the time.

Perhaps the most frequently cited concern among delegates was their inability to consult trusted friends and confidants on the matters under consideration in Congress. Adams conceded to a friend in June 1775 that "it would be a relief to my mind if I could write freely to you concerning the sentiments, principles, facts and arguments which are laid before us in Congress."[99] Before the onset of his fear about intercepted mail, Adams had made exceptions to the secrecy rule when writing to his trusted wife, Abigail—a practice indicating that women in particular may have been considered exceptions, inherently an extension of the private sphere and thus legitimate holders of secrets. On June 10, 1775, he informed her that though "in Congress we are bound to secrecy," he could tell her "under the rose" that he expected ten thousand men would be kept stationed in Massachusetts.[100] Even after he became afraid of committing news to writing and seemed to have stopped conveying much of substance to Abigail, Adams continued to wish he was able to confer with those he trusted. Writing to Warren, he drew a stark contrast between their "debates and deliberations" and "the conversations in the city and chat of the coffee house," which he described as "free and open," and which, it should be noted, were the bread and butter of newspaper reports.[101] "Indeed, I wish we were at liberty to write freely and speak openly upon every subject," he complained, "for there is frequently as much knowledge derived from conversation and correspondence as from solemn public debates."[102]

The desire to open up about what was happening in Congress soon exceeded wishes to write to trusted friends for advice. While they debated whether to declare independence in the spring of 1776, the delegates were careful to seek out evidence of public opinion before acting.[103] Given that most of the delegates had been sent with instructions to not declare independence, Congress trailed a shift in public opinion that spring, moving in a cautiously responsive fashion.[104] Not long thereafter, the confidence Rakove cited as a reason for the delegates' willingness to withhold their proceedings from the public was dwindling. Facing the prospect that Philadelphia might soon be occupied by British troops, the Congress decided to relocate to Baltimore in the winter of 1776–77. Once they had left, the problem of feeling cloistered became especially acute. Writing to fellow delegate Robert Morris that February, Benjamin Rush noted that "we live here in a convent, we converse only with one another. We are precluded from all opportunities of feeling the pulse of the public upon our measures." He was worried because the delegates were relying "upon the committee in Philadelphia to feel it for us."[105] The problem of feeling distant from the sentiments of the public may not have been of immediate concern in the early months of the Congress's deliberations. But by 1777, this was no longer the case, as the colonies had descended into a difficult and prolonged military conflict and Congress was responding to military, financial, and diplomatic crises as they arose.[106]

Beyond desiring a better connection with the broader public, it was the sense of duty they owed to their formally established constituents—state political officials—that led delegates to begin seriously challenging the adherence to secrecy. In January 1777, Maryland delegate Samuel

Chase sent the state Council of Safety a copy of a letter John Hancock had laid before Congress, noting that "I have no leave to make it public. I send it to give you all the intelligence in my power; it may be shewn but not printed."[107] A month later, he wrote again to the council with "intelligence necessary for your information, but the communication of it to our General Assembly must be made with every caution of secrecy."[108] Only a few days later, it was Chase who first proposed a resolution calling for the Congress to work with greater transparency. His proposal called for all resolutions, whether they passed or not, to be recorded in the journal and for the record of yeas and nays also to be printed at the request of a state delegation. The proposal went even further, calling for the doors of Congress to be opened and "except on particular occasions—all debates held in public."[109] The motion was seconded by the delegates from North Carolina and, as one of them, Thomas Burke, recorded in his notes that day, they "observed that it was very proper the Congress should have the public check on them, and that as every member was liable to be impeached by the state he represented, it was a justice to him and to the state that his votes should be entered on the journals."[110] This was necessary so "that the state might be furnished with testimony to prosecute, and the delegates with testimony to defend himself."[111] Here, Burke articulated a link between the representative function the Congress was playing and the necessity of working in view of constituents for the sake of accountability. But the vote on this resolution was postponed and never took place. A month later, Burke wrote to the governor of North Carolina lamenting that "By the rule of secrecy, you know, Sir, I am not at liberty to communicate anything before it is determined and therefore cannot consult the state upon it." Moreover, he reported that because limited information was entered in the journals, "nothing therefore can give testimony hereafter that such points were contested and even rejected by a majority as is indeed the usual case."[112]

In the wake of this failed attempt to publish greater detail of their deliberations in the journals and even allow the public to attend their meetings, some delegations began to violate the secrecy rule more flagrantly in reporting back to state officials. Such violations of the rule were perhaps understandable considering the lag in publication of Congress's journals. The Virginia deputies wrote to the speaker of the state's House of Delegates in May 1777 to deliver the "first volume of the last edition of the Journal of Congress." The volume, however, reached "no further than the 30th of December 1775." The delegates apologized for the deficiency of information they were able to send back: "As our duty directs, so our inclinations lead to an immediate compliance with the desires of the House of Delegates, but we apprehend insurmountable difficulty in getting the manuscript journal, because the many secret articles cannot be exposed to a copier, and neither the secretary or ourselves have time to do it."[113] The printing of the official journals had been further stalled, they reported, because "the printer has hitherto been delayed for want of paper."[114] Adams made the same explanation in a letter to Thomas Jefferson a week later, noting that "nothing gives me more constant anxiety than the delays in publishing the journals." In this case, he assured Jefferson—then serving in Virginia's House of Delegates—the delay was a mere matter of lacking manpower, as "we have too many irons in the fire," though "the committee are now busy every day in correcting proof sheets, so I hope we shall soon do better."[115]

Beyond the delay in publishing the journals, there was also the matter of what they contained or, more critically, what they did not contain. The process of preparing the journals for publication entailed decisions about what would appear in print and "what ought to be excepted," as Adams explained in a letter.[116] Back in December 1775, as the delegates reviewed for publication the journals that would appear in the spring of 1777, the diary of New Jersey delegate Richard Smith regularly noted that those "excepted" portions were almost daily selected.[117] A nineteenth-century study of the multiple versions of the journals showed how Charles Thomson, secretary to the Congress, had actually kept and revised the journals. In a note left at the beginning of the first volume of the "Transcript Journal," Thomson explained that "the passages and resolutions, which in this and the following books are crossed . . . were ordered to be crossed or marked so as not to be transcribed for publication."[118] Although it is thus possible to trace what was deemed unfit for publication, it is difficult to ascertain how Thomson composed the "Secret Journals." Frequently in the "Rough Journal," resolutions would be marked "with the usual dotted lines in the margin to indicate that this was matter of a secret nature," suggesting that it might be later moved to the "Secret Journal," so as to collect them in one place for reference.[119] The journal system was complicated and discerning secret from public content was an ongoing process.

Soon a series of leaks brought factional divisions within Congress to light and led to increased pressure from outside for delegates to abandon their strict observance of secrecy. In December 1778, an angry Silas

Deane, recently recalled from his duty as commissioner in France, published a long critique of his colleague Arthur Lee in the *Pennsylvania Packet.* Deane, who was himself under suspicion within Congress for his role in negotiating financial aid from the French, pointed the finger at his erstwhile colleague in Europe. "What I write to you, I would have said to your Representatives, their ears having been shut against me." As the possibility of a treaty with the French had become imminent earlier that year, Deane alleged that Lee "was dragged into the treaty with the utmost reluctance." "It was agreed that this important matter should be kept a profound secret," Deane recounted, but a few days later British member of Parliament Charles Fox—who, Deane was careful to note, was a good friend of Lee's alleged confidant Lord Shelburne—declared it in the House of Commons. This happened shortly after "Mr. Lee's secretary went to and from London, charged with affairs which were secret to your other commissioners." The reader was left to connect the dots. Upon his return that summer, Deane recalled, he had gone to Congress to inform delegates of these suspicions but found he was no longer able to obtain an audience.[120] Repeatedly referring to Congress as the reader's "representatives," Deane suggested the public was being misled and it was time to make the truth known.

The publication threw the Congress into convulsions as delegates split over what to believe, whether Deane should be penalized for having gone to the press, and what to do with Lee. In response to the allegations, Paine—then a secretary for the Committee of Foreign Affairs, formerly the Committee of Secret Correspondence—took to the pages of the *Packet* repeatedly to admonish Deane and vindicate Lee and his allies in Congress. In his first response, signed "Common Sense," Paine countered Deane's claims about Lee and questioned his trustworthiness: "A public man, Mr. Deane's former character, ought to be as silent as the grave; for who would trust a person with a secret who showed such a talent for revealing?"[121] He proceeded to state that over the coming days he would "lay before you some very interesting facts and materials," because "the public should know the whole, for upon that only can they form a proper judgment."[122] Two weeks later, Paine suggested the public might ask why Deane saw fit at this time to come out with these allegations; the answer, he indicated, would reveal that Deane himself was under suspicion in Congress for his behavior.[123] Despite accusing Deane of violating the integrity of his public position by disclosing secrets in print, Paine proceeded to set the record straight by revealing information he had obtained in his capacity as committee secretary. Deane had not, he disclosed, sought a third audience with the Congress. In fact, he was facing an investigation by Congress into his accounts, which he had not yet produced. "There is something in this concealment of papers that looks like an embezzlement," Paine suggested. He then laid out the precise suspicion that Deane had portrayed a deal made with the French royal agent Pierre August Caron de Beaumarchais as a loan when it was actually a gift. Paine repeatedly urged the public to trust him as secretary for the Committee of Foreign Affairs. Eventually, he lost his job over this revelation of what delegates considered secret information, though Paine argued he was actually vindicating the people's "representatives" from the false insinuations made against them.

When a vote was finally taken on whether to recall Lee (which failed), the records of yeas and nays mysteriously appeared in the *Packet*. Laurens railed in his notes on May 8, 1779, that "the whole truth should have been published, if publication was necessary or right, and the whole truth will be published—and Gentlemen remember this repeated offer on my part."[124] Even though Paine had been dismissed for exposing confidential information in the press, some members were beginning to reconsider their adherence to secrecy in light of repeated leaks.

Immediately following the resolution of the Deane-Lee dispute—at least for the time being—the Congress voted to publish its journals on a weekly basis.[125] Although this was a significant step considering the lag in publication up to then, the weekly journals were still by no means intended to present a full view of deliberations. As delegate William Floyd noted in delivering the first weekly journal to New York governor George Clinton: "All matters of a secret nature are put on a separate journal and will not be printed until the war is ended."[126] This statement implied that the secret journals were perhaps intended for publication upon the conclusion of the military conflict. In the meantime, delegates continued to be frustrated by the limitations of the published journals for the purposes of explaining themselves to their constituents—specifically state officials—back home. Later in May, delegate James Lovell wrote to the deputy secretary of the Massachusetts Council noting that "the published journals will in part explain my grounds; the secret ones would fully do it."[127] In mid-June, he complained to John Adams that "you will be scarcely able by our motley journals to understand what we are about."[128] Though it ultimately amounted to a token gesture, the Congress had nonetheless taken a small step toward opening its work to public view by printing the journals weekly after the upheaval caused by the leaks.

However, pressure continued to mount as further leaks seemed to prove how inadequate the weekly publication of the journals was to revealing what was actually taking place. On June 19, 1779, as the delegates opened discussion of a set of proposed peace terms that had been under consideration for a few months, Gouverneur Morris reportedly "said our pretended private business was no secret, it was known and talked of in every one of the states," to which Thomas McKean "confirmed this as to every county town in Pennsylvania," according to Laurens's personal notes.[129] The French minister in America had prodded Congress early in 1779 to prepare its conditions for peace after Spain had declared it would inform Britain of its intent to serve as a mediator or else enter the war.[130] In his notes Laurens reported having announced that he had "reason to believe [the proposed terms have] been transmitted to South Carolina, but not by me. I have hitherto held myself restricted from speaking or writing on the subject."[131] For months, the delegates had been discussing the possible peace terms, with one of the main sticking points being access to fisheries off the coast of New England.[132] As with all the deliberations, the peace conditions and thoughts on them were closely guarded, but internal disagreements led some members to bring the issue to the press.

In the June 23 issue of the *Pennsylvania Gazette*, "Americanus" picked up a report that had appeared in the *Maryland Gazette* nearly a month earlier, which had suggested there would be a strenuous military campaign over the summer that could be avoided had the Congress acted more wisely. "If the present distresses and ravages of war, and the expence of our blood and treasure, is owing to the dishonest and unwise practices and conduct of any man, or sett of men," Americanus wrote, "they ought to be exposed to the public, and the measures they have so fatally pursued to be reprobated and condemned." There was a dangerous faction at work within the Congress, he suspected, and "if so, it is high time that not only the Journals of Congress and the ayes and noes should be published, but that the doors of the House should be thrown open." If this were done, "their constituents [would] have an opportunity of judging for themselves who are the men who oppose themselves to the peace and happiness of the states." Though he proclaimed to be "very sensible of the impropriety and danger, as well as of the absurdity, of debating in public on the terms to be proposed in a treaty," Americanus concluded that "when this bleeding country is told that an execrable faction prevents peace, it is but natural to enquire where this faction is, who compose it, and what are their views."[133] It was an overt call for Congress to open its deliberations to public view, based on an insinuation that the delegates were using secrecy as a tool to subvert the best interest of the states.

The summer only got worse for the delegates, as the proposed peace terms were not the only issue for which they were coming under scrutiny. In the *Pennsylvania Packet*, a letter signed "Leonidas" lamented the state of continental money, which was leading to massive inflation, and asked why Congress, though aware of the problem, did nothing. Set up in the form of a speech "which ought to be spoken to Congress" on the issue, "the speaker first emphasizes the fact that the people are their masters, Congress their servants." A bold pronouncement of the relationship assumed between delegates and "the people," Leonidas's letter cast the Congress as a representative body of the population, not just of state governments. "Rouse then gentlemen, to a sense of danger of these infant states that are committed to your care," he urged. "Let us read something more than the Yeas and Nays and questions for recommitting and postponing business in your journals," Leonidas implored, tying the delegates' representative function to an obligation to work in public view.[134] Another anonymous piece in the *Maryland Journal and Baltimore Advertiser* printed on June 29—and subsequently reprinted in at least five additional newspapers over the coming month—tied together the Deane-Lee spat and the rumors about the proposed peace terms into a general distrust of Congress. The author, "O Tempora! O Moses!," alleged that there was a "junto early formed in Congress" that was managing to manipulate the proceedings to block all progress.[135]

The "Leonidas" letter went too far for some of the delegates, who called on July 3 for the printer of the *Packet* to be summoned before Congress to answer delegates' questions about the publication. According to Laurens's notes, Massachusetts delegate Elbridge Gerry proposed the measure after noting that "if such infamous publications are to pass without proper notice, tis time for Congress to go home and other men to come in their stead."[136] But others counseled restraint, noting that "it would be lowering and disgracing the dignity of Congress to take any notice of the printer or author," as Thomas Burke—who had previously supported opening the doors—reportedly declared. In a letter to Virginia delegate Richard Henry Lee, dated June 22, Laurens, though acknowledging the appeal of open doors, feared that such openness was not tenable: "As to the hearing and open doors I believe it would be a proper means had we the proper men—but alas!"[137]

Laurens's reflection laid out a problem he and likeminded delegates wrestled with over the following months. It seemed the only way to counter the leaks would be to release more information, which risked betraying secrets. In a letter back to Laurens the next month, Lee referred to the recent publications in the *Packet* and *Maryland Journal and Baltimore Advertiser* as cases where authors were "so artful in garnishing falsehood with truth that the varnished tale goes on with perhaps the greater number, who neither are, or will take pains to be informed." He seemed at a loss when it came to determining how to combat what he characterized as a pernicious problem. "I know the knaves who write these things have the advantage, because they cannot be completely exposed without exposing secrets that it would be very unwise to publish at present," he lamented. "This the true friends of America will not do, and this those Scribblers know well, which induces them to come forward with so much effrontery."[138] But given what had been introduced into public discussion, other delegates' thinking seemed to be evolving when it came to the necessity of maintaining secrets.

For his part, Laurens came to believe the time had come to work in full public view. With the steady stream of leaks and what he felt to be manipulation of the truth based on a conviction that the Congress would stick to secrecy, he thought it would be best to simply remove the restrictions. Reporting to the governor of New Jersey on July 5, Laurens urged him to take action "if this sketch for reformations shall not meet your Excellency's judgment." "Order our doors to be opened that our masters may discover what we leave undone," he concluded. Laurens's word choice was identical to that of Leonidas in his published call for greater publicity in Congress and suggests a particular conception of the representative function Congress was fulfilling.[139]

Over the coming years, the push for greater publicity in congressional work did make strides. The Articles of Confederation, ratified in 1781, included a provision requiring regular publication of the journals, with clearly defined exceptions of "such parts thereof relating to treaties, alliances or military operations, as in their judgement require secrecy."[140] It is noteworthy that this caveat was more specific in delineating when secrecy was justified than the Federal Constitution would be later that decade. Still, the articles did not necessarily result in greater public communication of information, though there does appear to have been a more frequent flow of facts from the president and/or the committee at headquarters—which was traveling with the army—to the governors and state assemblies in the early

1780s. Many of these missives requested secrecy due to the military nature of their contents, but state governments were being let in on those secrets to a seemingly greater extent.

When the war finally drew to a close, the matter of peace negotiations posed yet another test for congressional delegates. As news arrived of the negotiation, it was officially considered secret. The Pennsylvania delegation apologized to the state's Executive Council, as late as December 1783, for not being able to provide details of recently arrived letters from abroad. "As they consist principally of steps taken by our ministers in their negotiations for peace, and of conversations of a secret nature, which they have had with the ministers of some European courts, we are not at liberty to copy them for your inspection," they wrote.[141] Yet other delegates saw fit to share the information with people they believed had a need to know. Writing earlier that year to George Washington, the commanding general of the army, Arthur Lee noted that though "Congress have thought proper to enjoin secrecy with regard to communications of some of our ministers . . . I apprehend, the secret will be at least as safe with your excellency as with us; and it seems to me as necessary that you should be circumstantially informed."[142] With the end of war, it seemed the pressure to keep secrets lessened.

Though the Congress continued to exist until 1789 when the new federal government was put in place after the ratification of the Constitution, the center of political life shifted to the states after the war. It was there that American republics were being formed and the problems of political representation were primarily being worked out. Even efforts to open Congress to public view seemed to shift to the states. In a letter to the Massachusetts Assembly in June 1784, congressional delegate Francis Dana urged the state legislature to "require their delegates in Congress to keep them informed of what passes there not of a real secret nature, especially of all money matters." He suggested that "An apprehension that their proceedings will be carefully reviewed by those bodies, will introduce into Congress more circumspection, more prudence, and oeconomy; and will serve to establish them in the full confidence of the whole union."[143] Aside from the occasional effort like Dana's, the spotlight largely shifted away from the Congress.[144] In the meantime, congressional papers languished in "iron chest[s]," according to Thomson's papers.[145]

Keeping secrets had been central to the operation of the Continental Congress during the American War of Independence, even as a general suspicion of secrecy swept through communities up and down the eastern seaboard. During the war, publicity was primarily prized as a tool by which committees of safety exercised vigilance within their localities. Surveillance was used by interim governmental entities to expose enemies, while simultaneously proving to be a specter for political officials who guarded their communications closely. In the midst of a military conflict and conducting diplomatic negotiations abroad, delegates to the Congress were cautious to maintain confidentiality. And at the outset, they seemed to face little criticism for doing so. Perhaps this was because they were perceived to be a temporary body, to represent the colonies rather than the people, and to be generally responsive to expressions of public opinion.

But when people perceived a government to be permanent and, more importantly, to be representative, its use of secrecy was less tolerated. As Congress became a more entrenched entity with the drafting of the Articles of Confederation in 1777, even though the war was still waging, the delegates faced increasing scrutiny for working behind closed doors and limiting the publication of their journals. A series of leaks in 1779 pushed the case for greater publicity, as delegates themselves began to consider the benefit of bringing more into public view. Though Congress never did open its doors, that may have been primarily because its importance waned during the confederation period. When Americans set up republican governments in the states, built around representative legislatures, most affirmed a view that publicity was necessary and expected. While some state constitutions went further than others in guaranteeing publicity in the work of legislatures and carving out a role for the press in scrutinizing government operations, even those that allowed for secrecy suggested that some degree of publicity was expected. Allowing for public scrutiny of representative legislatures was increasingly normalized as multiple states officially endorsed it.

Yet as the framers met to reform the confederation government in 1787, publicity was still far from a standard expectation. In fact, at least one of the most prominent men at the time felt that one of the Continental Congress's deficiencies was a lack, not an excess, of secrecy. Writing to General Henry Knox in the winter of 1787, Washington diagnosed the problems with the existing government as such: "[the present government], from experience, we find is not only slow—debilitated—and liable to be thwarted by every breath, but is defective in that secrecy, which for the accomplishment of many of the most important national purposes, is indispensably necessary."[146] Though he confided in the same letter that he did not wish to participate in the coming convention and declared that he doubted it would succeed, Washington concluded that "after what I have seen, or rather after what I have heard, I shall be surprised at nothing."[147] Indeed, Washington would go on to preside over the Federal Convention—which would be held behind closed doors and under obligation of secrecy—to produce the United States Constitution.

Meanwhile, across the Atlantic, the American Revolution had stoked tensions and raised new challenges for the French monarchy. Long before anyone anticipated a revolution breaking out in France, similar questions about the nature of representation and the place of state secrecy were bubbling up.

CHAPTER TWO

Cracking the *Secret du Roi*

A FEW MONTHS BEFORE the British surrendered to the Americans at Yorktown, a shocking publication appeared in Paris. In early 1781, Royal Finance Minister Jacques Necker published for the first time the royal budget. On the very first page of the *Compte Rendu au Roi*, Necker stated that "shadows and obscurity favor nonchalance: publicity, by contrast, cannot but become an honor and a reward, in as much as one has felt the importance of his obligations and has endeavored to fulfill them."[1] Necker certainly intended for the airing of the royal accounts to burnish his own reputation—his numbers were not entirely clear, to say the least. But he also extended publicity into a general principle by which administrators could be held accountable for their performance.[2] He took care to note that he would not publicize such material were he not confident it would help the king by facilitating public confidence. As the crown confronted crises and calls for new administrative, legal, and legislative structures, such discussions of the need for visible governance became central to imagining solutions. In laying out proposed structures for provincial assemblies, Necker again linked the potential effectiveness of such organs to their publicity. In a recommendation to the king a few years later, Necker noted: "it is the publicity of deliberations that force honesty."[3] It was an ironic declaration considering he himself deployed publicity to dissemble. The episode encapsulates some of the paradoxes inherent in the concept, which would become more glaring as publicity was valorized.

As Americans celebrated their newfound independence, their French allies grappled with the fallout from having supported a revolution that established representative republics. Necker's bold publication marked the collision of the two primary components of that fallout. The first, of course, was the financial crisis the monarchy was facing as a result of having supported the colonists in their struggle against the British. By 1781, the country was nearly bankrupt and bold action would be needed to stem the losses.[4] But perhaps even more important than the contents of the budget, Necker's publication marked a culmination of decades of mounting pressure for greater publicity in government, which by then accompanied calls for the establishment of formal representative institutions within the French state. By publishing the budget, Necker defied the foreign minister—the Comte de Vergennes warned that the state's debts should not be publicly revealed, "for publicly exposing royal accounts would surely undermine that most critical religion of monarchy: secrecy."[5] In fact, the publication of the budget did violate this principal tenet of the crown and, in so doing, helped foster a new notion of accountability.[6]

Under the Bourbon monarchy, most politics were considered secret. The designation given to Louis XV's covert diplomatic agenda—the *secret du Roi*—could be aptly applied as the official modus operandi in many realms of state activity.[7] Dating especially to the reign of Louis XIV (1643–1715), the operations of the royal government and administration of justice were confined to a complex system of centralized control. From the dawn of the eighteenth century, the French press operated under an elaborate royal censorship regime, and political information was tightly controlled.[8] The reign of the Sun King also marked a rise in the use of *lettres de cachets*, which were sealed letters conveying clandestine royal orders, whereby subjects could be imprisoned without explanation.[9]

Secrecy had been built into the expansion of the royal administration under Jean Baptiste Colbert (comptroller general of finance and then secretary of state from 1665 to 1683), becoming a core ingredient of the absolutist state.[10] The absolutist ideal, though never fully realized, divested power from deliberative bodies and concentrated authority in a web of relatively anonymous administrative operatives who were meant to carry out the king's orders in the provinces and pass information back to Versailles.[11] The prevalence of confidentiality in government was predicated, at least in part, on the theoretical underpinnings of absolutism. The king was divinely sanctioned, his will bounded only by God.

His subjects, then, had no need to be privy to the political workings of the kingdom because the king's relationship to them was representative in a pre-modern sense: he embodied the nation.[12] His will was by definition the will of his people; "there is no public apart from the person of the king," as Keith Michael Baker put it.[13] Louis XV, crowned in 1722, was thus theoretically under no obligation to present or defend his decisions to the population he ruled.

In practice, the state's ability to maintain secrecy was imperfect at best. The growth of state censorship coincided with the blossoming of the public sphere. A rising supply of periodicals operated beyond the reach of the government, either illicitly or outside the country's borders.[14] The emerging salon culture in Paris and the ever-present circulation of rumors, court gossip, even poems, represented an additional realm of oral exchange that, despite the monarchy's best efforts, remained difficult to control.[15] By mid-century, public opinion was gaining political salience and manifesting in various forms to the point where people appealed to it as a legitimate authority. A politicized public sphere took root and public opinion blossomed particularly out of ongoing battles between the crown and the *parlements* legal courts, especially the *Parlement* of Paris, where clashes over religious doctrine and practice and taxes dominated the century and culminated in constitutional conflict. These courts, which registered royal edicts, laws, and taxes—in addition to serving as final courts of appeal—were a real check on royal authority. Positioning themselves as repositories of fundamental law and the voice of a national will distinct from that of the king, the parlements were also spaces where politics spilled into the open through published pamphlets and crowded courtrooms. Amidst these developments not only the capacity for, but the wisdom of, the monarchy's adherence to secrecy was called into question.

Historians of eighteenth-century France have long been concerned with how public opinion emerged, what constituted it, and what effect it had on the unraveling of the monarchy. The concepts of "the public" and "public opinion" remained nebulous even as they grew increasingly powerful through the last decades of the Old Regime. While some scholars argue that public opinion came to refer to a sort of tribunal of enlightened men—a reasoned opinion greater than the sum of its parts—others have suggested it was a force constructed by police spies intent on recording chatter in Parisian cafes, embodied by rowdy crowds in the pits of Parisian theaters, made up of readers of legal trial accounts, or those who penned letters to the editor throughout the kingdom.[16] Although there was certainly a developing politics of contestation and an increasingly public discussion of politics intensifying especially from the 1750s, it was mainly by the monarchy recognizing these developments and beginning to appeal to "public opinion" that the phenomenon was vested with political significance.[17] Many viewed the press as the central medium of this new political sphere that had been opened by public opinion, which in turn was increasingly considered by those who followed government as the ultimate pillar of authority.[18] It was this new concept—ironically at least in part the creation of a royal administration which sought to ground its legitimacy elsewhere—that made the French Revolution thinkable, as Keith Baker argued.[19]

Certainly, the monarch's own willingness to recognize and appeal to public opinion was crucial in undermining the regime's reliance on secrecy and restriction of politics to a closed government sphere. But it was also essential that there was in fact an expansion of printed material with growing readership. Moreover, the content of much of this material began to highlight and critique the monarchy's association with secrecy. Over the course of the eighteenth century, for instance, the French grew increasingly aware of the supposed contrast between their government and that of their neighbors across the English Channel. It had long been common for British writers to gesture to the French administration's strict censorship laws and opaque judicial and legislative systems to bolster their claims to be a comparatively free people.[20] As French philosophes began to echo this comparison, they stoked a new curiosity about other political systems and fed an emerging trend of associating clandestine government with tyranny. This would provide an intellectual foundation for critics of the royal regime to point to covert operations as evidence of its supposedly despotic tendencies. The critique was then further advanced by an underground literature that promised to lift the veil off the secret machinations of power at Versailles.[21] In fact, state secrecy was a common theme both in philosophical writing and in the genre of court intrigue.[22] The royal regime was increasingly associated with clandestine forces, inscrutable motives, and opaque administration. These characteristics were becoming linked with accusations of despotism.[23] Eventually critics would portray the royal administration and its private tax collection body, the General Farm, as screens blocking lines of sight between the king and his people, preventing accountable governance.[24] As calls for representative institutions mounted in the 1780s, they were linked to cries for more publicity in government, and secrecy became anathema.

Already in the first half of the eighteenth century, the forerunners of the high Enlightenment philosophes were comparing governments and using state secrecy and degrees of publicity in politics as barometers. Despotism, as defined by Montesquieu in his widely circulated *De l'Esprit des Lois* (1748), was predicated on an ignorant public. The less informed and educated the population, the easier it was for tyrants to remain in power.[25] The Ottoman Empire, a commonly deployed example of a supposedly despotic state in French writing, was associated with the secrecy shrouding the sultan's *Seraglio*, or palace—notably a space with a female presence.[26] In such states, the operations of the sovereign were hidden from public view. In free states, by contrast, information flowed without hindrance. Looking across the Channel, French writers constructed an example of an open state, characterized by free thought and a circulation of information. In his *Lettres Philosophiques* (1734), Voltaire marveled at the English government enabling denizens to communicate their thoughts freely, saying it gave letters a place of honor unlike in France: "Everyone can print what he thinks about public affairs. As such, all the nation must necessarily inform itself."[27] Of course, the French characterization of English government and politics was much closer to an ideal than reality. But these types of comparisons were increasingly used as tools to critique the French government as slipping toward despotism, as evidenced by its reliance on secrecy.

Growing calls for *publicité*, or more transparent government, in France eventually began to appear in addition to these more intellectual critiques of secrecy. They became prevelant in the struggles that intensified over the structure of the French state. Structural, or what contemporaries called constitutional, challenges defined the eighteenth century. Despite real tendencies toward administrative modernization and centralization unleashed under Louis XIV, the French state was a patchwork of overlapping jurisdictions, precariously negotiated power relationships, and unwritten customs.[28] The sheer number of institutions can be dizzying. While there were no explicitly representative institutions that could claim to speak for the people or nation—outside the king himself—royal authority was functionally constrained by the negotiation required with various legal courts, provincial estates and assemblies, and court dynamics that often influenced the royal council comprised of the king's ministers.

To understand the emergence of the interrelated concepts of public opinion, accountability, and a national will separable from the king that demanded representation, it is necessary to home in on a power struggle between the crown and specific courts called parlements. This struggle took many forms but played out predominantly through conflicts over religious practices and taxes, especially in the 1750s.[29]

Often confused by eighteenth-century foreigners and historians alike with the British Parliament, the parlements were in fact legal courts. They did play a somewhat legislative function in registering the monarch's edicts and new taxes, which nonetheless could be forced through on the king's command through a ceremony called a *lit de justice*.[30] There were thirteen of them by 1789 with the Paris Parlement atop the proverbial pile, though they did not operate as one institution with a formal hierarchy.[31] The lawyers who argued cases before the parlements were perhaps the most politicized corps of people in pre-revolutionary France and made up almost half of the deputies sent to the Estates General in 1789.[32] Judges in the courts were either appointed by the crown, bought their offices, or inherited their seats through family lineage. In short, the parlements were hardly a representative institution in the sense of their members being elected to voice the people or the nation's will. Nonetheless, they began to position themselves as such in the absence of any other official representative organ in the kingdom. Part of the reason they may have been able to do this was because they could boast one of the only relatively open spheres of publication and exchange of information in France. Lawyers could publish *mémoires judiciaires* without facing censorship and were thus able to critique the monarchy much more openly than other writers.[33] As courts, the parlements could also freely publish remonstrances against royal edicts, and they did so strategically in an effort to sway public opinion.[34] In fact, scholars have shown that publications related to legal cases were crucial to forming a public sphere and the idea of a tribunal of public opinion.[35]

The so-called Maupeou Revolution of 1771–74—in which a royal minister disbanded the parlements—was a turning point in the dialogue about publicity, explicitly linking the perceived problem of secrecy to debates over the (unwritten) constitution of the country. Legal historians and those looking to explain the failure of reform efforts in the waning years of the monarchy have extensively addressed the disbanding of the Paris Parlement and its replacement with *Conseils Supérieurs*, under the supervision of the royal chancellor René Nicolas Charles Augustin de

Maupeou.[36] The way in which the question of state secrecy was linked to this failed reform effort helps explain the emergence of the *Parti Patriote*, which supported the parlements' claims to be the representative body of the French people.[37] The event highlighted the threat of state secrecy and led to calls for publicity on two levels. Firstly, taking away the court's legislative function allowed the magistrates to argue that their registration of royal edicts was the one moment of visibility in the political decision-making process. This was a moment the Parti Patriote effectively claimed to constitute a form of political representation, based largely on its public visibility. Secondly, critics cited the way in which the ministry went about hastily disbanding the parlements as evidence of the secret motivations and methods of the royal administration.

Following their dismantling, many pamphlets portrayed the ability of the parlements to remonstrate openly against proposed laws as a process of communication, even illumination. During this process, the king's eyes could be opened to the sentiments of his people and the impact of the proposed edict or tax upon them. In one of the Parlement of Paris's published responses to the king's disbanding of the court, the ability to remonstrate against royal edicts was characterized as the one check the population had against the advance of tyrannical government. It might not have been much, "but it stops the rapid march of the arbitrary will; it holds at bay its effects; and it sheds a faint light on the truth, making it visible to the often blind eye of authority."[38] The Paris Parlement's ability to serve as a mediator between the people and the king, essentially to represent the people to the king, was predicated on its unique ability to make the people's interests visible to the otherwise blind monarch. This claim carried echoes of the grounds on which the Paris Parlement had defied the crown throughout the century, peaking in the 1750s by asserting its authority to weigh in on religious matters.[39]

Beyond this function of the Parlement, it was the secretive way in which the entity's authority was usurped that helped undergird its claim to represent the French people. Following the disbanding of the Parlement of Paris and the exile of its members to the provinces, a proliferation of pamphlets appeared, filled with suspicion of the secret motives of the chancellor and lamenting the clandestine methods he employed to fundamentally alter the structure of government. Responding to the royal edict demanding it register the king's action or be disbanded, the Paris Parlement pointed to the secret motivations behind Maupeou's plan as a reason the crown should reconsider its course of action. Such rash actions as disbanding the parlements were driven merely by personal interests and vengeance: "a supposed desire for authority is the only veil with which its authors cover themselves," the members asserted. "Never, Sire, has the veil been less difficult to penetrate than on the present occasion," they continued, urging the king to "set your sights on it; consult yourself only," and judge who really had the best interests of the state at heart.[40] If politics were run like this, the motivations for decisions would remain constantly hidden from the people and the king alike. The *parlementaires* cast the royal administration, particularly the ministry, as an obstruction between king and people, operating clandestinely and thus preventing representation of the people in, or to, the government.

Even supporters of the Maupeou reforms recognized the ubiquity of the discourse of secrecy, and they adopted it to vilify the parlements. A publication of the supposed "secret correspondence" between Maupeou and a counselor of the new *Conseil Supérieure* addressed the accusations of secrecy head-on. Designed to explain his motivation and justification for disbanding the Paris Parlement, the minister wrote that it was time he divulged the "most secret sentiments of his heart."[41] His correspondent laid out all the secret motives and machinations he was supposed to have undertaken, so that Maupeou could counter that the only secret motivation he had was love for his country. The parlements had usurped the power of representation and consent from the people, they were perhaps being paid by a secret enemy, and they had to be defeated.[42] Secret allegiances, secret motives, secret intentions—secrecy was the accusation du jour. In the struggle over the judicial reforms, secrecy and visibility were juxtaposed as governmental methods; secrecy was equated with despotism, while publicity, visible motives, and open communication between king and people were posited as tools of representation.

By the time the parlements were restored in 1774, soon after the accession of Louis XVI to the throne, tracts citing secrecy as the root of rotten royal administration were widespread. Reform advocates, among them royal officials, began advising the new king to adopt measures to publicize royal operations and eliminate secrecy from the state.[43] These tracts, most of them published, advocated more *publicité* of governance to promote an accountable administration, fair treatment of subjects under the law, and a sense of public confidence in the government. During Louis XVI's reign, some officials were beginning to imagine publicity as a mechanism whereby an administration perceived as increasingly unwieldy could be held accountable to the king and his subjects alike. The main targets of these reformers were the provincial administrators—such as intendants and their operatives—and tax-farmers (private contractors who collected taxes for a fee). By these accounts, the anonymity of these figures and the opacity of their operations were contributing to a complex, corrupt, and potentially unjust administration of the kingdom. Spurring such critiques of secrecy and calls for reform were revelations like the existence of Louis XV's long-running covert diplomatic agenda, the *secret du roi*, which he hid from his own ministers for years and ran counter to his administration's official policy. When, in 1776, a newspaper called the *Mémoires Secrets* chronicled the former king's duplicitous and mysterious maneuvers, Louis XVI had to confront yet another legacy of distrust fostered by his predecessor.[44]

Another particularly poignant complaint among reform advocates at the dawn of Louis XVI's reign concerned the use of lettres de cachet. These drew attention as arbitrary in no small part because they were secret acts that could put someone in prison for life.[45] One of the most notable complaints was *Des lettres de cachet et des prisons d'être* by Honoré Gabriel Riquetti, the Comte de Mirabeau. This work was composed in 1778 while Mirabeau was imprisoned at Vincennes (by lettre de cachet, for the third time) and first published in 1782. Disfigured by smallpox at a young age, Mirabeau was a rowdy youth who ended up absconding with a wealthy married woman, a misadventure which landed him in prison for the third time. As he wrote his critique of the lettres de cachet he also composed some erotic works, which further enhanced his estrangement from his noble background. Citing the lettres de cachet as evidence of arbitrary justice, Mirabeau highlighted how once one was delivered, the "most profound secrecy" was imposed on the prisoner's situation.[46] Though the tract focused on lettres de cachet and the prison system, Mirabeau used these to critique a royal administration he feared was becoming despotic, in no small part due to its secret activity. Tyranny made its shadowy advance through the concealment of palace mysteries, secret councils, and military orders, according to Mirabeau. Examples of this abounded throughout history dating to ancient Rome and, Mirabeau implored, "after such a large number of experiences, we should finally be convinced that the words THE SECRET OF THE STATE, THE SECRET OF THE ADMINISTRATION, applied to the interior and domestic government of nations, are used to conceal all types of robbery and the most atrocious attacks against even kings themselves."[47]

The perceived injustices of royal justice were frequent targets for critics of the monarchy. Prisons in particular became powerful symbols of secrecy. The Bastille prison—which would be stormed by armed Parisians on July 14, 1789, in the most iconic *journée* of the Revolution—was an emblem of arbitrary royal power, a place where a lettre de cachet could reportedly land someone for years without so much as a whisper of the prisoner's whereabouts. In the weeks and months that followed the storming of the Bastille, periodicals and pamphlets promised to expose the wrongdoing of the royal regime through prisoners' stories and artifacts found in the prison.[48] The municipal government also set to archiving records discovered there, establishing in 1791 a library for citizens to peruse evidence of royal perfidy.[49] This devotion to unveiling the stories of the Bastille built upon a tradition of prisoner narratives published over the course of the eighteenth century, which had made the prison a symbol of despotism. One of the most commonly cited cases in 1789 was that of a man who had been imprisoned during the reign of Louis XIV and taken up by Voltaire as an example of the despotic tendencies of the regime.[50] After gaining access to the prison's records, it was finally possible to identify this man, who had become a sort of embodiment of the secrecy shrouding the royal prison.[51] Though by the latter half of the eighteenth century the gap between the actual treatment of prisoners and perceptions of it had widened and only seven prisoners were freed in 1789, stories like that of this "man in the iron mask" had become iconic and the prison was firmly associated with despotism.[52]

Long before the fall of the Bastille, criticisms of state secrecy came from within the administration as well. In May 1775, a set of *Remonstrances des Cour des aides*, attributed to Chrétien Guillaume de Lamoignon de Malesherbes, lamented a pervasive corruption of the government rooted in its furtive nature. Malesherbes, who had protected the publication of the ambitious and subversive *Encyclopédie* in his role as head of the censorship apparatus known as the *Librairie*, was writing a remonstrance from another sovereign legal court in support of restoring the parlements in the wake of the Maupeou reforms. "It is the clandestine administration by which, under the eyes of a just sovereign, in the middle of an enlightened nation, injustice can reveal itself; or further, be committed notoriously," he wrote.[53] Though it was common to shift blame for corruption from the king to ministers, this case was particularly interesting because Malesherbes identified the king as a victim of government secrecy. The remonstrance pointed to two aspects of secrecy as facilitating such corruption: efforts to obscure the operations of the administration from the king and the nation, and the concealment of the personal identities of administrators. Hiding the operations of the government, Malesherbes argued, was a way to avoid public criticism of unpopular policies. Public outcry would be the only method for the people to express their interests to the monarch in a country where all representative institutions had been obliterated, and yet administrators concealed their operations to avoid even this.[54] Moreover, the anonymity of administrative operatives, especially at the lower levels, was contrary to the interests of the king himself and especially to the fiscal health of the kingdom.[55] Because royal instructions were hidden from the population, appointed officials cloaked with anonymity could essentially do whatever they wanted without being held accountable to the people or the king.

It was not by going after specific abuses that the monarchy could reform; systemic alterations were necessary, specifically opening operations to public view. Malesherbes advised the monarch to devote his time to "giving the People protections against despotism, and especially against *clandestinité*."[56] Motives for government acts needed to be publicized, and each act needed to be publicly linked to the person from whom it emanated and who was responsible for its execution.[57] Legal trials needed to be held in public view if justice was to remain inseparable from the king and judges were to adjudicate fairly.[58] Here was an argument for accountability; the core pillars of public trust needed to be transparency, visibility, *publicité*. As it was, the royal administration functioned as a curtain between the king and his people—Louis XVI and the populace needed to be able to communicate directly, but the "secrecy of the administration relentlessly opposed" this.[59] Malesherbes was not the only official to point to a need for direct communication between the monarch and the people, with visibility as the key component. In a less direct way, Anne-Robert-Jacques Turgot, the comptroller general of finance from 1774 to 1776, wrote a plan for municipal governments that emphasized the need to remedy the fact that there was no *esprit public* because there was no common and visible interest for people to identify.[60]

After the French involvement in the American Revolution, calls for publicity mounted even further as the crown found itself in a financial mess. It was under these circumstances that Necker published the royal budget in 1781, in an attempt to establish publicity as a standard of accountability. Necker's misleading numbers and his pretended publicity presented particular challenges for the crown going forward as it confronted the prospect of financial collapse and pressure to publicly consult some form of representatives of the nation in avoiding it. Some six years later, on the advice of his new minister of finance Charles Alexandre de Calonne, the king agreed to convene an Assembly of Notables, made up of deputies invited by Louis XVI to convey their opinions on Calonne's proposed taxes. After gathering in Versailles in February 1787, the notables quickly turned against the finance minister, leading him to bring the reform effort further into the public sphere. In a pamphlet widely distributed and strategically given to Parisian priests to read to their congregants, Calonne took his case to the public. "What is this strange darkness that surrounds the administration when all it wishes is to be just and beneficent?" he asked. "Why, in serving the people, should it keep the secret and impenetrable façade formerly used by those who betrayed the people's interests? Should the people's minister work in obscurity?"[61] His answer was an apparent and resounding no, which he made clear in publishing his plans along with these rhetorical questions. The Assembly of Notables was quick to condemn the pamphlet, which one described as "unworthy of the royal authority, which should speak to the people only by laws."[62] In the wake of the assembly, Louis XVI established a new royal council to reform the treasury and promised the regular publication of accounts—a further concession to demands for publicity in service of accountability.

As Calonne's successor, Loménie de Brienne, took a stab at solving the crown's financial perils through administrative reform and new loans, the pressure for publicity and consultation of representative institutions strengthened and further undermined royal authority. After refusing to sanction the proposed loans multiple times, the Parlement of Paris was exiled from the city in 1787. At this point, Brienne took his proposals to newly created provincial assemblies for approval.[63] Not only were the assemblies attacked for being appointed rather than elected, but they refused to sanction new taxes as well, leading the royal administration to another dead end. Brienne's proposed solution was a new Plenary Court designed to bypass the parlements as the locus of tax and loan approval; it was convened in May 1788. In response, many regional parlements as well as that of Paris continued to meet publicly, often drawing crowds to the *palais de justices* where they gathered.[64] As the parlements continued to claim representative status, supporters of the royal reforms began to call this claim into question in widely distributed pamphlets pointing out the personal interest of judges in resisting reform, echoing earlier critiques.[65] Amidst this constitutional confusion and persistent calls for convening the Estates General—a gathering of elected delegates from each order of clergy, nobility, and commons—the crown finally relented. The French were about to undergo a consultation of the national will through an institution many were casting as a representative entity despite its medieval origins as an advisory body.

In the middle of this turmoil, the American Revolution also proved to be an experiment to watch for *philosophes* who had long been ruminating on public opinion and the possibilities of greater publicity in the state. Crucially, writers examined American treatments of the idea of press freedom and the ways in which public opinion should be expressed from a vantage point of repression. Writing about independent America at this time was thus not directed at replication or practical problem solving; instead it was situated in an ongoing debate about whether censorship should be loosened and how much power should be accorded to public opinion in a theoretical representative system.

Looking at American state constitutions and, later, the Federal Constitution, writers in France used them to think through the possible consequences of loosening censorship and freeing the press in France. For example, the Italian Philip Mazzei published a four-volume work in Paris in 1788 that provided French translations of American legal documents, including the Federal Constitution drafted in 1787. Mazzei, a frequent correspondent of Thomas Jefferson and a strong supporter of American independence, discussed the establishment of press freedom as a useful tool to facilitate wise and stable representative government. Importantly, however, he cast it this way based less on how it was actually working and more on how it was intended to work. "In a country where much is printed with regard to public affairs, it is hard not to hope that the choices of districts will land on men who are worthy of representing their equals," he wrote.[66] In other words, giving people the power to vote for their representatives was not as risky as it might seem in a place where voters would be informed about public affairs. Furthermore, although the people could be misled by "general prejudices" or "passions," these would "easily dissipate in a country where the press is free, and where frequent use is made of it."[67] While the American case was cited as an example of the application of these convictions, Mazzei was not analyzing how or whether this had played out in practice; instead, he was elaborating the reasoning behind the establishment of these ideals.

It was a free press that made it possible to invest public opinion with power and facilitate a large republic where voters selected men to represent them. "The moderns accustomed to looking to the ancients as their models, have almost never understood how much the invention of the printing press could provide them advantages, by giving to dispersed men the ability to peacefully discuss affairs, and at the same time to remove the influence of misleading eloquence and instead augment reason, which is never misleading."[68] Mazzei looked at the American example of basing government on public opinion as possible and safe because he believed the press had the power to soundly shape it and guard against error. If one professed to support republican government, one must also support absolute freedom of the press. "Nothing is more important for this type of government than the freedom of the press. It is necessary to learn useful information, to correct abuses, to unveil vices of the government, to ground the dispositions of the people and to prepare minds for necessary reforms."[69] Mazzei went on to suggest that regulation of the press only led to the propagation of error and mistrust of the government. "The example of all the good that the freedom of the press has done and will do in America, will be much more useful for Europe as it is more applicable than that of England to reassure against all the supposed inconveniences of this freedom," Mazzei contended.[70] Though he himself did not cite concrete outcomes of the American commitment to press freedom so much as the beliefs motivating its establishment, Mazzei still treated what the Americans had done as evidence that freedom of the press could promote enlightenment and that public opinion could thus be vested with political power in a republican government.[71] It was a fundamentally optimistic vision, likely buoyed by the lack of attention to practical application.

The understanding of *publicité* and its potential to promote accountable administration served as a foundation for discussions that began to take place once Louis XVI called for a convocation of the Estates General in summer 1788, inviting opinions on the coming assembly.[72] As soon as the king announced the convening of the Estates General, the censorship apparatus proved unable to cope with the mass of printed material contemplating the structure of the Estates General and the reforms it should undertake.[73] This material included numerous tracts on the value of a free press to the deliberative process, particularly in the circumstance in which France found itself—attempting to consult the will of the nation. Malesherbes composed a six-part treatise considering the questions of whether to free the press and what complications could arise from such a decision. His opinion, written in 1788 but not published until after his death in 1809, was that freeing the press was absolutely essential to ensuring a successful meeting of the Estates General.[74] Anticipating arguments to come, Malesherbes asserted that without a free press, the supposed representation of the popular will would never be accurate. To support this contention, he cited the unpopularity of decisions of former Estates General, which, he claimed, were not adequately representative because they were sealed off from the public.[75]

Records of the Librairie reveal an agency conscious of its waning authority, unsure of how to manage the explosion of interest in the unique political event about to take place. Starting in January 1789, the Librairie began receiving prospectuses for periodicals dedicated to chronicling the meetings of the Estates General. The agency was receiving so many requests that by early April an official passed one along to his superiors with exasperation: "Yet another Journal of the Estates General!"[76] The prospectuses for these publications and their plans to publish were based on the need to satisfy curiosity and keep not only the people but the deputies informed—that is, to provide a forum for the exchange of information and ideas. Many portrayed themselves as attempting to provide unbiased and reliable information amid the slew of pamphlets flooding the streets in the lead-up to the big meeting. Like most of the requests, one from the Abbé Barret in mid-March proposed to chronicle "all that was relative to this National Assembly," from its organization to "its deliberations, its *arrêts*, its edicts, the *arrêts de conseil*, declarations, etc. that receive the sanction of the sovereign, and the way in which they are executed by particular Estates or provincial assemblies," in addition to offering a list "of the works that might appear on the Estates General and what they are about."[77]

Strikingly, there seem to have been relatively few mentions of the United States as an example in the publications leading up to the meeting of the Estates General or in the deliberations of what would become the National Assembly in 1789. Contrary to the assessment of some historians of the American Revolution, the American example remained of limited use in France.[78] More commonly, England was put forward as a model for or foil to French plans. However, there are some notable exceptions, and one is precisely on the topic of press freedom and the relationship of public opinion to representative government. When he launched a periodical dedicated to chronicling the meetings of the Estates General in the spring of 1789, Jacques Pierre Brissot de Warville cited precedent across the Atlantic. "Without gazettes, the American

Revolution . . . would never have been accomplished."[79] He depicted the wide reprinting of Paine's *Common Sense* as a crucial intervention in the course of the movement for independence. Unlike those publications that had examined the American example before the convening of the Estates General, Brissot was actually using the American case to demonstrate the way a commitment to free press and reliance on public opinion had operated in practice. In doing so, he was a rare example of a French thinker and politician who looked to actual experience in America with a free press and the effect it had on shaping public opinion. Perhaps he had been influenced by his trip to the newly independent states in 1788, when he had dined with George Washington and James Madison.[80] Crucially, French thinkers and politicians were looking at America in the revolutionary and confederation period, and at the state constitutions, without much evidence for how ideals enshrined in them played out in the post-revolutionary states, let alone in the federal republic (which had yet to be founded). As Brissot would discover, publicity was not a simple solution to the challenge of implementing a legitimate representative government.

The importance of publicity to the foundation of the National Assembly as a representative legislature in 1789 can only be understood as a result of this erosion of the legitimacy of government secrecy during the preceding decades. During the years leading up to the outbreak of revolution, state secrecy became firmly linked in the popular mind with despotism. By the time revolution broke out, closed-door governance would simply not be an option for the deputies sent to the Estates General in Versailles. To be considered accountable, and especially to be seen as representative, politics had to be visible. Before we explore how this played out in France, the rise of similar concerns about state secrecy and political representation in North America necessarily draws our attention back across the Atlantic, where the American Constitution was being drafted.

PART II

Performing Publicity

CHAPTER THREE

Behind the Veil of Secrecy

IN THE SUMMER OF 1787, eminent men from across the American states made their way to Philadelphia. There they shut themselves inside the Pennsylvania State House on Chestnut Street. As they set to work on a new federal framework for the United States, no one outside knew exactly what they were doing. And that was no accident. The delegates worked with urgency and the utmost secrecy. Other Americans were left to wonder what was being discussed behind closed doors, anxious to see the outcome of the mysterious deliberations. As the deputies neared the end of their work, James Madison wrote to Thomas Jefferson, then in Paris, to give a sense of the scene: "Nothing can exceed the universal anxiety for the event of the Meeting here. Reports and conjectures abound concerning the nature of the plan which is to be proposed. The public however is certainly in the dark with regard to it. The Convention is equally in the dark as to the reception wch. may be given to it on its publication."[1] Darkness. Mere days before it was printed and delivered to the Confederation Congress, Madison described the Constitution as shrouded in shadows.

Most of the decisions made by Madison and his colleagues, who met through that hot summer to produce what would become the Federal Constitution, have garnered extensive scholarly and legal attention since the moment the delegates disbanded. But their decision to hold their meetings in secret has been the subject of far less scrutiny.[2] When the delegates convened in Philadelphia, there were numerous circumstantial and pragmatic reasons motivating their decision to keep the doors closed. But an underlying understanding of how delegates were meant to undertake deliberation on the people's behalf also moved several of them.[3] Some deputies explained the decision to meet in secret as a way, first, to avoid confusion among the public until a complete product could be presented for evaluation and, second, to protect the integrity of deliberations from external influence. Such reasons were constitutive and expressive of a vision for how representatives of the people should work. Not only was meeting in secret partly motivated by a notion that political representation was best carried out by delegates insulated from popular pressure; it also had the effect of translating that vision into practice. The convention having worked in secret facilitated a deliberation more or less free from considerations of public opinion and the presentation of a final product for public evaluation as opposed to a participatory framing process.[4] It also created an aura of disembodied unanimity behind the document. This allowed framers to later portray the Constitution as accomplishing incompatible goals: for instance, some went on to insist it protected slavery, while others argued it might limit the institution.

Yet another important effect of the convention meeting in secret was the tethering of attitudes about secrecy to what came to be competing conceptions of representative government. During the ratification debates, critics of the Constitution seized upon the secrecy surrounding the Federal Convention as a problem, but they did so not just to conjure suspicion in a conspiracy. The Constitution's opponents began to question whether the use of secrecy in the process of political deliberation was ever legitimate in a representative government. For many, the answer was no. The political expediency of harping on secrecy as a way to generate suspicion in the Constitution cannot be underestimated; secrecy had, after all, been characteristic of alleged conspiracies and corruption in Great Britain.[5] But these detractors did more than paint secrecy as suspicious; they articulated a critique of secrecy, which would blossom further in the early republic, as incompatible with political representation. The sheer prevalence of the secrecy issue demands attention. Precluding discussion in ratifying conventions and the related concern of press freedom, it comes up in at least sixty pieces published during the ratification debates. How and why secrecy was linked with political representation begs for analysis.

Many Antifederalists, as opponents of the Constitution were called, deemed secrecy illegitimate in a republic because they defined political representation as a mirror, or microcosm, of society. Beyond advocating for frequent returns of elected officials to their home districts, more numerous legislatures, shorter terms, and smaller districts, Antifederalists pushed for greater transparency in the political process as a way to make representative institutions reflective.[6] In contrast, Federalist proponents of the Constitution defended secrecy's utility to a representative republic in which elected men were to determine the best interest of the whole without facing popular influence. This debate over the place of secrecy in the construction and operation of the new federal government reveals deep-seated disagreements over what it meant for politics to be representative and, more precisely, what it meant for representative politics to be a tool of popular sovereignty. At issue were not simply procedural questions of whether doors should be opened or closed, whether printers should publish proceedings, or whether delegates were obligated to communicate with constituents—all political practices discussed by contemporaries using the language of secrecy and publicity. The very nature of political representation was at stake.

Even when procedural decisions or polemical positions about secrecy were not wholly motivated by ideological commitments to a particular understanding of political representation, they carried ideological implications and shaped the translation of ideas into practices.[7] Secrecy in the deliberative process was increasingly associated with what came to be identified as a Federalist vision of representative politics in which elected officials were to deliberate independently of ongoing influence from the people for whom they claimed to speak. While committing to secrecy could be, and often was, a matter of political expediency for politicians on both sides of the factional divide, in the wake of the Federal Convention it became a politicized position. The Antifederalist contention during the ratification debates that secrecy was illegitimate in a representative republic grew into a tenet of the emergent Democratic-Republican party in the 1790s. Calls for greater publicity in government and the rejection of all manner of concealment were tied to a vision of political representation in which elected officials were to reflect the views of those they represented, who were to have an active role in the deliberative process. The delegates' decision to meet in secret over the summer of 1787 thus had the lasting effect of tying procedural decisions about secrecy and transparency, and debates over them, to divergent visions for how political representation was to work in the new republic.

More importantly, the use of secrecy in the Federal Convention was a crucial procedural decision that not only reflected a particular ideal of representative government but effectively helped to establish it in practice. Gordon Wood called the Constitution the final act of revolution, whereby the Federalists successfully co-opted the rhetoric of democratic radicalism to justify an essentially aristocratic system. Sovereignty of the people came to mean that government was derived from their consent but carried out in the hands of an elite.[8] This was, by Wood's estimation, the unique invention of the American Revolution, though he did not proceed to explain how or why this solution stuck. Looking at uses of and debates about secrecy allows us to penetrate the opacity of this legitimization. Secrecy became a tool to translate the Federalist vision of insulated political representation into practice. Critics of the Constitution advanced a competing conception of representation as a process whereby the elected were to consult and reflect public opinion, a process which required transparency. Highlighting these critiques of secrecy illuminates the endurance of challenges to the framing of representative government as democratic.[9] In the aftermath of the Federal Convention, debates about when and whether secrecy could be used in a representative republic became tantamount to defining what it meant for government to speak for the people.

Our story starts with fifty-five men making the trek to the Pennsylvania State House in May 1787, hoping to save what they saw as an endangered political experiment—and closing the doors behind them once they arrived.

The tale of these chosen men making their way to Philadelphia is a fixture of American lore. Prominent landowners, merchants, lawyers, political and military figures—they were among the most elite members of American society. Nearly half of them held enslaved people; for at least sixteen delegates from the southern states, this made up the core of their wealth.[10] The ranks of attendees were already thinned of any who doubted the project enough to refuse a spot, thus ensuring that those who did make the journey were predisposed to favor serious reform.[11] Traveling from their distant homes, deputies gradually trickled into the city in the waning days of May. The bustling mid-Atlantic city was on the verge of summer, known for its sticky heat and yellow fever outbreaks. Delegates who gathered there did not agree about the precise task at hand or the authority granted them by the Congress and state

Depiction of the Federal Convention in *A History of the United States of America* by the Rev. Charles A. Goodrich (Hartford: Barber & Robinson, 1823). (Source: The Library Company of Philadelphia)

legislatures. Under these inauspicious circumstances, they convened and soon vowed to keep the contents of their deliberations strictly amongst themselves.[12] From that moment on, the doors were kept shut and "sentries [were] planted without and within—to prevent any person from approaching near—who appear to be very alert in the performance of their duty."[13] Despite some vague leaks, details of the deliberations remained almost entirely absent from the press.[14] Reports on the convention that did appear in newspapers over the summer noted—some with alarm and some with approval—the intense secrecy with which the proceedings were guarded.[15] With the paucity of records due to the secrecy measures, it can be daunting to determine why the delegates insisted on shielding their debates from public view.

Precedent certainly afforded one reason; meeting in secret was not uncommon for a legislative body in the eighteenth century. As we've seen, both the Continental and Confederation congresses worked behind closed doors, only four state constitutions contained explicit requirements to either publish legislative journals or keep open doors during meetings, and even the House of Commons in England had only recently, and begrudgingly, begun allowing reporters to publish accounts of its proceedings.[16] But thinking about public access was changing. The inclusion of two provisions in the Constitution that would address public reporting of government activity—one requiring periodic publication of congressional journals and the other the publication of accounts—suggests a sense among those in the room that some degree of public visibility would be necessary in the government they were establishing.[17] Yet even in adding these requirements for transparency, the framers slipped in a caveat allowing for secrecy at Congress's discretion. Despite a seeming awareness of changing attitudes about the propriety of officials meeting in secret, the deputies decided to close their doors and to establish a capacious provision allowing for congressional secrecy in the framework they produced.

Immediate concerns about the tenuous nature of the convention's mandate and the possibility of foreign government spying were also undoubtedly factors.[18] So, too, was the fact that the deputies were not elected directly by the people but sent by state governments, which made their status as representatives distinct from those in a legislature—even more so because they were a constituent body rather than a regular legislative chamber.[19] Still, in the dozens of letters they sent to family members, friends, state officials, and overseas correspondents, deputies often explained the secrecy rule as a useful measure to create space for political deliberation, the public exposure of which could tarnish the results. Take for example deputy Alexander Martin, who wrote to Richard Caswell, the governor of North Carolina, explaining that the injunction of secrecy "was thought prudent, lest unfavourable [sic] Representations might be made by imprudent printers of the many crude matters & things daily uttered & produced in this Body, which are unavoidable, & which in their unfinished state might make an undue impression on the too credulous and unthinking Mobility."[20] George Mason, delegate from Virginia, similarly emphasized the ugly nature of deliberations in a letter to his son in which he called the secrecy rule a "proper precaution to prevent mistakes and misrepresentation until the business shall have been completed, when the whole may have a very different complexion from that in which the several crude and indigested parts might in their first shape appear if submitted to the public eye."[21] The reasons they provided reflected underlying understandings of how deliberation among officials was meant to work and of the ideal relationship between deputies and the broader public. Theirs was an insulated vision in which the messy process of exchanging and amending ideas was best carried out among delegates before proposals were presented in a finished state for evaluation by the broader public, which Martin referred to as "credulous and unthinking." This is not to say that the deputies were not motivated by political expediency or circumstance in deciding to keep the doors closed but that there was also a theoretical justification to their decision to meet in secret that summer. Regardless of the motivations that spawned it, this was a reasoning that would take on a life of its own, one requiring fidelity to its precepts by its Federalist backers and demanding intellectual engagement from its Antifederalist opponents.

In a letter to Jefferson penned on June 6, Madison elaborated on the reason for keeping the proceedings closed, writing: "It was thought expedient in order to secure unbiased discussion within doors, and to prevent misconceptions & misconstructions without, to establish some rules of caution which will for no short time restrain even a confidential communication of our proceedings."[22] The idea that secrecy was necessary to allow for "unbiased" discussion among the delegates, in addition to preventing the spread of false information or speculation among the populace, also reflected a particular, insulated understanding of the ideal relationship between officials and the public. According to his convention notes, Madison made a similar point in the meeting roughly a week later, declaring that "no member of the Convention could say what the opinions of his Constituents were at this time; much less could he say what they would think if possessed of the information & lights possessed by the members here." He went on to conclude that the delegates thus must "consider what was right & necessary in itself for the attainment of a proper Governmt." Meeting in secret allowed him to argue that "if the opinions of the people were to be our guide, it wd. be difficult to say what course we ought to take" and made it possible for him to assert the wisdom and sense of the delegates themselves as the proper guide for their decisions.[23] Again, he was articulating an ideal of insulated representation. Madison came to the convention sharing concerns about an "excess of democracy" in the state legislatures, where debt relief measures had frequently been passed and paper money issued in response to popular pressure.[24] Many delegates were demonstrably intent on insulating key government powers from popular influence, which some historians have interpreted as limiting democracy.[25]

Other scholars have suggested that Madison in particular never saw democracy as a problem to be solved. Some point to an unwavering commitment to majority rule to suggest that he never intended to limit popular participation in government.[26] Most compellingly, Greg Weiner has suggested that Madison viewed majority rule as inevitable and therefore sought to guarantee it would function as justly and wisely as possible. His concern was with passions and impulsivity, and he viewed time as a remedy; Madison aimed to create "speed bumps" not "roadblocks" to delay decision-making as a way to ensure majorities cohered over time and were founded in reason.[27] Whether or not Madison fundamentally distrusted democracy, it is unquestionable that he aimed to stabilize political representation as a durable form of popular sovereignty. As he would outline in *The Federalist* No. 10, Madison differentiated between a republic and democracy, stating explicitly that the former could avoid the pitfalls of the latter by refining public views through representative institutions.[28] Furthermore, he argued that an extended republic could endure where others had failed by enlarging the political sphere to elicit the election of "fit characters" who would have enough distance from popular pressure and factional interests to make sound decisions on behalf of the nation.[29] Shielding the details of political deliberation from public view, along with increasing the size of the polity, aligned with this vision of political representation.[30] Secrecy became, in effect, another crucial way to create distance—or time by Weiner's analysis—to allow for legislative decision-making without ongoing pressure from the unelected public or impulsivity within assemblies.

Though Madison would later change his views on the utility of secrecy in political deliberation, they remained linked to his evolving understanding of political representation. In fact, the evolution in thinking about government secrecy for someone like Madison—or, for that matter, George Mason, who would also later change his mind—further highlights the issue's relationship to conceptions of representative politics beyond merely pragmatic concerns.[31] In 1787, Madison was looking to relieve popular pressure on elected officials by creating space for calm deliberation. But in the 1790s, Madison would generally support the open doors of the House of Representatives, play an instrumental role in founding an opposition newspaper, and publish essays advocating an active role for public opinion in a "free" government.[32] This apparent change in thinking is the basis for what Wood called the "James Madison problem."[33] Perhaps Madison never did wish to separate the actions of the government from a reliance on public opinion.[34] However, his views on what constituted public opinion and the degree to which elected officials should be bound to it changed with the introduction of policy proposals he considered dangerous and unpopular in the 1790s.[35] Such a shift in thinking amounted to a re-conception of representative politics and its legitimacy. This was certainly related to the changing context, particularly the shift from writing a constitution to regular law-making.[36] The degree to which elected officials should be bound to public opinion was the defining feature of divergent understandings of how representative politics was meant to work. Federalists did not contend that representative government should be entirely divorced from public opinion, but they did attempt to concentrate the legitimate expression of that opinion to the moment of election and reduce its active role in decision-making by elected officials. After the Federal Convention, however, Antifederalists and subsequently Democratic-Republicans alleged that without an ongoing reflection of an actively expressed public opinion, political representation was not legitimate. Madison's take on precisely this question, along with his view on the proper use of secrecy in the process of law-making, evolved as he was serving in the House of Representatives.

To further illuminate the deputies' thinking about secrecy in the deliberative process that summer of 1787, it is useful to turn to debates over the two provisions in the Constitution that directly address the topic. The first version of Article I, Section 5—the provision requiring publication of journals—stated that the House and Senate, "when acting in a legislative capacity," should keep journals and publish them from time to time. According to Madison's notes, a short debate on August 10 over whether records of the yeas and nays should be entered on the journals was followed by some controversy over the requirement to publish them. Elbridge Gerry (MA) first proposed adding the line "except such parts thereof as in their judgment require secrecy."[37] The next day, Madison and John Rutledge (SC) proposed a version that stated each chamber would publish a journal of its proceedings from time to time, "except in such [part] of the proceedings of the Senate, when acting not in its

Legislative capacity as may [be judged by] that House [to] require secrecy."[38] This version of the secrecy clause suggests the two men believed secrecy necessary only for the Senate and only when it was acting "not in its legislative capacity," which likely referred to making appointments, presidential advising, or voting on treaties. However, this proposition elicited near unanimous rejection from the delegates, possibly on the grounds expressed by John Mercer (MD), which were that it "implies that other powers than legislative will be given to the Senate."[39] Gerry and Roger Sherman (CT) then proposed the line read that they should publish the journals, "except such as relate to treaties & military operations," which they hazarded should be possible in both houses.[40] The only state delegations to vote in favor of this were Massachusetts and Connecticut. Madison's notes do not provide any detail of the discussion surrounding this vote, but it is curious that when the cases requiring secrecy were delimited specifically as "treaties & military operations," the delegates overwhelmingly rejected the proposal. These seemed to be considered obvious cases where secrecy was justified, yet the delegates were unwilling to delineate them as the only instances in which it may be necessary. Notably, no factional divisions on this question are apparent in the discussion.

At this point, Oliver Ellsworth (CT) suggested that "as the clause is objectionable in so many shapes, it may as well be struck out altogether. The Legislature will not fail to publish their proceedings from time to time—The [people] will call for it if it should be improperly omitted."[41] But other delegates quashed this idea before it could get off the ground, citing the necessity of elected representatives reporting their actions to the people. James Wilson (PA) asserted that "the people have a right to know what their Agents are doing or have done, and it should not be in the option of the Legislature to conceal their proceedings." Wilson rejected outright any provision that allowed for secrecy, referring to representatives as "agents" who by implication were accountable to constituents who elected them. "It would give a just alarm to the people, to make a conclave of their Legislature," Mason noted. Nonetheless the clause was changed, with the support of six states, to require publication of the journals "except such parts thereof as may in their Judgment require secrecy."[42] The clause was brought up again just three days before the convention disbanded, on September 14, when Gerry and Mason proposed to allow for secrecy only in the Senate, "so as to require publication of all the proceedings of the House of Representatives."[43] But this proposal was quickly shot down: "It was intimated on the other side that cases might arise where secrecy might be necessary in both Houses—Measures preparatory to a declaration of war in which the House of Reps. was to concur, were instanced," according to Madison's notes.[44] The ability to maintain confidential deliberations remained open-ended as opposed to clearly delineated.

Shortly after this debate, the delegates added the provision requiring that "a regular statement and account of the receipts & expenditures of all public money shall be published from time to time."[45] At first, the clause called for annual publication, which was deemed impossible and impracticable by Wilson, Gouverneur Morris (PA), Rufus King (MA), and Thomas Fitzsimmons (PA). Once again, the deputies preferred vagueness in setting requirements for publication of government activity, ostensibly on the basis that it would make such information more accessible and intelligible to the public. Madison suggested that rather than requiring accounts to be published annually, the Constitution should specify that they were to be published "from time to time." This, he argued, would "enjoin the duty of frequent publications and leave enough to the discretion of the Legislature."[46] Congress had to have the ability to determine exactly what to publish and when. Although the framers ultimately specified that elected officials had to publish their activities, they were careful to guarantee that secrecy could be used when necessary. We have hints as to when some deputies believed it might be needed: in negotiating treaties or discussing military plans. But, generally, we must look to what they wrote and said during and after the convention to understand what they might have been thinking when they left this ambiguity in the Constitution.

Of further note is that all provisions mentioning secrecy or publication requirements had to do with the legislative branch, with nothing explicitly outlined in the Constitution regarding the executive or judicial. The delegates likely had secrecy in mind as an inherent power of the president given the debates over whether to form an executive council and their ultimate decision to vest executive power formally in only one person. Backing this interpretation are delegates' statements in the convention that the executive required "powers of secrecy, vigour, and dispatch" and the fact that in a number of *The Federalist Papers* Hamilton, Madison, and John Jay seemed to suggest the balance of powers would serve as a check on potential abuses of otherwise necessary secrecy used by the executive.[47] In *The Federalist* No. 64, for example, Jay referenced the "secrecy of the president" as an asset in "cases where the most useful intelligence may be obtained, if the persons possessing it can be relieved of the apprehensions of discovery."[48] On the other hand, the delegates did specify that the president was to receive advice in the form of written opinions, perhaps a gesture toward ensuring a degree of transparency in the president's work.[49] In addition to the lack of clarity on executive secrecy (which would very quickly crop up as a challenging ambiguity in the early republic), there was silence when it came to the judiciary, which today remains perhaps the least transparent of the three branches and also the least representative in a reflective sense.[50] A general focus on the legislature would largely carry through to the ratification debates where, aside from mentions of the potential for concealed advising to the president, concerns regarding secrecy would be focused on Congress as, not coincidentally, the directly representative branch.

When the delegates disbanded in September of 1787, keeping their deliberations secret remained a paramount priority in order to maintain a public perception of unanimity.[51] Though there was talk in the Confederation Congress of sending the Constitution to the states with proposed amendments, the idea was rejected. Moreover, that proposition was not to appear in the journal and the word "unanimously" was inserted into the resolution calling for the framework to be sent to the state legislatures.[52] Virginia congressional delegate Richard Henry Lee lamented that although the word "unanimously" only applied to the decision to transmit the Constitution to the states, it was inserted as a way to imply that Congress had unanimously approved of the framework.[53] Washington replied to news of this decision with approval, seeming to confirm Lee's suspicion of the intent behind presenting the Constitution with the apparent mark of approbation: "Not every one has opportunities to peep behind the curtain; and as the multitude often judge from externals, the appearance of unanimity in that body, on this occasn. will be of great importance."[54] Though his implied approval of working "behind the curtain" was surely rooted in a perception of its strategic utility in the situation at hand, it was a position that aligned with an insulated vision of political representation and, furthermore, had the effect of translating this vision into practice.

The importance of appearing unanimous in their decisions led convention delegates to respect and use the metaphorical curtain between them and the public as they disbanded. In Benjamin Franklin's oft-cited speech, which Wilson delivered at the convention's conclusion, he declared that "the opinions I have had of [the Constitution's] errors, I sacrifice to the public good—I have never whispered a syllable of them abroad—Within these walls they were born, and here they shall die."[55] The three delegates who refused to sign the Constitution in the end—George Mason (VA), Edmund Randolph (VA), and Elbridge Gerry (MA)—did so under harsh criticism. Randolph apologized, according to Madison's notes, assuring the delegates that "he did not mean by this refusal to decide that he should oppose the Constitution without doors." Gerry, too, apologized and declared that "if it were not otherwise apparent, the refusals to sign should never be known from him."[56] Ironically, perhaps, one of the main reasons Gerry cited for refusing his signature was the "power of the House of Representatives to conceal their journals."[57] Randolph and Mason would come under fire for not publicly divulging the reasons for their dissent and would eventually do so. But the initial intent to present a public face that obscured what they had argued behind closed doors speaks to a sense, shared across factional lines at this point, that representative bodies, particularly in constituent moments, could and should shield the deliberative process from public view. The curtain that Washington spoke of created a liminal space between elected officials and the public, where appearances could be crafted for public perception as opposed to an unfiltered display of the law-making process. In cases like these—both the drafting of the Constitution and Congress's decision to propose it to the states—politicians considered the appearance of unanimity crucial, which presented a pragmatic reason for their decision to use secrecy. Yet even if it was pragmatism rather than theoretical commitments that motivated the move, the effect was to put into practice the vision of representative government with which the procedural use of secrecy aligned.

The myth of unanimity remained long after the convention dissolved. When the delegates disbanded on September 17, the convention's secretary gave Washington the journals and "other papers which their vote directs to be delivered to His Excellency" after "burning all the loose scraps of paper which belong to the Convention."[58] Washington would keep the journals under wraps until 1796, at which point he deposited them with the State Department. Still, they remained unpublished and largely unexamined until 1819 when John Quincy Adams oversaw the editing and first publication at the direction of Congress.[59] A couple of years later, New York delegate Robert Yates's notes from the convention were published amidst a political battle over the revision of

New York's state constitution, prompting Madison to prepare for an eventual publication of his own.[60] Writing to a friend just two days shy of the thirty-fourth anniversary of the convention's disbanding, Madison noted that it was true that he possessed extensive notes and that "it is true also that it has not been my intention that they should for ever remain under the veil of secresy."[61] Some historians have speculated that immediate publication of the proceedings would have been politically disadvantageous, as many of the framers would go on to serve not only in ratification conventions but in Congress and the federal administration and would use ambiguity to advance conflicting goals. Madison, who heavily edited his notes, wrote in 1821 of his belief that the publication should be posthumous, or "at least that its publication should be delayed till the Constitution should be well settled in practice, & till a knowledge of the controversial part of the proceedings of its framers could be turned to no improper account."[62] Time, he believed, would make publishing the proceedings safe. Once their visibility would not impede the delegates from deliberating freely, nor their statements from being presented or misconstrued for political purposes, they could be released. Madison also clearly understood that a certain degree of mystery surrounding the framing of the Constitution afforded flexibility both in presentation and interpretation. In terms of presentation, Mary Sarah Bilder has identified the ways in which he significantly revised his own comments in the convention to make them intelligible and palatable within a post-ratification context.[63] In a deeper sense, he also aimed to dislocate constitutional interpretation from the Philadelphia convention to the ratifying conventions, where, he argued as early as the 1790s—perhaps due to political expediency—"life and validity were breathed into [the Constitution] by the voice of the people, speaking through the several State Conventions."[64]

It is worth pausing to consider the extent to which Madison was right about the effect of the convention's deliberations being kept secret, both at the time and long after the convention had completed its work. In the immediate aftermath of the convention, the fact that what had happened inside was not widely known did allow for malleability—to put it kindly—in addressing the intentions behind, and implications of, certain provisions in the document. There are numerous examples of this, but perhaps the most consequential concerned the institution of slavery. Because it was not clear how the clauses were crafted, "key proslavery and antislavery delegates like Charles Cotesworth Pinckney [SC] and

Gouverneur Morris [NY] turned the deals, and the ambiguities, into virtues," as David Waldstreicher has pointed out.[65] Deputies on both sides of the slavery question could report that they had done what was possible within the constraints of the convention and claim that the document either protected the institution or laid the foundation for its eventual elimination, based on their audience.[66] In South Carolina, delegates reported to the state legislature that the new federal framework secured slavery, while in the northern states, Federalists responded to critiques of the Constitution's treatment of slavery by blaming it on the Deep South and effectively absolving themselves of agency in the compromises made.[67] Perhaps unsurprisingly, Madison was a prime example of this approach, crafting his position sometimes in contradistinction to what he had said in the convention that summer.[68]

Moreover, the effects were long-lasting. The secrecy around the deliberations allows debates about the place of slavery in the American republic to endure to this day. The uncertainty stemming from the fundamentally opaque origins of clauses defining enslaved people as three-fifths of a person for determining congressional representation or ensuring the return of a person "held to Service or Labour in one State" who escaped across state lines, among other provisions, enables a multiplicity of interpretations. Some historians have since seen the use of secrecy as a way the framers attempted to absolve themselves of guilt and obscure what was in reality a deliberate, or at least knowing, protection of the institution of slavery. The omission of the words "slave" and "slavery" from the document, in this view, should be read as an indication of shame and a deliberate attempt to hide what was done in Philadelphia.[69] This interpretation is bolstered by the fact that once Madison's notes from the convention were published in 1840, leading abolitionists like William Lloyd Garrison concluded that the Constitution was in fact a "covenant with death."[70] Others have suggested that the secrecy surrounding the convention's deliberations actually obscures both the concessions exacted from southern delegates and a deliberate fight to prevent defining enslaved people as property in the federal framework.[71] As Sean Wilentz argued: "Because the Federal Convention deliberately worked in secret . . . the delegates weighed every word in the text all the more carefully."[72] Omitting the words "slave" and "slavery" in the document was not due to shame, Wilentz suggests, but was rather the result of a deliberate effort to prevent the enshrining of property in man within the Constitution.[73] Because the origins of the wording were for so long concealed and can even now only be pieced together within the confines of available sources, the question of slavery's status in the Constitution remains difficult to settle definitively. What is sure is that secrecy was used as a tool to throw a veil over the institution and keep it off the table, so to speak—a practice which would continue through the 1790s and unquestionably perpetuated the system of human bondage.

The secrecy surrounding the Constitution's origins rendered, and continues to render, many of the framers' intentions and the document's legacies inconclusive. This, if we take Madison at his word, was by design. It may well be an important ingredient of the federal framework's longevity, as silences and ambiguities in the Constitution have afforded it a degree of dynamism.[74] For example, the framers' use in most cases of gender-neutral terms such as "persons," "inhabitants," and "citizens" rather than "men" left open the eventual possibility of women claiming equal membership in the political community. Yet the fact that the term "women" was not included also provided a basis for their exclusion from formal political participation.[75] In terms of determining the document's relationship to Native Americans, the limited acknowledgment of "Indians" in the text has obscured both their profound influence on the shaping of constitutional provisions and the relationship of the federal framework to land dispossession.[76] In this and many other instances, the Constitution's opaque origins and strategic silences pose problems in a polity so bound by its foundational text.[77] Originalism as a mode of constitutional interpretation makes the secrecy shrouding the convention and the concomitant limitations of the historical record particularly salient. Without reliable records, and given the intentional confidentiality surrounding the framing, the method in fact leaves ample room for judicial interpretation.[78] The many ambiguities within the Constitution, and the significance of them, did not go unnoticed at the time; numerous critics pointed to the document as deliberately vague and difficult to understand, arguing that it concealed the extent of many powers it vested in new federal institutions.[79]

Madison's belief that keeping deliberations secret protected their integrity was not an understanding of representative government that everyone shared. Writing to John Adams from Paris on August 30, 1787, Jefferson proved prescient about how a significant portion of the public would react to the convention's closed-door deliberations: "I am sorry they began their deliberations by so abominable a precedent as that of tying up the tongues of their members. Nothing can justify this example but the innocence of their intentions, and ignorance of the value of public discussions. I have no doubt that all their other measures will be good & wise. It is really an assembly of demigods."[80] Many beyond the doors of the Pennsylvania State House would agree only with the first part of what Jefferson had expressed. Antifederalists, it turned out, were not so sure that "all their other measures would be good & wise," sometimes precisely because they had been formed in secret. In the wake of the convention, deliberating in secret was explicitly tied to what was soon deemed a Federalist conception of how political representation was meant to work, and opinions about its propriety began to differ along factional lines.

Once the convention had disbanded and the Congress had forwarded the Constitution to the states for consideration, the framers' measures for secrecy became the subject of extensive public debate. Antifederalists pointed to the withholding of the Federal Convention's deliberations and provisions in the Constitution allowing for secrecy as evidence of a conspiracy to subvert the confederation. But more importantly, criticism of the delegates' use and authorization of secrecy was deployed first as a reason to rebuke the all-or-nothing ratification process due to the public's inability to weigh in during the formation of the framework; and second, as cause to challenge the legitimacy of the convention and the government it proposed on the basis that government in the name of the people must be carried out in the public eye. In their critique of the convention's use of secrecy, Antifederalists articulated their vision of how political representation was supposed to work.[81] They cited secrecy as an impediment to popular input throughout the process of crafting the document and to informed public opinion with regard to the delegates' proposal. They also identified its use as a fundamental violation of the relationship between representatives and represented. But Federalist defenders of the Constitution did not recant in the face of such criticisms. Rather, many mounted a defense of the convention's commitment to secret (closed-door and unpublished) deliberations and their utility in the new government, arguing that it was useful and even necessary to avoid proceedings compromised by external, factional pressure. This debate over the propriety of secrecy mapped onto divergent understandings of what made government representative, specifically with regard to the role of the unelected in political decision-making—a divide that increasingly fell along hardening factional lines.

From the moment the Constitution was printed, many writers took to the press, urging people to scrutinize the text with their own eyes. This emphasis on examining the proposed framework personally was often linked to suspicion of the framers due to their deliberations having been concealed. Why, writers asked, did the deputies shut their doors? For some, the answer was all too obvious. Pieces that addressed the secrecy of the convention often did so briefly only to immediately draw the conclusion that the framers' intentions were nefarious. "An officer of the Late Continental Army" (who was allegedly William Findley, a staunch opponent of the Constitution), writing in Philadelphia's *Independent Gazetteer* in November 1787, questioned particularly the validity of what the public had been told about the unanimity in the convention. "The thick veil of secrecy with which their proceedings have been covered has left us entirely in the dark, as to the *debates* that took place." The deputies could not be trusted to present an honest account of what had happened inside the meeting when "the unaccountable SUPPRESSION OF THEIR JOURNALS, the highest insult that could be offered to the majesty of the people, shows clearly that the whole of the new plan was entirely the work of an *aristocratic majority*."[82] He construed the lack of knowledge about what happened inside the deliberative chamber as showing clearly that the result had not been a unanimous agreement as the delegates claimed. Adherence to secrecy in the process of drafting the Constitution was portrayed as a tool to trick the people in whose name the framework had been produced rather than facilitating the advancement of their interest.[83] While it may seem odd that writers making these arguments about secrecy were writing under anonymous pseudonyms, this was a common practice in eighteenth-century Anglophone print culture. Pseudonyms were selected to convey particular messages and meant to let the content stand for itself rather than resting on the reputation of the author.[84] Significantly, the use of pseudonyms stood in contrast to the way supporters of the Constitution often justified the secrecy surrounding the convention as acceptable precisely because of the reputations of those who had been in the room.[85]

A most basic concern to many Antifederalists was that without knowledge of how the Constitution had been developed and debated in Philadelphia, people were utterly unprepared to make a decision on it. During Pennsylvania's ratifying convention, "Columbus" noted in the December 8, 1787, *Pennsylvania Herald* that the Federal Convention had carefully considered each clause and sentence over several months of daily discussion and debate, a process into which the public did not have any insight. At the end of this period, the "members of the General Convention," as he called them, produced an unanticipated upending of the existing system with the expectation that people would adopt it wholesale. The people were deprived of the opportunity to pore over the component parts of this new Constitution and suggest amendments as the deputies in Philadelphia had done. Furthermore, he asserted, they could not properly evaluate the framework because the Federal Convention's deliberations "were kept within their walls with the secrecy of a conclave."[86] Likening the convention to the Catholic assembly of cardinals that met privately to select the Pope was certainly calculated to sow suspicion given long-held, rampant anti-Catholic sentiment.[87] But more than merely taking a jab at the convention based on its adherence to closed-door deliberations, Columbus was arguing that secrecy prevented the public from being prepared to make any decisions on the Constitution. Such assertions of the need for the public to have insight into the process of deliberating legislation or, in this case, the Constitution, in order to properly evaluate its merits and assent to its adoption, amounted to a different articulation of how political representation should work—a vision of representation as reflective. Representatives (or members, as most Antifederalists called them) needed to work in public view in order to facilitate informed popular participation when evaluating the work of government officials.

The claim that withholding records of the deliberations led to confusion among the populace was repeatedly cited as a reason to alter the ratification process—an ironic twist considering many of the convention delegates had initially explained secrecy as a way to prevent public confusion. A "Republican Federalist" wrote in the *Massachusetts Centinel* in January 1788 that the surreptitious manner in which the convention was convened and had proposed the Constitution led to the population being caught off-guard with the resultant proposal. If the delegates had consulted the public on their project, "the important question would have been previously canvassed; and understood by Congress and the Legislatures; and explained to the people; and the publick opinion would have been thus united in some salutary measure." The author considered knowledge of the deliberative process essential for the purposes of preparing the public to weigh in on the task its self-proclaimed representatives had undertaken and presented to them for approval. But "as the matter has been conducted, a *system of consolidation* has been formed with the most *profound secrecy*, and without the *least authority*."[88] Secrecy was an impediment to public engagement throughout the deliberative process, engagement which would have facilitated an alignment of public opinion with the proposals of representatives, vesting them and their product with legitimate authority.

Not only would having access to the deliberative process have informed public opinion when it came to evaluating the result of the meeting, it would have facilitated active public participation in the crafting of the legislative product, in this case the Constitution. In the spring of 1788, "A Plebeian" noted in a pamphlet that the debates of the Federal Convention were kept "an impenetrable secret, and no opportunity was given for well informed men to offer their sentiments upon the subject. The system was therefore never publicly discussed, nor indeed could be, because it was not known to the people until after it was proposed."[89] Now that the Constitution had been published, a free discussion had brought to light its defects as well as its strengths. The author used this to advocate that another convention be called based on this open conversation. Indeed, in addition to calls for another convention, the view that amendments should be proposed and considered as part of the ratification process was a common refrain throughout the debates over the Constitution. Deliberating on behalf of the people to produce a document in their name required their input. This could not be obtained when the process of deliberation was concealed from public view and only a finished product presented for their affirmation or rejection. The sense that the public should have an active role in the deliberative process of its representatives was central to an Antifederalist understanding of how political representation was meant to work, and it would endure in the early republic, especially among members of political societies.[90]

The debate over whether amendments should be allowed during the ratification process amounted to a contest over the degree to which the broader public should be involved in the process of law-making in a representative republic. As early as the fall of 1787, an acrimonious back-and-forth on this question unfolded between "Cato," writing in the *New York Journal*, and "Caesar," writing in the *New York Daily Advertiser*.[91] On September 27, Cato told readers to "teach the members of that convention, that you are capable of a supervision of their conduct. The same medium that gave you this system, if it is erroneous, while the door is now open, can make amendments, or give you another, if it is required."[92] Four days later, Caesar retorted that the door was not always open for suggestions and was in fact presently closed. He asked why Cato had not offered his expertise while the Federal Convention was meeting, at which point, he insinuated, the door had been open for alterations to the Constitution.[93] Cato responded directly to this question by pointing out that, contrary to what Caesar seemed to believe, the door during the meeting of the convention had quite literally been shut: "The Convention too, when in session, shut their doors to the observations of the community, and their members were under an obligation of secrecy—Nothing transpired—to have suggested remarks on unknown and anticipated principles would have been like a man groping in the dark, and folly in the extreme."[94] Tellingly, Caesar's retort, printed five days later, did not address this point whatsoever. He responded to all other aspects of Cato's argument but apparently had nothing to say regarding the secrecy of the Federal Convention's deliberations, much less how this might have prevented someone like Cato from offering his input on the formation of the document.

But Cato's complaints did not go unnoticed. On October 18, the *New York Daily Advertiser* featured a letter signed "Curtius," wherein the secrecy of the framers' deliberations was listed as among his most "consequential" charges against the convention. Cato had decried the "secrecy of their business" and lambasted the delegates for "shutting their doors," which Curtius called "dreadful impeachments!" Moreover, he suggested, "had not those doors been shut, Cato would have been among the first, to have imputed every section of their system to the party influence of Philadelphia." Here, Curtius used a counter-factual to suggest the utility of closed-door deliberations. While Cato cited the secrecy of the convention's proceedings to suggest a violation of the people's active participation in the deliberative process, Curtius argued that shutting the public out was an instance of "prudence," which protected the convention from accusations of undue external sway. He lamented that Cato "sees the Saviour, under God, of his country; but instead of the immortal laurel, he wears the tiara of an unresisted despot."[95] Underlying this joust over the issue of closed-door deliberations were divergent conceptions of how political representation should work. While Cato affirmed a need for public input in the deliberations of representatives, Curtius viewed such input as a dangerous opening for inappropriate influence over delegates' decision-making.

More than a month later, in the *Poughkeepsie Country Journal* in New York, another writer accused those who focused on the secrecy of the convention's deliberations of attempting to divert the population's attention from the content of the Constitution and "poison the whole plan by insinuations against the integrity of its authors." Like Curtius, "A Country Federalist" (who was Poughkeepsie lawyer James Kent) attempted to drain these suspicions of their potency by suggesting that the link between secrecy and conspiracy was not only false, but absurd. "From the circumstance that the Convention conducted their deliberations in private, for the purpose of a more free and liberal discussion, [critics] assert that it originated in the absolute conspiracy of a set of false detestable patriots (for these are their epithets) to erect a despotic government over this country," he wrote. Closing the doors was, again, characterized as a cautionary measure to protect and facilitate the deliberative process, not evidence of conspiratorial intentions or a violation of republican principles. Those who argued that the doors should have been open "appeal with a winning address to the most powerful passions of the heart," the Federalist author argued, and, in so doing, attempted to prejudice the public view of the Constitution based on insinuations that the circumstances under which it was developed were questionable.[96]

This assertion was bolstered by suggestions that had the delegates to the Federal Convention adhered to secrecy for nefarious purposes, they would not have published the Constitution for ratification. "Honorious" advanced precisely this argument in the *Independent Chronicle* in Massachusetts on January 3, 1788: "Fellow citizens! These secret councils are published upon the House-Top. This Draconian Code, these bloody laws, this terrible system, is in your own hands; see, think and judge for yourselves—be not gulled out of the blessings of a good government by such base and abusive misrepresentations." He went on to write that the Antifederalists were not only unfairly focused on the use of closed-door deliberations; they were using language calculated to sow suspicion in the product of the Federal Convention. "The idea of '*Conclave*' originated with the antifederalists at the southward!—it is a term fraught with *chicanery*, *roguery*, and *villainy*, and is an *insult* upon those *twelve States* who were represented in Convention!"[97] His claim that the language of secrecy was calculated to generate suspicion in the Federal Convention and its product was astute. Yet Honorious was missing the underlying concern that led Antifederalists to focus on secrecy as a problem in the first place. Publishing the completed Constitution for public consideration, to them, was not the same as allowing the people a window into the process whereby it had been created. Not knowing how the framework had been devised meant, first, that the public lacked necessary orientation to evaluate the document; second, it made the prohibition on offering amendments indefensible because the people had not been given a proper opportunity to actively contribute during its framing.

Despite such defenses of secrecy's utility in framing the Constitution, the more formal state ratifying conventions committed to procedures ensuring transparency—namely open doors and published deliberations.[98] Such measures may have been adopted to obviate challenges to legitimacy similar to those faced by the Federal Convention on the basis of its having convened in secret, and they surely reflected changing attitudes about the propriety of secrecy in representative government. The ratification process was meant to lend the legitimacy of the people's deliberation and approval to the framework, and, in such a circumstance, some scholars have suggested the open doors of the conventions were taken for granted by the public.[99] The case of the Pennsylvania Convention proves a particularly poignant example of how the decisions of the ratifying conventions to work with open doors were made based on the need to project legitimacy as representative entities. Facing criticism that the convention was being forcibly convened under what appeared to be hurried circumstances and that it did not adequately represent all parts of the state, delegates decided immediately to keep their doors open and provide for publication of their journals. A report in the *Pennsylvania Herald* noted that the convention could not have decided otherwise, as it was a representative body. Because it was not possible to convene the entire population to decide on the Constitution, authority was delegated to a convention of their choosing. "Whatever therefore is transacted by the Convention is, in fact, transacted by the people," the paper proclaimed. As such, if the people were to be excluded from hearing what happened there, they would in effect be excluded from their own decision-making process. Concealing deliberations of a representative body threatened to undermine the entire logic of reflective political representation. Moreover, the writer continued, the secrecy of the Federal Convention had cut delegates off from the people's guidance and "has probably been the source of all the opposition that is now made" to the Constitution. This clear articulation of the relationship between publicity and representative legitimacy was, significantly, reprinted outside Pennsylvania seven times in newspapers from Massachusetts to New York.[100] And although the secrecy of the Federal Convention was by no means the source of all the opposition to the Constitution, it was indeed a significant one. Not all ratifying conventions were open to the public either, and the often partisan, selective, or downright error-ridden records of the proceedings published in most states beg the question of how effectively publicized the conventions were in practice.[101]

For Antifederalists, a commitment to open doors in the ratifying conventions was necessary, though insufficient. The outcome of the Pennsylvania ratifying convention would be challenged as illegitimate on the grounds that proper debate had been hindered and the process had been rushed. Clearly, the process by which the Constitution had been framed still mattered to its opponents. Using a justification similar to that of the Pennsylvania newspaper about the need for representatives to act in public view, those challenging the legitimacy of the Constitution continued to point to the procedures of the Federal Convention as flawed. Of special concern, as Honorious had lamented, was an emphasis on the convention's use of secrecy. In the aftermath of the Pennsylvania convention's decision to ratify in December 1787, many of those who felt they had lost the battle hoped they might yet win the war by continuing to question the process by which the Constitution had been drafted. Pamphlets and newspapers both in Pennsylvania and other states suggest the strategy was at least somewhat successful, especially when it came to citing secrecy as a cause for suspicion.

The published dissent of the minority of the Pennsylvania Convention, which was widely circulated throughout the states during the ensuing ratification debates, prominently and repeatedly featured the confidentiality of the Constitution's drafting as prime evidence of its nefarious nature and the despotic intentions of those who produced it. "The convention sat upwards of four months. The doors were kept shut, and the members brought under the most solemn engagements of secrecy," they wrote, painting an image of the Federal Convention as a group exhibiting conspiratorial behavior. "Whilst the gilded chains were forging in the secret conclave, the meaner instruments of despotism without were busily employed in alarming the fears of the people with dangers which did not exist," the dissent continued. "The proposed plan had not many hours issued forth from the womb of suspicious secrecy, until such as were prepared for the purpose were carrying about petitions for people to sign, signifying their approbation of the system, and requesting the legislature to call a convention." A footnote in the dissent further drove home the minority's concern: "The Journals of the conclave are still concealed."[102] The purpose of this dissent, printed originally in Philadelphia, was undoubtedly to raise suspicion about the Constitution based on the process whereby it was drafted and debated. Highlighting the opacity of its origins and the ongoing confidentiality of the deliberations that produced it appears to have been a popular mode of sowing doubt.

A letter by "Hampden" (likely also William Findley, who was one of the signers of the Pennsylvania dissent) printed in the *Pittsburgh Gazette* on February 16, 1788, suggests that such suspicion in the process was prolonged. Hampden noted that many people who had initially invested their "unsuspecting confidence" in the convention and were pleased with the result had since changed their minds after "having by a more strict scrutiny penetrated the mystery with which much of it is enwrapped." In addition to gesturing toward a common refrain that the ambiguities in the language of the Constitution amounted to a form of secrecy in itself, this scrutiny was in no small part focused on the framing process: "But to be more particular; that honorable body, after entering into a bond of secrecy, which, however plausible and artful the reasons might be which brought that measure about, was certainly not necessary at least after their business was brought into form; because the secret transactions of government, such as making treaties, conducting war, and the like, was not the object of their deliberations."[103] Findley seemed to imply that establishing rules or verifying credentials could legitimately be done in secret, whereas deliberating ideas or proposals could not. Secrecy, he argued, was unjustified when it was used to conceal the actions of officials who were not explicitly dealing with "the secret transactions of government," which consisted principally of military or diplomatic issues. Given that these were not the purposes for which the Federal Convention had gathered, the delegates' debating behind closed doors was enough to give pause to the people in whose name the Constitution had been written.[104]

Eventually some of the men who had been in the room articulated concerns about secrecy having hindered the proper relationship between delegates and the people. When the Maryland legislature met to discuss the Constitution, Luther Martin—one of the members who had gone to the Federal Convention and left early—was called upon to discuss his experience. He began by lambasting the delegates for their strict adherence to secrecy, because "we were thereby prevented from corresponding with gentlemen in the different States upon the subjects under our discussion." Martin went on to detail how the delegates denied his request that during a recess the members be allowed to take copies of the proposed text to study while they were away: “But Sir, the same spirit which caused our doors to be kept shut—our proceedings to be kept secret—our journals to be locked up—and every avenue, as far as possible, to be shut to public information, prevailed also in this case.”[105] The adherence to secrecy, to keeping information from the public, was so stubbornly upheld that it ended up preventing the delegates from ascertaining the necessary information to deliberate in the people’s interest. Here, Martin was building upon and advancing a sense that the secrecy of the convention was cause to question the legitimacy of the entire process of framing the Constitution. It was the same argument that had been made in a letter printed in the *New York Journal* in November 1787, when “A Citizen” wrote that “by keeping from the world a knowledge of the important business which they had assumed upon themselves, they were precluded from all opportunities of receiving light or information, upon so interesting a subject, from the animadversions which their constituents would probably have made upon the different points under their deliberation.” Because it had been drafted in such a way, the Constitution “must therefore be considered as an unauthorized essay, which can only receive sanction from the assent of the people,” he concluded.[106] Behind this assertion was, again, an understanding of representative politics as reflective and thus requiring active public input throughout the deliberative process.

As the people—or, more accurately, their representatives—did consider granting their assent in the state ratifying conventions, the provisions for secrecy in the Constitution also drew the attention of deputies who were concerned that a repeat of the Federal Convention’s tactics would be authorized in the new government. “I appeal to this Convention if it would not be better for America to take off the veil of secrecy. Look at us—hear our transactions,” Patrick Henry, the ardent revolutionary, declared on the floor of the Virginia ratifying convention in June 1788. “I believe it would have given more general satisfaction, if the proceedings of that Convention had not been concealed from the public eye. This Constitution authorizes the same conduct,” he asserted, referring to the possibility of closed-door deliberations and concealed treasury accounts, which he feared the Constitution authorized by not providing adequate requirements for the publication of these items. Over the course of the convention, Henry declared that the people’s liberties would be in danger if the “transactions of their rulers may be concealed from them.”

To shield the "common routine of business" from the public was nothing short of an "abomination" and would lead to the perpetration of "wicked and pernicious . . . schemes," and "iniquitous plots."[107] In the Massachusetts convention, concerns over the lack of provisions for transparency were also raised, and in New York, delegates proposed an amendment that journals should be published "at least once a year, with the exceptions of such parts relating to treaties or military operations as in the judgment of either House shall require secrecy." The delegates went on to state: "both Houses of Congress shall always keep their doors open during their sessions, unless the business may in their opinion require secrecy."[108] The only state to do so, the New York convention attempted to establish a requirement for the day-to-day operation of Congress that would ensure the visibility of its activity on an ongoing basis. Some delegates in the states not only worried about the secrecy of the Federal Convention but also feared that the Constitution had not gone far enough in ensuring that representatives would work transparently.

Citing the House of Commons and American state legislatures, Madison argued in the Virginia ratifying convention that there was not an extant government that did not allow for discretionary confidentiality in its activity. In this sense the Constitution was going further than existing frameworks by requiring any publication of proceedings and accounts. Moreover, secrecy would not pose a problem in a government like the one designed by the Constitution, he asserted, noting that "There can be no real danger as long as the Government is constructed on such principles."[109] But just as his views on what it meant to represent the people evolved during the 1790s, Madison would change his mind on this determination that the government working in secret was not threatening in a representative republic. In fact, disagreements about the propriety of secrecy in the work of governing, particularly in the deliberative process of representatives, only deepened in the early republic. Keeping secrets became a central allegation advanced by Democratic-Republican societies against Federalist policies they claimed were not representative; to them, secrecy in government was nothing more than a trick to undermine reflective political representation.

Discussions of government secrecy—specifically closed-door, unpublished deliberations—during the ratification debates show how the question of what should be publicly visible was integral to the foundation of a national representative government. Delegates to the Federal Convention in the summer of 1787 discussed provisions for banning the publication or communication of the body's proceedings as measures to maintain secrecy. Many spoke freely among themselves and with their correspondents of their obligations to keep their deliberations secret and explained the necessity of these precautions for preserving the integrity of the deliberative process and its product. Secrecy would prevent confusion and misrepresentation of their work among the public and would shield the deputies from the influences of factional passion, preventing "biased" debate amongst themselves. In explaining to their correspondents the reasons for maintaining secrecy, delegates articulated an understanding of how political deliberations were meant to work, particularly among representatives. Their adherence to secrecy was rooted to some extent in shrewd political calculation, but it also aligned with a conception of political representation as a process wherein enlightened individuals deliberated calmly, secluded from popular sway in order to determine the best interest of the polity.

Once the Constitution was put to the public for debate, Antifederalists seized on the secrecy of the convention's proceedings as cause for suspicion of the document, a reason to propose amendments, and, ultimately, a justification for questioning the legitimacy of the convention and its proposed framework. As some Federalist writers noted at the time, Antifederalists amplified their concerns by talking about secrecy in language with increasingly negative connotations. The convention was a "conclave," which continued to "suppress their journals"; the Constitution had been born in a "womb of mysterious secrecy" and thus could not be trusted. But we would be wrong to conclude that Antifederalists focused so much on the secrecy of the Federal Convention and provisions for it in the Constitution because it inherently sounded suspicious. In fact, Federalist adherence to secrecy and the long precedent for its use in government suggest that there was nothing essentially suspect about it. Antifederalists focused on secrecy because it was central to an understanding of representative politics they were articulating in contradistinction to what the framers had effectively enacted and constructed with the federal framework. To reflect the will of their constituents, delegates would require ongoing dialogue with them and visible decision-making. At the heart of the disagreement between Antifederalists and their opponents were not just procedural questions of what could be secret in politics but more fundamental questions about what it meant to have a representative government.

The use of secrecy in governance was explicitly called into question over the course of debating the American Constitution. It was through this debate over how politics should function—in public or private—that divergent visions of a representative republic were articulated. Certainly, the framers produced theories of political representation that illuminate their thinking. But focusing on procedures sheds light on what this actually meant in practice as theories clashed through the process of implementation. Federalist commitments to the use of closed-door political deliberations and the insulation of elected officials were a practical extension of their political theory. Meanwhile, Antifederalist insistence on the need for transparent deliberations and dialogue between elected officials and their constituents illuminates a fairly coherent rival theory about what it meant for politicians to be representatives. As such, they were meant to reflect the will of their constituents and respond to public opinion, which required them not to be isolated but to remain under constant surveillance.

Once the Constitution was ratified and the federal government formed, there were no clear guidelines as to how newly elected officials were to balance a need for secrecy with an imperative for visibility in their daily activity. Other than being required to publish their journals and an account of the public receipts and expenditures "from time to time," elected officials would be free to determine the methods of their meetings and how decision-making in a representative government was best carried out. Yet these determinations would be made with the bitter debates about the Federal Convention's secret deliberations still fresh in the minds of those who were elected and their constituents. Pressure to publicize political activity was pervasive after the ratification debates, though the benefits of shielding decision-making remained integral to Federalist visions of representative politics.

CHAPTER FOUR

Building a House of Glass

IN THE SPRING OF 1789, Versailles hosted the deputies sent to the Estates General. Thousands of curious onlookers gathered alongside them and many more sought news of their activity in the press. "A national assembly in France, after an interruption of nearly two centuries, is such an unexpected event; the circumstances that made it necessary and that have led to it . . . are exciting so much interest among us and curiosity abroad that already all of Europe has its eyes fixed on the memorable scene which has just opened," the Abbé Ducros wrote in the prospectus for a proposed periodical in May. Having all eyes on it quickly became a central component of the representative function the Estates General was meant to fulfill. And to Ducros, as to many others, it made complete sense: "What spectacle was ever more worthy of attracting all gazes than an Assembly of the representatives of a powerful and enlightened nation, deliberating on the greatest interests of the state?"[1] Amidst this widespread attitude, the deputies' claim to represent the French nation rested in no small part on facilitating the public's gaze upon them.

A revolution was underway. A new era of politics was beginning, and this one, unlike the last, would have no secrets. Defining themselves in opposition to a monarchy that clung to secretive practices even in its last throes, the deputies of the Third Estate in particular proclaimed their commitment to transparency. Delegates deployed a discourse of publicity as evidence of their dedication to political representation. Adhering to transparent decision-making was at the heart of what was to make them legitimate; secrecy had no place in a representative regime. And this was not just idle talk. Members of the Estates General, which became the National Assembly as deputies claimed sovereign legislative power in June 1789, established procedures guaranteeing open meeting chambers; designed systems to print, distribute, and translate decrees; maintained access for journalists and the ability for them to print records of legislative debates; and set up a process whereby petitioners could speak to the assembly directly during their meetings.

Yet the impact of this multifaceted commitment to publicity was paradoxical. Though it was championed and implemented to attain legitimacy, the publicizing of its proceedings tended to undermine the representative regime rather than bolster it. Outside the halls of government, the notion of publicity was infused with a vigorous culture of vigilance and was taken up by radical journalists and club activists as an active process whereby elected officials could be held accountable for their every action. Daily independent reports of what happened inside the National Assembly allowed for constant commentary on all aspects of governance, which in turn heightened tensions when the deputies and "the people" did not seem to agree. Journalists and polemicists made it their task to hold representatives accountable by exposing their operations to the public and purporting to reflect the public's opinion back to the deputies. Visibility fed this vigilance and helped to engender an active political culture that blurred distinctions between the government and the population for whom it spoke—itself a contested and variously defined entity.

This adherence to *publicité*—a term with fluid meaning that left room for multiple interpretations—facilitated the persistence of a theory of representative politics that the deputies theoretically jettisoned in June 1789. After having been convened as the Estates General for the first time in 175 years, the deputies of the Third Estate and some supportive nobility and clergy quickly seized authority as the representatives of "the nation," declaring themselves the National Assembly and vowing not to disband before completing a written constitution. As spring gave way to summer in 1789, the remainder of the clergy and nobility gradually and grudgingly joined this assembly as equal members. In the process of transforming itself from a body of corporate estates carrying binding mandates and meant literally to incarnate the nation into a sovereign legislature speaking on behalf of the French people as a whole, the National Assembly necessarily and fundamentally reimagined representative politics. Led by Emmanuel Joseph Sieyès, the deputies in June of 1789 argued their way toward an insulated conception of political representation. Elected officials were to determine the will of the nation while shielded from popular influence. To that end, they discarded their binding mandates, insisting that each delegate was to speak for the interest of the entire nation rather than on behalf of a particular constituency.[2]

Writing about this transformation in the theory of political representation and its establishment as a form of popular sovereignty, Paul Friedland identified a central paradox in the articulation of what came to be called "representative democracy": it was "from its very inception a contradiction in terms, for the basic reason that a true democracy precluded representation."[3] The observation is astute in the case of both the French revolutionaries and the American framers in 1787; both were essentially attempting to wed the concept of popular sovereignty to a version of insulated, rather than reflective, representation.[4] French deputies attempted to overcome this contradiction by asserting a clear division between elected representatives and the general population, turning the people into passive spectators and rendering democracy compatible with stable political representation. American Federalists also made this attempt, relying in no small part on a theory of secrecy's utility to representative government. Across the Atlantic, however, French revolutionaries' commitment to acting transparently perpetuated a widespread expectation of reflective political representation whereby elected officials were to align themselves with public opinion.

In not only "attracting all gazes" but welcoming and encouraging them, the deputies enabled the unelected to watch *vigilantly*, believing that they, too, were part of the political decision-making process. Over the course of the early Revolution (1789–1791), a radical club culture rooted in this notion of vigilance burgeoned across the country, especially in Paris.[5] Though there were social dimensions to the radical movement, a focus on the rhetoric and activities of vigilance on the part of political clubs—like the Jacobins, Cordeliers, and Cercle Social—during the early Revolution reveals a political aspect of their activity that was based on an Enlightenment intellectual tradition of associating publicity with good government.[6] Parisian radicals tapped into a common conception of the utility of transparency to political representation, which created an opening whereby a broadly defined, and constantly contested, category of "the people" could assert an active role in politics. This opening facilitated by transparency rapidly posed problems for the legitimacy of the regime.

Even though the deputies eventually chose an insulated form of representation, it is no surprise that they still disavowed secrecy. Doing so was necessary to gain public trust in the context of Old Regime political culture. Even before they convened in Versailles, pamphleteers, aspiring journalists, and some deputies themselves were linking publicity to the success and validity of the representative process. State secrecy was not only politically untenable; it was intellectually moribund by 1789. Yet many deputies gradually began seeing it as practically valuable, if not necessary, to implement the new type of representative politics they imagined. Throughout the first two years of the Revolution, the monarchy continued to be associated with secrecy as the king was constantly suspected of dissembling. When he denounced the constitutional project and attempted to flee the country in June 1791, these fears seemed proven valid, prompting calls for more vigilance. Yet it was precisely at this moment, when the secrets of the monarch were exposed, that deputies of the National Assembly seemed firmly convinced of a need to expand their own use of secrecy in government. Enlightenment thinking about the place of secrets and the primacy of publicity to politics fundamentally shaped, and was reshaped by, the foundation of a new type of representative government whereby the people were to be made sovereign. The clashing of ideas (new conceptions of political representation with thinking about secrecy and publicity in the state) was intensified by the attempt to simultaneously implement publicity and political representation starting in 1789.[7] Battles over the balance of confidentiality and transparency in politics were inherently tied to a contest over what it meant for politics to be representative—and what it meant for representative government to be a tool of popular sovereignty.[8]

From the start, the deputies of the Third Estate, and supportive nobility and clergy, continually proclaimed the centrality of publicity to representative politics in order to define their legitimacy in opposition to a monarch adhering to the principle of confidential politics. Not only did the royal administration attempt to block and then control reporting on the proceedings of the Estates General, but it also attempted literally to conceal the meetings by keeping onlookers out as tensions reached a crescendo in late June. But even before this, questions of who could witness deliberations, and from where, came to the fore in the deputies' debates. Maintaining an open meeting chamber, access for reporters, and open lines of communication with constituents were central to the deputies' efforts to establish themselves as a representative body and to define whom they were representing. Royal efforts to control the flow of information merely intensified commitments to maintaining transparent operations. Yet the deputies' insistence on the centrality of publicity to the representative process soon clashed with their definition of representative politics as an insulated formation of the national will rather than as a reflection of popular sentiment. While attempting to control what "publicité" meant seemed one possible way to align the disavowal of secrecy with the type of representation they were professing, it was quickly evident that the way it functioned was not entirely in their control.

The meetings of the Third Estate, which took place in the Salle des Menus Plaisirs (a vast storage building converted into an assembly hall) in Versailles, were opened to the public from the beginning. Estimates put the average number of non-deputies in the room at anywhere between 2,000 on an average day and 4,000 for the opening session.[9] To give a sense of the magnitude of this group, there were 1,200 elected deputies, including the clergy and nobility, most of whom did not join the sessions until late June, after the declaration of the National Assembly.[10] Etienne Dumont, a Genevan writer who was politically active in France in 1789, described the early meetings of the Third Estate as near bedlam. By his account, "The chamber was continually inundated with visitors, with curious onlookers, who walked around everywhere, placed themselves on the floor of the chamber that was to be dedicated to the deputies, who were not jealous of this and did not complain that it violated their privilege."[11] The contrast with the closed-door calm of the Federal Convention in Philadelphia could not be starker.

A resolution adopted on May 28, before any other internal policing plans, attests to the potentially problematic presence of unelected people in the chamber. The assembly ordered that "the large number of visitors leave the interior of the chamber open for the deputies." The resolution went on to note that no opinions should be followed by tumultuous applause or signs of disapproval, which suggests that from the earliest days of the meetings, the chamber was relatively full of engaged attendees.[12] Though the resolution marks an early effort to begin separating the elected from the unelected during the meetings, it also reveals the deputies' dedication to keeping their sessions open to an audience, which

Engraving of a scene from the National Assembly over the summer of 1789, dedicated to patriotic women. Drawn by Antoine Borel, engraved by Nicolas Ponce, and entitled "Assemblée nationale: Constituée à Versailles le 17 juin 1789, six Semaines après l'ouverture des Etats Généraux; Dédiée aux Femmes Patriotes" (Paris, 1790). (Source: Bibliothèque nationale de France)

was to sit in the benches on the upper level of the room. Many deputies saw the presence of people in the meetings as encouraging and empowering, allowing them to keep the public abreast of their proceedings and putting them in a position to seek demonstrations of popular support.[13] This concern about the need for demonstrable backing was another marked difference with the American delegates to the Federal Convention, who did not have to worry about a king shutting down their deliberations.

But the value of having an audience in the meetings was not uncontested. For some, sequestering spectators was not sufficient; having them present was threatening. Pierre Victor, baron Malouet, a well-known Third Estate deputy from Riom and staunch royalist from the outset, interjected after the passing of these regulations, pleading that "given the importance of the subject being discussed, I ask that we deliberate in secret, that we make strangers leave." As one of the rare efforts initiated by a deputy to clear the chamber, his request was roundly rejected. "Strangers! Are there any among us?" Constantin-François Chasseboeuf de Volney exclaimed. "Do they not have the greatest interest in having their eyes fixed upon you? Have you forgotten that you are all but their representatives, their proxies (*fondés des pouvoirs*)?" Volney equated the request to deliberate in secret to an outright violation of their role as representatives, which he described as being agents for the people in whose name they deliberated.

A Third Estate deputy from Angers, Volney was known from the beginning for his incendiary commitment to voting by head (as opposed to by estate, which was what the crown and more conservative deputies favored).[14] Already a political division between conservative and more radical deputies was reflected in disagreements over public access and the legitimacy of secrecy in the deliberative process. Volney proceeded to ask whether the deputies really believed they could turn the people away. "I cannot respect he who seeks to hide himself in the shadows," he declared; "the grand day is made to shed light on the truth, and I am proud to think like the philosopher who said that all his actions never had anything secret and that he wished that his house was made of glass."[15] This idea that deputies should work in a glass house—that secrecy was anathema to representative government—was being articulated as understandings were evolving about both who was being represented and how to represent them. These questions came to the fore in mid-June when the deputies officially proclaimed themselves to be the National Assembly.

The deputies had been convened at Louis XVI's invitation as the Estates General, which was meant to embody the entirety of the people with the king at its head. In Old Regime society, "the people" was not conceived of as a group of individuals but rather as three corporate estates: the clergy, nobility, and the Third Estate—which, as the Abbé Sieyès wrote in a popular pamphlet published before the meeting, was "everything" and yet seeking to be "something" politically.[16] The Third Estate's demand that the orders meet together and vote by head contributed from the outset to breaking down the idea that estates were the unit being represented in Versailles. Two days before the deputies of the Third Estate, joined by some clergy and nobility, declared themselves the sovereign legislature of France on June 17, Sieyès proclaimed that the deputies in the room had been sent by 96 percent of the population and that they must get to work. It was up to them to "form the will of the nation."[17] Structurally speaking, the deputies had been chosen by electoral assemblies in some 190 constituencies, within which half the delegates were selected by the Third Estate, a quarter by the nobility, and another quarter by the clergy.[18] Each estate had its own electoral qualifications and procedures, but they were broadly inclusive; in most places, men over the age of twenty-five who paid direct taxes could select electors for the Third Estate.[19] As the deputies in Versailles dissolved these social distinctions and formed a single legislature, vigorous debate over what to call themselves ensued. It reveals varying conceptions among the deputies of whom exactly they were representing—ranging from the specific "25 million French people," "the majority of the nation, acting in absence of the minority," or "the commons" to the more encompassing "French people," or "the nation," which ultimately became the basis for the name National Assembly.[20] Such a definition expanded the conception of their constituency beyond the specific electors who had sent them to a much more abstract entity, one which entailed both exclusive and inclusive potential depending partly on how they resolved the concomitant question of how to represent these people.[21]

With the convening of the Estates General, two strains of thinking about representative politics jostled for primacy. One held that deputies were strictly beholden to the specific will of their constituents through binding mandates and that they literally incarnated the people—an extreme form of reflective representation. The other called for deputies to represent the will of the nation as a whole, giving the deputies the right to speak for the nation without having to sociologically define or actually consult it in any concrete way, amounting to insulated representation.[22] When they discarded the binding mandates (which were lists of instructions many of them carried from the assemblies that had elected them) and proclaimed themselves to be the National Assembly, the deputies leaned toward the latter conception of representation.[23] But despite defining political representation as an abstract concept whereby the people's will would be decided rather than mirrored, most deputies maintained that the process of determining that will should be performed publicly. The "visitors" and "strangers" who showed up in Versailles to watch deputies deliberate thus became important manifestations of the "people" or "the nation," as were reporters who reproduced accounts of what happened in the chamber for a broader imagined "public."

Throughout the repeated relocations necessitated when the king closed off the assembly chamber, the presence of crowds as the deputies deliberated was always guaranteed and, in retrospect at least, cited as a legitimating factor. Jean-Sylvain Bailly, who was at the time a member of the Third Estate representing the commune of Paris and who would soon become its mayor, recalled in his memoirs that the oath taken June 20 on the royal tennis court to not disband before completing a constitution was sanctified by the presence of large crowds. "The galleries filled with spectators, the crowd of the people surrounded the door and filled the streets, at a great distance," he wrote, "and all announced that it was the nation that honored the tennis court with its presence."[24] Jacques-Louis David, in his painting of the oath (begun in 1790 and never fully completed by him) would depict all the deputies surrounding Bailly, beneath light streaming in from the open windows, where crowds—including women—watched the tumult enthusiastically. On June 22, the deputies met in a nearby church after again being locked out of the Salle des Menus Plaisirs. "We first declared that we would let the public enter, and the church was soon full," Bailly recalled in his memoirs.[25]

Rhetoric emphasizing the importance of the public being able to witness the deputies' proceedings intensified when the crown attempted to stop crowds entering the chamber. In the royal session of June 23, wherein Louis XVI tried to conciliate the three estates and prohibit the formation of the National Assembly, guards surrounded the room and public entry was prohibited.[26] In his speech to the deputies, the king stipulated that the public could not attend the meetings of the Estates General, in the interest of "Good order, decency, and the freedom of suffrage."[27] The attempt to ban public attendance was an extension of royal precedent. But the monarch was also expressing an ideal of representative politics that aligned with the one deputies had adopted when they abolished their binding mandates. Deputies needed to be insulated from public view if they were to freely determine the nation's interest.

In his memoirs, Bailly noted that the admission of strangers (as the unelected were called) in meetings had been a nagging concern for royal ministers, who had often voiced this to him prior to the king's declaration. He replied that he was aware of both the benefits and the drawbacks of letting the public attend their deliberations, but "we were in a

Depiction of the swearing of the oath not to disband before completing a written constitution, begun by the artist Jacques-Louis David in 1790 and completed after 1791 by an unknown artist, entitled "Serment du Jeu de Paume, le 20 juin 1789." (Source: CCØ Paris Musées / Musée Carnavalet, Histoire de Paris)

time when no advantage could be neglected, nor outweighed by inconveniences." Moreover, "it was impossible to prevent this publicity." When the ministers suggested the implementation of a ticketing system to let in only selected people, Bailly reportedly balked, arguing that as the nation's "proxies," they did not have the power to hide themselves. "The free opening of the doors was an indispensable obligation," he wrote, essential to political representation as a process of echoing the will of constituents and carrying out their wishes.[28] In this statement, Bailly used the concept of "proxies" to describe the function of the representatives. When considered this way, hiding was simply untenable. But the reality was that the deputies had rejected such an understanding in declaring themselves the National Assembly.

This dedication to transparency and the repeated disavowal of secrecy was perhaps a way for the deputies to offer an assurance of accountability after having discarded the binding mandates. However, it was also a crucial way in which they failed to enact in practice the insulated vision of representative government to which they were committing. It also reveals the importance of studying theory and discourse in tandem with practices; the reality of politics often does not allow for ideological consistency. In his study of representative government during the Revolution, Friedland argues that although the deputies of the assembly operated with effusive praise for democratic ideals of popular sovereignty and claimed the will of the people as the basis of their legitimacy, "they constructed, brick by brick, a political edifice predicated on the exclusion from active political power of the very people in whose name their government claimed to rule."[29] In fact, the deputies did not use bricks to construct a wall between them and the people they claimed to represent; they insisted on trying to construct such a wall out of glass. While Friedland proceeds to explain how corporate interest groups, crowds, and petitions increasingly posed a challenge to the wall the deputies had erected, the weakness of such a wall was inherent in its nature. Insisting that the public be able to see their representatives, while simultaneously declaring that the deputies themselves were not beholden to listen to the people or react to their wishes, created a precarious situation from the start.

The insistence on publicity was not just empty rhetoric either. When soldiers ordered to keep the public out surrounded the chamber the day after the king's June 23 announcement, the deputies responded with a resounding commitment to open their doors. Not only did they immediately establish a "national printer" to print the assembly's decrees, but on June 25 they also resolved to convey to the king their objections to the presence of soldiers around the assembly and the barring of public entry. In calling for the deputation to the king, Antoine Barnave, Third Estate deputy from Dauphiné, exclaimed that "It is strange and surprising that we would wish to deny the nation entry into the national chamber. It is in this august place that we are stipulating its interests, that we are deciding its future: it is thus under its eyes that we should act; it is in front of the nation that we must operate."[30] Though he echoed earlier declarations of the impropriety of suggesting that the public be barred from witnessing their representatives deliberating, Barnave did not link this to the representatives being proxies for the nation. In fact, all the action in Barnave's statement was clearly to be taken by the deputies, while the nation, manifested in the people there to watch, was present as an audience. Here, a passive conception of publicité, of the public as mere spectator, was articulated—evidence of how the commitment to transparency could potentially coexist with the conception of representative politics not as reflective of public opinion, but as insulated from it.[31]

For onlookers though, publicity was not passive—it needed to be secured and enforced. Just after the resolution was taken to send the deputation to the king, it was noted in the assembly proceedings that "the people, irritated by the spectacle of bayonets, were threatening to go to great lengths to force their entry."[32] The assembly then sent three deputies outside to calm the crowd, which they reported they were able to do by informing them that the assembly had resolved to protest the king's closing of the meeting hall in order to ensure that access would no longer be barred.[33] One of those onlookers was none other than Thomas Jefferson, who narrated the event in a letter home to New York politician John Jay, explaining that the deputies "have named a deputation to wait on the king and desire a removal of the souldiery from their doors, and seem determined, if this is not complied with, to remove themselves elsewhere."[34] Indeed, the deputies were committing to open, transparent governance as a tool by which to establish their legitimacy, despite the lack of clarity on how this was to be enacted and its potential to clash with the type of representative government they were attempting to form. As the crowd outside suggested, what it meant to govern without secrets would not be defined solely by the legislators.

Throughout the summer and once they relocated to Paris in October 1789, the deputies of the National Assembly continued to profess a commitment to publicity and set up procedures designed to facilitate the visibility of their deliberations. Yet the meaning of "publicité" remained confused and contested as it was put into practice. Deputies established and maintained procedures to assure public attendance at their deliberations and to directly distribute their decrees through the summer of 1791, even guaranteeing publicity as fundamental to the function of the legislature in the constitution they promulgated that fall.[35] But they also soon began to limit the bounds of transparency by pushing some work to closed committees and more tightly controlling journalist access, thereby honing the definition of publicité as a controlled distribution of information. To many with their eyes fixed on the assembly, publicité meant more than having information delivered to them. A sense of visibility as vigilance infused popular understandings of what it meant to render government transparent. What publicity meant became a process of constant negotiation between deputies and the crowds and journalists who made it their mission to keep watch over the assembly's activities. The questions of whether to open doors to deliberations, if and how to regulate the press, and what work to keep secret were informed by underlying disagreements about how political representation was to work.

Not all manifestations of publicity were contested. The first official regulations for the chamber, voted into effect on July 29, 1789, banned non-deputies from the floor of the chamber but continued to facilitate their attendance in the meetings, which had been guaranteed since May. Moreover, the regulations accounted for the inflow of "petitions, requests, letters, and addresses," declaring that non-deputies arriving with these would either be admitted directly to the speaker's bar or sent to the appropriate secretary.[36] Over the course of two days in October, this welcoming of petitioners onto the floor of the assembly was taken to an extreme. Thousands of Parisians, mostly women, marched to Versailles to demand the deputies address food shortages. Some women later even entered the palace, making it all the way into Queen Marie Antoinette's bedroom. Earlier that evening, the crowd had invaded the National Assembly's meeting, overrunning the deputies, halting the deliberations with their demands, and even participating in debates and voting alongside deputies—illustrating the radical potential of publicity.[37] It was an early example of women using the accessibility of the meetings to assert their presence and priorities, even though they would remain formally disenfranchised as "passive citizens." In showing up and making demands of the representatives, women in their march to Versailles as well as through their regular petitions, offerings, and attendance at meetings claimed their status as citizens to whom representatives owed accountability.[38] Publicity made this claim to membership in "the people" or "the nation" possible as the women could embody the public in meetings, even if they could not vote for representatives. And the women that fall wielded significant political power. The October Days ended with promises of grain deliveries from the deputies and king. Louis XVI also sanctioned the *Declaration of the Rights of Man and of the Citizen* and the constitutional project, and he declared he would move his family to Paris with the deputies following suit.[39]

As the delegates set up in the capital, guaranteeing public access to their meetings remained a priority. Even before moving to their permanent location, there was an effort to accommodate onlookers during the two weeks they met in the *Archevêché*, next to Notre Dame Cathedral.[40] A letter signed by Joseph Ignace Guillotin, who was a Third Estate deputy from Paris and member of the team of deputies delegated to investigate possible meeting places in the capital, took into consideration the ability to host an audience when determining a location. In addition to his logistical work, Guillotin's name would soon be given to the mechanism he endorsed as a more humane method of capital punishment: the guillotine. Before this machine took on its symbolic power, the deputy may well have been better known in the assembly for his efforts to set up its meeting spaces. The committee deemed the Manège of the Tuileries (a horse racing track in the heart of Paris) the only spot that was possibly big enough to hold the meetings, with the caveat that the number of unelected attendees even there would be limited to five or six hundred.[41]

Located in the center of the city, the structure where the deputies began meeting was adjacent to the royal residence and, soon, next to many of the nascent political clubs. Galleries dedicated to holding onlookers were immediately constructed, lining the chamber on all sides. The hall was vast, crowded nonetheless, and loud. There was a constant concern with lighting the room and with devising a system whereby speakers could more effectively project their voices.[42] It is important to keep in mind the sheer number of deputies—more than twice the size of the British House of Commons and eighteen times the size of the House of Representatives that had recently been established in the United States.[43] With the deputies alone, the room would already have been packed and noisy, but there was also no shortage of curious passersby who showed up eager to fix their eyes on the deputies' deliberations.

Public attendance at the National Assembly was clearly valued by Parisians, as it had been by crowds in Versailles, as an essential component of the revolutionary project. The composition of the audience nonetheless changed with the move to the city. No longer made up of mostly elite, aristocratic viewers, large crowds gathered daily to secure a spot in the chamber. A letter written by an officer with the battalion of *Petits Augustins* recounts his service at the door of the assembly on a day when the crowd attempted to force its way inside after being held back. "The number of curious people is always at least double that who can find places in the galleries," he wrote. This led to tumult, especially "when it was necessary to turn away some two or three hundred people whom it is not possible to seat in the galleries, though they arrived the previous morning and evening."[44] A letter addressed to the assembly president seeking reformed rules for public entry declared that "the primary wish of all good French people is, without a doubt, to be able to constantly witness the work of the august assembly over which you preside." The letter, signed by more than thirty-five people, claimed that reforming the process by which the public was let inside would "guarantee the most zealous the full and peaceful enjoyment of the publicity of your sessions," by better accommodating people like "the old man, weak but burning with patriotism" and "the mother, drawn by a virtuous sentiment, aspiring to the honor of being at least once witness to the work of the assembly."[45]

The presence of an audience in the meetings was central to the emergence of a new type of popular politics. Deputies made their names, and careers, by their orations on the floor of the assembly. Public speaking became a key component of political popularity, itself a creation of the revolutionary period.[46] The meetings in the *manège* were raucous; onlookers were far from silent spectators and deputies catered to the crowd when speaking. There was a pervasive concern with the theatricality of politics in the National Assembly and many deputies were certainly savvy about playing to the crowd.[47] Committee records reveal that some deputies may have hired spectators, providing them with cues for when to applaud.[48] Despite concerns, this was a form of publicity the deputies of the National Assembly never ceased to endorse, repeatedly declaring the importance of, and making provisions for, the unelected public in their midst.[49] There was a regular corps of guards, or ushers, employed by the National Assembly to keep a degree of order in the chamber, particularly in the public galleries.[50] Though there would be sporadic attempts to remove "strangers" from the chamber through the year 1790 and first half of 1791, no comprehensive efforts to ban the public from its meetings were made until the summer of 1791 in the wake of the king's failed escape.[51]

Of course, there were many who could not make their way to the legislative chamber to watch the meetings. Chief among them were the hundreds of thousands of enslaved people in French colonies. The story of publicity in the early National Assembly is complicated by the inclusion of the colonial context, which sheds light on the limited nature of "the public" constituted by attendance in legislative meetings or even access to reports of deliberations. From the outset, deputies sent by planters and provisionally accepted from the Caribbean sugar-producing colony of Saint-Domingue, expressed concerns about news of what was taking place in Paris reaching the enslaved population on the island. In August 1789, the deputies wrote home with warnings urging local officials to seize "writing in which the word 'Liberty' appears."[52] After the adoption of the *Declaration of the Rights of Man and of the Citizen* that summer, colonial planters reacted, according to Laurent Dubois, "as if it were a disease to be quarantined."[53] Indeed, members of the slavery-protecting Massiac Club in Paris moved to clamp down on movement across the Atlantic, asking merchants in port cities to bar Africans from leaving for the colonies in an attempt to prevent news from circulating.[54] In the spring of 1790, officials on the island began a secret surveillance of letters addressed to people of color or enslaved people in order to suppress the flow of information and uncover evidence of any knowledge indicating conspiracies to act on it.[55] Considering the colonial context serves as a useful reminder of the limits of even a broad commitment to transparency in revolutionary legislatures and the way in which secrecy was often deployed to construct bounded political communities by excluding certain groups.

Back in Paris, rather than pushing the public out of assembly deliberations, deputies seemed more focused on determining what activity would be carried out there versus what would be managed outside the meeting hall. In Versailles, delegates immediately confronted the challenge of how to work efficiently as a group of 1,200, giving rise to questions of whether they should split off into smaller groups to deliberate. That June of 1789, the assembly had decided to establish twenty bureaus, which were small groups of thirty deputies each that were to discuss issues before they came to the floor. Later that month, after most of the nobility and clergy joined the meetings, the number was expanded to thirty bureaus with forty members each. Deputies partial to the monarchy, such as Jean-Joseph Mounier and Stanislas-Marie-Adelaide, comte de Clermont-Tonnerre, cited the relief of pressure from spectators as among the benefits of the bureaus, while more radical deputies saw danger in discussion happening "outside the public eye," as Timothy Tackett put it.[56]

A similar division of opinion occurred over the creation of committees, which were formed one-by-one to deal with specific issues, starting in June with four temporary committees and solidifying in mid-July with the Constitutional Committee and Finance Committee.[57] The development of the committee system reflected the emergence of a sophisticated effort on the part of the deputies to define publicity and limit its bounds. There seems to have been a realization, though limited at first, of the benefit to using committees as staging grounds where measures could be discussed and crafted for public presentation before being brought to the assembly as a whole.[58] Despite such conceptions of the value of closed-door deliberations, there is little indication that secrecy was openly discussed as a benefit, nor immediately enforced in the committees.[59] Other than a debate about whether the *Comité des Recherches* (created to receive denunciations and investigate threats) should be anonymous and meet in secret, there is no evidence of the assembly deciding to explicitly bar onlookers or reporters from committee meetings. Once the committees were set up in Paris, however, there is evidence of a controlled system for access to their meetings, with requests for badges, or tickets, to enter particular rooms and even corridors within the *manège*.[60]

Deputies received constant reminders that they were being watched. They sought legitimacy in the stream of letters received and read daily in the assembly meetings, sometimes actively courting them before making decisions.[61] Constituencies closely followed their deputies, even forming "information committees," which were charged with maintaining correspondence with their delegation in order to keep abreast of news and voice their opinions.[62] Sometimes those watching did not agree with what they were seeing. For example, as the deputies debated the matter of whether to grant a royal veto in the constitution, they received a letter claiming to voice the opinion of "the citizens convened at the *Palais Royal*," that a royal veto was not just and that the convened citizens thought it was time to "recall the ignorant, corrupt, and suspect deputies."[63] Another letter read into the assembly record right after the first expressed that those convened were ready to "*enlighten* their chateaux and houses" should the deputies continue to "trouble harmony" and wish to maintain royal sanction.[64] The letters, purportedly drafted to express the desires of a crowd at the Palais Royal, set off a frenzy of concern and sparked the arrest and detention of two men.[65] It is little wonder the deputies were concerned; the Palais Royal had been an origin point of uprisings that led to the overthrow of the Bastille on July 14.

Many deputies asserted that this kind of threatening pressure ran counter to the ideal of free deliberation. Such a response reflected the theoretical elaboration of representative legitimacy as it had been outlined with the declaration of the National Assembly in mid-June. That view held that representatives of the nation were meant to form the national will within the assembly, as opposed to reflecting a will formed outside its walls. In this instance, however, a popular will existing outside the Assembly was being asserted as the proper guide for the representatives' decision-making, thus advancing a conception of representative legitimacy as reflective of public opinion. This resulted directly from the deputies' commitment to publicity. Not only did their welcoming of petitions and maintenance of correspondence imply a dialogue with the unelected, but the transparency of their debates and decisions empowered people by informing them of what was at stake. It showed them who agreed or did not agree with their viewpoints, and granted them an opening to make their views known to deputies.

Indeed, pamphlets defending one detained author asserted that he was merely expressing popular opinion to make it known to the representatives who were, after all, meant to be the people's operatives. Camille Desmoulins, who would build a reputation as a radical journalist over the course of the Revolution, published a pamphlet in defense of the second accused author of the letter, arguing that "the menaces of the Palais Royal were paternal, and were intended to open your eyes. They were warning strikes, and advice."[66] He expanded upon this conclusion, writing that "In the middle of a nation so clairvoyant, it will become harder and harder day by day to hide yourselves from the vigilant gaze of 48 million eyes; for my part, Messieurs, nothing can stop me from following you with my lantern, and illuminating your every step."[67] Both the letters from the Palais Royal and Desmoulins's defense of the accused author show how the standard of publicity as central to representative legitimacy was made into an active process, taken up by people outside government to imply a dialogue between elected officials and those over whom they governed.

When the assembly moved to Paris that October, deputies found themselves at the epicenter of a culture of vigilance that had been percolating throughout the summer. Emerging from those who regularly convened in the Palais Royal and across the city in some of the municipal districts, a radical club culture was coming into being. The assembly of electors in Paris, which had met in the spring of 1789 to select deputies to send to Versailles, had decided not to disband, believing in the need to correspond with the deputies they had selected for the Estates General. This body eventually became a provisional municipal government, composed of representatives from separate districts across the capital. In some of these districts, being vigilant was their raison d'être. These groups stayed on the lookout for counter-revolutionary threats and tricks of the royal regime; they were also explicitly dedicated to watching their representatives. Focused mainly on the municipal representatives at first, the assembly of the Cordeliers district, which would grow into one of the most radical clubs of the Revolution, insisted from July 1789 on the need for daily reporting on every aspect of the municipal assembly's activity.[68]

After the National Assembly relocated to Paris, more clubs were immediately formed, initially among deputies themselves. But they quickly became large groups with varied membership. The Société des Amis de la Constitution, which soon became known as the Jacobin Club, began meeting in the fall of 1789 on the Rue St. Honoré, just steps from the Manège des Tuileries. Here, rhetoric of vigilance permeated the club's activities and avowed purpose.[69] Moreover, the activities of the network of clubs that formed—often in connection with the Paris Jacobin Club—throughout the country in 1789–90 reveal an overriding concern with obtaining information. Many were in fact formed to stay on top of political events in the capital, reading newspapers together in their meetings.[70] Their gatherings were generally also open to the public, unlike contemporary types of societies in both Britain and the United States.[71] There is evidence that even women were welcome in the Paris Jacobin Club, with space reserved for them.[72]

Over the course of 1790–91, these clubs would grow increasingly vocal about their roles as watchdogs. At a meeting of the Cordeliers in November 1789, attendees discussed their recent efforts to require the election of new members to the municipal government who would take oaths to follow the will of the districts. Elysée Loustalot, editor of the radical newspaper the *Révolutions de Paris*, articulated an understanding of political representation that underpinned the group's calls to vigilance:

> The representatives of the nation think themselves to be the nation, and those of the commune, to be the commune in reality; this is a major error which will abort public liberty in the first moment of its existence. All power comes from the people; the people are everything; they constitute a boss of the representatives.[73]

In refusing to issue an opinion on the Cordeliers' demands of the municipality, Loustalot noted that "the National Assembly was either prudent enough to not touch such delicate questions, or did not do so for reasons unknown to us." This understanding of what political representation meant was backed up with repeated calls to maintain "surveillance" over officials. The Cordeliers repeatedly cited the belief that "PUBLICITY IS THE SAFEGUARD OF THE PEOPLE" and noted their dedication to "an indefatigable vigilance."[74] In March 1791, James Rutledge, who had been arrested for making incendiary accusations against royal minister Jacques Necker, even called the club's surveillance committee "the eye, the sentinel of patriotism," which had penetrated into the "most hidden, of the vile municipal plotters."[75] Once the districts were disbanded and the Cordeliers became a society, formally called the Société des Amis des Droits de l'Homme et du Citoyen, its declared purpose was "denouncing to the tribunal of public opinion the abuse of different powers and of all kinds of threats to the rights of man."[76]

This vigilance was at least partly facilitated by a highly politicized press, not infrequently linked with these emergent political clubs. As historians have long noted, the periodical press expanded exponentially in the early years of the Revolution and much of it was focused on the politics of the National Assembly. With the fall of the Bastille in July 1789, some twenty new newspapers immediately sprang up; by the end of the year, Paris alone had seen the advent of 130 new periodicals.[77] Moreover, whereas in January 1789 only one daily periodical had existed in Paris, by the end of the year there were more than twenty politically oriented dailies and at least as many bi- and tri-weeklies on top of that.[78] In 1790, more than three hundred new titles appeared and almost that many more were started in the first nine months of 1791.[79] In his study of the revolutionary press, Jeremy Popkin argues that these prolific periodicals were considered an "indispensable link between the government and the public: it was at the heart of the new political culture of publicity and openness that was meant to ensure that rulers truly reflected the will of the people."[80] His point is worth exploring further, for the press was far from monolithic in the nature of its ambitions; the "culture of publicity" was murky.

Starting in January 1789, the Librairie (the royal agency in charge of censorship) began receiving prospectuses for periodicals dedicated to chronicling the meetings of the Estates General. The Abbé Ducros, quoted earlier as noting a universal curiosity in the assembly, prefaced his request to publish by warning of the danger of not sanctioning such reporting: "It will be difficult for any human power to stop the communication of news from [the Estates General], such that it will perhaps be dangerous to constrain it."[81] The royal administration would not heed his warning, instead denying all requests to publish accounts of the meetings in Versailles. On May 6, the king banned all reporting on the Estates General in unsanctioned periodicals. But efforts to stop the circulation of news only seemed to bolster the position of those who asserted that reporting on the deputies' deliberations was an essential component of the representative endeavor, either as the responsibility of the elected to their constituents or as an external check on delegated authority. There was a sense that political representation could be more effectively facilitated given the possibility of dialogue across time and space that print made possible. Moreover, 80 percent of the *cahiers de doléances* composed in localities throughout France on the eve of the Estates General asserted the need for a free press and, following the king's invitation to offer opinions on the convening of the Estates, there was no shortage of authors who took up the task. A clear market and expectation for political information emerged in 1789.[82]

Le Patriote françois, run by Jacques-Pierre Brissot de Warville, was one of a number of newspapers that appeared in the spring of 1789 without having sought permission and despite the Librairie's efforts to stop them. Confident that a declaration of press freedom was imminent and that chronicles of the assembly could not wait, Brissot went ahead and launched his periodical as planned. He portrayed the endeavor as vital to the assembly's potential success in constructing a constitution for France.[83] Brissot laid out the goals of his chronicle, chief among which was the accurate reporting of all issues having to do with the Estates General, from debates and resolutions taken within the assembly to analysis of the questions being considered.[84] He proclaimed that "This precious publicity will be the only way to make known to the nation its defenders and to stop betrayal by its enemies."[85] The periodical built on his recently published "plan of conduct" for the upcoming assembly, in which he emphasized that the deputies' "opinions need to be public so that the people can judge whether their representatives are fulfilling their intentions."[86] Brissot, born to a modest family in Chartres, had spent time in London in the early 1780s and traveled through the young United States on the eve of the Estates General in 1788. Having tried for years to break into literary life, Brissot had been briefly imprisoned in the Bastille in 1784 for penning *libelles* and had debt to pay off. He was an aspiring philosophe who found himself more often on Grub Street.[87] He had failed to obtain a spot in the Estates General as a deputy; launching a periodical dedicated to chronicling the assembly gave Brissot not only a way to make some money but also the possibility of breaking into the publishing industry and being a part of politics.

This sense that publicity was necessary for the deputies to fulfill their functions as elected representatives was also taken up by Honoré-

Gabriel Riqueti, the comte de Mirabeau. A friend of Brissot and deputy from Provence, Mirabeau was a well-known public figure who had already published tracts denouncing the despotism of the absolute monarchy after being imprisoned by lettre de cachet. When he arrived in Versailles, Mirabeau immediately began printing a periodical account of the proceedings, elaborating its purpose as that of fulfilling a responsibility of the elected to report back to their constituents. In the first issue printed on May 2, Mirabeau wrote that free peoples relied on the proliferation of periodicals and that "many good citizens, including many who are sitting among the representatives of the nation, adhere to this truth and have resolved to publish a paper that can provide at once an account of the proceedings to their constituents and a testament to civic zeal that good citizens bring to France."[88] For Mirabeau, providing an account of the proceedings was an essential duty of a deputy. It was also, undoubtedly, a way to build his name, advance an advantageous interpretation of events, and build popular support for specific political goals.[89]

Though Brissot and Mirabeau both articulated the value of publicity to the representative endeavor, their conceptions of it were slightly different due to their roles. It mattered whether the publisher was an outsider or a deputy. Publicity in the mind of someone looking in on the meetings was a tool to actively ensure accountability, whereas to a deputy with a vote and a voice in the assembly, it was often a way to broadcast his views and build a brand. This difference would only grow in importance as the spring of 1789 turned to summer and the deputies in Versailles discarded their binding mandates, declaring themselves to be a sovereign legislature.

The assembly's move to Paris in the fall of 1789 certainly proved a boon to journalists who had made it their mission to chronicle the deputies' actions, especially those whose stated purpose was to hold the nation's representatives accountable to what they perceived to be public opinion.[90] In line with the many proposals for periodicals in the spring of 1789, newspapers launched through the summer and fall that year continued to proclaim their centrality to the representative process by guaranteeing the publicity of the deputies' deliberations. In keeping with the difference between deputies self-reporting and journalists attending the meetings as outsiders looking in, a distinction emerged between those who claimed simply to report on assembly deliberations and those who explicitly asserted a watchdog role. However, in line with the point that a wall of glass is inherently destabilizing, both types of reporting had the effect of bringing the unelected into the political process and undermining the insulated theory of representative politics as it had been articulated by deputies in forming the National Assembly. Publicity, whether enacted as an aggressive publication of facts with the polemical intent of criticizing or correcting the actions of officials, or as an evidently benign recitation of information, posed challenges by making the population aware of what elected officials were doing.

Framing the mission of reporting as a mechanism of vigilance, Desmoulins, in his paper the *Révolutions de France et de Brabant*, declared that the National Assembly was not infallible and that its members had been elected by the vote of the people and could be removed by it. "It is to he who institutes, the right to depose," Desmoulins wrote in his first issue, the implication being clear: watch your deputies to ensure they stay in line.[91] It was his intent, his job as a journalist, to facilitate this process: "Here I am, a journalist, and this is a very fine role. It is no longer a contemptible profession, mercenary, slave to the government: today in France, it is the journalist who has the stick, the book of the censor, and who passes review of the senate, the consuls, and the dictator himself."[92] In *Le Publiciste parisien*, which would become the famously radical *L'Ami du Peuple*, Jean-Paul Marat also framed his writing in such a way as to suggest his publication was a tool of accountability. Reporting the opinions held by deputies—noting some directly by name—Marat in his first issue on September 12, 1789, followed this with his own understanding of what the right stance was in the debate over the royal veto. To him it was obvious that handing the king a veto was a bad idea; he implied that those deputies who thought otherwise were clearly mistaken. Those on the wrong side of the question were being actively watched: "The nation can appreciate today the virtue of its deputies; it knows those who are worthy of its confidence," he wrote.[93]

Dozens more newspapers dedicated themselves to chronicling every detail of the deputies' deliberations less aggressively, some purporting to offer no commentary at all. The *Annales patriotiques et littéraires de la France*, edited by Louis-Sebastien Mercier and Jean-Louis Carra, promised to provide "the most exact and reasoned results of the operations of the National Assembly, as well as those of the Commune of Paris, purged of all the minutia and unimportant details," which the editors claimed would only bore their readers.[94] By the fall of 1791, Etienne Le Hodey would launch a newspaper dedicated solely to chronicling assembly debates, as close to word-for-word as possible; *Le Logographe* was predicated on the belief that documenting the activity of the deputies, without comment, was a worthwhile endeavor. Given the technological limitations of the time, even a purportedly verbatim record of the deliberations involved significant reconstruction and interpretation—a notable caveat when considering how a reader, then as now, would encounter assembly debates.[95]

At first, the deputies welcomed reporters into their chamber, constructing a number of small offices within the room in Paris where they could have dedicated space to take notes and produce their periodicals. An undated document, likely in the handwriting of Guillotin, records the journalists who had guaranteed seats in each of four "enclosed platforms" in the corners of the chamber and which staircases and doors they were permitted to pass through.[96] Over the course of 1790–91, Guillotin and his colleagues developed an increasingly formalized process for regulating reporters' access and movement inside the chamber. Enforcing publicity through the printed press became a sophisticated and booming business, leading the deputies of the National Assembly to carve out a role as mediators and monitors of the process. What it meant to govern transparently was yet again contested in the negotiations between journalists and deputies over who could have access to what and what it was possible to print.

In addition to closely regulating reporters' access to their deliberations, deputies struggled to limit the bounds of transparency by defining press law via legal action against journalists they believed took their roles too far. Though there were no legally defined restrictions on the press before the summer of 1791, printers, journalists, and distributors continued to be pursued by police, denounced in the National Assembly, and tried in Parisian courts for libel, sedition, treason, and calumny. The Châtelet, the principal municipal court of Paris, which remained responsible for criminal and political justice through December 1790, rendered regular criminal judgments on eleven speech cases during the last five months of its existence.[97] The typical punishment for the printer or journalist was a requirement to pay a fine and to print a copy of the court's judgment in the next issue of his newspaper. Furthermore, the injured parties were permitted to have a certain number of copies of the judgment printed and posted around Paris, at the cost of the offending printer.[98]

The Châtelet was also charged with the investigation of crimes of *lèse-nation*, essentially high treason, throughout the last year or so of its existence, from October 1789 through December 1790.[99] These cases were ones in which government officials, or the government itself and thus the nation and Revolution, were deemed under threat. The legal category of *lèse-nation* was ostensibly a translation of the concept of *lèse-majesté*—which entailed a crime violating the dignity of the king or an attack on the state—though the National Assembly never did clearly define it.[100] More than a quarter of the cases pursued as crimes of *lèse-nation* between the fall of 1789 and December 1790 were challenges to free expression, three of them sparked by printed material.[101] It is significant that what were essentially cases of libel, defamation, or publication of secret information were treated as crimes of treason. Surely it was a matter of convenience to some extent given the lack of press laws in place at the time. Yet, at the least, treating press cases in this way required casting such offenses as treasonous. These conflicts with journalists were one way the National Assembly was struggling to define the bounds of publicity by limiting the role of the press in enacting it.

On the morning of June 21, 1791, Paris was thrown into confusion as news spread that the royal family was missing. Plans had been in the works for months for them to leave Paris, but it was not until June 20, the last possible night General François Claude Amour, marquis de Bouillé, advised it would be possible, that the king and his family snuck out of the Tuileries Palace.[102] In full disguise, with a passport signed for travel to Frankfurt, the king, queen, their daughter, the dauphin, and the king's sister made their way to a waiting army assembled in Eastern France.[103] Stopped in the town of Varennes after a patriotic postmaster recognized his face from a rendering on the new currency, Louis XVI was escorted back to Paris, arriving just five days after embarking on his long-planned escape. Upon reaching the capital on June 25, the royal family was met by a nearly silent crowd of thousands, according to an anonymous account of Louis XVI's entry into Paris.[104] Their king had fled; after hiding his feelings about the Revolution, he had physically tried to hide to get out of the country. The fiasco proved a turning point in the Revolution, irreparably damaging the monarchy in the public mind and initiating a genuine republican movement.[105]

The king ultimately proved to be the fulcrum of debates about the problem of secrecy and the function of publicity in the representative regime. Louis XVI's failed attempt to flee France in June 1791 intensified popular fervor for vigilance while revealing the potential instability caused by transparency of government operations. In the midst of crisis, the National Assembly began to change its practices in earnest, sealing itself off and attempting to control the flow of information through the press to the public. Deputies deemed publicity as a means of vigilance too great a threat to the stability of France's representative regime, especially as distrust between the population and its representatives intensified over the summer of 1791.

When the National Assembly learned of the king's departure on the morning of June 21, calls mounted immediately for calm and direct communication with the people in Paris and the provinces. Yet these directives were accompanied almost immediately by a resolution that their chamber be closed off to all but the deputies themselves. Third Estate deputy Armand-Gaston Camus, who was in charge of the archives, immediately suggested the measure, which was reportedly met with applause and adopted without debate.[106] Camus himself cited the need to "deliberate with calm" as the reason to shut out the public. Though there is no recorded discussion of any other reasons for sealing off the assembly deliberations, the deputies' actions in the ensuing hours and days suggest a sense that controlling the flow of information and public perception of the missing king was their priority. While they did not themselves yet know the details of the situation, there seemed to be an immediate concern that information could not be uncovered in front of the assembly and the public simultaneously. Although they did not articulate it, the deputies' decisions with regard to handling the king's flight suggest the emergence of a conviction that publicity needed to be restricted and secrecy employed in governing, particularly during an unstable situation.

The deputies quickly drafted a decree aimed at staunching rumors and panic, declaring the missing king a victim of kidnapping. Assuring the people that the situation was under control, the remainder of the decree offered no further details on the deputies' plans or intentions; rather, people were implored to trust them and to remain patient, while waiting for instructions.[107] In a very clear effort to establish their status as sovereign leaders in control of a crisis, the deputies of the National Assembly were creating distance between themselves and the public through their rhetoric, paired with their resolution to seal off their deliberations. Details seemed dangerous; presenting a united and firm front was paramount. Barnave, who would soon be exposed for working with the royals to try to maintain the constitutional monarchy, cautioned the need for extreme care in the drafting of the decree, warning that "the publicity, the extreme publicity, which your proceedings will receive, will become the veritable account of the grand event that occupies us."[108]

Concentration on carefully crafting their decrees, with the awareness that they would be the official word from the deputies on what had happened, further suggests a concern to manage the story for public consumption.

Soon the deputies would have more reason to control the flow of information. The revelation of the king's secrets—that he disavowed the constitution and intended to flee—posed a problem for his legitimacy as head of state under the system the deputies had been crafting.[109] Within hours, the assembly was made aware that the minister of justice possessed a letter in the king's handwriting, prohibiting him from affixing the state seal to anything. The existence of such a letter immediately cast doubt on the story of a kidnapping and suggested a clear intent on Louis XVI's part to leave the capital. Over the course of the afternoon, evidence mounted that the king had fled. A declaration left with his servant turned out to be a long revelation, written by Louis XVI with the avowed purpose of exposing his and the government's conduct "before the eyes of the French, and all the universe."[110] The king wrote with vitriol of what he considered the many mistakes of the National Assembly, the emergence of a threatening political club culture, and the wave of libel and offense the press was propagating.[111] He believed the National Assembly had become dominated by the culture of political clubs designed to force deputies to follow their whims. He then detailed what he considered to be all the aggressions committed against him and his family since the advent of the Revolution in Versailles. At the heart of the matter, he wrote of being forced to go along with decisions made by the assembly though he did not freely support them—essentially revealing all his endorsements of the constitutional project to have been disingenuous. He concluded by stating his belief that the French people loved their king and would endorse his diagnoses of the Revolution and warmly welcome him back.

But the Revolution had gradually radicalized with developments like the nationalization of church property in the fall of 1789, the 1790 Civil Constitution of the Clergy and subsequent requirement for clergy to swear an oath to the new constitution, and the ongoing emigration of much of the nobility. The king was increasingly perceived as being on the wrong side of such developments: slow to accept decrees, seemingly suspicious of the constitutional project, and suspected of plotting with foreign powers to reverse the Revolution. Whispers of republicanism had been percolating among members of radical political clubs and Parisian districts, and even among some National Assembly deputies. Louis

XVI was wrong; his people did not rally to his side, and he was instead apprehended as a traitor.

To the journalists and polemicists who had been skeptical of the monarchy for months, Louis XVI's letter was a secret exposed, evidence that the nation had been tricked by the dissembling monarch. In fact, the revelation that the king had been hiding his disdain for the Revolution came as little surprise. But the failed flight seemed to prove that vigilance on the part of the people was desperately needed. Most periodicals contained an account of the king's declaration in their June 22 editions, and few used the language of "kidnapping" to describe what had happened, despite the official language of the assembly's decree. Clearly reporters had not been expelled from the assembly's deliberations on June 21; many periodicals cited the king's declaration as evidence of his intent to flee and discussed the treatment of this news within the assembly. The revelation was proof that the nation had been tricked and that more vigilance was needed to prevent such eventualities.[112]

What irked many radical journalists more than the king having been able to keep such a secret for so long was that the National Assembly seemed to be in league with the reviled monarch, intent on keeping his secrets. Indeed, the National Assembly repeatedly declared the king's flight the result of a kidnapping. Their reasons for doing so are clear; the deputies needed a trustworthy king for the constitution they were near completing, which retained the monarchy.[113] A traitorous king would not do and the deputies knew it. Responding to the king's declaration on June 22, the assembly conclusively referred to the flight as a kidnapping and addressed his letter as if it were left by conspirators responsible for taking him.[114] The address went on to respond to the points made in the letter, framing the response as one to "those who dictated" the letter to the "seduced king."[115] This type of language led many editors to question why, in the face of such blatant evidence of his intentions, deputies continued to use an ill-fitting term to describe what had happened. "At first we called (I do not know if it was due to politeness or to politics) the flight of Louis XVI a kidnapping! But it was really him who kidnapped himself with his family, and with his family alone; the description of kidnapping is thus wrong, a lie," the *Annales patriotiques* declared.[116]

Calls for Louis XVI to be removed from the throne, even for a republic to be established, increased. But the National Assembly did not align its actions with these requests. Rather, on July 15, the assembly finally issued a decree blaming Bouillé and some low-ranking military officers for the flight. The deputies decreed that if a king retracted his oath to the constitution or conducted an army against the nation, he would be considered to have abdicated.[117] A king who had abdicated, they declared, could be considered as a "simple citizen, subject to charges according to the regular procedures."[118] The deputies concluded that while Louis XVI could be considered to have abdicated based on his denunciation of the constitution, the law defining that act as grounds for abdication had not existed at the time and thus could not be applied to him.[119] Yet the debacle was a manifestation of the challenge revolutionaries faced in claiming the mantle of representatives of the nation from the monarch, who had traditionally been considered the very embodiment of the people, his will inseparable from that of the nation.[120] That notion had come under stress since 1789 as the assembly's very existence posited both a nation and a will distinct from the king.[121] Now they were ostensibly at odds, a conflict that would culminate in the king's trial and execution a little over a year later.

Word of the decree and the decision not to further investigate or try the king was not well received by those with radical leanings. Following its passage on July 15, a massive crowd gathered outside the assembly, shouting insults and threats at the deputies. The July 16 meeting of the National Assembly was focused on the need to explain and justify the previous day's decree in the face of public upheaval. But the deputies' effort to ease tensions failed; public dismay came to a breaking point on July 17. That Sunday, some fifty thousand people gathered on the Champ de Mars to sign a petition against the assembly's decree excusing the king.[122] After two people were killed, Bailly—by then mayor of Paris—declared martial law and sent the National Guard to break up the crowd. When the guards arrived and called on the group to disperse, they were met with yelling and stones.[123] In response, the Marquis de LaFayette ordered the guards to fire into the crowd, which they did, killing fifty.[124]

In the days leading up to what was quickly labeled a massacre, the deputies had already begun discussing the threat posed by their loss of control over the spread and interpretation of the story of the king's flight. A man was arrested at the Palais Royal for reading from *L'Ami du Peuple* to a group of some twenty women.[125] Throughout June and July, peddlers were arrested for crying out news that was inflammatory, such as negative reactions to the July 15 decree.[126] The assembly had made some efforts in the two years prior to the summer of 1791 to define limits to the free press. However, immediately following the massacre, it passed a law that authorized arrest and trial for anyone who "provoked murder, pillage, fire or formally counseled disobedience of the law, either by placards and posters, or by writings published or peddled."[127] Finally, on August 22, 1791, comprehensive regulations of the press were put into action. Press violations were defined as "provocation of legal disobedience, inciting degradation of constituted powers, resistance to public powers, voluntary libels against public functionaries, and libels against private individuals."[128] These definitions were refined and inserted into the constitution that was signed in September 1791.

A steady flow of reporters' requests for space and cards granting access through that summer of 1791 shows how formalized the admittance process became during the waning months of the Constituent Assembly's existence.[129] In late June, a request addressed to Guillotin—at that point in charge of the *Inspecteurs de la salle*—from the editor of the *Journal du Soir* asked for two spots in a tribune. He had been unsuccessful in securing one for the past year and he believed justice required his receiving a dedicated space to report.[130] On July 2, Guillotin wrote to the editor and informed him that he could establish a small partition for one person to sit in the corner of the public galleries on condition that he deliver a copy of his paper to the archives daily, that he not yield the space to any others, that he would not make noise or other disturbances, and that he would inform the committee the moment the space ceased to be useful to him.[131] In September 1791, Guillotin issued permission to the editor of the *Mercure universel* to take up a place in the tribune on the right side of the president, on condition that he deposit a copy of the paper each day with the archivist and the *Bureau des Commissaires*.[132] This was done following a request from the editor to be accorded a place where he could "see and, above all, hear because without this advantage, I will be involuntarily drawn to commit grave errors harmful to opinion."[133]

The Legislative Assembly, which began meeting in October 1791, proceeded to establish increasingly complex and strict procedures to regulate access to their deliberations. By the spring of 1792, there was a corps of guards with extensive responsibilities and regularized organization in charge of upholding rules in the chamber. Two guards were assigned to keep the public out of restricted areas and charged to "maintain silence among those who raise their voices, and if there is noise in the corridors or if they find them to be too crowded, the officer will bring in the guard to clear them."[134] The flow of information from the assembly floor to the streets of Paris was a site of contestation, where the functioning of representative government was daily worked out.

The theory of representative government articulated by the deputies to the Estates General who declared themselves the National Assembly in the summer of 1789 required a separation between the population and elected officials that was never effectively actuated due to a widespread and intense aversion to secrecy. The deputies in the National Assembly repeatedly emphasized the importance of publicity to the representative process and committed to practices ensuring the public could watch them. In practice, being able to watch deliberations and follow constant reports on the actions of the deputies fostered a culture of vigilance. Journalists and club members asserted a duty to ensure the government remained representative in the sense of officials reflecting public opinion, which contradicted the deputies' articulation of representation as a process whereby officials themselves formed the national will (and should therefore be insulated from popular pressure). By 1791, it was becoming increasingly clear that two different understandings of representative government were competing for primacy. The deputies undermined their ideal of political representation with their rhetorical and practical commitment to publicity; it was not possible to form the national will at a distance when the public could see every step of the process.

Deputies received regular reminders that they were being watched not only by constituents back home but also by journalists and crowds in the capital who often did not agree with their decisions. A culture of vigilance swept over Paris; keeping watch over the nation's representatives was a way to ensure they followed the opinions and desires of those whom they represented. Publicity thus became a central axis upon which the meaning of what it meant for politics to be representative was negotiated. As the problem of disagreement between the representatives and the people cropped up, defining what publicité meant and how it would work in practice became a focus among deputies struggling to establish their legitimacy. As they tried to redefine publicity as a one-way process, a careful and calculated distribution of information to a passive audience, deputies began limiting the bounds of transparency. Gradually, from the summer of 1789 through the spring of 1791, the National Assembly recognized a need to close its doors and control the flow of information more closely if it was going to establish a stable representative legislature as a legitimate tool of popular sovereignty.

Even as they continued to profess the importance of publicity to the new regime and proclaim the necessity of eradicating secrets from society, elected officials accelerated the reintroduction of secrecy into more aspects of governance. They did so increasingly in response to the mounting pressure created by the radical insistence on vigilance over the deputies as representatives of the people. Throughout the Legislative Assembly's existence—over the course of a year starting in the fall of 1791—new procedures were established to limit the flow of information from the assembly floor and to assert greater control over who could see what as the political process unfolded. This was done amid escalating calls for vigilance over the deputies as they made decisions out of concert with apparent public opinion, particularly in regards to maintaining the constitutional monarchy in the face of loud cries for a republic.

Redrawing lines between visible and concealed, public and private, was a core activity of the revolutionary government. The process informed understandings and shaped the nature of representative government in France. As time wore on, the Legislative Assembly found itself in an increasingly precarious situation. With a king trusted by ever fewer people and a persistent pressure to publicize government operations and reveal counter-revolutionary plots, tensions were rising. The balance between secrecy and publicity would require recalibrating with the declaration of a republic in September 1792, three years after deputies in Versailles had proclaimed *publicité* as vital to representative politics.

CHAPTER FIVE

Mere Spectators of Events

As the revolution continued to roil France, the meanings of publicity and vigilance underwent a remarkable transformation. Political leaders worked to redefine publicity and reintroduce secrecy as a valuable tool in governance. Building on the belief that some degree of secrecy was necessary to effectively combat hidden conspiracies in a time of revolution, deputies in the National Convention—which convened in the fall of 1792 as France declared itself a republic—began to shield more government work from public view. Publicity was increasingly advocated as a calculated broadcast of information whereby public opinion could be molded for distinct political purposes. Whereas during the early Revolution, radicals—particularly Jacobins—had posited publicity as coterminous with vigilance enacted by citizens over their elected officials, by late 1792 they were refashioning it as a tool to be deployed strategically by the government itself. Vigilance was increasingly considered a virtue and responsibility of elected officials—over the monarchy, over each other, and over the people. The government during the period of the Terror (1793–94) was geared toward achieving transparency in society but, ironically, it carried out vigilance from behind closed doors.

In redefining the meaning of publicity, deputies of the National Convention were bringing practices into greater alignment with the theory of representative government they had undermined since 1789 with a relentless emphasis on publicity. As they shut doors and publicized information with the aim of shaping public perceptions, Jacobin deputies in the National Convention attempted to enact political representation as a relationship in which elected officials were to determine the best interest of the nation and guide public opinion rather than reflect it. Though allied with insurrectionary Parisians and committed rhetorically to a reflective style of representation based on popular surveillance, in practice, Jacobins moved toward an insulated, even directive, form of representation.[1] It would, surprisingly, bring their political practices closer to articulations endorsed by more conservative deputies and American Federalists across the Atlantic.

This shift can only be understood as a result of the rapidly evolving political dynamic from 1792 to 1794. It coincided with the integration of many of the most virulent watchdog journalists into the National Convention as representatives. Furthermore, it was a result of both Girondins (a faction constructed as enemies of Jacobins and allied with Brissot) and Montagnards (the radical left-wing faction associated with Jacobins) finding themselves at odds with what appeared to be public opinion, in the capital and provinces respectively. Contesting the assertions of radical Parisians claiming to voice the will of the people, both factions sought to redefine publicity in practice and reintroduce secrecy into governance as a way to free political decision-making from having to reflect public opinion—or, practically speaking, whoever was loudest in claiming to express it. Jacobin leaders never stopped championing publicity, but it was an altered form: representatives were now vigilant on behalf of the people because they could see more, and better.[2]

Histories of the Terror—generally characterized as 1793 through the summer of 1794—have tended to focus on answering the question of why. Why did the French Revolution devolve into political violence?[3] But what if we shift the focus to how: how did the government change during the period later defined as the Terror, and how did revolutionaries conceive of and justify these changes?[4] Focusing on the ways in which the meaning and implementation of publicity was limited and on the reintroduction of secrecy into government directly links the repressive tactics of Jacobin leaders to their thinking about political representation.

This story begins with the exposure of a stash of royal secrets. The discovery in November 1792 of an iron safe stuffed inside a wall of the Tuileries Palace quickly became a symbol for the shadowy maneuvering of the monarch, especially because the papers it held implicated many formerly popular political leaders as royal collaborators. The way deputies handled the contents of the *armoire de fer* and trial of Louis XVI indicates a mounting effort to control the public's access to information in order to ensure a desired political outcome. As winter gave way to spring in 1793, the foundations of what became the Terror were laid with new committees, defined to a great extent by their secrecy. Facing a population that, in large part, did not seem to agree with the Convention's decisions and wanting to avoid the perception of being subject to crowd pressures in Paris, Jacobin leaders sought to move the decision-making process from the floor of the Convention to a closed committee room.[5] Though the Constitution of 1793 affirmed the importance of publicité as crucial to ensuring that representative government would be bound by expressions of the people's will, Jacobin leaders did not consider this possible under current circumstances, and the constitution was suspended. Their determination to represent a nation, a people, that they were simultaneously trying to bring into being led them to adopt an insulated vision of political representation.[6] To achieve democratic ends, Jacobin politicians justified the adoption of means they themselves had defined as undemocratic. Representatives could not be reflective if they were to be revolutionary, and secrecy was essential to this state of exception.

By the summer of 1794, the revolutionary government had restricted the meaning of publicité and had thoroughly reintegrated secrets into its work as part of its attempt to assert in practice the long-held theory of political representation as insulated from, rather than reflective of, public opinion. Though this alteration in the practice of representative politics was justified as exceptional, there seemed no end in sight. In July, paranoia reached a crescendo and many deputies decided that the way this state of exception was functioning was no longer sustainable. On 9 Thermidor, Year II—or July 27, 1794—Maximilien Robespierre, a key leader of this period, was ejected from the Convention. The regime was once again altered, opening the possibility of repudiating the type of political representation Jacobin leaders had been attempting to impose, in no small part through the reintroduction of secrecy into government.

Three months after the king had been effectively deposed in the storming of the Tuileries Palace on August 10, 1792, and two months after France was declared a republic, Minister of the Interior Jean-Marie Roland announced to the National Convention that he had discovered a stash of Louis XVI's papers. "They were in such a particular place, such a secret place, that if the only person in Paris who knew of them had not indicated their presence, it would have been impossible to discover them," he relayed on November 20.[7] A blacksmith who was commissioned to construct an iron box and lock reportedly led Roland to a hollowed-out space in a palace wall, where they found a safe filled with some seven hundred documents. Evidently placed in the secure box for safekeeping, the files were a physical manifestation of all the king's supposed secrets. Though they would not be cited extensively during his trial and contained little explicitly damning material beyond what was already known, the documents found in the so-called *armoire de fer* became a powerful symbol of state secrecy.[8] Moreover, the way in which they were handled, particularly debates over who should have the ability to access the documents and what should be revealed to the public, led to the first significant contests over the meaning of publicity and the place of secrecy in the National Convention. Debates about how to treat the documents revealed disagreements over defining the meaning of political representation in the new republic; representatives were now the ones who could legitimately unveil and exercise vigilance, using publicity to display select information to the public. This new conception of the place of state secrecy and meaning of publicity laid the foundation for deputies to assert their primacy over the people in deciding the king's fate.

It is unlikely that Louis XVI's primary motivation in constructing the safe was to hide papers; he was probably attempting to safeguard them against theft or destruction. Still, the fact that the safe was hidden and locked created a perception of intentional concealment.[9] Given that the king was already suspected of lying and plotting, especially in the wake of the Flight to Varennes, the armoire de fer proved a powerful symbol of monarchical secrecy. Reporting on its discovery on November 21, Louis-Sébastien Mercier and Jean-Louis Carra wrote in the *Annales patriotiques et littéraires* that not all the papers regarding the Civil List (the royal register of paid clients) were where they had previously been found: "several were hidden in an excavation made in a wall of the Tuileries Palace."[10] Fitting in with a narrative of the Revolution constructed since 1789, the revolutionaries were yet again unveiling royal perfidy and shedding light on previously hidden political maneuvers.[11]

The significance of the armoire de fer was at first largely symbolic but it quickly became about more as the contents were catalogued. The safe contained mostly letters addressed to the king from members of the clergy about religious reforms and reports from various officials providing strategic proposals, as well as policy analysis from Arnaud II de La Porte in his capacity as intendant of the Civil List and notes from some escaped nobles offering professions of loyalty. Though the materials confirmed that Louis XVI was generally not in favor of the revolutionaries' religious reforms and that he had labored to preserve the power of the monarchy in the face of the radicalizing Revolution, the documents did not show anything about the king that was not generally known. What they did show was the monarch's extensive efforts to sway public opinion and engage in political persuasion under the Constituent and Legislative assemblies. Among the documents most scrutinized in the Convention and the press were records outlining money spent on hiring spies, polemicists, and people to sit in the galleries of the legislature and applaud at particular points. "These pieces prove that the heretofore king never walked in good faith in the direction of the Constitution, that he was himself at the head of all the plots against it," Brissot, now a deputy himself, wrote in the *Patriote françois*.[12] "While his brothers prepared a counter-revolution from outside, he deployed a vast plan of corruption within, the goal of which was to affect a moral counter-revolution," he continued.[13] The documents did demonstrate a keen awareness of the importance of shaping public opinion in Paris and maintaining influence within the legislature. More troubling, perhaps, was that the king had been acting behind the scenes to mold political discourse and decisions. In doing so, the monarchy was living up to its reputation for shadowy dealings, in contrast to the highly valorized centrality of publicity under the new regime.

Even more concerning to the deputies was not that the crown had been operating in the shadows to influence the political process but that the king and his ministers had been working with elected deputies. Dozens of current and former deputies were implicated in the files, seemingly confirming that even the most ardent of patriots could merely be wearing a mask.[14] Moreover, the evidence suggested that all the talk about representatives acting in view of the people had been just that: talk. In reality, some of the most prominent deputies of the early Revolution had been dealing with the monarchy behind closed doors, essentially engaged in a political process that was entirely, and intentionally, shielded from public view. All the warnings of the radical clubs and calls for vigilance over elected officials seemed to be validated with the unveiling of the information contained in the armoire de fer. It was not only the king or aristocrats over whom surveillance and vigilance needed to be exercised but also elected representatives of the people.

Perhaps the most prominent, and surprising, of the political figures implicated in the armoire papers was the comte de Mirabeau, who had died a hero in the spring of 1791. On December 5, the committee cataloguing the papers read two letters in the Convention that detailed royal ministers' dealings with Mirabeau and other unnamed deputies. A letter to the king described one royal operative's efforts to win deputies to the king's cause, which, the author reported, many were willing to support secretly, for no other reason than to help the monarch. The group he had been able to form "remained enveloped in impenetrable veils, and left their majesties with a sort of small army in Paris always ready to act in their service."[15] A second letter, written by La Porte, named Mirabeau as a deputy who was helping to ensure the king's influence among the members of the assembly. Along with these letters, the chairman of the committee also revealed an accounting of money spent on planting spies, paying people to cheer in the galleries of the National Assembly and certain cafes, and printing pamphlets designed to sway public opinion in favor of the king.[16] An outraged Convention voted to investigate Mirabeau further to determine whether his remains should be removed from the Pantheon, where they had been laid to rest following his death. In the meantime, the deputies placed a veil over his bust in the assembly hall.[17]

There were also members of the current Convention who had their names mentioned or insinuated in the papers found in the armoire, which fueled suspicion that deputies were still hiding their real loyalties. When "the most prominent members" of the legislature were mentioned in letters without being named, it spurred rampant speculation about whom they might be and whether they were currently sitting in the Convention. On November 29, a number of deputies reported that they had read speculation that they personally had been implicated or that certain deputies had been arrested based on being named in the armoire de fer papers. Deputy Charles François Delacroix, father of the famous Romantic painter Eugène Delacroix, asked that the commission investigating the papers make a report as soon as possible on who was implicated, because his enemies had taken the opportunity to try to smear his name.[18] "Trust is easily altered," Delacroix declared, citing concern that the people's faith in the National Convention was tenuous.[19] Those whose names were specifically mentioned defended themselves by citing their commitment to transparency. Montagnard Bertrand Barère, whose name had appeared, declared that "A Roman Citizen said: 'I wish that a house open to all gazes would be constructed for me, so that all my

Depiction of a skeleton with Mirabeau's head sitting atop a pile of papers and holding a crown while Roland and the locksmith who had led him to the palace break open the *armoire de fer*. Entitled "Apparition de l'ombre de Mirabeau: trouvé dans l'armoire de fer au chateau des Thuileries" (Paris, 1792); artist unknown. (Source: Bibliothèque nationale de France)

fellow citizens can witness my actions.' Citizens, I would have wanted to live in such a house during my time as a member of the Constituent Assembly."[20] The metaphor of the glass house, cited during the early months of the National Assembly's existence by Third Estate deputy Constantin-François Chasseboeuf de Volney as an explanation of why the doors to its deliberations should remain open, was here referenced as a personal virtue of an individual deputy. He should be trusted, Barère claimed, because he had made a concerted effort to live in public view and make his loyalties transparent.

As Barère's self-defense indicates, not all the revelations of the armoire were trusted, and certainly not by all the deputies, which raised the question of how state secrets were to be handled. From the day Roland revealed the existence of the armoire de fer, suspicions of the process whereby these secrets were unveiled began to circulate. Why had Roland gone to the Tuileries Palace alone with the blacksmith who exposed the safe? Why had he not taken with him members of the legislative committee appointed to catalogue the contents of the palace? Was it possible he had tampered with the contents of the safe? Roland was, after all, an appointed minister. He was also closely allied with the Girondin faction in the assembly coalesced around Brissot, which was at odds with the more radical Montagne (the faction that included most Jacobins by the fall of 1792).[21] Mere minutes after Roland had made his announcement in the Convention, Desmoulins, a prominent member of the Montagne, asked Roland rhetorically whether he really thought "we did not find it strange that one single man examined [the papers] before us?"[22] In the *Patriote françois*, Brissot responded to this challenge by pointing out that the committee created to catalogue the papers had only been created that day; the reason Roland had not taken any members of this committee along to uncover the armoire was simply that he had not known of its existence.[23] Even if this had been the case, others persisted, why would he still have gone with only the blacksmith and one other person to uncover what was apparently such an important stash of secrets? "The care he took to be accompanied in this expedition by only two of his own creatures, leads to all the conjectures we could wish to draw," Marat reported in his newspaper.[24]

Now that the Convention had the papers from the armoire in its possession, regardless of the manner in which they had been discovered, the deputies adopted precautions to guarantee the integrity of the evidence. Following the recommendation of a deputy who noted that even the affixing of state seals on seized papers was no safeguard against tampering and fraud, Roland stayed in the Convention Hall until one o'clock in the morning along with appointed commissioners to register each page of paper he had delivered earlier in the day. A committee of twelve deputies was then appointed to systematically comb through the documents and report to the Convention on their contents. Control over the unveiling of state secrets was thus firmly lodged in the legislature and wrested from the hands of the minister of the interior. Though factional divisions were perhaps the main motivation for questioning Roland's ability to control the contents of the armoire, it was also his status as an appointed minister that undergirded the contestation. Roland was a member of the executive branch of the government and was thus considered an improper, even dangerous, keeper of any secrets. Shortly after the discovery of the armoire, Marat called attention to the dangers of the ministerial cabinet, which "like under royalism or despotism," he wrote, was the "master of all." "It is thus in his hands that all the state secrets are placed, of which he communicates none to the representatives of the sovereign and into which he never allows any insight other than when they support his views."[25] This sort of argument was further bolstered by the concurrent debates taking place in the Convention during the late fall months of 1792, which cast suspicion on Roland's role in the lack of resolution to the ongoing subsistence crisis. "Public functionaries under the new regime are worth even less than those under the old regime," Marat irately concluded.[26]

Though the deputies seized control over the secret files from the ministerial branch, they just as swiftly drew a curtain to control their public exposure. Immediately after the committee was created, Jacques Defermon des Chapelières, a moderate, proposed that "except for the members of the commission, no one can come into the room where the analysis of the papers found in the Tuileries is being done."[27] The Convention enacted this rule without debate and the handling of state secrets was transferred to a select committee of elected representatives. Two days later, the committee was directed to make a report of the pieces it had discovered that it "estimated to be important and worth verifying."[28] In the process, a slow release of the documents contained in the armoire began. The committee would periodically report to the Convention on the papers it found the most incriminating, particularly those pieces that implicated members of the sitting legislature or prominent figures from earlier in the Revolution. This was how the evidence against Mirabeau came out and what led Barère to defend himself by claiming he had always wished to live in a glass house. But fewer than half the documents found in the armoire were ever printed and only a carefully curated number were even used during Louis XVI's trial.[29]

The trial of the deposed king marked a turning point both for the type of political representation that deputies, especially Jacobins, advocated, and for the way in which they defined and practiced publicity.[30] Specifically, the issue of whether to refer the question of the king's fate to the people—in the form of an "appeal to the people"—engendered nothing less than a debate over the very mechanics and legitimacy of representative government. Once the Convention had decided on Louis XVI's guilt, the appeal meant that its decision would then be sent to the primary assemblies for consideration. There, delegates would either vote for or against the Convention's decision, and the king's fate would ultimately be determined by them.[31] In what became one of the most salient conflicts between Girondins and Montagnards, deputies had to balance strategic and ideological commitments in their decisions about whether or not to support an appeal.[32] It was generally Girondins who urged mechanisms to determine a pre-existing popular will and reflect it in government.[33] Though allied with insurrectionary Parisians, Jacobins in fact began to express a vision of representation that would preclude and invalidate popular intervention.

It was a crucial moment at which strategy and ideology shaped one another in a feedback loop, making it pivotal to the articulation of ideas about representation. Many of the deputies' reasons for supporting the *appel au peuple* in the king's trial were likely tactical, despite being articulated as ideological commitments. From a purely strategic standpoint, sending the decision to the primary assemblies for consideration would buy time at the very least and could possibly save Louis XVI's life. Undoubtedly, many deputies supported the appeal for this reason alone. Moreover, an appeal would present a challenge to the Montagne—which had been closely linked to Parisian radicals—by breaking the debate out of the capital. On the opposite side, many who rejected the popular appeal likely anticipated the possibility that it could save the king's life and thus complicate the founding of the republic and raise tensions with crowds in Paris who wanted Louis XVI gone for good. We should also not minimize the role of fear in the deputies' calculus both of what to say and how to vote.[34]

A few short weeks after throngs stormed the Tuileries Palace and forced Louis XVI's imprisonment that summer, crowds driven by conspiracy theories massacred hundreds of prisoners across Paris. It was in the wake of this confusion, and no doubt fear, that deputies devised a process for trying the king.[35] Many of them changed their minds about the appeal from the first time it was introduced to the vote on whether to move forward with it.[36] This suggests the fluidity of theoretical commitments in the face of political realities; it also shows how a public audience shaped stances and their justification in ways that could lead to interesting ideological acrobatics. The elaboration of theories of political representation in what may have been a strategically motivated debate attained significance going forward. The deputies' decision to reserve the determination of the king's fate to themselves was the strongest assertion yet of an insulated type of representative politics.

This vision was justified partly based on changing understandings of how publicity worked. Deputies argued that representatives were more qualified than the population to make weighty decisions because of what they could see that the public could not. But they also deemed their decisions legitimate because of what the public *was* able to see: namely, their deliberations and votes. This determination was a key turning point in the definition not only of representative politics but also of publicity and how it ought to function in a republic. The incident highlights a tension within the concept of transparency: authenticity was distinct from, and sometimes even conflicted with, the public performance of political representation, despite both being considered essential to republican government.[37]

On the opposing side, the case for conducting a referendum might have remained for many a strategy to save the king. But it is still significant that the argument was ultimately advanced by articulating a vision of political representation as necessarily reflective of public opinion, in the sense that Parisian radicals and American Antifederalists had advocated. Supporters of the appeal argued that the deputies' authority was delegated and thus necessarily limited. If the deputies did not utilize a mechanism whereby the people's sovereignty could be explicitly expressed and then respect the outcome, they were nothing more than a new style of tyrant. Jean-Paul Rabaut de Saint-Etiénne advocated letting the primary assemblies vote on how the king should be punished by framing it as a necessary consultation of the nation: "The nation sent you, without a doubt, but to delegate powers, not to exercise them all;

because, I repeat, it is impossible that it wished simply to change masters."[38] Representative government was only legitimate, according to Girondin Armand Gensonné, because the people could not practically govern themselves. "But [the people's] rights are violated every time that we make them do something by representation that they could do on their own," he argued.[39] By this logic, the very legitimacy of representation simply vanished when it was possible to consult the people directly on a decision.

This notion of political representation as necessarily reflective relied on an active style of publicity, in the form of a dialogue—importantly, with the entire country, not just those in close proximity to the Convention. In cases where public opinion was "formed and well known," the deputies' relationship with those who had elected them was simple: "We have but to be its interpreters, and as soon as it is manifested, it is up to us simply to provide the last degree of evidence."[40] Here, Girondin François Buzot also conveyed an understanding of political representation as a reflective process, in which elected officials were to ascertain public opinion and form their decisions accordingly. In the case of the king, it was possible that public opinion had been formed but was not yet known to them. "I am far from thinking the clamors of one portion of the inhabitants of one city are the expression of the national wish," he declared, referring to radical Parisians who were eager for a conviction. "For too long our *départements* [provinces] have been mere spectators of events that have influence on the destiny of France as a whole."[41] In calling provincial citizens "spectators," Buzot seemed to acknowledge that watching alone was not good enough, that the Convention conducting its business transparently was not sufficient to guarantee the proper relationship between public opinion and political decision-making. Instead, it had to be a two-way street, an active process whereby spectators had an opportunity to offer their input on decisions.

As others, mostly members of the Montagne faction, argued forcefully against the referendum, they too articulated an understanding of what being a representative meant. Their vision also relied on publicité, but a more passive form of it. The dangers of secret maneuverings in the primary assemblies and of the population being blinded were cited as reasons to restrict decision-making power to the Convention. Within its walls, all the evidence could be properly seen and carefully considered.[42] Moreover, this could be done in public view, whereas referring the decision to the primary assemblies created opportunities for intrigue and secret influence over the decision. It was the all-seeing ability of the representatives, backed by the fact that they had been elected to make decisions, that made the popular consultation a threatening proposal.

For those against the appeal, inviting the primary assemblies to affirm or reject the Convention's decision was dangerous. It would create the possibility of civil war by exposing rifts within the population, and it threatened to delegitimize the decisions of previous legislatures and hamper the future exercise of popular sovereignty through representative government. Once they appealed to the people, it would be difficult to draw the line between what needed to be considered directly by the population and what could be carried out by its elected officials. This could call into question all the previous decisions made by representative legislatures throughout the Revolution. It fundamentally threatened the entire basis and legitimacy of representative politics. On January 2, Carra, who was actually allied with the Girondin faction and had long edited a newspaper, cautioned against the *appel au peuple* because it was "risking, in this occurrence, putting the people and its representatives in formal contradiction."[43] If the primary assemblies did not agree with the decision the Convention had made, the disagreement would be evidence that the elected officials were not representative, which could provide ammunition to foreign enemies who had already been claiming this. It would not be unlike the situation of the National Assembly in the wake of the Flight to Varennes, when its decisions had been distinctly out of sync with expressed public sentiment on the king.

Some scoffed at the idea that whatever decision the primary assemblies made it would simply provide a check of public opinion for the Convention. Montagnard Marie-François Moreau responded to claims that if the primary assemblies voted against the execution of the king it would only prove that the people remained unenlightened. Such discord would be proof that the population "does not see its own interest; that it is still blinded by its prejudices, or duped by royalist intrigues," he declared. Moreover, as representatives, it was "up to you to enlighten and to prevent [the people] from falling into the trap that is being prepared."[44] Robespierre also suggested that in the primary assemblies, there was likely to be "unreasoned and heated deliberations," where the people could not clearly foresee the outcomes of their decisions.[45] For this reason, the people had elected representatives to the National Convention to make decisions on their behalf, in their best interest. Delivering the last word in the debate over the referendum, Barère made an even more literal claim about the ability of the Convention to see what the primary assemblies could not. "The citizens of the primary assemblies, do they know as you do the pieces of the trial? Have they heard, as you have, the accused? Have they seen him?" For Barère, the qualification to make a decision on the king's fate came down to having literally seen him and all the evidence against him, which was not possible on a mass scale. As the nation's representatives, they could simply see more. "Do they have before their eyes the political considerations and the revolutionary events that surround you?" he asked. The answer was implied: that the people simply could not see enough to judge.[46]

But it was also what the people *could* see that made the Convention's determination legitimate, according to Barère. Though it was not an active publicité, wherein a dialogue between the representatives and the people was to ensue, the Convention had conducted the entire trial in public view. In taking on a judicial role, the deputies had ensured that a core tenet of legal protocol was adhered to: "Publicity is the essence of criminal procedures for all citizens," he declared, "and who would be judged more solemnly and with more publicity than Louis Capet?"[47] Being the people's representatives, they had diverged from traditional judicial practice to guarantee even more transparency. Whereas in a court, the deliberation was conducted in secret, in the case of the king it was and would be done in front of an audience. "The nature of our functions, our responsibilities, our mandates, all necessitate publicity; it is the safeguard of the nation, it is also ours," Barère declared.[48] Here, he posited publicité as the mechanism that protected the Convention against accusations of usurpation of power. Performing its decision-making process in view of the public was sufficient to guarantee the legitimacy of the outcome as an act of popular sovereignty. By this measure, publicité was fully neutered, becoming a passive process of reception. It maintained its value as a principle of representative politics, but shifted in meaning so as not to undermine the government's stability. Moreover, in practice, this publicité was in fact limited; what the public saw of Louis XVI's trial, particularly the evidence used against him, was carefully controlled.

The procedures observed during the trial and the voting on the king's fate match a pattern of the political trials of the period known as the Terror. Evidence was prepared in secret, but once the accusation was made, deliberation and judgment were public, as was the punishment. As previously mentioned, the committees that combed through the evidence and prepared the accusation against Louis XVI met in secret with only a fraction of the evidence ever printed for public consumption. Once the king was accused, he was brought for questioning in front of the National Convention, where he was also presented with evidence for the first time. Though they had concerns about security during the trial, the Convention maintained open doors throughout the process—from the numerous appearances of the king himself to the deliberations and roll call voting on his fate. A meeting record of the *Comité des Inspecteurs de la salle* on December 10 details the extra precautions taken for the king's appearance the following day, from checking to make sure no one carrying weapons or batons was admitted to combing the galleries the previous night to ensure no one was hiding.[49] Depictions of Louis XVI appearing to answer questions show the crowds in the galleries at the time, further emphasizing the importance of publicity to the process. When it came time to vote on whether the king was guilty, how he should be punished, and whether the decision should be sent to the primary assemblies for ratification, Buzot suggested that regular voting procedures would not be sufficient for such a solemn occasion. Rather, he proposed that, in addition to holding a roll call vote, each deputy should verify the recording of his vote and the list should immediately be printed and distributed throughout the country.[50] The Convention decided to do this and proceeded to declare the king guilty on January 15, 1793, and condemn him to death a few days later.

Louis XVI was publicly guillotined on the Place de la Révolution, now the Place de la Concorde, on January 21. His severed head was held up to the crowd, evidence of the regicide performed before the eyes of those gathered to witness it. Just two days later, Roland delivered his resignation from the office of minister of the interior. Though he maintained that he had never tampered with the evidence found in the armoire de fer, he acknowledged that he had lost the public's trust, or at least become a distraction. "It is time to remove myself from the public eye and the concern of one party in the Convention," he wrote. "Heaven is my witness, posterity will judge me."[51] He declared that he would hand over all his accounts to the Convention and to the public, which he maintained would prove his innocence in the face of the allegations of corruption leveled against him. "I present myself to my contemporaries as to posterity, with my works; they speak for me."[52] Later considered guilty of the accusations against him, Roland would escape from Paris in the spring of 1793, only to commit suicide upon hearing that his wife had been guillotined.

Beginning with the trial of Louis XVI, the National Convention built on measures implemented during the previous year under the Legislative Assembly to more tightly control access to its meetings and began to reinstate secrecy in certain parts of governance. While continuing to champion the value of publicity to guaranteeing the legitimacy of representative politics, Jacobin deputies especially moved to circumscribe its meaning. It was to be the deputies themselves who would exercise vigilance—over the ministries, over the citizenry, and over each other. The Convention would broadcast information directly through printed accounts of its meetings that were produced by its own employees and printed by the national printer. While the deputies created their own organs of publicity, they simultaneously began to restrict access to their chamber for journalists who did not fit a particular political profile. The formalized Comité des Inspecteurs de la salle took on an increasingly robust role monitoring access to the chamber, though Parisians continued to populate the galleries at the Convention's meetings and their right to do so was seldom contested. But through the spring and summer of 1793, the deputies moved more of the work of governance off the floor of the Convention and into newly created committees, which met in secret.

This reintegration of secrecy into the governing process and the ever more limited definition of publicité, which were justified as exceptional measures, can only be understood in relation to the political dynamic in 1793. The struggle between two factions in the Convention significantly contributed to new attitudes about the place of publicity and secrecy in government, which entailed different articulations of what it meant to represent the people. Though the deputies of both the Girondin and the Montagne factions maintained a rhetorical commitment to publicité, the political reality they were facing made it increasingly untenable for either side to support in practice. The first shift in the meaning of publicity was linked to the integration of many of the most prominent journalists into the Convention as representatives themselves. No longer outsiders, these reporters were thus not able to claim to exercise a watchful eye over the government as a whole; instead, they watched over one another from factional vantage points. Simply due to the fact that so many of the self-proclaimed watchdog journalists of the early Revolution became deputies in the National Convention, the meaning of publicity evolved from being a process whereby vigilance was exercised upon elected officials from without to being an internal vigilance strategically projected outward. Moreover, the underlying link between publicity and legitimate political representation—through the guarantee of aligned public opinion and political decision-making—was increasingly called into question.

Both factions began to ask how publicity was functioning and what their commitment to it meant for the legitimacy of representative politics. To Girondins, it was not a matter of shutting doors but of changing who was let through them. Throughout the winter and spring of 1793, they grew increasingly concerned about the limits of the dialogue they were holding through their commitment to the transparency of their deliberations. Confident that the voice of the country as a whole would be more aligned with their views, they focused on expanding access to their deliberations and limiting the role of radicals in close proximity. Meanwhile, the deputies of the Montagne faction found themselves in a complicated position as the months wore on. They remained rhetorically committed to publicity because the notion of active publicity, of vigilance over elected officials, had arisen largely among their radical Parisian supporters. It was largely these avid citizens who populated the galleries in the Convention on a daily basis and to whom the Montagne mainly owed its growing political dominance. Yet in an effort to control increasingly violent Parisian radicals and deny the implications of the mounting resistance to them in the provinces, Jacobin deputies began to reconceive publicity and the very legitimacy of representative government. These deputies did not want to be perceived as being directed by the passions of a crowd, and they also did not want their decisions called into question by the apparent disagreement of vast portions of the provincial population. The way out of this bind was a reintroduction of secrecy into government and a total transformation of the meaning of publicity from an active dialogue into a process of strategic broadcast. The role of representatives could no longer be to reflect when the people did not seem to have the right opinions. Instead, their role would be to insulate themselves and to direct opinion, to shape the people anew—a goal similar in some sense to the ideal of American Federalists.[53]

The meaning of publicity began to mutate as soon as the National Convention convened. Among both the Girondin and Montagne factions, a number of deputies were already established newspaper editors by 1792.[54] Though they had begun their revolutionary careers by calling for vigilance over elected officials, they were now elected themselves. This role began to change as Girondins like Brissot, Carra, Mercier, and Gorsas and Jacobins like Marat and Desmoulins adjusted their reporting based on their new roles. Newspapers like the *Patriote françois*, run by Brissot, and the *Annales politiques et littéraires*, edited by Mercier and Carra, took on new tones. Now run more as party mouthpieces than before, the periodicals presented particular versions of stories and responded to critiques of allied officials with defenses of their actions. On the left, Marat launched a new periodical and Desmoulins dropped his altogether until late 1793. In the prospectus for a new periodical, Robespierre declared that the representatives deserved "a gallery more accessible than that of the National Convention, from where they can be heard by the entire universe."[55] He intended to create this with his periodical—to provide a place where deputies could speak to the entire population and where he would himself "trace a faithful tableau of the operations of the assembly."[56] He would "expose to your eyes the outcomes of all the grand events" and uncover the intrigue that threatened the pursuit of liberty.[57] These authors were still calling for surveillance and claiming to unmask enemies, but they were now insiders. Casting a vigilant gaze on colleagues, their claims carried implications for themselves as well.[58]

Beyond the effect of journalists integrating into the Convention as deputies, there were also explicit measures taken that were designed to limit the bounds of publicity. Before the trial of the king even began, the Comité des Inspecteurs de la salle had formalized the process of regulating access to the galleries through the use of entry cards signed by members of the committee themselves.[59] Journalists were required to obtain signed access cards, which they would turn in to the guards during the meeting and pick up on their way out.[60] In an apparent effort to monitor the reporters regularly attending the meetings, the committee decided on January 5, 1793, that it would take the names of all the journalists who worked in the desks (*loges*) inside the Convention and post a list at each end of the chamber.[61] Gradually, the committee was setting up a sophisticated system to monitor access to the Convention's meetings. Even employees of the Convention's various committees were required to carry cards, which were given to only two secretaries from each committee. The rest of the employees were granted passes that would allow them to make their way through the hallways to their offices.[62] Deputies also were required to present access cards to enter the chamber. An undated letter from the corps of ushers to the committee noted their increasing workload with these restrictions. They were frequently called to the doors or hallways to identify deputies who had forgotten their entry cards or to accompany citizens to the speaker's bar or to speak directly to the president.[63] When the Convention moved into its new meeting space in the converted Tuileries Palace in the spring of 1793, the Comité des Inspecteurs de la salle once again outlined the procedures for regulating access into the room. Anyone would be allowed into the adjacent gardens, except those who were not wearing a cockade (a red, white, and blue bundle of ribbons pinned to hats or clothing). Once the sessions began, the guards were to clear the hallways of any groups or individuals walking through.[64]

Despite the growing efforts to control access to the Convention meetings, the right of the public to attend was seldom seriously questioned. Instead, deputies focused on how they could change the composition of the crowds and minimize interruptions coming from the galleries. On December 14, 1792, Girondin deputy Louis Pierre Manuel made a proposal designed to politically balance public attendance at the Convention's meetings. He first prefaced his proposal by saying that "without a doubt, the Convention wishes that its meetings were vast enough to contain all the citizens of the republic; without a doubt all the members of this assembly would wish to see themselves surrounded by all their constituents." After carefully assuring the deputies that his proposal was in pursuit of this unquestionable value, he noted that "several citizens of Paris and of the *départements* claim to not be able to enter into the temple of liberty." To ensure that citizens who were unable to spend time in line would still be able to access the meetings, Manuel called for the prior distribution of a limited number of tickets to each section of the city and to départements, such that the audience would be ticketed in advance of arriving.[65] Faced with shouts from the galleries and opposition from his fellow deputies, Manuel asserted that "surely this plan cannot be justly opposed," since it was merely designed to allow a greater number of citizens to attend their meetings. "The more people see us, the more they will respect us," he concluded.[66] But he was promptly accused of being an aristocratic sympathizer for wanting to control public access to the meetings through the select distribution of tickets. Radical deputy Jacques-Alexis Thuriot replied that while securing access for citizens from the départements was indeed desirable, in the present circumstances, if deputies granted tickets, the galleries would be filled with corrupt factional supporters.[67] The underlying question, according to Louis-Michel Lepeletier, marquis de Saint-Fargeau, was whether "the National Convention can exercise influence over the composition of the galleries, without thereby altering the grand principle of the publicity of its sessions."[68] The Convention did not even vote on Manuel's proposal—the presumed answer to this question being a solid no.

If the effort to change the composition of the crowds in the Convention was unsuccessful, the concurrent struggle to impose silence was also doomed to failure. Throughout the early meetings of the Convention, the president would frequently interject to remind the audience that onlookers were not permitted to exhibit any signs of agreement or disapproval with the deputies. The problem of applause or shouts also occupied the Comité des Inspecteurs de la salle, who sought out possible structural remedies. In a letter to the committee dated January 18, 1793, a "citizen of the commune of Paris" acknowledged that stopping such expressions of opinion would be difficult. But perhaps if the Convention constructed smaller sections within the galleries, using a partition to cut off voice communication and sightlines, the commotion could be tempered. He was not sure such steps would accomplish the goal, but "if I was able to contribute to ensuring the respect due to the assembly and its deliberations, and the deliberations were no longer troubled by the insolent clamor of the tribunes, I would see myself as a useful citizen."[69] The prohibition on spectators making noise went unenforced by late winter of 1793, particularly because it was impossible to control following the vote to declare war on Britain and the Netherlands and the annexation of Nice.[70] Yet the effort was not entirely abandoned. When the Convention moved to its new meeting hall that spring, the balconies were further removed from the floor of the chamber, delineated by columns, and the ones closest to the speaker's bar were reserved for visitors from the departments outside Paris.[71]

These efforts to change the composition of the audience and to keep it quiet during the Convention's deliberations represented attempts to refine the meaning of publicity so that it facilitated a specific type of legitimate political representation. The Girondin deputies who supported Manuel's proposal to impose a ticketing system designed to attain geographic and political variety within the audience believed that the way publicity was currently being guaranteed actually undermined the process of representative politics. If the only people in the audience were

Parisians, and among them only those dedicated enough and able to spend hours in line, the deputies were getting a skewed vision of the public's opinion and the entire population was being deprived of the ability to watch its representatives. The notion that the Convention should work transparently was not in itself problematic, but because its visibility was only a reality for those in the immediate vicinity, transparency was not having the intended effect of maintaining a dialogue between representatives and the population. Similarly, concerns about signs of approbation or disapproval from the galleries during deliberations were not rooted in disavowals of the utility of publicity to the political process writ large. They were about trying to make the value a more passive one. The deputies were to perform publicly, but the public was not meant to respond outside the established form of electing deputies.[72] These efforts reveal the evolving conception and implementation of publicity in the Convention and how it was manipulated to underpin a style of representative politics that was more insulated from, and directive of, public opinion, rather than reflective of it.

While the public's presence during the meetings was generally taken for granted, there were nonetheless some points when it suddenly came under threat. On March 28, 1793, for example, following a proposal of the *Comité de sûreté générale* (the committee tasked with domestic security and surveillance), the inspectors declared that all the citizens who currently had access to the galleries or anywhere inside the chambers would be required upon leaving to show their "*cartes de section ou de civisme*," which were akin to identity cards vouching for the individual's patriotism or loyalty.[73] This rule would be extended later in the spring, at which point all visitors entering the chamber would be required not only to show their *carte de civisme* but also to prove they had paid their taxes.[74] Alain Cohen has argued that this was tantamount to a restriction of press freedom as it gave the deputies a way to deny reporters access to their meetings.[75] While there was no formal exclusion of reporters from the meetings, it is true that the requirements for gaining entry were certainly designed to ensure that only a particular type of reporter was able to enter.

It was no coincidence that this measure was first implemented in late March 1793, when the government faced what appeared to be a confluence of shocking and dangerous circumstances. General Dumouriez—who had led French troops to an unlikely victory over Austrian and Prussian forces mere months earlier—defected across enemy lines after his troops refused to rally to his proposed march on Paris to dissolve the Convention.[76] In response, the stunned deputies first took steps to uncover and publicize the record of his perfidy. On April 2, deputy Pierre-Joseph Cambon declared "at this hour, it is necessary to tear off the veil." He called for the publication of all of Dumouriez's correspondence with the Committee of General Defense, especially all papers relative to the declaration of war against Austria. "It is important that France knows what happened; and it is only by the publication of all the pieces that she will be able to judge between us and this felon general."[77] The Convention then moved that all the letters and memos that Dumouriez had written to the minister of war, the committees, or the Convention as a whole would be printed and that the Committee of General Defense would be charged with combing through them. Following a pattern set in the early Revolution, the general's correspondence was published as a way to expose him, to unmask his underlying disloyalty and to make known its extent. As had happened with the revelations of the armoire de fer, it was the deputies themselves who were doing the unveiling, revealing evidence to the public to illustrate their foregone conclusion of guilt.

After Dumouriez had defected, an understandable suspicion of other officials also fed into the sense that there needed to be a reorganization of leadership and an internal investigation of members of the Convention. The country was facing a crisis. With the troops at the front lacking a leader and with reports of uprisings against the National Convention in regions across France, calls for decisive action mounted. On April 3, Marat proposed the creation of two new committees, each one composed of twelve members, which he requested meet "*à huis clos*," behind closed doors.[78] This measure was proposed to "expedite the arrest of traitors who were within the country, the agents of enemy powers, and of all suspect people."[79] After insisting that the newly created committees should meet in secret, Marat immediately declared that he believed they should be "granted the most extensive powers, the most formidable to do good."[80] In response to this proposal, Girondin deputy Jean-Baptiste Boyer-Fonfrède zeroed in on the proposed secrecy of the committees. "It is important that all the measures you take are taken unanimously; and, would they be if your committee deliberated in secret?" He doubted it, despite the obvious utility of secrecy in projecting the *appearance* of unanimity. "If the measures that need to be presented are formed in a secret committee, you will have neither confidence, nor union, and you are lost without them."[81]

But three days later, in a plan presented by a segment of the Committee of General Defense, secrecy was proposed as foundational to the new committee. Article 2 of the plan presented to the Convention stated that "this committee will deliberate in secret." Immediately following this declaration was an articulation of the committee's fundamental, and vast, purview, which was to "oversee and accelerate the action of the administration confided in the provisional executive council, whose acts it can even suspend, when it believes them to be contrary to the national interest, as long as it informs the Convention without delay."[82] Though there was some resistance to the creation of such a powerful committee, there was, remarkably, no further recorded concern in the Convention about the committee being allowed to conduct its work in secret. Even Buzot, who warned against yielding too much authority to so few deputies, noted that the new committee with its proposed secrecy was a necessary improvement over the Committee of General Defense. The existing committee was too large and unable to deliberate efficiently, "and additionally, could not keep its deliberations secret, because it is with great difficulty that twenty-five people can keep a secret, and because all the deputies, members of *départements*, the municipality, and even foreigners could attend."[83] If the Committee of Public Safety was to be more effective than its predecessor at preventing abuses of power, searching out traitors, and taking executive action, it would need to start by closing its doors. Article 2 of the plan for creating the new committee was passed without any further debate and thus the Committee of Public Safety was, by definition, an organ of government that would work entirely in secret.

From the outset, the committee's dedication to maintaining confidentiality was serious. In addition to the declaration that it would meet in secret, the plan for operations laid out in its first session detailed that the national treasury would guarantee funds for "secret expenditures."[84] The committee was to report to the Convention weekly on the situation of the republic and the general measures it had taken to ameliorate it. But on a day-to-day basis, there were very limited notes taken within the committee, such that little record of deliberations exists beyond a register of its decisions. In the days immediately after its establishment, there is also evidence that the committee took new measures that elaborated on what it meant to meet in secret. The Comité des Inspecteurs de la salle was tasked with finding a room where the new committee could meet, which needed to close by key.[85] In a more detailed list of its own procedures, the Committee of Public Safety also declared on April 7 that "no citizen will be admitted during the meetings" and that an official would be appointed "to hear from citizens who have something to propose."[86] In cases where the committee needed to confer with the *conseil executif,* they were to meet in an intermediary room and "no citizen, other than the members of the committee, can be present during the deliberations."[87] Furthermore, specially hired couriers who were supplied with identity cards and *certificats de civisme* would carry the committee's communications.[88]

In a document detailing the organization of the offices under its auspices, the members of the committee even took care to outline how incoming correspondence and internal documentation should be kept confidential. The head secretary of each office was to convey to the central bureau all papers that he did not consider "reserved for the secret examination" of the committee itself. Within the central bureau, another secretary was then to comb through this material, determine which documents required secrecy, and then maintain those within the central office. A note in the margin of this directive gave further instruction: "All secret pieces that the committee did not keep within its confines, should stay within the central bureau."[89] This was especially true with, though not limited to, documents having to do with foreign affairs. If this rule were not carefully upheld and "the pieces passed into the other bureaus for registration, it is to be feared that the secret will be violated, simply by strangers who come and go in the bureaus and could indiscreetly catch a glimpse of these pieces."[90] The Comité de sûreté générale, for which very few internal records survive, was careful to maintain absolute secrecy of its sessions as well. With offices in charge of taking in materials by region, the committee declared that only the two head secretaries and principal secretaries of each office were allowed to enter into the committee's meeting room to provide information about what was happening in each office. A guard, stationed in a separate room next to the general secretariat, would keep a list of all those who wished to address the committee and would then pass it along in secrecy.[91] These two committees, which were in no small part concerned with surveillance over the population and deputies, took extensive precautions to carry out their work outside the public's view.[92]

As the Committee of Public Safety expanded its scope of work and staff over the following year, it became a de facto executive branch of the revolutionary government, marking a transformation in the conception and implementation of representative politics. The fact that it worked in secret is of paramount importance to understanding both why this shift occurred and the way in which it was effected. The dedication to working behind closed doors was aligned with a model of representative politics whereby the elected were to light the way for the people, rather than reflecting an expression of public opinion formed externally. The committee did not need to meet in public view because it was not designed to align itself with the public's input. Rather, secrecy would allow it to act nimbly and with wisdom in safeguarding public safety. This was justified, significantly, by reference to the extraordinary circumstances in which the republic found itself: facing rebellion from within and invasion from without. In this sense, then, secrecy was an exceptional measure; the type of representative politics it facilitated was a temporary exigency rather than a permanent transformation.[93]

The primary activities of the committee can be boiled down to two: the exercise of surveillance over and direction of other government officials, the military, and the citizenry; and the shaping, or enforcing in some cases, of a particular vision of public opinion. Its iconography reflected this role of vigilance and broadcast—the committee's stationery bore the image of an eye shining light at the top of the page. Both realms of activity were aimed at overcoming challenges to the representative republic in its current form. From its inception, the Committee of Public Safety would be directed at coping with the reality that a vast portion of the population did not seem to agree with the actions of the representative government. Soon after the committee was formed, the republican government faced uprisings, particularly in the western part of the country. As a result, Jacobin understandings of representative politics were changing from a vision akin to that of American Antifederalists—and, by that point, Democratic-Republicans—of reflecting public opinion to an ideal long held by more conservative deputies in France and by American Federalists, of insulating political decision-making from outside pressure. If public opinion did not seem to agree with the direction the deputies were headed, the public must be wrong. Rather than reflecting public opinion, it then became the representatives' duty to shape it.

In pursuit of this goal, the committee asserted publicity as a strategic broadcast of information to the public with the purpose of molding opinion and working to bring it into alignment with the committee's own views. Members of the Committee of Public Safety were not interested in carrying on a dialogue; instead they took pains to deliver their

Seal from the top of a register of edicts issued by the Committee of Public Safety, dated 6 Frimaire, an II (November 26, 1793). (Source: Archives Nationales [France], AN/AF/II/23, dossier 181; photo by Joanna Hope Toohey)

message to the provinces—even if it required force. An official *Bulletin* of the National Convention was established in the spring of 1793, to be produced by the national printer in the number of 18,000 copies daily.[94] Employees of the *Comité de pétitions, dépêches et correspondances* were assigned special seats near the Convention president to record deliberations for the periodical.[95] Memos from the Committee of Public Safety to the committee charged with producing and distributing the *Bulletin* outlined the aim of their reach with the periodical: from the armies at the front to popular societies throughout the country.[96] But the deputies did not stop at distributing an official periodical. Immediately after its establishment, the committee decreed that "secret agents" would be sent into the départements to ascertain the public sentiment in the region, the army, the administration, tribunals, and local political societies.[97] Soon, members of the committee themselves were being dispatched to areas considered to be in rebellion. In places where the population was not aligned with the Jacobin majority in the National Convention, it would be forced into subservience.[98]

Importantly, the Jacobin deputies were not only reintroducing secrecy into governance and redefining publicity because it seemed that much of the population did not agree with their vision or decisions. There was also the concern that even those who did back the Jacobin faction could pose a threat to the legitimacy of representative government by not respecting elected officials as legitimate decision-makers. Repeated insurrections on the part of Parisian radicals and their constant interventions in the audience of the National Convention fueled concerns about the representatives' legitimacy. In early June 1793, an armed crowd demanding the expulsion of the Girondin deputies surrounded the Convention. Though they attempted to present the expulsion as a willful decision, the Jacobins in the Convention essentially had no choice but to carry it out, under threat of violence. Friedland has analyzed this incident as a crucial breaking point between Jacobin deputies and radical Parisians, who he argues had a fundamentally different conception of what representative government meant.[99] While radicals saw the deputies as their delegates, charged with carrying out the expressed wishes of the populace, the Jacobins in the Convention increasingly asserted an understanding of political representation as an embodiment of the nation rather than its reflection.[100] "The Jacobins had achieved the most hermetically sealed representative space that the Revolution had yet known," Friedland argues, "a space where spectators were not welcome because everything that they could possibly say worth listening to was being said for them."[101]

Indeed, the Committee of Public Safety in particular strengthened its authority in the wake of the expulsion of the Girondins. When it came time to renew the committee in early July, Desmoulins raised some concerns that it had not been entirely effective in confronting rebellion and that it may be growing too powerful.[102] Member of the committee Jean Bon Saint André, apparently sensing a critique of the committee's secrecy, replied: "You are lamenting the secrecy the committee uses in its deliberations; but the importance of the measures treated therein requires it."[103] He challenged the Convention to disband the committee entirely if the deputies found it rotten, "but if you conserve it, do not debase it."[104] The deputies responded by limiting the number of members on the committee to nine and, after hearing a report on its work and progress the next day, issuing a vote of confidence in its efficacy.[105]

There had been remarkably little concern about the Committee of Public Safety articulated in the press from the time of its inception, and certainly none about it meeting in secret. But by the summer of 1793, some questions about its secrecy began to crop up. In a meeting of the Jacobin Club, a member proposed on June 18 that administrative committees, including those of the Convention, should be required to meet in public view. In response, Robespierre reportedly retorted that making all committees public was unnecessary and dangerous. "I ask if it is really important that the people leave the Convention to spend the rest of the day in the committees," he responded, suggesting that this would distract public attention with insignificant things. He went on to call the proposal somewhat absurd given the small size of the committee meeting rooms, declaring that the Committee of Public Safety could accommodate no more than fifty people at a time. Besides, who would actually show up in the committee meetings? According to Robespierre, it would be the spies of foreign courts, aristocrats, and agents of foreign powers who would fill them. "The deliberations would thus suffer the disadvantages of publicity, without advancing its advantages," he concluded.[106] By this stage in the Revolution, a figure who had long advocated the necessity of publicité to guaranteeing the legitimacy of political representation was explicitly defining its bounds.

The extraordinary circumstances in which France found itself were repeatedly cited as justification for limiting transparency and for abjuring the reflective basis of representative government. The changes were not meant to be permanent. In fact, the Constitution of 1793, which was never implemented, upheld the value of publicity to representative government as constitutive of a particular type of political representation wherein officials were to be restricted by the expressed wishes of the people at large. The Constitution was clear that the "population is the only base for national representation" (Article 21). Such assurance that sovereignty ultimately rested with the people themselves, rather than with their elected representatives, was the theoretical basis for ensuring that the work of governance remain publicly visible at all points. Not only was freedom of the press protected in the new *Declaration of the Rights of Man and of the Citizen*, but multiple articles of the Constitution guaranteed that elected officials would work in public view. Article 45 declared that the meetings of the national assembly would be public and Article 46 stated that its deliberations would be printed. The sessions of administrative bodies appointed by primary assemblies—at the municipal and departmental levels—were also to be held in the presence of the public, according to Article 84. Perhaps most indicative of the way publicity was conceived as a tool to implement representative government as a strict reflection of popular sovereignty, expressed in primary assemblies, was the process outlined in the Constitution for passing laws. All laws proposed in the national legislature were to be printed and sent to all communes in France under the title of "proposed law" (Article 58). If, after forty days, half of the departments plus one had not protested the proposal, it could then be passed into law (Article 59). In the event of complaints, the primary assemblies would be convened to consider the proposal and deliver a judgment (Article 60). Not only was the political process to be performed publicly, but also the public was to be provided a structural opportunity to deliver its feedback before any proposals could become laws made in its name.[107]

But this constitution was immediately suspended and the government declared "revolutionary until the peace." Though the understanding of representative politics as reflective of public opinion, guaranteed through publicity of the political process, was enshrined in the framework, it was not the understanding under which deputies were functionally operating in 1793. Restricting publicity, governing in secret, was essentially justified as an exceptional measure, necessary in exceptional circumstances. "The republic will be founded," the young dynamo Louis de Saint-Just declared in calling for a revolutionary government on October 10, 1793, "only when the will of the sovereign envelops the minority of monarchists, and wins it to her side by right of conquest."[108] His clear message was that the government was filled with traitors, the population with counter-revolutionaries and passive subjects, and the enemies were at the gates. Though he did not explicitly cite the need for secrecy, Saint-Just at least implicitly called for it. The Committee of Public Safety needed to continue its work, which consisted in no small part of exercising surveillance over the other organs of government from behind closed doors. Saint-Just lamented that the "representatives of the people, the generals, the administrators are surrounded by offices just like the old men of the palace." The proliferation of correspondence and government orders was a "mark of its inertia"; "the demon of writing is waging war on us and we do not govern."[109] There were too many procedures, too much concern for documentation and communication. "It is impossible that revolutionary laws will be executed," Saint-Just declared, "if the government itself is not revolutionarily constituted."[110]

On the morning of July 26, 1794, Robespierre delivered a rambling speech in the National Convention, in which he warned of new counter-revolutionary plots and the need to eject more deputies from the legislature. Fearing for their lives, a group of deputies—including members of the Committee of Public Safety—banded together and decided it was time to stop the cycle of political trials that had been intensifying over the previous year. The next morning, Robespierre was arrested in the Convention, along with his younger brother, Saint-Just, Georges Couthon, and Philippe Le Bas. Rumblings of what had happened began to spread across the capital, and people poured into the streets to take part in what promised to be another momentous revolutionary *journée*. A confusing twenty-four hours ensued, which have since caused many a headache for historians attempting to explain the end of the phase of the Revolution that came to be known as the Terror. The story of Robespierre's overthrow was carefully curated during the ensuing period of conservative backlash against the Jacobin-led government. Though his ouster has been previously considered the work of more right-wing deputies within the Convention facilitated by an indifferent Parisian population, Colin Jones has recently pointed to the hitherto neglected centrality of popular reaction against Robespierre and the Commune government.[111] Though he asserts the importance of Parisian people to Robespierre's downfall, Jones concludes that the popular turn against him marked a rejection of this one man rather than of the Jacobin government.[112] The gap that had opened between Robespierre's rhetoric and the way the government worked over the preceding year complicates interpretations of this turning point. Could popular support for the overthrow of Robespierre on 9 Thermidor at least partly mark a rejection, if not of its policies, of the type of representative politics and the reintroduction of state secrecy that government had accomplished over the previous year?

The details of the day are clear enough. After being arrested, Robespierre was turned away from the prison where he was taken and whisked to the *Maison de la Commune*, or the city hall. There, officials of the Commune holed up to try to devise their next steps, while troops sent from the Parisian sections amassed in the courtyard. That night, Robespierre perhaps attempted unsuccessfully to commit suicide, shooting himself through the jaw—a desperate act that left him in agony and effectively unable to speak. It appears that as news spread of what was happening, the amassed troops began to dissipate and the sections sent men to the National Convention in droves to support its calls for the trial of Robespierre and his closest allies. "In a sense, then, 9 Thermidor was a highly inclusive moment of democratic decisiveness," Jones writes.[113] The following day, Robespierre was guillotined on the Place de la Révolution, falling victim to the processes he had been instrumental in establishing.

In the immediate aftermath of 9 Thermidor, the press was considerably freed, the Committee of Public Safety and Comité de sûréte générale were divested of much of their power, and the Commune was reformed, its role in government of the capital diminished. The government of the Terror was abruptly dismantled and it was not done solely by conservatives with conservative aims. "Overthrowing Robespierre was not an act of 'Thermidorian Reaction,' " as Jones writes. "The 'Thermidorian Reaction' came later."[114] The Thermidorian period leading to the establishment of the Directory tends to be considered as a rejection of radical politics and restriction of the more democratic elements of representative government. This is undoubtedly true. The Directory would mark a further turn away from the type of political representation rooted in reflection of public opinion and toward a more insulated understanding of representative government being legitimated by election but executed by a small group of enlightened elites. Yet the end of the Terror, the takedown of Robespierre, could have actually marked a repudiation of this very type of political representation. There was a gap between the rhetoric of publicity as vital to reflective representation—enshrined in the Constitution of 1793—and the procedures of secrecy used to implement an insulated style of representation. Even though overthrowing Robespierre was later portrayed as a rejection of what the rhetoric entailed, there was a brief moment when it instead could have been read as a rejection of the practices. The meaning of political representation and the proper place of secrecy and publicity in government were far from settled in July 1794.

CHAPTER SIX

Politics Behind the Curtain

JUST WEEKS BEFORE ROBESPIERRE'S downfall in France, Americans celebrated the eighteenth anniversary of independence. On July 4, 1794, members of the Democratic Society of Pennsylvania drank a toast to "Governmental secrecy; May it be banished [from] the land of freedom, and be hereafter known only to a conclave or a court." Five sips earlier, they had toasted "the representatives of the people; May they never forget the source of their power and the end of their appointment."[1] With each toast, these men were outlining a conception of representative politics—one in which secrets had no place. Printing these toasts in Philadelphia's *American Daily Advertiser*, the club was also warning its representatives that they were being watched.

Representatives were not, however, of one mind on what they ought to be revealing. Deciding who should see what was a dilemma. Their answers to this question, like the declarations of the popular society, were shaped by their understandings of what it meant for politics to be representative. Moreover, their determinations shaped the way representation worked in practice. Examining how the place of secrecy in politics was debated highlights the extent to which the meaning of political representation was unsettled as Americans embarked on their republican experiment in 1789. Foregrounding the strategic use of secrecy in the new republic sheds light on the intentionally undemocratic structure of the government, in the sense of limiting popular participation in politics. The debates such uses of secrecy engendered show how the projection of the republic as a democracy was not altogether convincing to many who continued to push for open doors and a more reflective form of representation.[2]

Politicians made daily decisions about which pieces of the political process they saw fit to share and with whom. They did this individually every time they wrote home and structurally as they established procedures in the new government. In Congress, determinations about who could watch them deliberate, whether printers would be allowed to publish their proceedings, and which issues were better kept off the floor were tantamount to defining their relationship to the public as representatives. In the House, where members were elected directly by people in the states, secrecy had become all but untenable following the bitter debates over its use in the Federal Convention. Speaking for the people seemed increasingly to require speaking in public view—though not everyone agreed. Federalists, like the Jacobin leadership during the Terror, continued to envision representation as enlightened men determining the best interest of the public while removed from popular pressure. This ideal persisted among some in the House, who made efforts to carve out spaces for decision-making outside the public eye. It predominated in the Senate, where the doors to the chamber remained shut until 1795. Here also, though, perennial debates during the first few years of the republic over the propriety of deliberating in secret reflected and shaped competing understandings of the body's representative role.

Beyond Congress, there was also the open question of how secrecy would be used by the republic's elected executive, himself considered a representative of the people.[3] George Washington's judgments about what would be done in public view were similarly linked to his understandings of what it meant to be a representative, and they significantly shaped perceptions of the president's political relationship to the population. In addition to Washington's determinations about the place of secrecy, his appointed secretaries also played a part in defining the executive branch and, more particularly, how making policy in a representative republic ought to relate to public opinion.

The unelected, those supposedly being represented, had opinions about secrecy too. Printers, constituents, and those in popular clubs like the Democratic Society of Pennsylvania often propounded a model of political representation as directly reflective of, and accountable to, public opinion—views that propelled a growing cry for more transparency in politics. Many saw secrecy as a ploy used by representatives to intentionally subvert the will of citizens. While there were those who continued to advocate its utility to the representative process, confidentiality was increasingly discredited as it was linked to a series of apparently unpopular government decisions in the mid-1790s. In the realm of diplomacy especially, the Washington administration and its congressional allies strategically employed secrecy to pursue policies that were often not popular. In doing so, they advanced an understanding of representative politics as determinative of the best interest of the people, without too much external influence. The emergent Democratic-Republican party, however, adopted an opposing position (which had earlier been championed by Antifederalists), decrying state secrecy as a violation of political representation as a reflection of public opinion. These contests over what would and could be kept secret versus what should be done in public mirrored and shaped underlying disagreements over the way in which political representation would work in the new republic.

In 1794, the young federal government faced a test. Or rather, a series of tests. The ongoing war between France and Great Britain was making it difficult for Americans to navigate the seas. Sailors were being impressed into the British navy and American merchant cargo seized. War seemed a distinct possibility and President Washington intended to avoid it. The threat of war loomed abroad, but also, it seemed, at home. Many Americans, vocal ones, did not agree with the course their government was charting in this conflict. As an unpopular treaty was negotiated with the British in 1794, the new republic confronted not only an international test but a domestic one: what would happen when the representative government made a decision that did not appear to align with public opinion? The administration used secrecy to attempt to mitigate the blow to its legitimacy that such discord could potentially inflict. Secrecy largely proved to be useful in this endeavor. But the resultant criticism of the government's measures also demonstrated the vitality of an alternative conception of political representation, one in which public opinion was to be faithfully reflected in government. This incident forced to the fore difficult disagreements that had simmered from the first convening of Congress in 1789, which is why we start our story here, in the spring of 1794.[4]

It was then that Washington dispatched John Jay, the chief justice of the Supreme Court, to London to hash out an agreement with the British. Throughout the negotiation, administration officials were careful to keep details of the treaty and its progress confidential. Eight months after sending Jay, Washington reported to him that Congress had been calm given that no agreement had yet been reached. “As yet no details have been handed to Congress on this subject,” he wrote; “indeed, no communication of that business has been made to any body except those immediately about me in the Executive departmts [sic].”[5] Details of the transactions were restricted to trusted members of the executive branch, with no information flowing outward at all, even to Congress. Secrecy was being used not only to keep the public at bay regarding the treaty but also to demarcate power within the government between the executive and legislative branches. As the negotiations neared their end, the only people with information that permitted them to follow the progress and details of the agreement were executive officials.

Outside the halls of government, people were not entirely blind to what was happening. Knowledge that a secret negotiation was taking place fit into a pattern of government concealment that newly created popular societies claimed was threatening the legitimacy of the republic. It was the people’s right to “examine the proceedings of the legislature, or any branch of government,” the Republican Society of Lancaster declared in its January 1795 constitution.[6] It was “not only the right,” professed the Democratic Society of the City of New York, “but *the absolute duty of the people*, to have a jealous eye over the conduct of the government.”[7] Writing in the *Newark Gazette* in March 1794 on behalf of the Republican Society of that town, “Cato” claimed that inspecting government proceedings was essential to maintaining a legitimate relationship between representatives and the people. “We are told that our rulers are men of our own choice,” he wrote. “In private life if a man employs any agent to transact his business for him, he does not abandon all enquiry into the situation of his affairs, and the conduct of his agent, or if he does, the agent soon becomes master.”[8] Representatives were agents of the people, responsible for their actions to the public that had elected them.

When text of the treaty finally arrived in Philadelphia in spring 1795, Washington and Secretary of State Edmund Randolph agreed to keep the document strictly between the two of them. Randolph wrote to Vice President John Adams on April 2, 1795, discrediting press speculation on the treaty by saying “not one word of which, I believe, is known thro’ a regular channel to any person here, but the President and myself.”[9] Taking up the treaty for consideration, the Senate voted to keep the terms secret as they deliberated, at the urging of Federalist members.[10] Thus the circle of those with knowledge of the treaty’s components was enlarged to include the Senate but not the House and certainly not the unelected public. Secrecy was used throughout the treaty negotiation and ratification to withhold details from the public but also to differentiate between the executive and legislative branches, and even between the Senate and House.[11]

Shortly after the Senate voted in favor of ratification in June 1795, a summary of the treaty suddenly appeared on the streets of Philadelphia. It was printed in the *Aurora General Advertiser*, which was run by Benjamin Franklin Bache, an active member of the city's Democratic Club and grandson of Benjamin Franklin. Soon thereafter, Bache printed a full copy of the treaty prefaced with a letter from Senator Stevens Mason of Virginia, who had furnished the text, urging people to obtain an accurate knowledge of what "I think has already been improperly withheld from them."[12] Though the Senate had voted to prohibit senators from authorizing the printing of the treaty text or any articles, it had lifted the demand for full secrecy after the vote on ratification was taken.[13] Mason violated the Senate prohibition in giving the copy to Pierre-Auguste Adet, the French foreign envoy, who turned it over to Bache. The Washington administration had actually decided to print the treaty at this point, believing that secrecy was doing more harm than good, but Bache beat them to it.[14]

The printer immediately set off north with the text to foment opposition in clubs and town meetings of other cities.[15] Outrage ensued, with a flood of pamphlets and press reports calling the agreement unfair, a betrayal of the country's French ally, or even an outright surrender of American sovereignty. Petitions from popular societies poured into the president's office, and burning effigies of Jay lit many a town square. Amidst this torrent, a persistent criticism emerged regarding the use of secrecy in the process of negotiating and deliberating on the treaty. The concentration on the secrecy surrounding the treaty drew upon and contributed to a political discourse that linked corruption of political representation with state secrets.

Up and down the coastline, popular societies fumed about the secrecy surrounding the treaty. That fall, the *City Gazette* of Charleston published resolutions adopted by the Republican Society of Pendleton County, which highlighted secrecy as the primary problem. "The constitution of the United States gives to the president and Senate the power of making treaties," the resolutions acknowledged, "but it communicates no ability to hatch those things in darkness." Secrecy and mystery were suited to monarchies and conclaves but were "*opposite to open and republican principles.*" "There is no authorized secrecy in *our* government, and to infer such a right from the practices of other nations, is a prostitution of republican principles," the society members declared. Its use made "twenty greater than the whole," they proclaimed, referring to the twenty senators who voted to ratify the treaty contrary to what they perceived to be the public will. The Constitution had restricted the right of ratifying treaties to the Senate, partly on the basis that negotiations required "the greatest secrecy," the society conceded, but nonetheless the members pronounced a "curse on such secrecy! It has undone our country!"[16]

At this point, it is worth stepping back to answer some questions. Were the members of the South Carolina society right? Did the Constitution dissuade the use of secrecy in concluding treaties? How often was secrecy being used in the young federal government? Why was it being used and what effect was it having? To understand how and why the use of secrecy became so central to the conflict over the Jay Treaty in 1794–95, we must go back to the founding of the republic and trace what had taken place since state conventions had ratified the Federal Constitution in 1787–88. Over the course of the intervening years, the government's use of secrecy had been constantly contested as part of a negotiation over the function and legitimacy of representative politics in the United States.

When Congress first slowly convened in New York City in the spring of 1789, the question of whether its activity would be publicly visible remained unresolved. The Constitution required a periodic publication of its journals, "excepting such parts as in their judgment may require secrecy," but did not detail how often or what could properly be withheld from them. Coming off the bitter ratification debates—which remained ongoing in Rhode Island—the country's newly elected representatives were far from agreed on these questions. Federalists had maintained the utility of secrecy to the deliberative process throughout the ratification debates, while opponents of the Constitution had increasingly emphasized a belief that the deliberative process had to be publicly visible in order for political representation to be considered legitimate. Though the Constitution had been agreed to, little else had; the proper balance of secrecy and publicity in the new government had yet to be worked out.

There was, however, one thing the country's newly elected officials did seem to agree upon and it was that they were being watched—whether they liked it or not. Like their counterparts across the Atlantic who were gathering in Versailles at the same moment, elected officials often noted the feeling of having eyes on them. This pressure bore down as the opening of their meetings lagged due to missing members. As Pennsylvania Senator William Maclay wrote home to Benjamin Rush: "I never felt greater mortification in my life, to be so long here with the eyes of all the world upon us and to do nothing, is terrible."[17] Like his colleagues in Congress, Washington also reflected on the pressure of this gaze, writing to a trusted correspondent in July that "the eyes of America—perhaps of the world—are turned to this Government."[18] He was far from unaware of the weighty implications of even seemingly small, procedural decisions, repeatedly noting in his letters the importance of establishing good precedents. In January 1790, he would reflect on this in a letter to English historian Catharine Macaulay, writing: "In our progress towards political happiness my station is new; and, if I may use the expression, I walk on untrodden ground." Every decision, every action, "any part of my conduct," he wrote, may "hereafter be drawn into precedent."[19]

Despite this sense that the world was watching, the lack of consensus over what exactly should be visible was stark in both the legislature and the executive administration. In the newly created Congress, the balance of secrecy and publicity was primarily considered in terms of regulations over public access to deliberations, especially for printers who sought to publish debates. On April 8, "the doors to the House of Representatives were thrown open for the admission of the citizens."[20] Meanwhile, the Senate shut itself up across the corridor in the newly renovated Federal Hall. Reporting back to the French minister for foreign affairs, the French envoy in New York, the Comte de Moustier, wrote that "Democratic spirit still prevails in the House; the Senate is guided by Aristocratic principles, and even tends toward monarchism." This division was reinforced by "the way debate proceeds in the two Houses," he wrote: "Those in the House are open to the public who can hear their debates in the galleries. The Senate holds its séances behind closed doors."[21] Historians have tended to agree with Moustier's determination, stating as fact that the House was open because it was the more directly democratic wing of the legislature, while the Senate remained shut off from public view because it was meant to represent the states rather than the people. The decision to maintain open doors and publish deliberations in the House has even been called inevitable, given that the body was to be directly accountable to the people.[22]

In fact, the House's decision to open its doors and allow printers to publish deliberations was far from a foregone conclusion. Writing to her husband in May 1789, Abigail Adams offered a reminder of the contingency: "When I read the debates of the House, I could not but be surprised at their permitting them to be open."[23] Granted, the Adams family tended to be cautious when it came to interaction between politicians and the people out of doors, but her surprise was not misplaced. Precedent in the American states and Continental Congress would have suggested doors would likely be closed, not to mention practices back in London. And yet the decisions of the House fit within a slowly shifting tendency for legislatures to open doors and allow debates to be printed, as we've seen in preceding chapters. In the states, some legislatures had established a precedent for holding public deliberations—most notably the Pennsylvania Assembly—though this practice was not carried on without criticism or concern. Changes were also afoot across the Atlantic. But a nascent trend does not an inevitability make. Moustier's report, for example, also asserted that "this arrangement is appropriate . . . but in a sense it is due only to chance, because it derives from the stylistic whim of the architect."[24] Because Pierre Charles L'Enfant had added galleries to the House chamber and not to that of the Senate, Moustier mused, the rules of public accessibility were determined by the building, ultimately reinforcing a theoretical difference between the chambers, even if not intentionally designed to do so.

In reality, these decisions were neither obvious nor were they matters of mere chance based on the architecture of the halls where legislators met. Though there is little record of the debates within these bodies over the initial establishment of these rules, persistent contestation and skirting of them yield insight into the intense disagreement over the propriety, degree, and form of transparency in the legislature. Many constituents were hungry for insight into the political process, believing it to be a crucial component of guaranteeing political representation as reflective of their wishes and input. But elected officials in both the House and Senate were often hesitant to open dialogue or reveal too much, instead guarding an insulated conception of representation. Working out what it meant to speak for the people was thus negotiated among elected officials in both houses, printers, and constituents, partly through struggles over which aspects of the legislative process could be legitimately kept secret. Moreover, the question of how publicity was best guaranteed—whether through the presence of an audience in the room, the reporting of debates in the press, or correspondence with constituents—was an open one.

From the moment Congress convened, there was a small cadre of entrepreneurial printers with potent civic pretensions who stationed themselves in the galleries. John Fenno launched his *Gazette of the United States* with a promise to provide "impartial sketches of the debates of Congress" and to "leave no avenue of information unexplored" in his mission to bring political information to the public.[25] Thomas Lloyd, who had developed a reputation for his shorthand in recording the debates of the Pennsylvania Assembly, also set up shop in New York with the intention of publishing verbatim congressional debates. Despite conceiving of their role as impartial transmitters of information, as opposed to vigilant watchdogs—like moderate printers operating in 1789 in France—the effect was nonetheless to spread information about the activity of elected representatives. Newspapers across the country picked up the proceedings of the House from the papers in New York and, starting in 1790, Philadelphia, creating "a kind of whispering gallery and acts and speeches are reverberated round from N York in all directions," as John Adams characterized it.[26]

These printers were concerned with the commercial success of their periodicals only in so far as newspapers tended to be expensive to produce and rarely turned a profit. Their motives in publishing were predominantly political.[27] The notion that printing the proceedings of Congress was a civic endeavor worthy of great personal sacrifice is evident in many of the private letters and public comments of printers and reporters who set themselves to the task. In letters to his son, Fenno's concerns about his competitors and financial worries were matched by evidence of his commitment to fulfilling what he considered to be an important political role in printing and disseminating news. In a letter written on June 6, 1789, after he had begun publishing, Fenno noted that the number of his subscribers was constantly growing and that he had been "sitting up *all Night*" every Tuesday since he began publishing to ensure his paper made the Wednesday morning post. When lamenting that it would be unpopular for the government to pay for the production of a newspaper, Fenno reflected in a letter to his son that "the management of the Paper is a task of such magnitude that few persons ever before undertook its equal—it employs all my time—it absorbs my *whole* attention in such manner, that I have not known a pleasing moment of relaxation since you were here."[28] Such extraordinary efforts were cast as patriotic duties. In publishing a guide to Lloyd's shorthand system in 1793, the Philadelphia printer John Carey urged the teaching of shorthand to enable any man (and he did use the term "man") attending political assemblies to record and then communicate to his family and neighbors what had transpired. This would "result in respect and obedience to the Laws of the Union, and grateful veneration for those who frame them; since their conduct and motives, in order to command the general approbation of their fellow-citizens, need but to be publicly known."[29]

It is worth pausing to reflect on the shortcomings of early reporting of congressional deliberations and limitations of the resultant records—for both contemporaries and historians. Despite enthusiasm for shorthand as a potential method for recording verbatim accounts of debates, reporters faced considerable practical challenges that often led to omissions and errors seldom acknowledged by historians who rely on the *Annals of Congress* for quotations from early lawmakers. While the Constitution required both houses of Congress to regularly publish journals of their proceedings, anyone interested in what was actually said in the course of deliberation had to turn to newspapers. Not only were the journals infrequently published and relatively inaccessible, but they contained only summaries of actions without any record of discussions.[30] An act passed in September 1789 further required that all laws be delivered to the Secretary of State, who was to publish them in at least three "public Newspapers," distribute copies to state governors, and "carefully preserve the originals."[31] While guaranteeing an official and accessible record of laws, this measure also did not provide any insight into the deliberative record. It was not until 1873 that Congress voted to have its debates officially recorded by note-takers in its employ and published as the *Congressional Register*.[32] Before then, unless interested constituents were in direct contact with their representatives, they would have to rely on reports of deliberations that appeared in the press. These reports could lag behind actual floor activity and were subject to omissions due to space constraints; in addition, according to many elected officials, they were often downright inaccurate. Lloyd's reports—which became a primary source for the *Annals of Congress* when it was compiled in the 1830s—were "not to be relied on," as Madison put it. "The face of the debates shews that they are defective, and desultory, where not revised, or written out by the Speakers," he warned a correspondent in 1832. Lloyd, Madison asserted, "was indolent and sometimes filled up blanks in his notes from memory or imagination."[33] Historians who have compared Lloyd's rough notes with what he published in his unofficial *Congressional Register* tend to confirm Madison's criticism, noting the frequent lack of any rough notes to indicate a record beyond memory for what he published.[34] This point is critical: reports of deliberations billed as verbatim were fundamentally constructions of the reporters who wrote them and, as such, presented an illusion of transparency that nonetheless shaped the operationalization of political representation.[35]

Even with all these limitations, the sense that recording and disseminating the proceedings of the country's elected representatives was useful for encouraging trust and obedience was a touchstone for the earliest congressional reporters. A staunch Federalist, Fenno conceived of his project as one of forming a national political culture and bolstering support for the new government. He seemed to believe that by publicizing the proceedings of the nation's new representatives, he could enhance their legitimacy as voices of the people. Fenno considered public opinion to be the basis of governmental legitimacy, but he also believed the government itself could shape that opinion—and he conceived of his effort as part of that process.[36] In endeavoring to present information for the purpose of shaping public opinion, rather than purporting to channel that opinion to express it to elected officials, Fenno essentially presented himself as an appendage of the government rather than as a watchdog on behalf of the people.[37] This approach calls to mind the efforts of some journalists operating at the same time in France, notably the comte de Mirabeau. The simultaneous development of a conception of passive publicity, as previously discussed in the French context, suggests similarly unsettled understandings of what it meant to render government transparent and the purposes of doing so in the United States. Just like Mirabeau, in providing this broadcast of information, Fenno did more than he realized. His effort to publicize congressional proceedings carried implications that surpassed his intentions. As with the more aggressively vigilant newspapers—which appeared in France starting in 1789 and would be launched by printers like Philip Freneau and Bache a few years later in America—even these more passive publications had the effect of feeding a public hungry for information and thereby empowering the formation of independent opinions about government activity with the implication that they should be heeded.

The importance assigned to publicizing the proceedings of the new nation's representatives was not a creation of the printers. Indeed, they were meeting a demand from all those who felt themselves distant from "the seat of government, the fountain of intelligence."[38] Dozens of letters poured into New York during that first session noting the newspaper reports with pleasure. Readers wrote to their representatives that the reports were "a great treat" and that they "brought the scene near to us."[39] Others were more elaborative in the reasons why they sought news from Federal Hall. Writing to Massachusetts representative George Thacher to establish a regular correspondence, Boston printer Thomas B. Wait emphasized that "should you but once convince me of your insensibility to the censure or applause of your constituents, I should from necessity at the time acknowledge a conviction that you was a very dangerous person to be employed in their service."[40] He then asked for regular letters so that he could fill his local gazette and meet the desire of the population for news from their representatives. In response to the thirst for information, members of Congress gradually developed a genre of circular letters, which were often printed, filled with assurances of fulfilling a duty to provide updates, and sent back to districts to be widely shared. Shortly after the passage of the Post Office Act in 1792—which incorporated the postal service as a central administration in the state and thereby expanded the postal network in addition to admitting newspapers into the postal system with a modest fee—North Carolina representative John Steele wrote home with hope for the potential of the new law to ameliorate communication.[41] "Hitherto the people of that state have been much in the dark in regard to the affairs of the general government, that time I hope is at an end." He went on to underscore his commitment to sharing information, noting "that the diffusion of knowledge is productive of virtue, and the best security for our civil rights are incontrovertible truths which cannot be too frequently, or too forcibly inculcated."[42] The publicity of congressional proceedings was what would give the population power to ensure their representatives stuck to their wishes. The number of people writing to their representatives for accounts of political happenings and the crowds of men and women who regularly attended in the galleries of the House suggest both how prominent this understanding of political representation was and how much of an impact it had on the way representation functioned.

Many politicians fretted over the potential for newspaper reports of congressional deliberations to be misleading and struggled to meet the demand for information from home with their own letters. But the written medium was generally less of a worry than actual audience attendance in the House. It bears emphasizing that the publicity of political deliberations did not take one form—not only was reading records of debates different from witnessing them in person for the curious constituent, but the impact of these different types of publicity on how representation worked was various. In discussing where to locate the new capital, for instance, many politicians harbored fears of crowd interference in big cities. As Maryland state senator Charles Carroll explained when he opposed moving the state capital to a big city in 1786, populous surroundings could place pressure on elected officials and "endanger free speech" in the legislature.[43] Carroll's uneasiness here was a common concern among federal officials as well, who no doubt had memories of the Continental Congress temporarily leaving Philadelphia to avoid intimidation by unpaid soldiers and who received news of popular disruptions to French assemblies in the early 1790s. While print presented the possibility of cool and reasoned consideration with the benefit of both time and isolated perusing without the influence of oratory, audience attendance had the potential to ignite passions and pose a threat with its immediacy.[44] One point of anxiety about the potentially dangerous effect of having an audience was the presence of women in Congress. In 1790, Virginia senator Richard Henry Lee lamented that while they discussed where to locate the capital, women in attendance seemed with their presence to say: "As you vote, so will we smile. A severe trial for susceptible minds. And a very unfair (if I may say that Ladies can do anything unfair) whilst the abundant beauty of Philadelphia had not an equal opportunity of showing its wishes."[45] In addition to worry about female presence, his reflection spoke to a general fear of influence exerted by those with access to the chamber versus the potential influence of more distant constituents. It also raises the point that publicity of the proceedings created an opening for some people who did not have the right to vote to play a part in representative politics.

In fact, the attendance of women in Congress—in the House and then the Senate once doors were open—illustrates the paradoxes inherent in the valorization of publicity. Historians have effectively dismantled the notion that women were relegated to the private sphere, demonstrating their centrality to politics and public presence in the early republic and arguing for a more expansive definition of politics to capture this activity.[46] From the outset, the House galleries often filled with so many women that they had space reserved for them.[47] Writing slightly later, once the Capitol had been erected, in 1806 Catharine Mitchill—the wife of Samuel Mitchill, a congressman from New York from 1801 to 1804 and then senator until 1809—noted a difference between the "green gallery" typically filled with women and the "upper gallery," which she described as populated with "the rabble, black & white."[48] Mitchill frequently attended debates with her husband, who referred to her in correspondence as a constituent, and she also spent time in the congressional library.[49] Women "helped constitute the public," as Jan Lewis put it. "They ratified and legitimized the proceedings of the new national government and they did so both as citizens and as women."[50] Furthermore, the wives of prominent politicians played an integral role in politics through the facilitation of salons where elected officials conducted business unofficially and where women were able to convey their views to representatives.[51] In this sense, gender was less the determining factor in political exclusion than wealth.[52] And yet women were excluded from formal, legal participation in representative politics because they were denied the right to vote. Publicity provided a degree of informal influence and the assertion of an extra-legal expectation of accountability. But it may well have simultaneously served to justify the continued formal exclusion of women from representative politics, rendering them essentially passive spectators rather than active citizens.[53] In a particularly striking articulation of this dynamic, Lewis points to women in Congress as "props," noting that "in the drama of American democracy, women were assigned the best seats in the house."[54] The possibility for publicity to engender passivity rather than the active dialogue its proponents hoped to enforce is nowhere more evident than in the image of women sitting as spectators in a chamber where they could not speak.

The members' decision to acquiesce to the yearning for publicity despite concerns must be placed in the context of attempts to quell critiques at the outset of the new government. Distance from the seat of government had been a fear of many Antifederalists during the ratification debates. Edmund Pendleton, a prominent Virginia politician, wrote to Madison in the spring of 1789, noting that he was glad to see reports of the House debates in the newspapers, "as it silences that part of Opposition which asserted our total ignorance of every thing which should be done."[55] The decision to allow publication of its proceedings was essential to securing the legitimacy of the new legislature as a representative body. Rhode Island judge William Ellery wrote to Connecticut representative Benjamin Huntington in July, noting that "if Congress had shut themselves up and concealed their proceedings three months, jealousies and suspicions would probably have arisen, and the people might not have patiently waited until their Moses's should have produced their table of laws."[56] Supporters of locating the capital in a big city appealed to the desire for publicity, frequently bringing up, like one of Massachusetts representative Benjamin Goodhue's constituents, that "if Congress met anywhere but in a large city, it would be able to decide the financial and other affairs of the federal government in profound secrecy."[57] The strategic necessity of allowing for the publicity of Congress's proceedings in order to obviate threats to its legitimacy cannot be discounted.

Yet the wish to avoid the kind of relationship with their constituents that demands for publicity rested upon also led members to begin carving out a private sphere of communication. Though the representatives generally professed their commitment to publishing their proceedings—and designs for the capital city accounted for a public presence—in their correspondence they were constantly calling for confidentiality.[58] Typically toward the end of letters, members would note that they expected the contents to be held in "the utmost confidence" or that what they had written was "confidential and not to be made public."[59] In a letter to retired general Horatio Gates in late April 1789, Virginia representative Alexander White wrote that while "I have from time to time forwarded to the Winchester printers all the Congressional news to be published for the information of the People at large, this is intended as a Tete a Tete and not to appear in Print."[60] He proceeded to detail his "astonishment" that so many members were in favor of using titles to indicate rank in the government, an opinion he apparently did not see fit for public consumption. While topics they wrote about confidentially varied, the line between public and private tended to be the same; when they explained their sentiments on a topic, it was not meant for public communication. Benjamin Goodhue, for example, wrote home that because he expressed "freely what I feel," he expected the recipient to "conceive it will not be prudent for you to divulge or shew this letter for fear they may call me hot headed impetuous &c and not careful in my conduct in such measure as are necessary for preserving the Union."[61] Representatives did not intend to show their hands when they hadn't prepared to lay them out.

Delineating physical space for the political process to unfold away from the eyes in the gallery also began in 1789. We know, partly from the complaints of elected officials like Maclay, that no small amount of business was carried out informally over dinners, in taverns, or at the *levées* held at the President's residence.[62] There were also committees created that would meet in the mornings, before the House convened as a whole, and there is no indication that non-elected people or printers were allowed to attend.[63] An inventory of furnishings prepared by the House clerk John James Beckley in November 1790 shows that each committee room contained meeting tables and bookcases with "drawers, locks, and keys" and that his office also contained a desk with "drawers, locks, etc."[64] Committee and administrative papers, few of which survive, were evidently safeguarded under lock and key. Moreover, already in the summer of 1789, when certain topics came up for debate the House shut its doors or restricted the circulation of information. From the beginning, negotiations over the location of the federal government and the related discussions of debt assumption were conducted in hushed tones. Pennsylvania representative Peter Muhlenberg reported to a correspondent that discussions about the capital, "which are not publickly transacted and will not appear in the papers," were "most agitated, altho' in private." He proceeded to relay what he had heard but emphasized the information was to be "considered as confidential."[65] Even the introduction of the proposed constitutional amendments comprising the Bill of Rights in the summer of 1789 was apparently kept quiet at first.[66] Coincidentally, perhaps, representatives also rejected the right of constituents to instruct elected officials as one of the amendments to the Constitution.[67]

One of the most significant topics members tried to keep quiet in the House during these early years was the question of slavery. Responses to an anti-slavery petition by a large group of Quakers in February 1790 show how conscious members were of the implications of their deliberations being public and their desire to avoid raising the issue. Representative Michael J. Stone of Maryland immediately urged rejection of the petition for fear that word the House was even considering such measures would depress the monetary value of enslaved people. South Carolina representative Aedanus Burke, likely gesturing to the public audience where members of the Quaker delegation were seated, said "the men in the gallery had come here to meddle in business with which they had nothing to do."[68] James Jackson of Georgia affirmed that "If Congress pay any uncommon degree of attention to their petition, it will furnish just ground of alarm to the Southern States."[69] These southern representatives attempted to keep such a petition from receiving any kind of formal acknowledgment from the House in order to prevent a public perception that it would move to regulate or ban slavery. In an example of how transparency can sometimes have the effect of hiding things, Madison urged members to simply admit the petition if they really wanted to keep it quiet. "Had they permitted the commitment of the memorial, as a matter of course, no notice would have been taken of it out of doors," he commented, emphasizing that "they excite alarm by their extended objections to committing the memorials."[70] Even Madison, in this instance, was seeking a way to keep the divisive issue off the table, so to speak, a reminder of the way in which slavery was partly perpetuated by pushing it off the political agenda and keeping the issue out of public view.

It was not uncommon, though also not uncontroversial, for the entire House to shut its doors and go into secret session. Very early, in August 1789, the House closed its doors to consider a message from Washington as it was determined it might contain secret information. This was not an infrequent occurrence over the ensuing years.[71] In early 1792, the House passed a standing order that "whenever confidential communications are received from the President of the United States, the House shall be cleared of all persons except the members and the Clerk," identifying a regular occasion when no audience or reporters would be allowed inside.[72] Despite this standing order, the practice of shutting the doors in such circumstances did not go unquestioned. When it was proposed in late 1793 to close the doors to discuss the president's communication with regard to a treaty being negotiated with Morocco relative to an ongoing piracy problem, the motion was carried only over substantive objections. "It was said, that secrecy in a Republican Government wounds the majesty of the sovereign people," the record recounts. Moreover, opponents of closing the doors maintained that "this Government is in the hands of the people; and that they have a right to know all the transactions relative to their own affairs." However, others emphasized that "because this Government is Republican, it will not be pretended that it can have no secrets." Those wanting to clear the galleries maintained that the executive in particular was the "depository of secret transactions" and that elected officials must weigh the rights of the people with their interests. "To discuss the secret transactions of the Government publicly, was the ready way to sacrifice the public interest," they concluded.[73] Though the motion to close the doors was passed that day, an amendment was made to the standing order allowing the House to determine whether it believed secrecy should be maintained after hearing the confidential communication.[74] Despite this seeming concession to greater transparency—or at least more discretion for the House to determine when to allow it—just a few months later the chamber passed another standing order that "in case of any disturbance or disorderly conduct in the Gallery or Lobby, that the SPEAKER (or Chairman of the Committee of the Whole House) shall have power to order the same to be cleared."[75] This broad provision allowing for closed doors was recorded without any debate.

Though members of the House of Representatives were often furtive despite their avowed dedication to publicity, most senators propagated no such illusions. Facing criticism from the start, senators would keep their doors closed and prohibit the publication of their proceedings until 1795. From the very beginning, the confidentiality of Senate activity was considered by many to be a "radical defect" of the chamber.[76] Before members had even decided on any controversial policies, the Senate was rendered suspect by its apparent belief in the need to hide its activity. Writing to Washington from Virginia in mid-July 1789, one of the president's regular correspondents noted that he found "the Senate in general, to be unpopular, and much censured for keeping their doors shut."[77] Answering this letter some ten days later, Washington said he could not explain why the senators had decided to deliberate behind closed doors, "unless it is because they think there is too much speaking to the Gallery in the other House, and business thereby retarded."[78] Indeed, the impact on deliberations and decision-making of a socially heterogeneous audience and the awareness of reporters recording speeches in the House was a concern even among members of the lower chamber.

Unlike Washington, others explained their reasons for supporting closed-door proceedings in more theoretical terms. For some senators, debating out of the public's view was essential to maintaining the people's confidence in any representative body. Paine Wingate, senator from New Hampshire, explained his thinking in a letter to Massachusetts Federalist Timothy Pickering at the end of April, stating simply: "I do not desire that the private conduct or public proceedings of this body should be exposed to the dayly inspection of the populace." Deliberating "a little more out of public view would conduce to [the Senate's] respectability in the opinion of the country who would then judge of that body by its public acts and doings," he wrote. This reasoning resonated strongly with the Federalist notion that finished legislation should be published as opposed to the process of forming it, which had been advanced by those who defended the decision to frame the Constitution behind closed doors. Wingate wrote that while he was "not a friend to mystery and hypocrisy," there were some foibles and faults of men "which had better be concealed from observation." He compared the Senate to a family and suggested that even "the best regulated family" would be degraded in the eyes of the public if all its "domestic transactions" were revealed. Anticipating the response that Congress was not like a family, since it was an elected legislature, Wingate responded that "you may reply that Congress should be very circumspect & exemplary," and while this was true, "they may be differently circumstanced in a federal Town from what they be in either of the two cities now contemplated."[79] Although he believed Congress should be able to withstand scrutiny, he thought it was unlikely they could maintain legitimacy in the public eye, at least in New York or Philadelphia, the cities where they might meet.[80]

In a letter to John Adams, the vice president and chair of the Senate, his frequent correspondent Richard Peters also approved of the decision to keep the doors to the Senate shut. Though he thought the Continental Congress had "better reasons for keeping their squabbles to themselves" than the current one due to the threat of internal and external enemies during the war, he concluded that "I believe the people continued their confidence in them longer, for not being acquainted with what passed behind the curtain."[81] By keeping the curtain drawn, so to speak, he hoped the new government would be able to accomplish a great deal and maintain legitimacy more easily. Notably, these defenses of closing the doors may have been composed in support of the Senate's practices, but they spoke of Congress more broadly. Rather than asserting that the Senate should close its doors to establish a distinction between it and the lower house, advocates of confidentiality in the decision-making process seemed to believe it would be beneficial for all government activity to be more carefully shielded from public view.

Senators voted against opening their doors to the public and printers four times before finally relenting to persistent pressure in a vote taken in February 1794. Attempts to pry open the doors got more explicit with theoretical reasoning over time. The first effort, made in April 1790, called simply for the Senate to open its doors while acting in its "legislative capacity" (meaning when it was not considering treaties or appointments) "that such the citizens of the United States as may chuse to hear the debates of this House, may have an opportunity of so doing."[82] No further note made its way into the journal, other than the resolution having failed. In February 1791, Virginia senator James Monroe, who had been an Antifederalist and would later be a leader in the Republican party, proposed that the doors to the Senate should be open when it acted in its legislative capacity, "except on such occasions as, in their judgment, may require secrecy." A roll call vote left a record of the nine members who voted in favor and the seventeen who shot it down.[83] The next attempt, also made by Monroe, in March 1792, was proposed in the same language and shot down by the same margin. By February 1793, the fourth proposed resolution contained a lengthy justification. Chief among the arguments was that "the Senate of the United States are, individually, responsible for their conduct to their constituents, who are entitled to such information as will enable them to form a just estimate thereof." Opening the doors was tantamount to asserting an understanding of senators as representative in the sense of being delegated by constituents. The journals were "too voluminous and expensive to circulate generally," nor did they contain "the principles, motives, and designs" of members, which the resolution presumed was important information for constituents in order to assess their decisions. By prohibiting the press from reporting on their debates, "the influence of their constituents over one branch of the Legislature [was] in a great measure annihilated."[84] Though only seven members voted in favor of the resolution, it was a powerful statement of their understanding of what it meant to represent the people and the necessity of transparency to ensuring their legitimacy.

The resolution that would ultimately pass a year later took this language further: "While the principles and designs of the individual members are withheld from public view, responsibility is destroyed, which, on the publicity of their deliberations, would be restored." Here political representation was defined as a process wherein the elected had a "responsibility" to the public that required disclosure of their decision-making process. The "abuse of power, mal-administration of office" would be exposed while "jealousies, rising in the public mind from secret legislation," could be avoided by allowing spectators to watch and printers to publish their deliberations.[85] After putting it off for more than a month, the Senate voted nineteen to eight to construct galleries and open its doors, except "in such cases as may, in the opinion of the Senate, require secrecy." Following the vote Adams wrote to his wife, Abigail, with apparent anxiety, noting that "What the Effect of this measure, which was at last carried by a great Majority, will be, I know not."[86] His son Charles Adams, however, had more ominous predictions. Writing to the vice president a month before the Senate's decision was made, he had issued a warning of sorts: "You know Sir that it is an idea cherished by many that a Republic should have no secrets. This doctrine carried to its full extent will no doubt lead us into some disagreeable scrapes," he wrote. Nonetheless, the pressure was such that "I also think we must pay the price of experience for all the wisdom we are likely to obtain."[87]

The procedures of the emerging executive administration, like those in Congress, elicited intense discussion both within the halls of government and among the population more broadly. Historians have often treated decisions made by and about the executive branch as they related to etiquette, honor, or the construction of a republican court culture. Placing focus squarely on the procedural use of secrecy in the cabinet highlights deeply held notions of what it meant to represent the people. While the president maintained a carefully regulated public visibility of his person, most of his business was guarded as confidential.[88] Considering the spaces in which daily political activity was carried out and the mechanisms whereby it was conducted, it is evident that Washington and his administration viewed secrecy as an important tool for defining executive power in contrast to legislative function and for attempting to establish the executive as representing the best interest of the people at a remove from popular pressure. The president was not primarily interested in reflecting public opinion in his decisions, even if he was aware of the need to appear in public and court it. As a consequence, the decision-making process and the daily governance of the country were not processes to be performed publicly.

From the moment he arrived in New York, Washington began confidentially soliciting opinions on the proper mode of behavior for the president to adopt when interacting with the public, other elected officials, and any individuals who might seek his attention. After posing a list of questions to Adams, he offered an excuse for his attention to what seemed to be mere details: "Many things which appear of little imp[ortance in] themselves and at the beginning, may have (great and) durable consequences."[89] In fact, the care Washington devoted to these questions and the well-developed responses of those he queried suggest that no one at the time believed these issues to be trifles. The problem of striking a balance, as Washington put it in a letter to Madison on May 12, between "the inconveniences as well as reduction of respectability by too free an intercourse" and the "charge of superciliousness, and seclusion from information by too much reserve" was paramount.[90] The question of secrecy lurked beneath the surface of these discussions as something whose appearance ought to be avoided so as not to generate suspicion. While there was a general sense among the president's advisors that distance from the population was required to establish an air of authority and dignity, there was a countervailing emphasis on the need to avoid appearing too hidden from public view. Hamilton, for example, suggested that senators, in addition to the heads of executive departments, ought to have individual access to the president, as a way to assure the people that there was "a safeguard against secret combinations to deceive him."[91] The conviction that such a precaution was necessary was likely informed by the trope of a king being deluded by a circle of ministers who concealed truths and restricted dialogue between the crown and the people. A republican executive, especially, needed to avoid the appearance of being unduly influenced or deceived, and achieving that would require some degree of open doors.

When the doors were open, determining what people should see was top of the president's mind when he took office in 1789. Washington thought strategically about the image he presented to the public, often using the metaphor of a theater, or stage, to talk about the world around him.[92] During the journey he took from Mount Vernon to New York for his inauguration, as thousands lined the roads to greet him before his celebrated arrival in the temporary capital, Washington performed a type of publicity familiar to European monarchs. "In a profound symbolic sense, he *was* the nation," according to T. H. Breen—it was a feat the French king Louis XVI was losing the ability to pull off at precisely the same moment.[93] Soon after arriving, he decided it would be beneficial to embark on tours of New England, where he traveled in the fall of 1789, and the southern states, where he completed an arduous journey in 1791.

Although there was a carefully crafted publicity surrounding the presidency, the business of governance was another matter.[94] In fact, secrecy—or confidentiality, as it was frequently put—was a distinguishing characteristic of the executive branch, especially compared to the legislative. The president and his secretaries held their meetings mostly in private and maintained confidential communications. There seemed to be a sense that taking information to Congress was tantamount to moving it into public view, especially when it went to the House. The understanding seemed to be that executive activity was to take place "behind the curtain," that it was up to the president to discern what would be conveyed, when and how, to the legislature and, beyond it, to the public. Washington tended to present finished policies to Congress, insofar as he could, and to limit the public exposure of matters, especially diplomatic and military, that remained unsettled.

Apprehension about the confidentiality of the conveyance of mail, the security of seals, and the malicious curiosity of prying eyes were constant referents in the correspondence of early American politicians. For those who had spent time overseas in a diplomatic capacity, notably Jefferson and Adams, the habit of worrying about the security of correspondence and writing in code was deeply ingrained.[95] But the potential leak of information sent on paper appears to have haunted most officials, if not from personal experience, then at least from the anecdotes of acquaintances. Before he even got official word of having been elected president, Washington explained to Virginia Antifederalist politician Benjamin Harrison why he had broken off a regular correspondence. He stated that "I found from disagreeable experience, that almost all the sentiments extracted from me in answer to private letters or communicated orally, by some means or another, found their way into the public Gazettes."[96] Though Harrison responded with assurances that their correspondence had "been long since buried in oblivion," Washington's fear of having something written in a letter later printed in the press was not unfounded—it happened from time to time.[97] Members of the executive administration brought these worries with them to their new posts.

Perhaps it is no surprise then that the vocabulary of secrecy saturates the correspondence of Washington's secretaries. Despite declarations of emotional transparency among correspondents, the lexicon of secrets more often appears without negative connotation and as directive.[98] Quite often, officials would jot down the words "secret," "private," or "confidential" in order to indicate that the information they conveyed was to be restricted to the recipient's knowledge alone. The phrase "Secret & Confidential" would frequently appear just above or below the dateline of a letter, setting the expectation of confidentiality. Other times a brief statement would appear toward the bottom of a letter, as if an afterthought, to remind the recipient that what he or she had just read was "strictly" or "perfectly confidential." The word "private" also commonly appeared at the top of letters and seems to have indicated one of two possible meanings. The first possibility was that the letter dealt with personal matters unrelated to the author's public capacity. But more often it seems to have been used in the same manner as "secret" or "confidential," to denote the delicate nature of the letter's contents. A rare direction of usage given by Alexander Hamilton to a correspondent in December 1790 confirms this reading: "When you write to me any thing confidential—Write over the Superscription or Direction the word 'private.' "[99] Washington's letters to cabinet secretaries in his second term are nearly all labeled "confidential" or "private and confidential," indicating his expectation that communications among his secretaries would remain secret. Writing to Timothy Pickering in 1799 from retirement, Washington delineated his own notation system: "First, such communications as you may conceive proper to make to me *alone*, and mark *confidential*, shall go no farther; those marked *private*, I may, occasionally, impart their content to well disposed characters; and those without either, will leave me unrestrained."[100]

There seems to have been an evolution toward more explicit notations of confidentiality in the correspondence of administration members as time wore on. While often their correspondence with individuals outside the cabinet would contain some mention of the intended secrecy of the letters, the initial correspondence sent between Washington and his secretaries in 1789 rarely contained any such notation, which begs the question of whether it was assumed. Given that they were generally residing in the same city it was likely that their letters were predominantly delivered by personal secretaries or messengers, which may well have guaranteed secure conveyance. Still, notations within the letters themselves were typically a directive to the recipient more than deterrence to prying eyes. The gradual increase in notations of confidentiality from 1791, but especially by 1792, suggests that while it may have been assumed before, as relations deteriorated within the administration there may have been a sense that it needed to be explicitly stated. The summer of 1792 did, after all, find Jefferson and Hamilton at each other's throats in the press—partly over a new partisan paper, the *National Gazette* printed by Philip Freneau, which he launched with Jefferson's support.[101] Mounting critiques of Hamilton reflected anxieties over the creeping-in of British-style government, and Washington responded by handling cabinet business with more discretion to avoid distrust of the institution.[102]

With the founding of Freneau's newspaper and the growing rift within the administration, the question of the proper balance between secrecy and transparency in government took on renewed centrality in deeper disagreements over the way representative government should be and was working. Freneau had launched the *National Gazette* in the fall of 1791, declaring that he intended to provide "a brief history of the debates and proceedings of the supreme legislature of the United States, executed, it is hoped, in such a manner as to answer the expectations and gratify the curiosity of every reader." The periodical was intended to deliver useful and true information to the besieged reader and, in that spirit, the same issue carried a list of senators and representatives by state. Printing this implied Freneau's intended purpose as a reporter; with the debut of the *National Gazette*, Freneau established a newspaper aimed at filling the role of a watchdog.[103] Unlike Fenno and Lloyd before him, Freneau advocated and practiced a more active form of publicity, in which he printed calls for vigilance and propagated suspicion of government secrets. During the spring of 1792, accounts of debate in the

House of Representatives and passages from Hamilton's *Report on Manufactures* were printed alongside scathing critiques of proposed policies.

In fact, it was partly in opposition to Hamilton's policies that James Madison, then serving in the House of Representatives, gradually articulated a new vision of how representative politics ought to work in a series of essays published in the *National Gazette* starting in late 1791. Madison, who in 1787 had been looking to relieve popular pressure on elected officials, was by the early 1790s reconsidering what constituted public opinion and the degree to which elected officials should be bound to it.[104] Though he had supported closing the doors during the Federal Convention and had written in *The Federalist* No. 10 about the benefits of a republic for filtering opinion through representative bodies, his alarm at Hamilton's proposed economic measures led him to re-evaluate how political representation was working in practice.[105] He suggested that maybe the new government was not bound closely enough to public opinion, which, he wrote in an essay published December 19, 1791, was "the real sovereign in every free [government]."[106] Convinced that an interested minority was advancing Hamilton's promotion of manufacturing funded by the national debt, Madison joined with Jefferson in opposing the Treasury secretary's policies.[107]

It was not merely out of partisan pragmatism that Madison began this thorough re-evaluation of the representative process. As he worked on the newspaper essays, he was also wrestling with political philosophy while composing "Notes on Government," which, though never finished, was the framework for a comprehensive structural analysis of popular governments.[108] As numerous scholars have observed, what Madison had thought unlikely in 1788 was happening by 1792. The extended republic theory was not functioning to dilute factions as he had predicted and the deliberative process was not refining as he had hoped.[109] In his writing, he was working through the implications of his experience in Congress and rethinking assumptions about how representative government ought to work.[110] By publishing this series of essays and calling for the "circulation of newspapers through the entire body of the people," Madison began an effort, in which he was joined by Jefferson, to break politics out of the confines of the halls of government. Embracing a more active style of publicity through the press was part of that process.

Aside from a budding opposition finding voice in new periodicals like Freneau's *National Gazette*, another factor contributing to more explicit labeling regarding confidentiality in executive correspondence may have been Congress beginning to flex its muscles when it came to requesting papers from the administration. The first instance of a congressional inquiry requiring the release of papers proved a test for how far secrecy would be guarded in executive transactions. In late March 1792, the House launched an investigation into the failure of a 1791 attack led by General Arthur St. Clair against a coalition of Native Americans in the Northwest Territory. Three days after the House had requested "all persons, papers, and records" related to the incident, Washington held a meeting with his secretaries before deciding how to respond. Jefferson, as he often did, recorded the general contents of the ensuing discussion. According to his notes, Washington declared that he intended to carefully consider how to handle such an inquiry to set a viable precedent. His main hesitation was that "he could readily conceive there might be papers of so secret a nature as that they ought not to be given up."[111]

Having considered the quandary, his secretaries unanimously advised the president to "communicate such papers as the public good would permit" but "to refuse those the disclosure of which would injure the public."[112] Furthermore, they concluded that "neither the Committee nor House had a right to call on the head of a department, who and whose papers were under the Presidt. alone," and that instead they should request information from the president directly.[113] Hamilton apparently balked at the notion that all secretaries should equally face the possibility of having to deliver information, especially papers, up to Congress. By Jefferson's account—which was followed by a lengthy rant of suspicion as to the reason why—Hamilton reportedly felt that if Congress believed it could request information from his department (the Treasury), "They might demand secrets of a very mischievous nature."[114] Despite this reservation, it was apparently quickly agreed that "in this case . . . there was not a paper which might not be properly produced" and thus copies of everything relative to the incident were transmitted to the House committee. The administration would thus in the future decide which papers were safe to release to the legislature on the basis that they would not "injure the public."[115]

While the case of a congressional inquiry was an extreme example, the president was constantly deciding what information to lay before Congress and how to do it. Inherent in these decisions was the issue of secrecy. When something was presented to the legislature, it lost its confidentiality—except, of course, in cases where Washington conveyed information as explicitly secret. In 1791, John Jay responded to Washington's solicitation of advice for what to include in his address to Congress upon the opening of the session with a warning: "As to *public* and *private* communications—it strikes me that the former should contain only important & public Information, and in generals [sic]; and that Details, as well as Intelligence of a more secret nature, or of lesser Importance should be conveyed by Message.[116] Keeping "details" and "intelligence of a more secret nature" (and unimportant information—a designation which, it should be said, involved some judgment) out of official messages to Congress seems to have been the standard practice. But there were also numerous instances where the president conveyed information and requested that Congress keep it confidential. The first case in which he did this appears to have been in January 1790, when he noted in his diary that he had transmitted to Congress all the papers relative to ongoing negotiations with Native Americans in the south, "but communicated in confidence, and under injunction that no copies be taken, or communications made of such parts as ought to be kept secret."[117] Throughout his tenure, Washington would convey information to Congress with calls for confidentiality (particularly when the information related to diplomatic negotiations), generating controversy in the House.[118]

It was precisely in this realm of governance that a test of the executive administration's theory and use of secrecy was looming on the horizon in the form of a Frenchman and his politics of publicity. Edmond-Charles Genêt landed in Charleston, South Carolina, in April 1793 to acclamation. Fervor for the French Revolution pervaded the streets of American cities; Genêt would write home that he found himself "in the midst of perpetual fêtes."[119] Seeking support for raiding British ships, attacking Spanish and British holdings in North America, and repayment of French war loans, Genêt would whip up a wave of popular support in his quest to sway American foreign policy. But the news, which just barely preceded him, that the French had executed their king and declared war against Britain immediately brought Washington and his cabinet together to reconsider the course the United States would chart in the rapidly escalating conflict. The possibility of discord between the people and the men who purportedly spoke for them suddenly arose. This discord, far from the first but arguably one of the most intense instances, had the potential to unsettle the legitimacy of the new government's claim to represent the people. Though it would prove Genêt's downfall rather than the president's, the threat was far from lost on Washington and his cabinet.

The administration's navigation of diplomatic relations over the course of the next two years would prove how essential secrecy was to its conception of what it meant to represent the nation, but also how that was changing. In handling the establishment of neutrality, engineering Genêt's recall, and subsequently negotiating a treaty of amity and commerce with the British, the Washington administration and its supporters in Congress strategically deployed secrecy to circumvent hostile expressions of public opinion. In doing so, they exhibited an understanding of political representation as independently determinative of the best interest of the population rather than reflective of public opinion. While members of the administration on both sides of the emerging party divide would use and advocate secrecy through the summer of 1793, by the new year, Jefferson was charting a different course—one Washington briefly considered as well. Releasing information could guide public opinion, and Jefferson advocated a responsibility for the executive to do so. Despite this brief flirtation with transparency, Washington and his supporters in Congress attempted to shape the meaning of political representation in practice by strategically shielding deliberative processes and decisions. They did this in order to determine what they believed to be in the best interest of the country when it appeared to contrast with public opinion as manifested in popular clubs, newspapers, and petitions.

Accusations of the executive using secrecy to undermine the will of the people began as soon as Washington issued the Neutrality Proclamation in the spring of 1793. An anonymous essay printed in the *National Gazette* on June 1 lambasted the proclamation as contrary to the nation's obligations to its French allies and challenged the administration: "it might reasonably have been expected that you would have rendered yourself clearly intelligible to the citizens of America." Americans expected, the author asserted, "that nothing mysterious or of double meaning would have been promulgated by the elective executive of a free country." The type of "monarchical mystery" he saw in the issuance of the proclamation "ought surely to be rejected with abhorrence"[120] Such accusations foreshadowed the types of criticism the administration would face over the ensuing few years, boosted with the rise of popular societies that made watchfulness over the government their mission. Starting that spring of 1793, clubs calling themselves Democratic and/or Republican societies began to issue constitutions and mission statements calling for government to be "watched with the eye of an eagle," lamenting that "the vigilance of the people has been too easily absorbed in victory" and asserting the importance of "republican vigilance"

Satirical cartoon depiction of a Democratic-Republican club, entitled "A Peep into the Antifederal Club" (New York, August 16, 1793); artist unknown. (Source: The Library Company of Philadelphia)

to securing "just, mild and equitable government."[121] These clubs were formed in Genêt's wake and often gestured to their perception of popular society movements in France, which by 1793 had become immensely powerful as politicians aligned with the Jacobin Club moved to consolidate power in the National Convention.[122] Making a toast to the French and American revolutions, the Democratic Society of Pennsylvania declared "those events have withdrawn the veil which concealed the dignity and happiness of the human race."[123] Emerging from the shadows, these societies—much like their counterparts in France—urged their members to awaken and watch their elected representatives to guard against creeping tyranny. Ironically, Federalists criticized the societies for their adherence to secrecy in their meetings, an allegation pitched (not unsuccessfully) to undermine their claims to speak for the people.[124]

Though the rhetoric of these societies and opposition newspapers like the *National Gazette* was intended to inflame, allegations that the administration's policies were being formed outside the public's view were not unfounded. The Neutrality Proclamation had been issued while

Congress was not in session and had been developed among the members of the administration, if not necessarily under any special measures of secrecy. As Hamilton labored to swing public opinion against Genêt over the summer, the administration proceeded to put teeth to the proclamation, devising an intricate set of rules when it came to shipping, privateering, and maintaining treaty obligations. Meanwhile, Genêt threatened to take his case to Congress and then to the American people, who, he believed, were more sympathetic to the French than the president's official neutrality accounted for. Asserting that republican politics had deserted the "crooked paths" of "old diplomacy," he played to a swelling sense among the emergent Democratic-Republican societies that political decisions ought always to align with the will of the people.[125] As public opinion gradually began to turn against Genêt and in favor of the president's determination to keep the country neutral, the administration even began to consider releasing the envoy's correspondence with Jefferson to further bolster its case against him. It was apparently at Jefferson's insistence that the administration decided against this disclosure, an illustration of the way in which opinions about the utility of secrecy did not always fall neatly along emergent party lines. Nor were these opinions ideologically consistent; they could also be crudely strategic, as the Genêt affair illustrates. And yet it was only when officials believed that public opinion could be swayed by exposing details of political transactions that they considered doing so.

Feeling scorned after failing in his mission, Genêt wrote to Jefferson asserting his intention to have all his correspondence with the federal government, as well as his instructions from French officials, translated and printed for public distribution. "Monsieur, frankness, candor, and publicity are the only basis of politics in France," he proclaimed, asking Jefferson to ensure the president would distribute his publications to Congress for its further consideration.[126] In declaring this, Genêt was indeed delivering a line that resonated with the political values espoused by revolutionaries in the National Assembly and, up to then, in its successor, the National Convention. What he did not seem to grasp was that there were limits to these values in the United States. Not all aspects of policy-making were to be laid before the public for its inspection. In engineering Genêt's recall and rejecting the notion that his appeal to the people could ever be legitimately made, American officials made a statement that their French counterparts were never able to effectively assert, despite their best efforts: in a representative republic, representatives spoke for the people. Secrecy proved, and would continue to prove, a critical tool to asserting this distinction.

In late November 1793, as Congress was finally about to reconvene in Philadelphia after a disastrous yellow fever outbreak that summer, the executive secretaries met to determine what the president should relay with regard to Genêt and the broader conflict between the French and British. The French envoy's recall and the details of the neutrality policy were to be presented as faits accomplis, but the recent decision of the British to seize American ships carrying corn or flour to French ports posed some problems. In the meeting, Hamilton was apparently "against the whole, but insisted that at any rate it should be a secret communication, because the matters it stated were still depending." According to Jefferson's notes from the meeting, Secretary of War Henry Knox agreed with this assessment and Attorney General Edmund Randolph seemed on the fence. "I began to tremble now for the whole, lest all should be kept secret," Jefferson reported. His motivations were surely strategic; he wanted the world to know that the British had been violating neutrality, especially after much had been made of French incursions. Apparently, Washington "took up the subject with more vehemence than I have seen him shew" and decided all communications should be made publicly, which surprised Jefferson.[127] But a few days later, the president was reconsidering his decision, noting that he did not see any danger in making a public communication regarding Britain but with Hamilton insisting that the British were more lenient in their regulations than the French, he did not want to "take ground we cannot maintain well."[128]

In response, Jefferson began to advance a theory of political representation that rested on transparency. Concealment was not acceptable for a politician conscious of his constituents:

> If they could be kept secret, from whom would it be? From our constituents only, for Gr. Britain is possessed of every title. Why then keep it secret from them? No ground of support for the Executive will ever be so sure as a complete knowledge of their proceedings by the people; and it is only in cases where the public good would be injured and *because* it would be injured, that proceedings should be secret.[129]

It was unacceptable for the executive to keep information from his constituents, Jefferson argued. The public's knowledge of the grounds upon which decisions were made would bind the people to their elected leader. He asked whether the president did not have the same duty to communicate to his constituents as congressmen and, moreover, "if they were desirous of communicating [the proceedings], ought the President to restrain them by making the communication confidential?"[130] Washington seems to have agreed in this instance, making a public report on the situation with France and Britain in Congress just three days later. But the escalating tensions he outlined would prove the beginning of another turn in public opinion. It seemed to push Washington further toward a belief in the need to strategically employ secrecy in charting a course for the United States, whose best interest, he believed, did not always align with the people's professed wishes.

This conviction led to the procedural secrecy used in the negotiation and ratification of the Jay Treaty. As noted earlier, the process in this case showed both how the government was using secrecy to bolster a less reflective style of representation and how that style of representation was being contested through critiques of such secrecy. Before the treaty was released, in the spring of 1795, "secrecy itself, as much or more than the possible contents of the treaty, became the dominant issue," according to Todd Estes. The belief that secrecy was illegitimate in a republic sparked a debate that spring between the popular and anonymous Franklin writing in Eleazer Oswald's *Independent Gazetteer* and William Cobbett, an increasingly well-known Briton writing in Philadelphia. The letters of Franklin began appearing before the treaty had ever been published. He harped on the secrecy surrounding the negotiations as a violation of the republican nature of the government. "The extreme secrecy which enshrouds Executive transactions, has the strongest tincture of anti-republicanism about it," he wrote in May. "If the People have the right and the capacity to govern themselves, they are certainly entitled to a knowledge of their own affairs." Franklin even admitted that sometimes there may be legitimate reasons for the public to be kept temporarily in the dark with regard to a treaty, but he wondered why the Senate was not even "entrusted with the objects of Jay's mission." "If the People are unworthy of having *their own secrets* confided in them," he asked, "did the same unworthiness extend to *the Senate?*"[131]

Later that year, Cobbett printed a lengthy rebuke of Franklin's letters. In response to the assertion that the Senate should have been informed of the details of Jay's mission while it was in progress, Cobbett said "it would be slandering the Constitution, to suppose that it contained any thing approaching so near to the anarchical, as to subject the particular object of negotiation to an assembly, not obliged to secrecy, before the negotiation is opened."[132] Suggesting that the public had a right to be informed of the details of the treaty was even more absurd: "It would be mere nonsense," Cobbett contended, "to pretend that they have a right to be informed of all the secrets of a negotiation, without having a right to break it off."[133] The people, in electing their representatives, yielded to them the ability to make decisions. If they had no right or ability to change course with regard to treaty negotiations, what use would it be for the people to be informed of the details? Knowing what was happening while not having the ability to stop or change it, because they had already abdicated the decision-making power to their elected officials, was useless. "What satisfaction could they derive from being tantalized with a view of dangers, that they could not avoid?" he asked. Though framed slightly differently, this was a classic Federalist interpretation of the place of secrecy in a representative system: transparency had little use if the people who could watch were powerless to act.

In the *New York Journal* that fall, a speech that had been delivered in the local Democratic-Republican society noted that "few things are so evil as to be unproductive of any good." The treaty had at least aided in "stimulating the public mind, hath produced occurences, furnishing a clue, by the guidance of which their labrynth of delusive artifice is further explored and detected." The government in this case, as in many others, had operated with "ambiguity, obscurity, complication, and secrecy" to hide from the inspection of the people. This manner of operating "implies that the plans or measures so concealed or disguised are against the general will and interest."[134] The treaty, as these republican partisans claimed, was a pivotal point after which government secrecy, the depths and purposes of which had been revealed through the fiasco, proved increasingly difficult to justify.

Though Washington did sign the treaty in August, there was a greater sense in which the Federalist administration may have won a battle that summer but had begun to lose an ideological war. The Federalists prevailed in the dispute over the treaty itself in that it was ratified, but they were pushed to adopt strategies of popular politics to achieve an acceptance of the agreement.[135] The contest over the treaty was linked to a deeper debate about the proper relationship between citizens and representatives.[136] As public opinion shifted in favor of the treaty, Federalists adopted the reflective vision of representative politics they had long rejected in theory.[137] The treaty debacle also marked a turning point in Federalist political tactics because key components of the broader political culture were renegotiated at that time. Federalist leaders were forced to reconsider their practices, particularly in regard to the place of confidentiality in the political process. They had, after all, decided in late June to finally publish the treaty, which is significant—even if they were beaten to it by Bache and the Republican senator who supplied the text.

In the wake of the Jay Treaty debate, the Senate opened its new galleries and people showed up to see a previously closed aspect of the political process unfold.[138] Through persistent challenges to its legitimacy as a voice of the people, specifically through critiques of the use of secrecy, the practices of the new federal government gradually evolved to more nearly reflect an understanding of political representation that the framers had initially rejected. Federalists continued to envision a representative government made legitimate in the moment of election, after which enlightened men were to determine the best interest of the nation free from popular pressure. Being able to shield much of the political process from public view was crucial to this conception. In order to divorce the decision-making process from public opinion, "it was best for the people to be both absent and unaware of just exactly what it was their representatives were doing," as Trish Loughran put it.[139] While she pointed to the disjointed space of the early national public sphere as facilitating this separation, it was also by theorizing and using secrecy that political figures asserted this conception of representative politics.

In the daily decisions they made about who could see what, elected officials advanced their visions of what it meant to represent the people. When the House of Representatives decided in 1789 to open its doors and allow printers to chronicle its proceedings, it did so partly to counter the fears of Antifederalists who had warned during the ratification debates that the new government would operate beyond the sight the people. By performing the deliberative process in public view, representatives were living up to an understanding of political representation as a process that required publicity. Yet in simultaneously carving out spaces for politics to unfold outside the public eye, they calibrated how much to respond to public opinion. The Senate relied on secrecy to establish its legitimacy as a representative body in an insulated sense, keeping its doors shut until 1795. Although there were senators who persistently argued the need for their deliberations to be publicly visible, it was not until five years into the republic that they won over their colleagues. Washington and his administration, also, carefully crafted the meaning of a representative executive as one that was publicly visible but governed in private.

To be sure, this was a style of government that many Americans were intent on chipping away. Viewing secrecy as incompatible with political representation, many printers and popular societies decried what they perceived to be the pervasive use of concealment to undermine public opinion's proper influence on government. These critiques took on particular poignancy in the realm of diplomacy, where it appeared the government was contradicting popular will at every turn. Homing in on the common thread of secrecy, emergent Democratic-Republican partisans called for greater publicity in politics. These calls were tantamount to asserting an alternate conception of how political representation was meant to work and what made it legitimate. Secrecy was pernicious precisely because it impeded the reflection of public opinion in political decision-making, which partisans of publicity upheld as the proper foundation for representative government.

PART III
Spectatorship

CHAPTER SEVEN

Surrounded by Spectators

As the house of Representatives debated requesting confidential materials from President Washington in the spring of 1796, tensions around secrecy once again ran high. While no rule of thumb had yet been established, Representative Abraham Baldwin announced in Congress that "he thought the importance of having many Governmental secrets was diminishing. The doctrine of publicity, he said, had been daily gaining ground in public transactions in general, and he confessed his opinions had every day more and more a greater tendency that way." Baldwin was a Georgia Republican and his declaration came in a speech defending the request for materials relating to the negotiation of the Jay Treaty, which Republicans still hoped to scuttle by withholding appropriations. "The passion for mystery was exploded," he went on, "and what experience he had had in public matters confirmed him in the opinion that the greater the publicity of measures the greater the success."[1] Though motivated by his party's desire to prolong the fight over the initially unpopular treaty and likely driven by the conviction that nefarious or embarrassing material lurked in the requested papers, Baldwin's assessment of publicity was not wrong. Over the preceding few years, secrecy had repeatedly proven a liability for Federalists as the opposition pushed for greater transparency.

Yet deep disagreement persisted. Both houses of Congress still sometimes closed their doors and cleared the galleries throughout the latter half of the decade. A standing rule allowed a representative to request that this be done "when any Message shall be received from the President which shall require secrecy, or when any member has any communication to make which, in his opinion, required secrecy."[2] Still, these decisions were not without controversy. For example, when Massachusetts representative Samuel Sewall motioned in January 1798 to clear the chamber and shut the doors to discuss a recent, violent altercation on the floor between two members—Matthew Lyon and Roger Griswold—he was rebuked. Desiring privacy because "it was a subject which would considerably affect the feelings of the members of the House," Sewall succeeded in having the public removed only to bring up the topic and immediately see the doors reopened. In the Senate, which now met by default with open doors, there were also some lingering efforts to limit the publicity of its proceedings. For example, in January 1796, a motion was made to direct the secretary of the Senate to keep a "Secret Journal . . . in which shall be entered such parts of the proceedings of the Senate, in their Legislative capacity, as they shall deem proper to be kept secret."[3] The motion was, however, defeated without any debate recorded. In short, the question of when secrecy was warranted and legitimate had still not been settled.

In the wake of the Jay Treaty debate, the pressure for publicity was greater than ever because the Federalists had also conceded its importance over the course of the debacle. Yet they retained a propensity for secrecy and continued to articulate its value in protecting elected officials from what they considered undue popular pressure. This remained true even though the publicity of diplomatic material proved strategically advantageous to their party on several occasions throughout the latter half of the decade. While these instances would test both factions' theoretical positions about secrecy and publicity, neither abandoned its ideological inclinations either to advocate publicity or guard material with secrecy. And yet, in repeatedly being pushed to publicize documents and deliberations, Federalists ultimately contributed to broadening the expectation of transparency and its concurrent implication of a more reflective and responsive political representation in government.[4] By the time Thomas Jefferson took office as president in 1801, publicity was central to a broad understanding of the government as representative in a reflective sense.

Jefferson's election is commonly considered a turning point in the early American republic.[5] It certainly was. But in order to understand the nature of what Jefferson proudly called the "Revolution of 1800," it is essential to examine the Adams presidency in the preceding four years. In fact, to make sense of 1800, we must dive deeper especially into 1798 to understand the backlash created by Federalist attempts to control the effects of greater publicity in politics with the Sedition Act. The election of 1800 swept the Democratic-Republican opposition into office, leading Jefferson to declare victory for the type of reflective political representation he and his allies had long advocated. Publicity was the order of the day and the shields provided by secrecy were supposedly torn down. But Jefferson's administration cannot be so simply understood. As in many aspects of his life, Jefferson was full of contradictions on the question of secrecy in government.[6] In the widening disjuncture between his rhetoric and behavior, the third president contributed to redefining publicity as a passive process, whereby a carefully curated show for public consumption was meant to satisfy demands for transparency.

Historians have often noted a shift toward more democratic conceptions and forms of politics as the nation advanced into the nineteenth century.[7] Greater publicity of the process can and should be classified as part of this evolution. And yet it is worth pausing to consider the enduring effects of the use of secrecy at the origin of the representative republic. Once galleries were constructed, was the "radical publicity" advocated by popular societies dead?[8] If not entirely lifeless, the deliberate theorization and use of secrecy through the early years of the republic had rendered an active notion of public opinion marginal to establishing the foundational legitimacy of the representative republic.[9] Moreover, publicity itself was thoroughly redefined and vacated of its more radical implications by the time Jefferson espoused it from the White House.

As Washington neared the end of his momentous presidential term, the republic was rocked by yet another roiling debate about the proper place of secrecy in the government—an eventuality the president probably lamented. Perhaps unsurprisingly, the debate arose again around the controversial Jay Treaty, which remained an open discussion even after the president affixed his signature. In March 1796, as the House took up the question of allocating funding to fulfill treaty obligations, ardent New York Republican Edward Livingston motioned to request from the executive all papers related to the negotiation of the treaty. He initially gave the reason that "some important Constitutional questions would be discussed" and that it was "very desirable, therefore, that every document which might tend to throw light on the subject should be before the

House."[10] His proposal launched a weeks-long debate over the House's role in treaty ratification, the nature of the Constitution, and, most importantly for our purposes, the representatives' right to request confidential material from the president. A back-and-forth ensued, broken down mostly along party lines, between those who maintained the legislature's right and duty to view and expose such material and those who believed executive privilege militated against sharing documents outside very specific circumstances. On numerous occasions over the course of the debate, the discussion boiled down to blanket statements on the propriety of publicity in a republic. It was to Washington's great annoyance that he was yet again dogged by these questions. He aimed to settle them definitively as he made the decision to retire and secure sound precedents.

A significant episode in the fourth Congress, the debate over whether to request executive materials lasted weeks. Once the demand had been made, the first major looming question was upon what basis such a request could be justified. When pushed a few days after the initial proposal to offer a reason, Livingston asserted that "he did it for the sake of information." It was not possible to state the specific purposes to which that information would be used before seeing the material; the papers themselves would reveal the purpose for which they were needed.[11] Even if they were not requesting the material to launch an investigation of officials' behavior, "the right . . . of superintendence over the officers of Government, gave a right to demand a sight of those papers, that should throw light upon their conduct," Virginia Republican John Nicholas argued.[12] Those in favor of the request frequently cited an oversight role as justification for which further explication would be gratuitous.

Others emphasized that the request was prompted less from an oversight capacity and more from the need for information in order to allay persistent concerns about the treaty. Supporters of the request noted at various points that they "did not wish to pass judgment on [the treaty] without knowing the circumstances under which it was made," as William Giles of Virginia put it.[13] Expanding on this point, the outspoken Pennsylvania Republican Albert Gallatin noted that "it was supposed that the President and the Senate were the best judges, because they possessed the best information: to render this information public, must then answer a valuable purpose."[14] A number of Republican representatives suggested that releasing the papers related to Jay's mission would at the very least serve to assuage widespread public anxieties surrounding the treaty.[15] The request was "founded upon a principle of publicity necessary in this, our Republic, which has never been opposed, that I have either heard or read of, since the first organization or operation of this Government," Virginia representative John Heath argued.[16] That the treaty was so controversial was a reason to double down on the principle of publicity, which Heath presumed would have "so agreeable an effect as to reconcile fully the feelings of the people to the propriety of the negotiations as well as the instrument itself."[17]

But if the intent was to publish the papers, Connecticut Federalist Nathaniel Smith asserted, surely that would require a separate act. Though many members were suggesting that "nothing was more desirable than publicity in all governmental proceedings," he hoped it "would be admitted that there was a great difference in that respect between the Executive and the Legislative."[18] It ought to be left up to each branch of government to determine whether to release material. In short, Smith suggested that Congress did not have the ability to impose publicity upon the executive branch. Robert Goodloe Harper of South Carolina made a similar point. After avowing his general commitment to publicity, he urged his colleagues to think about what would happen if the situation were reversed. Imagine, he went on, that the House had adopted a ban on printers being present in their chamber "and that the President had sent a message informing the House, that publicity in the proceedings of Government was a very desirable and necessary thing" and urged representatives to open their doors. He did not think such a request would be well received in the chamber. If the House believed it had the power to request the papers from the president, why did it not "have a right also to direct the Senate"? "We ought, therefore, if we act consistently, to request the Senate to let their gallery remain open for general information while they discuss executive subjects."[19] Harper likely misfired with this strategy since he was aiming to convince those who articulated blanket beliefs in publicity and would probably have welcomed such principles being asserted across government. Nonetheless, his underlying point about the separation of powers tied the question of publicity and secrecy to fundamental prerogatives of each branch.

Those arguing against requesting the papers also reasserted the value of secrecy in government, especially in the executive branch, and the danger of setting bad precedents. There was an ever-present belief that exposing the papers "might lead to a disclosure to foreign nations, through this House, of certain points in our foreign relations, and in the estimate of our own, domestic interests which might do us mischief," William Vans Murray of Maryland argued.[20] Because the request was related to foreign affairs specifically, many believed it would be improper to disclose the documents. Ezekiel Gilbert of New York noted that "as long as there are despotic governments to be negotiated with, secrecy was necessary."[21] Toward the end of the debate, Gilbert adopted another line of argument, stating that "however inclined we might be to expose all our own secret negotiations and Cabinet transactions, he said it could not be proper, contrary to the practice of all other nations, to expose wantonly the Cabinet negotiations and concerns of another nation." The reason for secrecy, these representatives concluded, was to protect the integrity of the United States and its relations with other countries who had a reasonable expectation of confidentiality in their dealings. Their defense of secrecy was circumscribed, allowing them to purport a general support for publicity in most matters.

But others were more comprehensive in their arguments against requesting the documents. It would be for the purposes of satisfying "vain curiosity," according to Daniel Buck of Vermont.[22] Harper stated that though he wished to see the papers, "he could not consent to call for them, because that implied a right to possess them, which he could never admit."[23] In the end, many opponents of the resolution came back to their conviction that the reason for calling for the papers was suspect. "If a requisition of this kind could be ever justifiable, it certainly would be proper to accompany it with precise and specific reasons, stating the real objects," Uriah Tracy of Connecticut asserted.[24] The crux was that "in negotiations in time of war, confidential communications were necessary," as New York representative John Williams argued. "It was contended that in a Republican Government, there ought to be no secrets," he said, "but he would ask whether it was not specified in the Constitution that secrecy should be observed on particular occasions?" Moreover, "he believed if the Constitution of France were examined it would be found that their system admitted of secrets."[25] Requesting the papers would do nothing more than establish a bad precedent that would put the United States at a global disadvantage. Of course, at the time he made this statement, he was right about the French constitution, though such measures were not implemented there without similar conflict.

Most representatives rejected these concerns and the House voted to make the request on March 24, 1796. Once made, the question fell to the president to answer: Did the House of Representatives have the right to demand confidential communications from the executive branch? It was a question that had come up before, but this time Washington would not brook it. Once again, his response was both strategic and cast in terms of deeper theoretical implications about government structure and function. The conclusions of his trusted advisors varied based on their knowledge of what the material contained. Some cautioned that releasing the documents would be a strategic blunder, while others—with less knowledge of their contents—suggested that withholding the files could prove more politically damaging. Yet in recommending how to respond, Washington's advisors uniformly warned of the need to do so in such a way as to protect the executive ability to keep material confidential at the president's discretion. As Washington himself had repeatedly noted since he stepped into office, as the first president all his decisions had the potential to set precedent. It seems likely then that there was a genuine concern with the implications of being compelled to share private communications as much, if not more, than there was a worry with the immediate political implications of sharing these particular papers. The resulting decision had the effect of further cementing executive authority over the realm of foreign affairs and, more importantly, the legitimacy of secrecy in this realm of government activity. It was a precedent Adams would build upon once he took office, in spite of political exigencies.

Upon hearing about Livingston's intent to make the request, Washington's trusty advisor Alexander Hamilton initially wrote urging him not to comply based on the larger precedent it might establish. "It will be fatal to the negotiating power of the government, if it is to be a matter of course for a call of either house of congress to bring forth all the communication however confidential."[26] Hamilton ultimately made the case for withholding the diplomatic papers primarily based on his analysis of the potentially damaging domestic political effect of disclosing the particular documents in question. Even so, he had also gestured to what he perceived to be the dangerous precedent of Congress being able to expose confidential material at will.

While Hamilton's advice made the case for denying the House request largely based on the specific papers in question, Washington remained interested in the underlying principle: could the House compel the exposure of executive records? In his reply to Hamilton after he had ultimately issued a denial of the request, Washington clearly articulated this deeper concern, stating that "from the first moment, and from the fullest conviction in my own mind, I had resolved to resist the principle wch was evidently intended to be established by the call of the House of Representatives."[27] In seeking the input of his cabinet, Washington seems to have been interested less in the immediate political implications of releasing these particular papers and more in the broader principle and precedent. Writing to his secretaries, the president asked for their opinions on whether Congress had the constitutional right to ask for the papers at all; whether even if it did not have the right it would nonetheless make sense to furnish the papers; and lastly, in what terms he should reply to the request whether it be to fulfill or refute it.

Attorney General Charles Lee, who acknowledged that he was "not acquainted with those papers," asserted that while he did not believe Congress had a right to demand them, he nonetheless counseled the president that "it will be expedient under the circumstances of this particular case to comply with the request." Yet even in advising the delivery of the papers, Lee encouraged the president to submit an explicit stance on the power of Congress to issue such requests in the future, something he clearly felt should be strictly delineated. Although he believed the House of Representatives did have "generally from the nature of its functions a right to demand from the President such statements of the transactions in any of the executive departments as they shall conceive necessary or useful in forming their laws," the right of the president to determine whether to comply with such requests remained imperative. "It does not therefore follow that this branch of Congress possesses a right to demand and possess without the consent of the President copies of all the instructions and documents in his custody relative to any subject whatsoever, whenever they shall be pleased to require them."[28] In this case, Lee conveyed a belief that strategic considerations should lead to the release of the confidential communications despite a broader commitment to safeguarding such material.

Other secretaries did not agree. In his recommendation, Secretary of the Treasury Oliver Wolcott first asserted his belief that the Constitution gave to the president and Senate the right of making treaties in large part because such business required "secrecy and dispatch," which were two elements not likely to be maintained in a "numerous public body." He warned of the danger of setting precedent and posited that "there may and probably do exist many particulars on which good faith and prudence require the observance of secrecy."[29] In refusing to disclose the papers, Washington would simply be fulfilling his constitutional duty to protect the public interest, Wolcott reasoned. "In the exercise of the duties committed to the president, secrecy and personal confidence are sometimes essential."[30] He admitted that "if there was reason to believe that a refusal would diminish the public confidence in the Government this would be a powerful argument in favor of compliance." Yet he saw an even greater danger in losing public confidence for submitting to what he called "improper demands."[31] In his recommendation, Wolcott was drawing on arguments made in *The Federalist Papers* about the fundamental assumed powers of the executive, chief among which were secrecy and speed of action.

In his response to the House of Representatives, Washington based his refusal to produce the files as the fulfillment of the intent behind constitutional structures. Prefacing his denial with the assurance that his "constant endeavor [has been and will be] to harmonize with the other branches," Washington attempted to protect himself from accusations of concealment. "I trust, that no part of my conduct has ever indicated a disposition to withhold any information, which the constitution has enjoined upon the president, as a duty, to give, or which could be required of him by either house of Congress, as a right," he wrote. Washington articulated a tendency toward transparency before bracketing the request for diplomatic papers as a particular case where secrecy was in fact expected and structurally accounted for in the Constitution. "The nature of foreign negotiations requires caution; and their success must often depend on secrecy," he went on, noting that even after they had been concluded, the "disclosure of all the measures, demands, or eventual concessions, which may have been proposed or contemplated, would be deemed impolitic." This necessity for secrecy "was one cogent reason for vesting the power of making treaties in the president, with the advice and consent of the Senate; the principle on which that body was formed, confining it to a small number of members."[32] In making this assertion, Washington referred back to the secret proceedings of the Constitutional Convention, a move Jonathan Gienapp has argued was crucial for shifting understandings of constitutional interpretation.[33] For our purposes, it is worth noting that in explicating the constitutional imperative to maintain secrecy in the case of foreign negotiations, Washington referred to decade-old proceedings that were themselves still not public.

Washington's refusal to disclose executive papers to the House of Representatives was, in many ways, a fitting conclusion to his presidency. Throughout his two terms in office, he and his advisors had worked to safeguard executive prerogative and assert independence from the legislative branch in particular. Though far from indifferent to public opinion, Washington carefully advanced and guarded the executive's right to diverge from it. He repeatedly relied on secrecy to do this throughout his term. Being the nation's top representative, to him, meant leading with wisdom rather than following any kind of will expressed outside official channels. Election was the proper expression of the people's will. As he stated in his Farewell Address in 1796, he had assumed office due to "a deference for what appeared to be your desire." Beyond that moment, he worked on behalf of the American people to do what he believed to be best based on the knowledge he had. As he left office, he warned Americans to beware efforts to "covertly and insidiously" undermine the federal government and urged them to be "watching for its preservation with jealous anxiety." Secrecy lurked among the people as a threat to the government, not as a danger within the government itself. He cautioned that there was a duty to obey a government established by the people, deeming a threat "all combinations and association, under whatever plausible character, with the real design to direct, control, counteract, or awe the regular deliberation and action of the constituted authorities."[34] Washington had steadfastly stuck to an understanding of representative government as insulated, even directive, rather than reflective of public opinion. His vision and the decisions he made to ensconce it laid a foundation for the role of the executive and representative government more broadly as the republic underwent its first transition of power in 1796.

The pressure for publicity continued to dog Washington's successor. More so even than that of Washington, John Adams's presidency was consumed by foreign affairs and repeated crises that brought the country to the brink of war. Specifically, the Adams presidency was characterized by a failed diplomatic mission to France and the fallout from it, which resulted in a "Quasi War" of ongoing tension and skirmishes on the seas between the two countries. A staunch Federalist, Adams had long been dubious about too much responsiveness to public pressure. Working as an American minister to Britain during the drafting and ratification of the Constitution, Adams returned and accepted the vice presidency under Washington. In this role, he served as chair of the Senate and little else. He and his family were among those skeptical of opening the doors to the House and later the Senate. In short, Adams was no advocate of reflective representation. The political dynamics of his presidency would test his commitment to insulated representation, however, as public opinion swung in favor of Federalist policies. Still, Adams remained wary of exposing too much to public view or of courting public opinion. Ultimately, he and his Federalist colleagues in Congress moved to crack down on the press and limit the extent of publicity in the political process. Adams's inclination to safeguard secrecy was clear from the beginning as he hesitated to expose diplomatic dispatches from France that chronicled the solicitation of bribes from American officials. That incident, which came to be known as the XYZ affair, launched a period of rough relations with the French and initiated preparations for war.

Upon taking office in 1797, Adams appointed three envoys to Paris with the aim of negotiating a commercial agreement to protect American shipping in the ongoing war between Britain and France. When they arrived, however, the commissioners were approached by French agents (who came to be known as X, Y, and Z) who suggested they offer a bribe to the French foreign minister and a loan as a precondition to negotiations. They refused and two of the commissioners left immediately, leaving behind Elbridge Gerry, who tried to keep open lines of communication.[35] When Adams received reports from his emissaries on what had happened, his inclination followed Washington's in the case of the Jay Treaty papers. Knowing the contents of the communications and conjecturing the effect of their release, Adams feared that if he were to make them public, war would be inevitable because public opinion would quickly swing in that direction.[36] Wanting to keep his options open, Adams elected to keep the letters under wraps. Despite the political advantage that would be derived from publishing official papers, the president decided to shield them from public view based at least in part on a conception of how the executive was meant to make decisions.

In a letter to Washington, retired Virginia politician Alexander White relayed a frustrating discussion he had with Adams over dinner about the XYZ dispatches. "[Adams] expressed his doubts with respect to communicating them; he said if the communication was confidential yet there were men in the legislature who would public everything." Apparently, Adams wondered aloud whether members of the House would take an oath of secrecy upon receiving the material, to which White expressed skepticism. Nonetheless, White apparently "took the liberty to say, that I thought everything explanatory to the relative situation of France and this country ought to be communicated." He reported making this case by emphasizing that because the contents could lead to war and Congress had the sole power to declare it, they ought to be let into the process.

Moreover, he argued, "withholding information would strengthen the ground of the opposition to effective measures." In the face of this assertion, Adams apparently replied that "the letters might have facts which would implicate individuals on either side of the water, or even endanger the personal safety of our ministers." Despite being advised that publishing the letters would be politically advantageous, Adams remained concerned with the effect it could have on the issue at hand. White concluded that Adams would likely "make no further communication to Congress on that subject" and, for a while at least, he was right.[37]

After Adams mentioned the dispatches in a March 1798 address to the House of Representatives, a debate arose there as to what exactly the president was asking the members to do and whether they needed to see the papers in order to take action. Giles noted that Adams had asked the House to prepare for war based on papers he had not shared. The president had essentially declared that "I have not sent [the papers] to you, but require you to act upon them," he pointed out. "The House has been thus obliged to take up the subject in the dark," Giles continued, alleging that "it left a strong impression on his mind that something was not correct, which was the reason the expected papers were not sent."[38] The proposal to request the documents was actually then made by a Federalist, Representative John Allen of Connecticut, who introduced the resolution "because there is a paper printed in this city which is continually insinuating that there is something in these despatches which, if they were made known, would show that the conduct of the Executive has been improper."[39] It was another example of the Federalists being pushed into adopting a policy of publicity due to the growing suspicion of secrecy promoted by the opposition party, specifically in this case the *Aurora General Advertiser*. If something were kept secret, it must be because some aspect of it was suspect. This stance forced the hand of Federalists like Adams who were not in fact trying to hide any specific information but rather were withholding material out of a theoretical commitment to decision-making sheltered from public pressure. Giles confirmed that he, for one, was not "satisfied as to the sincerity of the proceedings of the Executive of the United States toward France," and, as a result, he thought the House should inspect not only the official dispatches Adams had mentioned but also the instructions the ministers had received.

But most Federalist members resisted requesting the dispatches, believing that it would harm American negotiations with France and that it was an affront to the president. Delaware representative James Bayard stated his belief that "it was wholly a matter of Executive discretion to judge whether it would be proper to communicate them or not." He cited the leak of the Jay Treaty in 1795 as precedent that suggested the House could not keep the papers secret if required. He added that, besides, "he was one of those who had so much confidence in the Executive as to trust his candor, understanding, and integrity to determine upon the propriety of what he should send to or withhold from this House."[40] On this point, some Democratic-Republicans also agreed. Baldwin said he believed the request was futile because even if they made it, "it is well known that he will not be obliged to send them."[41] Gallatin noted Bayard's opinion and said that even if they did ask, "how did he know that it would be given, or, if given, whether it would not be in a mutilated state."[42] Livingston followed up by making the point that while he certainly wished to see the information, he feared it would be nothing but a waste of time. Obliquely citing Washington's refusal to provide papers related to the Jay Treaty, Livingston lamented the likelihood that "the information would not be sent," and thus deemed the request useless.[43]

Despite these concerns, which were undoubtedly strategically crafted for political effect, the House voted overwhelmingly to request the dispatches and instructions given to the commissioners. Adams complied the following day, though even then he asked Congress to keep the documents confidential. In transmitting them, he directed that they should be kept secret "until the members of Congress are fully possessed of their contents, and shall have had opportunity to deliberate on the consequences of their publication."[44] With this move, Adams relinquished to the House the responsibility of determining whether to publish the papers. For two days, representatives considered them in closed session before abruptly voting to print and publish 1,200 copies. The debate over doing so shows how the contents of the material ran up against politicians' theoretical commitments to publicity or secrecy. Federalists who had been against requesting the papers now called for publication and broad dissemination. On the other hand, Democratic-Republicans were quiet or even reversed course; Gallatin seemed to suggest that, after seeing the material, he was not sure it should be publicized for fear of negatively impacting relations with the French. It was a moment when ideological commitments clashed with political strategy for both proponents and opponents of secrecy. Representative Christopher Champlin of Rhode Island noted that "he could not understand how gentlemen could reconcile their wish for publicity with their opposition to the proposed publication."[45] The same could have been said of the Federalists who suddenly found themselves advocating printing the papers when they had largely been hesitant to request them.

Once the House did move to publish the dispatches, Adams was proven right. Calls for a declaration of war mounted as Democratic-Republicans found themselves reeling due to their strategic miscalculation. But it is worth emphasizing that despite the harm to their political position resulting from publication of the letters, Democratic-Republicans did not concede that their advocacy of publicity had been an error. Nor did Adams change his mind and adopt a policy of publicity given the boost this particular revelation gave his administration.

The dispatches stirred public opinion, feeding a hunger for war and concern about foreign influence in domestic politics. Following their release, a pamphlet by Philadelphia lawyer Joseph Hopkinson warned that there were bad actors out there who would mislead the public. With the publication revealing the truth of the failed negotiations, he claimed these actors were exposed. The faction friendly with the French were "our foes—let us understand them to be so, and no longer contend in the dark," he urged.[46] Making the dispatches public had the effect of correcting misconceptions; they were a reset that supposedly exposed the misleading artifice of the opposition. Writing to the president in the wake of the dispatches' publication, Adams's cousin by marriage Cotton Tufts reflected that they "have opened the Eyes of Many that were blind and have turnd them from the Error of their Ways." Despite this positive political outcome, Tufts qualified the "communication of these State Papers" by noting that the "Necessity of the Measure I regret much."[47] Even while acknowledging the strategic advantage of publishing the dispatches in the situation at hand, Tufts still conveyed a sense that this type of publicity should not be the default. He may have been playing to Adams's own reservations about making diplomatic material public, but even if he was, the caveat is crucial.

It becomes even clearer why Adams remained committed to shielding diplomatic decision-making from public view when we shift our attention to American relations in the Caribbean. On the heels of the XYZ revelation, the administration was pursuing a controversial plan of working to reopen trade with the sugar-producing island of Saint-Domingue. A French colony, Saint-Domingue was, by the end of the 1790s and after nearly a decade of warfare, on the verge of founding an independent nation led by formerly enslaved people. Despite widespread sentiment that the United States should ally with other European powers to suppress this development and reestablish slavery there, the Adams administration resolved that the best course would be to support the Black, formerly enslaved Toussaint Louverture in his aims at independence.[48] While Adams himself was less than enthusiastic about the possibility, he seemed resigned to the likelihood of Haitian independence and backed the advice of his cabinet to establish friendly relations with the emerging country.[49] In the closing days of December 1798, Secretary of State Timothy Pickering hosted a dinner at his residence with a man named Joseph Bunel, a merchant from Cap Français and envoy of Louverture. Bunel had been dispatched with the mission of getting the United States to end a trade embargo imposed by Congress six months earlier and to secure political and economic support for Louverture's independence movement.[50] This secret meeting launched three years of American relations with what would become the first independent nation led by formerly enslaved people, which Jefferson put to an end once in office. Officials considered secrecy essential in order to continue to pursue relations with the French, but perhaps more importantly, as Ronald Angelo Johnson notes, "this venue of secrecy was commonplace in the American capital at the end of 1798 and beginning of 1799."[51] Administration officials were aware that the course they were pursuing was unpopular, and they handled the diplomatic overture like they did many other issues as they attempted to head off Democratic-Republican opposition. The incident serves as a reminder that while secrecy could be used to subvert democracy in the sense of making policy against public opinion, it could also be applied for what might be considered democratic ends, like supporting a Black nation.

As the pressure for war with France mounted at home, the lines between public and private would be continually challenged and blurred. Just two months after the publication of the XYZ dispatches, Benjamin Franklin Bache—editor of the *Aurora* and persistent thorn in the side of Federalists—obtained a conciliatory letter from the French foreign minister Charles Talleyrand addressed to Adams. Possibly feeling that the letter demonstrated the French Republic's desire to avoid war, Bache printed the missive in June 1798. It was prefaced with the simple statement that "we hasten to communicate to our readers the following very important state paper."[52] Five days later, the periodical printed a reassurance that Bache had not received the letter directly from France but rather from an acquaintance in Philadelphia.[53] Once again, Republicans like Bache considered that more publicity, not less, was a solution to their political woes. If the XYZ dispatches had tended to bolster the administration's position, the Talleyrand letter posed problems for it.

It turned out that Adams had not yet processed or shared the letter with Congress when Bache published it. Upon being alerted to its circulation in the pages of the *Aurora*, the president probably seethed. Two days later (on June 18), he conveyed Talleyrand's letter, along with the commissioners' response, to Congress, at which point representatives George Thatcher of Massachusetts and Robert Goodloe Harper of South Carolina moved to have it printed. Once again, the Federalists moved to publish material only after, and seemingly because, it had been distributed through the Republican press first. Alluding to the belief that Bache was an operative of the French government, Harper called for "counteracting the effect of any of their machinations, by publishing the truth to the people."[54] The first lady shared these suspicions. Over the following days, Abigail Adams wrote to a number of correspondents with her interpretation of the Talleyrand letter having been printed. "In the mean time Talleyrand had sent out to Bache his Letter, for to be published here, & without, the replie of our Envoys," she relayed to her sister.[55] Writing to her brother the same day, she explained that she believed the letter was likely delivered to the government and Bache on the same day but that given the necessity of translating and making copies for Congress, Bache "caught the opportunity and sent his hand Bills on Saturday by the thousand."[56] By her estimation, printing the letter was a stunt designed to get an edge on the president. She had no doubt that it was a coordinated effort of Bache in league with the French minister. Writing to her sister, Adams immediately linked the publication to the need to crack down on these types of leaks, noting that "in any other Country Bache & all his papers would have been seazd and ought to be here, but congress are dilly dallying about passing a bill enabling the President to seize suspicious persons—and their papers."[57]

Weeks before the passage of the Alien and Sedition Acts, which were designed to prevent suspected foreign operatives from functioning in the country and to clamp down on what Federalists considered threatening publications, Bache was arrested on charges of common law sedition for his printing of the Talleyrand letter. Upon his arrest, Abigail Adams was careful to note in a letter to Tufts that the president had not had any part in the matter, though she was emphatic that "not a paper has he published for six month I believe a year, but what would subject him to a commitment."[58] She went on to convey her belief that "the Attorney Gen'll of the states ought to prosecute the constant libelous publications which issue from those fountains of Corruption."[59] Though the reference was general, her previous letters mentioning the publication of the Talleyrand letter clearly indicate this type of piece was among those she would have included as such publications. Throughout the spring of 1798, the first lady had repeatedly emphasized the need for legislation regulating the printing of seditious material and for monitoring the activity of foreigners. Fiercely protective of her family, she wrote frequently of material that appeared in Bache's paper in particular and tied it to the need for sedition legislation. "I wish the Laws of our Country were competent to punish the stirrer up of sedition, the writer and Printer of base and unfounded calumny," she wrote to her sister.[60] In the case of the Talleyrand letter, it was not so much what was said but the fact that the piece was printed at all that she considered so egregious a violation.

In fact, Bache's printing of a diplomatic letter addressed to the president before it had been received and processed was top of mind as legislators took up the possibility of both acts. His perceived treachery encapsulated the fears motivating both the Alien and Sedition Acts—a cluster of legislation that has long been regarded as a dark spot in American history. Could it be that he was a secret French operative working within the United States and taking direction from the French government? His publication of the letter seemed to prove that Bache had a direct connection with the French minister and that he was perhaps more loyal to him than to the commander in chief at home. Moreover, his publication of material that was traditionally kept private was yet another incidence of what the administration considered premature and unauthorized exposure of information related to policy decisions.

The Alien and Sedition Acts were technically four laws passed over the course of June and July 1798. Three were aimed at regulating immigrants and the fourth was geared at monitoring and restricting the press. The Naturalization Act increased the residency requirement to gain citizenship from five to fourteen years. The Alien Enemies Act permitted the government to arrest and deport male citizens of an enemy nation in the event of war, and the Alien Friends Act allowed the deportation of any non-citizen who was suspected of plotting against the U.S. government in peacetime. Finally, the Sedition Act took aim at writings against the government that were deemed dangerous—a prospect that posed many complications.

The Alien and Sedition Acts were, in part, an effort to root out secrecy among the populace and at the same time guarantee it within the government. The Alien Acts were motivated by a fear of secret conspiracies operating in league with foreign governments within the country; the intent was to expose and eliminate them. With regard to the Sedition Act, the concern with secrecy was less direct, though the law should still be understood as an effort to rein in the effect of publicity in government. While the final text of the Sedition Act did not directly mention the publication of confidential material as cause for prosecution, examining the debate over it and the cases prosecuted under it reveals that such incidents were among those legislators had in mind. The law technically deemed criminal "false, scandalous and malicious writing or writings against the government of the United States, or either house of the Congress of the United States, or the President of the United States, with intent to defame the said government, or either house of the said Congress or the said President, or to bring them, or either of them, into contempt or disrepute."[61] Historians have long treated the bill as either a political ploy on the part of Federalists to suppress opposition or as a principled attempt to impose civility in the public sphere.[62] It can be read as both of these things. But it should also be understood as part of an effort to mitigate the effects of a commitment to publicity in government, which Federalists believed was often forcing their hand politically.

Once the bill was introduced in the House, discussion quickly turned to letters that members themselves sent to their constituents—a practice that was becoming increasingly widespread and formalized. Allen referred to a member of Congress from Virginia writing home that the national debt had been intentionally increased, which Allen deemed a lie. Harper built on this point to express a concern about supposed falsehoods and calumnies being given weight by representatives spreading them. "He had recently seen a private letter [written by Congressman McDowell of North Carolina], he said, which had given administration measures the most vile coloring and had imputed to members the most abominable motives, which were contrary to what the writer knew the truth to be at the time."[63] The bill was meant to prevent the spread of what Federalist members deemed falsehoods, particularly those spread by members of Congress themselves. Because they could not restrict what was said on the floor, they turned their focus to what members communicated outside the chamber.[64] When Harper insisted that "it was not his intention to restrict the freedom of speech on that floor, but the consequences of it out of doors," Livingston called out the intent for what it was. If he did not mean to restrict representatives from speaking freely, Harper clearly meant to "prevent the people from knowing what has been said."[65] Considered from this angle, the Sedition Act was not just concerned with the opposition press but was also aimed more precisely at clamping down on the communication of elected officials with constituents through the press and the growing genre of circular letters.[66]

In fact, the examples of offending letters brought up in the debates over the Sedition Act had themselves already been the subject of legal battles the previous year, indicating both the increasing commonality and political significance of this form of publicity and the concurrent contestation of it. By the mid-1790s, the practice of sending circular letters was growing and it was not uncommon to have them printed and distributed widely back in districts and even sent to newspapers. Like other forms of publicity—such as audience attendance at deliberations or newspaper reports—circular letters engendered a particular type of transparency that made them contentious. They were not, of course, an unbiased transcript of government transactions. Rather, they came from the perspective of the member and reflected both what he wanted to tell and what he thought his constituents wanted to know.[67] These letters commonly speak of a sense of duty to share information and, as Virginia representative Samuel Cabell did in a March 1796 letter, invite readers to respond: "write to me and communicate your sentiments freely to me on the present awful crisis, as my greatest desire is to carry into effect the will and wishes of my Constituents."[68] In May 1797, a federal grand jury in Virginia indicted Cabell based on his circular letters, which the jury cited as among a genre of such letters that constituted "a real evil" intending "at a time of real public danger, to disseminate unfounded calumnies against the happy government of the United States." In reply, Cabell vowed persistence. "At a distance from my constituents, charged with their best interests, and bound to give them such information relative to their public concerns, as I possessed, I never before knew it was criminal to execute this duty."[69] In reaction to the indictment, Representative John Clopton, also of Virginia, disclosed in a letter that he believed the intent of the indictment was to "denounce the very act of letter writing as a species of criminality, when it is from a representative to his constituents—and as if those letters were particularly obnoxious, because they were *circular*; that is to say, for a distribution amongst the citizens at large." He protested that it seemed the court's goal was to "restrain and control *particularly* the intercourse between the citizens and their representatives while engaged in their official duties at the seat of government."[70]

If we think of the Sedition Act partly as an attempt to regulate this type of material, the backlash against it is cast in a new light too. The contestation of the law was, at least in part, motivated by the idea that a representative government should be entirely open to inspection by the public. Representative Nicholas went so far as to argue that, like all proposed regulations of the press, the intent was "to destroy the only means by which the people can examine and become acquainted with the conduct of persons employed in their Government."[71] To restrict the public's ability to inspect government work was a violation of the principle of representative government. "If you thus deprive the people of the means of obtaining information of their conduct, you in fact render their right of election nugatory," Gallatin argued.[72] When this was taken into account, he believed the bill could be seen for what it was: a Federalist attempt to "perpetuate their authority and preserve their present places."[73] Republicans in the House portrayed the bill as a mechanism designed to help Federalists hide unpopular policies from public scrutiny and to hinder the representative process as they understood it.

In opposition to the bill, Nicholas delivered a long and impassioned speech in which he touched on the nature of truth and rights guaranteed by the Constitution but fundamentally drove home his point by citing the importance of publicity. In a government in which all officials were elected, "the people have no other means of examining their conduct but by means of the press, and an unrestrained investigation through them of the conduct of the government."[74] Any restriction of the press was thus an attack on the principle of political representation. "You might as well say to the people, we, your Representatives, are faithful servants, you need not look into our conduct," he went on. "To restrict the press would be to destroy the elective principle, by taking away the information necessary to election." The core function of the press was to publicize the operations of government in order that people were able to make decisions about whom they wanted to elect to represent them. To regulate the press was to violate that central mechanism of reflective representation by blocking the work of government from public view. "If he found a power existing which trammeled the press, and prevented a free communication of whatever took place in Government, to the people at large, he should no longer see a possibility of abuses in the Government being corrected by the influence of the people," he declared. "There would no longer be reason to expect that uncontrolled government would consult the public good."[75]

Federalists, meanwhile, insisted that they had no intention of shielding government from public view or preventing communication between representatives and their constituents. "Every man will still be at liberty to print and speak at pleasure; but he must be prepared to prove those charges which bring disgrace upon his fellow-citizens," Harrison Gray Otis of Massachusetts declared.[76] The aim of the bill was not to close off communication but to alter it by requiring evidentiary defense of claims made. "Neither does the present bill restrain a free animadversion upon the proceedings of Congress, or the conduct of its members; it merely prohibits calumny and deception," he went on.[77] Despite this assertion, Otis seemed to acknowledge at other points that the bill would place some limitations on the way journalists covered Congress. Asking whether it was "not a restraint upon the freedom of speech that the people in the gallery are not allowed to join in the debate," he suggested that the present bill would not limit coverage any more than such a measure.[78] Finally, in answer to Nicholas's claim that not even Parliament had passed any such law restricting criticism of its actions, Otis proclaimed that "in Great Britain, Government is more able to protect itself."[79] Despite his protestations to the contrary, it seems Otis at least was thinking about the Sedition Bill as, in part, a way to protect Congress, if not by shielding it from public view, at least by controlling to some degree what was said about it. The legislation was thus taking a slightly different approach to regulating public access to the government. It was not blocking reporting; rather it sought to monitor the output about government for what the bill's authors considered false or dangerous.

Once passed and signed into law on July 14, 1798, the Sedition Act faced ongoing criticism as an instrument of undue government restriction on speech and the press. In the material produced to critique the law, the notion that it prevented people from inspecting the behavior of their representatives was prominent. Jefferson and Madison set to writing state-level legislation to build a movement against the laws, which has since been studied as a precedent for the idea of state nullification of federal laws—a tactic used and often threatened by southern states in particular going forward.[80] Concentrating his efforts in Virginia, Madison penned a declaration denouncing the Sedition Act for myriad reasons. Notably, one of the most prominent was that it prevented the proper function of publicity in a representative government. Calling the Sedition Act a violation of the First Amendment, the Virginia Resolution explicitly states that it "ought to produce universal alarm, because it is leveled against the right of freely examining public characters and measures, and of free communication among the people thereon."[81] The resolution then calls this right of inspection "the only effectual guardian of every other right."[82] This stance built upon a decade's worth of arguments about the proper relationship between representatives and the people, specifically how it was to be guaranteed in practice.

Despite the backlash, the act did go into effect and was quickly put to use in prosecuting Republican politicians and printers. Over the life of the legislation, from the summer of 1798 to the winter of 1801, some 51 prosecutions were pursued and at minimum ten convictions delivered, with those individuals facing jail time and fines.[83] Republican printers were often the targets of indictments, which were vigorously pursued by Secretary of State Pickering.[84] Of particular note is a subset of cases linked to the question of confidentiality being violated. In addition to Bache's indictment for printing the Talleyrand letter, which was not technically prosecuted under the Sedition Act, there were three indictments in particular that were rooted in some way in the exposure of what was considered confidential material. Of course, the contents of the material mattered, but the very fact that the information was published was the main bone of contention in these cases.

The first conviction under the Sedition Act was that of Matthew Lyon, a Republican representative from Vermont. Perhaps best known for getting into a physical fight with Federalist Roger Griswold on the floor of the House in which the two battled each other with a cane and fire tongs, Lyon frequently published his reflections on politics. He was tried in October 1798 on three counts of sedition. One of them concerned a letter he had written and the other two involved his publicizing a letter written by Joel Barlow, an American foreign envoy, to Georgia's Representative Baldwin. The second count had to do with the contents of that letter, which blamed the deteriorating relations with France in part on a speech Adams gave in Congress in which he criticized the French government. The third count was simply that Lyon had publicized the letter and caused it to be printed and published. Over the course of the trial, "several witnesses were called to show that the defendant, both in public and in private, had extensively used the letter for political purposes, and in doing so, had frequently made use of language highly disrespectful to the administration."[85] The district judge presiding over the trial, John Paterson, instructed the jury to consider only whether Lyon published the writing in question and whether he did so seditiously.[86] The second question was all but answered by the first, according to Paterson, who asked the jury to "consider whether language such as that here complained of could have been uttered with any other intent than that of making odious or contemptible the president and government, and bringing them both into disrepute."[87] At the root of this case was the charge that Lyon had inappropriately, with the intent of promoting sedition, publicized an otherwise private letter that contained harsh critiques of the president. Had Barlow's letter never been published, it would not have drawn the ire of Federalist officials. As it was, Lyon was fined $1,000 and sentenced to a year in prison, during which he was re-elected to the House of Representatives for a second term.

Bache never went to court over his publication of another private letter (from Talleyrand) because he died abruptly in a yellow fever outbreak in September 1798. After his death, the *Aurora* was taken over by William Duane, an Irish immigrant with a long history as the bane of whoever governed in the location where he was living. Born in rural New York, Duane moved back to Ireland as a young child, ultimately taking up a job as a reporter for John Almon's *General Advertiser* in London in the 1780s. It was while working for Almon—a major advocate for press freedom—that Duane learned techniques of legislative reporting and became involved in the radical London Corresponding Society. In 1786, he made his way to India as a private in the East India Company, only to be expelled from the colony in 1795 for critiquing the colonial government. He arrived in the United States in 1796, via another sojourn in London, and quickly made a name for himself by agitating against the Jay Treaty. In the summer of 1798, he was hired at the *Aurora* and that fall found himself the editor after Bache's untimely death.[88] In his new role, Duane set himself to exposing what he believed to be a deep well of wrongdoing in the Adams administration and turned the *Aurora* into an even more relentless scrutinizer of Federalist policies and actions. It was related to these efforts that Duane faced his first indictment under the Sedition Act.

Over the summer of 1799, he printed a claim in the *Aurora* that Adams and his administration had been bribed by British officials in making policy. The allegation cited a letter Duane claimed to have obtained in Adams's own handwriting that noted the existence of British influence in the selection of "an officer of the most confidential and important trust under the government."[89] Duane may have been referring to a May 1792 letter Adams wrote to Philadelphia lawyer Tench Coxe in which he supposedly noted that British influence had been exerted in the appointment of Thomas Pinckney as minister to Britain.[90] Duane was indicted, though his trial was postponed and the charges were dropped early in 1800. The printer later claimed that the fact that the charges had been dropped was proof of the truth of the allegation, despite later claims that the Adams letter had been a forgery.[91]

Duane nonetheless soon found himself back on the defensive for another news report, this time related to the upcoming presidential election. In February 1800, the editor printed news of a Senate bill proposing the creation of a special committee (composed of six senators, six representatives, and the chief justice) to review Electoral College ballots in the coming presidential election. The bill, which was ultimately rejected, was proposed in response to a deadlock in Pennsylvania as to the selection of electors.[92] Three Republican senators leaked the bill, which was backed by Federalists, to Duane who quickly exposed the story, casting it as an unconstitutional effort to rig the election. "We noticed a few days ago the caucuses (or secret consultations) held in the Senate Chamber," the article began.[93] Printing the bill, the paper declared it "an offspring of this spirit of faction secretly working" and suggested the effort was related to one in the state to diminish its say in the upcoming election.[94] In a curious move, Duane likened the faction he identified and the manner in which it worked as "in the perfect spirit of a jacobinical conclave" and warned that it could make of the American Constitution what the "self-created consuls" had made of the French constitution.[95] In casting the Federalist-led procedural modification to the electoral process as a Jacobin-like act, Duane was creatively flipping the script on his opponents. Throughout the 1790s, Federalists had lobbed the label of Jacobin at Democratic-Republicans. However, Duane put his finger on a major similarity between the Federalists and their avowed French enemies in pinpointing their use of secrecy. Federalists in the Senate were none too happy with his characterization.

Over the ensuing weeks, the Senate poured over Duane's report that alleged the existence of a secret committee working to fix the election. On March 4, Uriah Tracy of Connecticut (now a senator) acknowledged that it was legal to report on the proceedings, but he asked whether it was not a crime to "tell lies about transactions?" He maintained that because Duane reported that the bill had passed when it was merely under consideration, he had misrepresented the intentions and actions of members. If they could not punish the printer himself for the publication, Tracy urged an investigation nonetheless, by which "at least we can exercise the power of removing our officers, if we should convict him of a secret league to transmit intelligence which is confidentially entrusted to his care."[96] On March 20, the Senate resolved to summon Duane to answer questions and defend his publication of what they considered "false, defamatory, scandalous, and malicious assertions, and pretended information."[97] They declared that Duane had the intention to defame "the Senate of the United States, and to bring them into contempt and disrepute, and to excite against them the hatred of the good people of the United States."[98] His publication was tantamount to a "high breach of the privilege of this House."[99] Although Duane had incorrectly stated that the bill had already passed, the details about the piece of legislation were otherwise accurate. The Senate was thus essentially making an argument that it was improper to publish the contents of bills under consideration in the chamber, though it did so under the guise of the error of misreporting the status of the bill.

Duane did appear in the Senate four days later, only to be read the charges and voted guilty by the Federalist majority. After he was allowed two days to confer with his counsel, he did not return. Instead, he went into hiding until Congress adjourned. In the meantime, he continued to seek out and expose suspected Federalist wrongdoing. As the federal government gradually relocated to the new capital of Washington that summer and fall, he had no shortage of material to generate suspicion.[100] A fire in the War Department that broke out in November and another in the Treasury Department in January 1801 provided fodder for Republicans, who aimed to generate suspicion that Federalists were intentionally destroying incriminating material in anticipation of the election results.[101] Fears of violence and covert manipulation of the election were influenced by the memory of Napoleon Bonaparte's overthrow of the Directory government in France in the fall of 1799.[102] Over the summer of 1800 both parties had also held congressional caucuses, wherein they came together to agree on presidential candidates behind closed doors. These were treated with suspicion given their nature as extra-constitutional, back-room situations.[103] In the meantime, Duane was formally indicted under the Sedition Act for his publication of the Senate bill in October 1800. In the wake of the election that swept a Republican majority into Congress and ultimately put Jefferson in the White House, the will to pursue Duane ebbed, and the new president personally intervened to stop the case. Moreover, Duane had not been wrong to make note of the secrecy surrounding the presidential election.

The presidential election of 1800 was a test for the American Constitution and federal government. Conducted in an atmosphere of intense polarization, hobbled by a constitutional defect in the way elections occurred, and without precedent for a peaceful transition of power between parties, the event held all the makings of a crisis. To many on both sides of the political spectrum, the election seemed to represent a culmination of fears that the Constitution would not survive.[104] Though the electoral votes were not officially counted until February 1801, by the end of December 1800 rumors abounded that the election was a tie.[105] The Constitution dictated that in such a situation the decision was to be made by the House of Representatives. In this case, the House continued to be controlled by Federalists despite the thumping they had received in the elections. Suspicions mounted that the presidency would somehow be stolen.[106] Under these circumstances, the House set to deliberating behind closed doors.[107] Balloting in the House continued to produce a tie and, for a week in mid-February, representatives, in frustration, considered changing the process. Ultimately, they adopted new rules for balloting and agreed to limit the choice between Jefferson and Aaron Burr in the hopes of reaching a conclusion. This compromise finally put an end to the uncertainty when Jefferson was selected on February 17 and inaugurated on March 4, 1801.[108] It was fundamentally a tense, confusing process that was widely perceived at the time as marred by corruption and mystery.

With that, the "revolution of 1800" was complete and Jefferson was swept into office along with a sizeable Republican majority in Congress. What is most notable about this so-called revolution, however, is precisely that it was not revolutionary.[109] Instead, the election was carried out within the confines of the Constitution, despite the obvious deficiencies that made the process exceedingly complicated. The fact that the defects were worked out behind closed doors seems crucial to understanding how the constitutional structure held despite the irregularities. As Joanne Freeman has argued, the malleability of the situation was essential to achieving a resolution within the constitutional structure, and the outcome depended on friendship and personal loyalty rising above the politics.[110] This likely would not have been possible had not negotiations and decisions taken place behind closed doors. Unlike in France, where secrecy was used just a year earlier to overthrow the constitution and install a new order, in the United States it facilitated the endurance of structures with defects that would later be remedied through procedurally established channels.

Ironically, a man who was an avowed champion of publicity in representative politics was brought to power through a secretive process. Yet Jefferson, as countless historians and biographers have concluded, was a man whose life was rife with contradictions. The primary author of the Declaration of Independence, which proclaimed the ideal of equality, he also held more than six hundred enslaved people throughout his life, including some to whom he was related. He wrote of the inferiority of Africans with conviction and also fathered multiple children with an enslaved woman in his household, Sally Hemmings. Generally an advocate of restrained federal government, he nonetheless seized the opportunity during his tenure in office to purchase the Louisiana Territory, thus doubling the size of the country. His attitude about state secrecy and the proper function of representative government is no less contradictory. Throughout his public life, Jefferson constantly advocated publicity in government as the proper course and an invaluable mechanism to facilitate reflective representation. And yet he often strategically shied away from the public eye, operating behind the scenes and attempting to carve out a private sphere in which he could control policy debates and decisions. The contrast between his rhetorical commitment to publicity and his emphasis on privacy and confidentiality in his behavior effectively completed a process of redefining publicity in the American government from an active dialogue to a controlled, passive spectatorship.

Jefferson rarely wavered in his rhetorical commitment to publicity. Writing to the well-known journalist Mathew Carey in 1796 about his project to publish a history of the war of independence, Jefferson declared that he was "no friend to mystery and state secrets. They serve generally only to conceal the errors and rogueries of those who govern."[111] It was an echo of the stance he had taken throughout his time working as secretary of state in Washington's cabinet. Such a declaration was calculated in the sense that he was writing to a journalist whose stance on the question of publicity could be safely assumed. However, it is an important example of how Jefferson portrayed himself as a friend and champion of the people throughout his career. Disavowing "mystery" and secrecy were tactical ways of advancing this image of himself and his theoretical commitment to a reflective style of political representation, wherein public opinion was to play a directive role in government. His correspondence in the latter half of the decade is littered with disavowals of secrecy and with accusations that the Adams administration was stoking "passions & delusions" which "the federal government have artfully and successfully excited to cover it's own abuses & to conceal it's designs," as he put it in a missive to Madison late in the summer of 1799.[112]

The Virginian also had a number of pet projects aimed at enhancing the function of the federal government. Even before serving in the Continental Congress, he had been interested in parliamentary procedure and had studied it extensively.[113] When he took over as president of the Senate while serving as John Adams's vice president, he set to composing a manual of parliamentary practice, which he later published. It was a collection of the rules of the Senate and House, along with references to English parliamentary procedure as a way to supplement and fill gaps. "The President must feel, weightily and seriously, this confidence in his discretion; and the necessity of recurring, for its government, to some known system of rules, that he may neither leave himself free to indulge caprice or passion, nor open to the imputation of them," he wrote in the preface to the guide.[114] Jefferson was also heavily involved in the design of the new capital city of Washington, specifically the capitol building where Congress would meet. He was interested not only in procedure but also in the architecture of spaces where the legislature would meet.[115]

But there was another side to Jefferson as well. As the election of 1800 drew nearer and he worked to agitate against hostilities with France as well as the Alien and Sedition Acts, he consistently called for confidentiality in his communications. By 1799, Jefferson frequently lamented his lack of trust in the postal service, instead seeking out private couriers whenever he could or noting his suspicion about postal conveyance as a reason for his guarded letters. Writing to Gerry in January of that year in regard to his mission to France, Jefferson asked him "after reading it as often as you please to destroy at least the 2d & 3d leaves. The 1st contained principles only, which I fear not to avow; but the 2d and 3d contain facts stated for your information, and which though sacredly conformable to my firm belief, yet would be galling to some & expose me to illiberal attacks."[116] Highly conscious of what he was willing to tie his name to publicly, Jefferson was careful to instruct his correspondent to eliminate proof of some of his positions. As the election

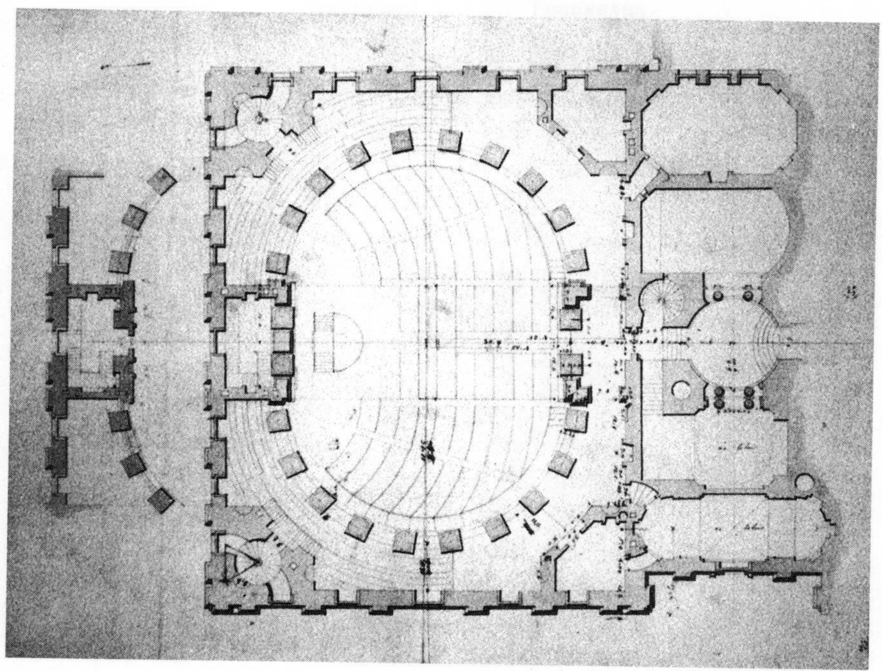

Benjamin Henry Latrobe (architect), "The United States Capitol, Washington, D.C. Plan, principal story of south wing," created/published between 1803 and 1814. (Source: Library of Congress)

drew nearer, he continued to carefully cover his tracks in disseminating "views which I am anxious should be generally exhibited," as he put it in a letter conveying pamphlets to Virginia Attorney General Philip Norborne Nicholas in the spring of 1800.[117] He trusted Nicholas "with the secret that these pamphlets go from me. You will readily see what a handle would be made of my advocating their contents. I must leave to yourself therefore to say how they come to you."[118] It was best he was left out of the story publicly. Instead, Jefferson sought to disseminate materials from behind the scenes to avoid public association with their contents. Concealed motives, covered tracks—these moves did not align with his avowals of the importance of publicity in the political process.

Still, contrast with the previous administration allowed Jefferson to convey the sense of a new direction. The new president took office in the wake of Adams's so-called midnight appointments, in which the outgoing president made a number of judicial selections in a last-minute attempt to ensconce Federalists in the judiciary. This action was easy to perceive as yet another attempt to violate the will of the people under cover of darkness. As Jefferson assumed office, he declared the dawn of a new day. Famously proclaiming that "we are all Republicans, we are all Federalists," Jefferson affirmed his conviction that the American government was the strongest on earth. "Sometimes it is said that man can not be trusted with the government of himself," he went on. "Can we, then, be trusted with the government of others?" A republic built on the foundation of reflective representation was the best way to safeguard the common good; trust was not to be assumed. Listing the "essential principles of our Government, and consequently those which ought to shape its Administration," Jefferson included "absolute acquiescence in the decisions of the majority," "the diffusion of information and arraignment of all abuses at the bar of the public reason," and "freedom of the press." These, among others, were the principles that had "guided our steps through an age of revolution and reformation," he said, and they ought to be "the creed of our political faith, the text of civic instruction, the touchstone by which to try the services of those we trust."[119]

In the early days of his presidency, Jefferson's victory was celebrated as a return to true republican principles, among them a commitment to publicity. Writing to the new president in July 1801, James Hopkins, a lawyer, drew a sharp contrast with the previous administration. "We know the Publick Good will ever be your Object," he declared; "the View of the People (when it is not fetterd or Deterr'd by Sedition Laws or Judiciary Persecution) will still Permit, thro' the Medium of a free Press, to the Means, as well as the Methods, of Promoting & Attaining the Desired End."[120] As the press was restored to its full function, the people's voice could again be conveyed to elected officials and thereby form the proper foundation for their decision-making. "Here then we see the Folly as well as the Wickedness of the late Administration!—by shutting up the Avenues of publick information or Deterring the free Citizens by Judiciary Punishments from speaking the Truth—they could not but expect, either to have no Information respecting the Opinions & Sentiments of the People, or to have them Represented in a False & Perverted light."[121] Hopkins viewed the Sedition Act as, at best, a way of perverting public opinion and, at worst, a means to entirely thwart it. Given these effects, the law fundamentally prohibited the Adams administration from reflecting the will of the people, thus rendering it fundamentally unrepresentative. His line of thinking calls to mind the critiques made of the Federal Convention having met in secret more than a decade earlier.

As president, Jefferson did decide to run the executive branch differently from his predecessors in distinct ways. Aiming to instill a sense of accountability and placing a high value in trustworthiness, Jefferson espoused an ethic of simplicity in government.[122] He was, by all accounts, deeply interested in the preservation of public documents, and he continued to make use of the partisan press to promote his policy positions publicly.[123] In general, Jefferson preferred decentralized government and had no taste for the trappings of society etiquette.[124] The *levées* and receptions characteristic of the Washington administration were roundly rejected. Jefferson viewed these occasions as sites of corruption, in no small part due to the presence and power of women in these spaces.[125] Instead, he made an effort to distinguish "society" as separate from the political sphere, entirely private and distinct.[126] His studied presentation of himself as a simple man of the people and his rejection of these often suspect locales of political activity were calculated to convey his commitment to publicity, accessibility, and straightforwardness in government.[127]

And yet the reality was much more complicated. Jefferson was more committed to publicity for show, as it were, than he was to genuine transparency. As Catherine Allgor put it, Jefferson maintained "iron control hidden under a velvet glove."[128] He blended his private social life with politics; his main mode of communication was through private, domestic visits, rather than official avenues.[129] Moreover, when he hosted dinners, the guests were only men and often of the same political party.[130] He served these dinners at a round table specifically to prohibit private conversations from taking place outside his observation. The president even took pains to employ deaf and mute waiters to guard against the possibility of leaks.[131] Jefferson held cabinet meetings in his private library in the White House, fostering the notion that appointed secretaries were invited at will into the decision-making process.[132] These were not the actions of a man who was dedicated to transparency. Despite his rhetorical stance on secrecy, Jefferson was quite clearly motivated to maintain it to the greatest extent possible in his administration as a method of control.

He also did a great deal to try to establish a boundary between the public and private life of an elected official. Despite projecting the image of a simple man, he led a shadow life with a family that included several children shared with Sally Hemings, a woman he enslaved. The relationship was initially publicly exposed in the 1796 presidential campaign through an anonymously penned article (by Hamilton) in the *Gazette of the United States*. It surfaced again during Jefferson's first term as president in an 1802 newspaper report and was taken up by Federalists as a way to undermine the president politically.[133] Jefferson never responded to the allegations publicly and worked hard to "make the Hemingses strictly a part of his private world," as Annette Gordon-Reed put it.[134] Starting in his presidency and stretching into his retirement, Jefferson closely guarded his private living quarters at Monticello behind multiple locked doors and later porticles that blocked views from the outside into his living space.[135] As Gordon-Reed argues, Jefferson "took the firm view that public officials should be judged on their actions as public men alone. His private life was not really the public's business."[136] This opinion has rarely predominated in American politics since.

While Federalists had generally remained committed to the use of secrecy as a way of protecting their vision of insulated representation through the 1790s, by the end of the decade that position was increasingly untenable. As publicity came to be routinely expected, the question of what it actually meant in practice came to the fore. Pulling back the curtain generally did not mean exposing all aspects of political decision-making to the public. When elected officials opened a scene for people to see, it tended to be curated for public viewing. As the federal government grew into an increasingly modern state apparatus, the spaces for secrets proliferated and the question of precisely where the political process unfolded became harder to determine. The proper place of secrecy in a representative republic remains, to this day, an open question in the United States, and one with profound implications for how we understand what it means to have a government that speaks for the people.

CHAPTER EIGHT

The Disastrous Effects of Publicity

The end of revolution in France proved more elusive than it had in the United States. Yet there were parallels. Like Jefferson's election, France's transition from the Directory to the Consulate—which Napoleon Bonaparte would soon dominate and overthrow—happened behind closed doors, in representative bodies. There were important differences, of course. Jefferson was elected within constitutional bounds, while Bonaparte and his allies executed a coup d'état; the Constitution was upheld in the United States but overturned in France; and Jefferson stepped down after eight years in office, whereas Bonaparte eventually crowned himself emperor. Nonetheless, focusing on the uses of secrecy and publicity through the latter half of the 1790s reveals some common threads in the way representative democracy was conceived of, and practiced, on both sides of the Atlantic. The gap between the celebration of publicity and practical use of secrecy in governing continued to widen. The result drained publicity and representative democracy of their more radical potential.

As many historians have pointed out, the Terror did not suddenly end with the fall of Robespierre.[1] It would perhaps be more accurate to say that he became a victim of the system that came to be defined as the Terror. The suspicion and calls for surveillance that had characterized the darkest days of the Year II persisted into the Thermidorian period. Though the leadership changed and the government apparatus adjusted, the rhetoric of publicity and vigilance was taken up by new orators with new ends. And just as it had in the Terror, this rhetoric remained at odds with a calculated use of secrecy in the governing process. Amidst a culture of unveiling and exposing past perfidy, deputies took steps to shield and insulate their work. In the days and weeks that followed Robespierre's demise, the gulf that had opened between the Jacobin leadership in the Convention and the popular movement of the Sans-Culottes and Parisian sections became a space in which curious realignments played out. Jacobin leadership had adopted a conception of representative politics in an insulated sense, in which reflecting public opinion was no longer necessary and thus secrecy was essential to governance. Though they denounced Jacobins and the government they had led, Thermidorian politicians in fact persisted with this insulated vision of representative politics, leaving disempowered Jacobins to take up the mantle of reflective representation again. After the fall of Robespierre, the divide between Jacobins within and outside government collapsed and they once again became a faction fighting for publicity, in an active form.

In the battle against them, Thermidorian deputies—many of them former Jacobins—struggled anew with the problem of legitimizing popular sovereignty through political representation. They faced the challenge of securing legitimacy for the government as a voice of the people while establishing stability amidst intense unrest and division.[2] With the Constitution of Year III, written and ratified over the summer of 1795, deputies redefined representative government once more. They restricted the franchise and refined the representative process, allowing much more room for secrecy. After declaring that two-thirds of the Convention would return to the legislature under the new constitution, many of them retained their seats. A government characterized by turmoil, political apathy, and bureaucratic expansion, the Directory emptied political representation of any sense that it was reflective.[3] At every level, officials worked much more extensively behind closed doors and moved to restrict the press repeatedly. Republicans, as the faction situated between royalists and neo-Jacobins was called, began to espouse the benefits of insulated representation. In doing so, they abandoned the rhetoric of publicity and began to explicitly theorize a utility for more secrecy in the representative process.

But this alignment of rhetoric and practice among Republicans would not stand. While neo-Jacobins continued to push for greater publicity to make political representation reflective again, another force was at work from afar. The victorious general who conquered much of Italy and occupied Egypt was shrewdly cultivating his image back home.

Bonaparte basked in publicity, deploying it to glorify his victories and foster personal loyalty.[4] No fan of reflective representation, he nonetheless harnessed publicity in the sense of broadcasting to a passive audience. When he returned to Paris, disaffected politicians saw him as the face of what they considered to be another necessary revolution—a chance to consolidate an insulated representative government. Unfortunately for them, the tool soon became the master.

The rolling of Robespierre's head sparked a culture of revelation. It was a period in which politicians and polemicists alike reasserted the press's role as a critical watchman to prevent government abuses. This championing of oversight and surveillance was bifurcated, however, between those who meant it and those who merely espoused it. In all cases, press freedom was posited against the excesses of the Jacobin government, which had closed its doors and restricted the press to a degree unseen since the outbreak of the Revolution. On the one hand, politicians refashioning themselves as opponents of the Terror took up the rhetorical mantle of vigilance, arguing that part of the way in which Jacobin leaders were able to perpetrate their projects was by hiding them. They were not wrong. And yet, these politicians were merely picking up the Jacobins' rhetoric and continuing their practices of secrecy within the government. Meanwhile, neo-Jacobins urged surveillance over the government and championed the free press from outside the corridors of power, directing their efforts at enforcing a reflective style of political representation. As they had throughout the Revolution, the meaning of surveillance and publicity differed depending on whether the individual espousing it was inside or outside the legislature. Deputies promoting the value of vigilance seemed to apply it backward chronologically, whereas those writing from outside made it an active force to be exercised over the current government.

Louis-Marie Stanislas Fréron, a character who would rise to leadership in the Thermidorian Convention despite having served as a *representative en mission* (a deputy sent to the provinces to evangelize) in 1793, immediately published a pamphlet in the wake of Robespierre's downfall that called for freedom of the press. All of France and Europe even, he declared, was awaiting an account of the deputies' conduct in the wake of the abuses that had come to light. The Convention should be embarrassed by what had happened, and in order to found the republic on solid ground, the time had come to expose misdeeds.[5] The Convention had finally unmasked Robespierre for the traitor he was and the moment was upon them to restore press freedom in order to continue their work of revelation. Moreover, it was the restriction of the press that had allowed Robespierre to commit the evils of the Terror. "If the press had remained free, this crowd of irreproachable citizens who, by [Robespierre] and his accomplices' orders were taken every day to prison, then the scaffold, would have had their voices heard; the details of all the horrors committed in the prisons would have been exposed before the eyes of a sensible nation."[6] Though they had never officially revoked the freedom of the press, Fréron asserted that, in practice, leaders had restricted it and thereby facilitated the Terror by hiding their actions. "Thus the tyrant at once choked the freedom of discussion that would have allowed the Convention to denounce him to the nation and the freedom of the press by which the nation could have denounced him to the Convention," he concluded.[7] "This terrible example teaches us how much the freedom of the press is necessary to intimidate, unveil, and arrest the plots of ambitious men."[8]

With such a stance, Fréron was ironically picking up the mantle of Jacobin polemicists like Marat and Desmoulins, who had earlier made similar cases about the utility of the press in exposing criminals and traitors. The press performed the crucial task of surveillance, without which ambitious and mysterious men could literally get away with murder. Later in his pamphlet, he went even further, declaring the free press to be a necessary component of representative government. Because it was impossible to convene all Frenchmen together to determine the general will, it had to be deciphered by a limited number of representatives sitting in a room deliberating. "By the freedom of the press," he reasoned, "this defect of representation is erased, or at least corrected: by it, the entire nation, even if it does not participate in the voting, can participate in the deliberations."[9] With a free press, "the representatives and the represented tend to continuously merge and democracy can exist in a nation of 25 million men though there are only 800 legislators."[10] The publicity of deliberations, made possible by the press, created a dialogue between elected representatives and those they represented, facilitating a reflective form of representation. It was an argument that recalled Brissot's in 1789 with the founding of the *Patriote françois* and Robespierre himself when he declared in 1793 that he wished it were possible to erect stands large enough that the entire nation could watch the deliberations of the National Convention.[11]

In this way, the Thermidorian Reaction did not represent a change in political rhetoric, so much as it was a realignment in terms of where it was directed—a point that has been made by many historians of the period. Fréron, who ran the most popular newspaper of the Year III (*L'Orateur du peuple*), "appropriated the radical language of the Terror to condemn the Terror," as Laura Mason put it.[12] As Mason shows, Fréron's newspaper "preserved the form and language of populist radicalism" all while he worked to disavow the legitimacy of club activity and exonerate the National Convention of any responsibility for the Terror.[13] In using the language of publicity and popular sovereignty to advocate the restriction of popular societies and bolstering of the government's surveillance power, Fréron was working to void the terminology of its radical origins and implications, instead rendering it the tool of an insulated style of political representation that would guide public opinion and survey the population for subversives.[14] However, in doing this, he was actually carrying on the project started by the Jacobin leadership during the Terror. Though Robespierre had continued to espouse the importance of publicity, in reality he was already running a government that worked largely behind closed doors, shaped opinion through a state-run press, and engaged in extensive surveillance. Fréron thus carried on the same jarring disconnect between rhetoric and reality that the Jacobin leadership had begun the previous year.

There were others, however, who were appropriating the language of revelation and publicity seemingly more to reclaim it from the projects of fallen Jacobin leaders. As restrictions on the press were lifted in the wake of the Terror, a proliferation of pamphlets took on the task of exposing the horrors perpetrated by the Committee of Public Safety and its *representatives en mission* in the provinces. A prominent example of this was Louis-Marie Prudhomme's multivolume *Dictionnaire des individus envoyés à la mort judiciairement*, published over the course of 1796–97. He promised to deliver charts and lists of crimes committed by every legislator, every faction, and to identify all the "victims assassinated judicially."[15] In the foreword to the first volume, Prudhomme declared that "this manner of writing history is completely novel."[16] He promised to unveil not just the crimes committed by those who had "succumbed under the weight of their own tyranny, but importantly the crimes of those who remain on the scene, and even those who continue to govern."[17] In a footnote to his declaration, Prudhomme asked the reader to recall the Constituent Assembly and how the representatives had tolerated Marat's abuses being hawked right outside their doors. "This assembly never formed itself into secret committee to take measures against journalists," he reminded his readers.[18] The government of the Terror—including those who remained in the current government—represented a fallen group who had distorted the principles of publicity, attacked the press, and worked to hide their evils from public scrutiny. His project was to restore publicity and surveillance over elected officials.

Those who published such catalogues of atrocities after 9 Thermidor were in many ways continuing practices that had been ensconced during the Year II.[19] Transparency, after all, had been an important pillar of the government of the Terror. Yet the purpose of such recordings during the reign of Terror was to display power and project fear—it was a publicity of passive spectatorship. The meaning of such publications changed after the fall of Robespierre. At that point, they became tools of retrospective transparency with an emphasis on revelation and vindication; there was a greater emphasis in this literature on classification and accountability.[20] Significantly, this material was published not by the government but by critics on the outside. Such revelatory literature was meant to shed light in an active, investigatory sense, as opposed to the symbolic and limited purpose of government record-keeping during the Terror.

A series of high-profile trials for perpetrators of what came to be defined as the Terror emerged from and fed into this renewed culture of unveiling. These began almost immediately over the summer of 1794 as a despised *representative en mission* formerly based in Nantes, Jean-Baptiste Carrier, was rapidly tried for gruesome acts he had overseen, including mass drownings in the Loire River.[21] Also put on trial that summer was Antoine-Quentin Fouquier-Tinville, the chief prosecutor of the Revolutionary Tribunal from 1793 through much of 1794. His trial similarly exposed a litany of "chicanery and manifold abuses behind the moralistic façade of revolutionary justice," as Howard Brown put it.[22] Just a few days after Robespierre was killed, another widely hated *representative en mission*, Joseph Le Bon was recalled from his post in the departments of Pas de Calais and the Nord and promptly arrested. Le Bon had many complaints filed against him even during the Year II, but powerful allies on the Committee of Public Safety had protected him. In the face of an effort to recall him in July 1794, just weeks before 9 Thermidor, Barère had excused his behavior by claiming that it was "not a good idea to look too closely into the actions of the representatives in the provinces," as Ronen Steinberg wrote.[23] This advice was completely disregarded in the wake of

Le Bon's arrest as a steady stream of pamphlets appeared recounting his alleged atrocities, including sexual violence.[24] The next summer, Le Bon was put on trial, during which he defended himself and refused to admit guilt for what he deemed acts to protect the republic. He was nonetheless sentenced to death just days before the Convention issued a general amnesty for "all acts related purely to the Revolution."[25]

Over the course of that first year after 9 Thermidor, the Convention would have preferred to move on, "to draw an impenetrable curtain over the errors in which the Convention and the entire people had been accomplices," as deputy Pierre-Florent Louvet advised.[26] But a stream of petitions and denunciations poured in, demanding retribution and justice. Despite some initial concerns that trying individuals would be akin to putting the Revolution, the Convention, and the French people on trial, deputies relented to pressure to provide some sort of justice by prosecuting individuals for crimes. These trials proved to be venues for airing grievances and constructing a narrative of exposure. The trials boiled down to a show of the government listening and responding to citizen grievances. They provided outlets for accounts of horrors, and the trials themselves—which happened in front of crowded galleries—served as a way for the Thermidorian government to gain legitimacy by marking a symbolic break with the previous regime despite the significant overlap in personnel that remained.[27] The trials ultimately allowed the Convention to repudiate the idea of collective responsibility and instead ascribe guilt to particular individuals who could be excised. They served as an official endorsement and indulgence in the culture of revelation and commitment to the publicity widely considered necessary to establish accountability and overturn the rule of the Terror. And yet, this approach proved temporary. Soon, the Convention granted a blanket amnesty and began to handle denunciations with quick expulsions from political positions as opposed to drawn-out public trials.[28] It was a trajectory away from publicity that the Convention followed in its own operations, too.

Within the legislature, there was initially a movement to unveil Robespierre's previously hidden perfidy and shine a light on it. At first, deputies maintained that secrecy was the element that had enabled him to carry out what they now deemed nefarious activities. In affirming the principles of the revolutionary government, the deputies declared on 14 Fructidor (roughly a month after 9 Thermidor in the summer of 1794) that Robespierre had perpetrated his system of Terror by maintaining different positions in secret and in public, "covering himself with masks, following the example of all usurpers."[29] As there had been with previous revolutionaries turned traitors, there was a thorough investigation of Robespierre's seized papers and a trickle of revelations based on discoveries made in the process. The Thermidorian deputies, like each successive victorious faction before them, positioned themselves in the role of investigators bringing to light hidden conspiracies. In March 1795, François Antoine de Boissy d'Anglas, a former supporter of Robespierre, rose to the speaker's bar to "unveil to your eyes; bring light into the paths of their thoughts, and to expose the secret of their plots."[30] The architects of the Terror had appealed to the passions rather than the reason of the people and had methodically worked to destroy the social order. It was time to expose the "odious mystery" to the people at large by detailing actions taken under the previous regime. Anglas called 9 Thermidor the turning point at which the "rays of justice and truth, pierced the thick shadows that obscured our political horizon."[31] The rhetoric of publicity undergirded the rejection of Robespierre's rule, implying a contrast with the Thermidorian government.

But outside the realm of retributive justice, Anglas's prizing of publicity—like that of Fréron—was not dominant. Nor was it practiced in the Convention, which maintained a continued commitment to limiting access to, and the visibility of, its proceedings. Pointing out the way secrecy was used during the Terror as a method to undermine the will of the people did not translate into disavowing it in present politics and, more importantly, it did not endure for long. In fact by late spring 1795, deputies charged with advising on how to reform the government came to blame publicity for the Terror, rather than secrecy. This line of thinking had arisen in the aftermath of Robespierre's fall, as the shifting whims of Parisian crowds renewed debates over whether an audience should be allowed in the chamber and whether members of the public could take the speaker's bar to petition. Once the question had been posed, some began to make the case that the audience might have been behind the Terror. In this account, the pressure of spectators in the convention—not the secrecy of the committee system—was to blame for the horrors of Robespierre's rule. It was thus first in the discussion of audience attendance at their deliberations that deputies began to propose that perhaps publicity was more to blame for the Terror than secrecy. By the summer of 1795, blaming publicity seemed to have overtaken the concern with secrecy, becoming foundational to the reform of the legislature.

The possibility that the audience played a role in the Terror was first raised just over a month after Robespierre's death. On 10 Fructidor (August 27, 1794), former Robespierre-supporter François René Mallarmé thundered that a constant stream of denunciations was coming from the Right and by that he did not mean his colleagues. "I am talking about the strangers who fill up a section of the chamber"; he likely gestured upward pointing to those in attendance that day. He went on to propose that no one without an explicit invitation from the Convention be allowed into the room, "especially not women."[32] Such a proposal a few years earlier would surely have been met with disdain, perhaps even a collective scoff. But times had changed. Jean-Michel Duroy, who would be executed nearly a year later, seconded his motion, asserting his shock that women especially were inside the chamber. "Since my return, I have been scandalized by the manner in which you hold your meetings; they resemble a public place where conferences are held," he went on. He pushed for barring the audience on the grounds that it was necessary for the Convention to "re-establish the dignity it warrants, that it cultivate the respect of citizens, and for this it is indispensable that it focus especially on its deliberations."[33] Concern with the effect of having an audience was bipartisan. After asserting that the guards had informed him that many of those in the audience were attending with access cards distributed by Robespierre, former member of the Committee of Public Safety Pierre-Louis Bentabole blamed disorder on spectators. "You must have remarked, like I have, that especially in important discussions, this room fills up with strangers, and part of the disorder that can sometimes reign in our deliberations is due to them."[34] Unlike previous conversations in 1792, in which Girondin deputies made efforts to change the composition of the audience rather than argue for barring it altogether, deputies no longer saw *who* was present as the heart of the problem. Though each faction was worried about adherents to the other side in the galleries, all agreed that the solution was to limit the audience altogether.

The problem, moreover, was not just that the public was disruptive but that there had been a calculated manipulation of the audience for political purposes. Another former member of the Committee of Public Safety, Jacques-Alexis Thuriot, claimed that the disgraced Robespierre, Couthon, and Saint-Just had distributed access cards to their agents, allowing them to regularly attend deliberations. "They sat among us, up above, in the middle, below," he went on, suggesting they had integrated themselves among the deputies. It was they, not deputies, who denounced elected officials and called for them to be sent to the revolutionary tribunals during the Terror. "They came here and followed us even after we left to follow all our proceedings, then they went to give an account to the tyrants they loyally served." Thuriot's theory served many functions: it displaced responsibility for the Terror from the Convention to external agitators who had supposedly infiltrated the body of deputies; it blamed commitments to publicity and access for undermining the authority of the elected government; and it insinuated that secrecy was necessary. When bad actors were "in on the secret of the government," they could manipulate it and lead representatives astray. His proposed solution was to bar anyone other than deputies and their employees from entering the chamber. This was decreed and it was further recommended that anyone who showed up with an access card who was not a deputy or authorized employee would be considered suspect. It was the hardest crackdown yet on access to the National Convention.

Restricting the publicity of the Convention's debates foreshadowed the way in which committees would be reaffirmed as necessary centers of confidential activity over the next year. Despite some disavowals of the use of secrecy, publicity was ultimately painted as the enemy when deputies considered restructuring the government in order both to build public trust and to promote efficiency going forward. Deputies insisted that attention should be turned from how committees worked to who was assigned to them. If those who were working on committees could be trusted, there was no need to introduce publicity into the process.

At first, when deputies discussed the future of the committee system, some were quick to raise the specter of secrecy as a threat to be avoided, despite the argument that it was necessary in particular realms. Reflecting on the government structure that had brought about the Terror, Jean-Lambert Tallien, a leader of the Thermidorian coup, noted that under a system in which there were no fixed rules, a committee that acted with secrecy, dispatch, and unity tended toward subjugation.[35] As they reconsidered the role of the Committee of Public Safety, however, many deputies reasoned that because diplomacy and foreign relations required secrecy to be successful, they should be placed entirely under the purview of that entity.[36] The committee had been created with these affairs in mind. Yet others echoed Tallien in questioning the necessity of such a mode of working. During the early years of the Revolution, Jean-François Rewbell reminded his colleagues, it had been partisans of tyranny who argued for the necessity of secrecy and since then, its use had gotten them nowhere. At the time, he recounted, its opponents had declared, "We can govern perhaps as badly as you without your secrecy, but never worse."[37] The case was the same today. In November 1794, deputy Paul Cadroy built on this argument, outlining Robespierre's use of secrecy to construct the architecture of the Terror. It was incumbent on the deputies to avoid a repeat of such uses of secrecy. He proposed that committees should be required to provide an account of all their activity, that "commissions and their agents no longer be permitted to use secrecy in their operations," and that representatives on mission in the provinces be required to report back to the Convention directly and regularly on their activities.[38]

But in general the committees continued to be granted a degree of secrecy in their work, especially the Committee of Public Safety. In renewing the committee on 18 Fructidor (early September 1794), no explicit mention was made of secrecy other than to note that the treasury would provide a credit for "secret and extraordinary expenses."[39] Although it is significant that the ability to work in secret was not explicitly delineated in the renewal of the committee, it was likely left out because it was assumed. As it had before, the committee appears to have continued working behind closed doors. Moreover, members defended this practice beyond the treatment of military or diplomatic affairs. As winter crept up on them and the food situation grew precarious, Jean-Jacques-Régis de Cambacérès, who would later be instrumental in the government of the Napoleonic Empire, assured the Convention that the Committee of Public Safety was working diligently on the issue. However, he reminded the deputies and the public that "it is infinitely delicate and even dangerous to speak of it."[40] "It is one of the parts of public administration that requires vigilant secrecy," he concluded, assuring the other deputies that there was not a single meeting of the committee that did not treat the issue. The same message—trust us—could just as easily been delivered a year earlier.

Nonetheless, controversy over the committee's use of secrecy was not entirely suppressed—in other words, trust had not been established. The question was raised anew in the spring of 1795 through a discussion about the way in which treaties ought to be negotiated and ratified. Some deputies held that the use of secret clauses in treaties was ill-advised, in part because they were often not kept secret for long and in part because it was the duty of the entire Convention to declare peace or war. "The French people should work like the Roman senate. There are no secrets to be kept," asserted the virulent anti-royalist Alexandre Edmé Pierre Villetard; "moreover, experience has proven that, even if we wanted to, secrecy would not be maintained."[41] Putting the ability to consider treaties in the hands of only a few deputies, he continued, would deprive the people and their delegates of the right to determine their own best interests. Other deputies echoed this concern, suggesting that allowing secret clauses opened the possibility of the Committee of Public Safety being the only entity in the know about the content of treaties. It could thereby run roughshod over the Convention as a whole. Furthermore, Villetard reiterated what Genêt had said when he had been in the United States two years earlier, asserting that, unlike the old ways of diplomacy, foreign affairs founded on justice would not need secrets.

But the reality, as many pointed out, was that secrecy remained a necessary component of diplomatic relations and it could, in fact, end up securing the people's interests better than publicity. Cambacérès complained that comparing France to the Romans was absurd, asking whether, like the Romans, they "debate on the public square?"[42] Moreover, eliminating the use of secrecy from diplomacy would require a change in the entire structure of diplomatic relations. In other words, if the French changed their ways, diplomacy would not work unless all other countries followed suit. Would the deputies really "want to refuse your government all the advantages that Pitt derived from the secrecy that covers all the operations of the British government?" asked former *deputé en mission* Joseph François Laignelot (now an ardent critic of Robespierre), referring to the British prime minister William Pitt.[43] It was an argument advanced by Federalists in the United States around the same time

Rather than limit the use of secrecy, many suggested the deputies should focus on appointing trustworthy individuals to serve on the committee. Whether the committee faced scrutiny of its operations or not, its responsibility would not be diminished, Cambacérès maintained. Essentially, transparency was not necessary to keep the Committee of Public Safety in check, a point Boissy d'Anglas made in the following days when he argued that the rotation of members on the committee would expose any dangerous secrets.[44] In fact, some deputies believed the goal of ensuring that the committee act in the public interest might actually be thwarted by greater publicity.[45] Emphasizing these points the next day, Louis-Marie de La Révellière-Lépeaux—who had been in hiding until 9 Thermidor and who would play a prominent role in the Directory—said that although some maintained that secrecy harmed the principles of democracy, it was in fact the opposite. "What is the wish of a people that names a convention to constitute a free government?" Undoubtedly, the people wanted that convention to take all reasonable, legal measures to pursue its best interests. Sometimes, he concluded, secrecy was necessary to arrive at "prompt and honorable peace," for example.[46] The Committee of Public Safety "knows better than anyone what is in the best interest of the republic," Jean-François Crassous argued.[47] Such an assertion is striking, given that the last eight months had been spent chronicling and denouncing the actions of that same committee. Once again, the idea was that trust could replace transparency, rather than being built with it. The deputies should focus more on whom they appointed to the committee and less on the way in which it worked.

The notion that trust could be restored in the Committee of Public Safety by focusing on the selection of members was central to the arguments made that summer for the value of investing power in a committee that worked outside the public eye. Late in the spring of 1795, Antoine Claire Thibaudeau, who had often voted with the Montagne but never joined the Jacobin Club, gave a report on behalf of a commission that had been created to recommend how to strengthen the current government. Once again, the commission's conclusions were surprising. As it was, the government was ineffective because activity was carried out within committees that were isolated from one another and thus sometimes acted in overlapping and contradictory ways. The solution, he went on, was to invest authority in a single committee: the Committee of Public Safety. Perhaps anticipating the backlash to such a suggestion, Thibaudeau recounted the origins of the committee, pointing out that it was never meant to replace the ministries in an executive sense; instead it was intended as a watchdog and orchestrator of administrative activity. "In effect, the Committee of Public Safety was created, in principle, only to replace the Convention in deliberations that needed to remain secret, such as those relating to military operations or foreign relations," he reminded the deputies.[48] Though the committee had surpassed its initial mandate, it was meant simply as a "council of state charged with the power of the Convention in matters not susceptible to public deliberation."[49] If it were confined to this role again, the committee could serve as the head of the government in situations not conducive to publicity, which appeared by the commission's estimation to be widespread.

A few days later, the commission came back with further recommendations for an interim government to be installed until a new constitution could be promulgated. The root of the tyranny that had reigned under Robespierre, explained the formerly imprisoned Girondin Pierre-Claude-François Daunou, was the "enormous influence given under the old government, to the deliberations of the National Convention and the destinies of its members."[50] It was not secrecy that had facilitated the Terror; excessive publicity was the culprit. This was an about-face from the rhetoric calling for exposure and blaming Robespierre's methodical secrecy in the days after his fall—though perhaps not a surprising conclusion for someone like Daunou, who had been ejected from the Convention and imprisoned following pressure from Parisian crowds. The commission proposed centralizing authority again and discontinuing the frequent late-night meetings of multiple committees, where Daunou said energy was wasted and "time that the government should be acting in secret and the legislature meditating far from tumult was lost in interminable debates."[51]

As the Convention discussed these proposals over the ensuing days, deputies advanced an explicit theorization of secrecy's utility to representative government. If his mode of operating is taken as evidence of his thinking, it may as well have been a theorization that Robespierre himself held but did not dare make public. "In all states, secrecy is necessary in most of the operations of government, in order to prevent obscure maneuvers and prepare successes," Frérrand maintained. It was not in banning secrecy that abuses of power were prevented, but in guaranteeing the proper personnel were invested with the power to keep secrets. Pointing out that the committees had not conspired since 9 Thermidor, Frérrand concluded that the "safeguard is in promptly renewing them, in the freedom of choice, in the freedom of opinions, and none of this existed under the decemvrit [the Terror]."[52]

Although the culture of revelation had been rhetorically co-opted by Thermidorians who were actually comfortable with keeping secrets, there were still left-leaning deputies, journalists, and members of the Paris sections who continued to claim vigilance as their raison d'être. For them, publicity and press freedom were not just tools to expose the wrongdoings of the past; they were necessary components of restoring reflective political representation. This reality highlights the distance that had opened between the Jacobin leadership on the Committee of Public Safety and the Sans-Culottes before the fall of Robespierre.

Those struggling to define themselves as Jacobins outside the confines of the Terror called for the Constitution of 1793 and repeatedly invaded the National Convention to demand food amidst famine conditions. Theirs was a vision of reflective representation, which they enforced partly by asserting their right to be present in the Convention chamber. Undoubtedly, these incidents influenced the deputies' ultimate rejection of publicity and endorsement of the importance of secrecy in the new constitution they ended up writing.

Establishing his newspaper shortly after the fall of Robespierre, a man going by the name Gracchus Babeuf took press freedom so seriously he called his chronicle the *Journal of Press Freedom*. Throughout its yearlong run, the periodical was oriented around the topic and the necessity of exercising surveillance over the government. In the prospectus, Babeuf made sure to note that even though Robespierre committed wrongs, there was still value to his ideas. Quoting the former Jacobin leader, Babeuf made a case for press freedom that could have been pulled directly from Fréron's pamphlet. "Especially under a representative government, which is to say when it is not the people who make the laws, but a corps of representatives, the exercise of [press freedom] is the only safeguard of the people against the scourge of oligarchy."[53] He went on: "the freedom of the press is the ONLY RESTRAINT on ambition, the ONLY METHOD to hold the legislature to the rule of legislation."[54] In citing Robespierre on this point, Babeuf was picking up the rhetoric of the Jacobins, just like Fréron. But unlike Fréron and the Jacobins at the helm of the government during the Terror, Babeuf was asserting its value in practice. Popular societies, he declared a few weeks later, performed the function of "exercising surveillance over the agents of social administration, redressing them when they mislead or when they tend to transcend the bounds of their mandates, making them know the general wish, which should inform the law."[55] Members of such societies were the people, he declared, "on guard, on watch to ceaselessly examine whether their agents are doing their will and not tricking them."[56] Babeuf became a leader in the Society of the Pantheon, one of the most prominent left-wing clubs of the Thermidorian period, which put him on the radar of authorities.

Though only representing one segment of it, Babeuf was part of a movement of avowed democrats struggling to redefine itself outside the Terror. Carrying forward a conception of reflective political representation that the Jacobins in the Convention and then the Thermidorians had decisively rejected, the popular movement continued to assert its presence. In the year or so following Robespierre's fall, the Convention was invaded three times by crowds disavowing its representative status and attempting to put forward their voices as not-so-gentle guides. The tumult began in the spring of 1795, just as the Convention was starting to profess more openly the value of secrecy and to defend the preservation of the Committee of Public Safety. Roughly two months apart, crowds led by Sans-Culottes invaded the Convention on 12 Germinal (in April) and then again on 1 Prairial (in May). The crowds, fueled by rumors that the government was organizing a famine amidst widespread food shortages, proclaimed their duty to rise up and make their demands.[57] The Prairial uprising turned violent as the crowds took over the deputies' seats and forced the passing of multiple decrees, killing a deputy in the process and parading his head on a stick.[58] These uprisings were seen by many as proof that "the people" were villains or had at least been led astray. The events stoked fears of a new Terror.[59]

In the wake of the Germinal uprising, deputy Antoine-Louis François Sergent likened it to the consequences of the Flight to Varennes for the late king; the representatives lost their legitimacy. Yet, he said, they had not to look to deputies in the Convention to blame for this. Rather, it had been the work of aristocrats and a secret society of *Feuillants* (referring to the *Club des Feuillants*, which had supported the retention of the monarchy).[60] Similarly, after the Prairial uprising, the Convention passed a proclamation declaring that those leading the insurrection had been secretly trying to overthrow the Convention.[61] The deputies subsequently purged a number of Montagnard members in an attempt to assign blame and reassert control in the wake of the crowd intimidation. Later in the fall of 1795, the Convention faced yet a third uprising in Vendémiaire (October). Partly in response to their declaration that two-thirds of the deputies would be returned to the new legislature, crowds once again threatened the chamber in the days leading up to the violent clash. When primary assemblies had convened to elect deputies in Paris, sections declared them to be sovereign in place of the Convention, which the sections argued was violating the sovereignty of the people with its policies.[62] Over the course of a week or so, crowds gathered outside the chamber, contesting the Convention's legitimacy as a sovereign legislature. The commotion culminated on 13 Vendémiaire when Bonaparte dispersed the crowds in an ominous precursor to the definitive rejection of reflective representation that was coming with the general's eventual ascent to power.

Ultimately, Thermidorian deputies were left with the challenge of straining to assert precisely what the Jacobin-led Convention had been aiming to establish, which was representation in an insulated sense. Their visions for society differed, but their conceptions of how political representation ought to be practiced were similar. As it conceived of what would come next, the commission charged with revising the Constitution of 1793 paid attention to the challenge of how to firmly redefine political representation as an insulated, passive process. Closing the doors and sealing off spaces of deliberation was no small part of this.

Over the summer of 1795, the deputies ultimately composed a new constitution aimed at stabilizing the situation in France and putting an end to the Revolution. As they combed through the proposed articles, the publicity of the sessions of the new Council of Five-Hundred (the lower chamber) elicited much debate. While the draft constitution stipulated that the sessions would be public, it limited the number of audience members to no more than half the size of the assembly. Some deputies replied that if the principle of publicity was upheld, the size of the audience could not rightfully be limited. "All citizens have the right to ensure first-hand that their proxies vote well," Louis-Joseph Charlier, a long-time Jacobin who had turned on Robespierre, declared.[63] But others responded that in fact the unelected did not need to watch their representatives work. Given that the entire population could not vote on laws, "I do not see why they would all come to the galleries of the body that proposes them," Boissieux pondered. In order for the legislature to make "wise laws," he continued, "they need to not have spacious galleries that trouble or command them."[64] The memory of the Terror, he said, proved this point. Former Girondin Jacques Antoine Creuzé-Latouche noted that "Robespierre said he wished the galleries could hold six thousand people; you know how he filled them."[65] Though their numbers were never so large, he reminded his colleagues how "they interrupted, yelled, threatened, and insulted all those who did not speak in support of their boss."[66] Admitting that the people had the right to prompt knowledge of what happened in the legislature, Boissieux suggested the proper way to guarantee it was through newspapers rather than audience presence. Though the proposed article maintained the possibility of audience attendance as long as it did not exceed half the size of the assembly, the idea of limiting publicity to the press as opposed to direct public presence was discussed more seriously than it had been up to that point.

The next article of the constitution explicitly provided for the possibility of shutting out the public and meeting in secret. This provision was a significant shift in procedural structure, as it provided for the first time since 1789 a regularized, legal method to close the doors of legislative deliberations. After Daunou noted the potential for the council to simply form itself in this secret committee constantly and thereby render null the publicity that gave it a "democratic character," the deputies shifted to discussing how voting would be recorded in such a session.[67] Article XLI of the constitution stipulated that all votes taken in a secret session would be recorded as roll call votes and published as soon as the need for secrecy had expired. But the article led to a more protracted debate about the aims of using secrecy in the legislature, where publicity was once again cited as a cause of the evils of the Terror.

Some suggested that requiring the publication of roll call votes would defeat the entire purpose of allowing a space for deliberation outside the public eye, which was necessary to avoid the kind of factional intimidation that had reigned within the National Convention. Louis Legendre, a Jacobin who had turned against Robespierre at the last minute, recalled the way committees had been renewed during the Terror because deputies were shamed and bullied into voting for their continuance. In order to ensure that deputies had the courage to vote how they genuinely wanted, roll call votes, he believed, should be banned entirely.[68] Indeed, the requirement to print roll call votes undermined the point of having secret sessions, Jean Denis, comte Lanjuinais, a steadfast opponent of the Montagnard faction, noted. The vote would already be taken by the time it was printed, so publication could not stop a bad decision and it would empower factions with the threat of public exposure. Moreover, he argued against the English model of allowing deputies to record their opinions on any issue in the legislative journal; this would only provide an avenue for factions to gain popularity.[69] "The liberty of the people can only be preserved by the freedom of opinion among its representatives, which can only be guaranteed in secret voting," claimed Jean-Baptiste Mailhe, who would develop royalist leanings. Once again, these deputies pointed to excessive publicity within the Convention—not the use of secrecy in the committees—as the cause of the Terror. To make decisions in the best interest of the people, representatives needed to be free to vote their conscience. Publicity of the deliberations and votes only empowered factional interests and intimidated deputies, which in turn undermined the people's interest. It was a theorization of secrecy's utility to the representative process that almost no one in French politics had dared make explicitly before that point.

A small number of deputies resisted the conclusion that secrecy would protect the legislative process, warning instead that it had the potential to undermine it. Jean-Baptise Quirot warned that after having defeated the worst excesses of demagoguery, they should avoid swinging too far in the opposite direction. "I fear that in keeping the operations of the legislature secret, we may facilitate the methods for an aristocratic faction to undermine the liberty of the people, by removing their ability to watch."[70] Most likely retreating into secret session to discuss war or to examine the conduct of executive power, the deputies would be free to dissemble and prevaricate on these important issues if their votes were not at least made public, according to some. Seizing upon this concern, Théophile Berlier suggested that they delineate the occasions upon which the council could legitimately go into secret session. Otherwise, aristocrats in the assembly would be able to manipulate and maneuver even more easily than if the sessions were conducted in public.[71]

Despite the worry about swinging too far in the opposite direction due to anxieties about the previous methods of working, the Constitution of Year III, adopted in the early fall of 1795, significantly expanded the authorized use of secrecy in the government. In this way, it reflected a shift toward open theorizations of the utility of secrecy to preserving representative politics. The meetings of both the newly created upper and lower chambers were declared "public," with the restriction that the size of the audience could not exceed half the size of the assembly, and their legislative journals were to be published.[72] However, voting in both chambers would be done first by asking deputies to stand; in cases of doubt, a roll call vote would be held but would remain secret.[73] Each chamber could convene in secret session at the request of a hundred members. The counterbalance that the councils could only discuss but not formally deliberate in secret session should be considered a hollow concession to those who were concerned about the lack of publicity. Like its American counterpart, the new constitution did not specify cases in which either house was allowed to go into secret session; however, there was one topic they were required to discuss only in secret: any accusation made against a member of either house.[74] All members were also bound to wear a uniform, and the legislature was barred from attending any public ceremonies.[75]

The internal procedures of the other branches of government were less explicitly outlined in the constitution. The five members of the Directory, who served as the executive and were chosen from among the lower house by secret ballot, likely worked behind closed doors by default as there was no mention of their deliberations being public. Though the executive body was made to appoint a secretary to keep minutes during its meetings, the members could also meet without him and record their own minutes on a separate register.[76] They were to appear in their official capacities only wearing the uniform assigned to them and were each to be accompanied by two guards.[77] When they sat in session, they were guarded by a corps of 120 men on foot and another 120 on horseback.[78] The Directory also had primary authority when it came to foreign relations, which included the right to agree to secret conventions and secret treaty conditions without the approval of the legislature.[79] The design of the Directory government was intended to set the executive apart from both the legislature and the broader public. From uniforms to restrictions on their public appearances and their extensive guard, the Directory was insulated to a greater extent even than committees had been earlier in the Revolution.

In practice, the institutions of the Directory began to operate in a much more systematic manner than earlier regimes, developing a highly regulated system for controlling access to legislative deliberations and segmenting work partly based on its visibility. The use of secrecy was repeatedly tied to the ambition to legislate with restraint and wisdom, as opposed to the earlier periods of the Revolution. In the way they used and discussed secrecy, members of the legislature and state-employed journalists began to theorize a utility for it, arguing that it was a boon in the representative system.

In addition to the uniforms worn by members of the legislature, all employees attached to the government had their own official attire. All secretaries were to wear a tricolor cordon with a medal attached to indicate their role. Messengers were to wear a long white jacket, blue belts and pants, and black hats with a feather in them; ushers would wear a similar uniform in black.[80] All employees thenceforth would be easily identifiable as such and their roles clearly indicated by their dress. Moreover, records of payment from the summer of Year V show that representatives were issued small medallions to use as entry cards in order to regulate their access to the chamber.[81] In meeting minutes taken on 27 Messidor in the Year IV (July 1796), the commission detailed the replacement of entry cards for representatives with small metal pieces, which "would have on one side the name of the representative and the

Sheet of entry passes for allowing people to access the area where the Directory met in the late 1790s. (Source: Archives Nationales [France], AN/C/455; photo by Joanna Hope Toohey)

designation 'representative of the people.' On the other side, it would say *Conseil des Cinq Cents*."[82] Access for journalists was also highly regulated. A document dated 17 Brumaire, likely in the Year IV at the outset of the Directory's work, established that "in order to be admitted to the journalists' tribune, each note-taker must give their names and addresses, as well as those of the journalist for whom they work."[83]

In the records of the Council of Ancients (the upper chamber), a long document lays out the composition of the guard charged with monitoring the chamber as well as the building and surrounding gardens. For almost every position inside the building, the guard stationed there was instructed to "let in only representatives of the people, secretaries with their cards, and ushers and *garçons de salle*."[84] In order to perform this duty, the guards were instructed to stop anyone claiming to be a representative who displayed an old entry card, which did happen.[85] In addition, secretaries and messengers were issued medallions with their roles emblazoned on them. On one occasion an individual without a medal who claimed to be an employee was stopped and held until he could be identified. This incident indicates a strict monitoring of the hallways around the meeting chamber.[86] Not only did guards keep a close watch on the interior of the building; records indicate a number of arrests of people in the surrounding gardens.[87] The guards were in regular contact with the Paris police to ensure they stayed abreast of security situations in the city and how they might impact the legislature they were charged with protecting.

Unlike denunciations, discussions of military and foreign affairs did not constitutionally have to take place in secret session, although they often did. Over the course of 1796–97, the Council of Five-Hundred went into secret committee fairly regularly to discuss treaty negotiations and developments in the colonies.[88] It is not always clear what exactly they were discussing in such closed sessions, but often the minutes specify that they were closing the doors to read a letter from the executive. Other times, officials acknowledged the pressures for publicity and worked to offset potentially negative exposure by compensating with speed. For example, a 1796 message from the Directory urged the council to counteract the publicity that was mandated for any measures proposed to the legislature by passing this particular action—the dispatching of agents to the West Indies—urgently.[89] The council voted to authorize the project and send it immediately to the Council of Ancients in order to hasten its adoption and reduce the intervening time period in which the country's "enemies" might hear about the plan.[90]

By far the most common reason for meeting in secret session under the Directory was to discuss financial affairs. Indeed, there were entire days in the legislative records where the legislature convened behind closed doors ostensibly to discuss such matters. Despite the frequency with which they did this, deputies were not always so sure that secrecy was the solution to the challenge of stockjobbers trying to profit from uncertainty based on the discussion of state finances.[91] In November 1795, conservative deputy Aaron-Jean-François Crassous stated his concern that bad actors were spreading word that the legislature was deliberating secretly to "hide the extreme embarrassment of the situation they suppose you are in, and that you are preparing violent measures to suddenly hit the citizenry."[92] As Villetard put it, there was no winning in this case. "Stockjobbers take advantage of the secrecy or the publicity of financial discussions equally," he advised. While Jean-Baptiste Mailhe believed that "nothing is more dangerous than speaking publicly of finances and diplomacy," he replied that the time had come to publish the financial plan they had devised behind closed doors. "It is even more dangerous to keep secret for too long the plan adopted," he reasoned. Having reaped all the benefits they could from working in secret, Charles François-Gabriel Morrison agreed that at that point, the plan was either good or it was bad. If it was bad, "in order to judge it, it is necessary that we collect the external light that good citizens can shed on it."[93] A few days later, there was another attempt to prevent the legislature from closing its doors to discuss the financial situation; a deputy unnamed in the record suggested that it was only by discussing the state of affairs publicly that those trying to sow suspicions could be silenced.[94] Despite repeated pleas that they finally open the discussion to public view, the council continued to deliberate in secret session over the next few months, at the urging of deputies who argued that exposing financial details would empower stockjobbers and weaken the position of the state in the eyes of citizens and foreign powers.[95]

Early on in the existence of the Council of Five-Hundred, a report in the government-sponsored *Moniteur* framed the lack of reporting on the legislative deliberations surrounding finances as something to be grateful for. The people were "impatiently awaiting the result" of the council's secret deliberations about a new financial plan, and it was a good thing they were being made to wait. The report noted that the Revolution had "too often lent to the representative corps a rapidity which was rendered dangerous by the unity of its composition." Hasty and unwise laws had been passed as a result and it was time the legislature delivered carefully considered, measured laws passed only after thorough reflection. If anything ought to temper the anxiety over the new financial plan, "it is the confidence inspired by the wisdom and slowness that the legislature is bringing to its deliberations. This slowness is already one of the main benefits of the constitutional order," the report pronounced. Under previous regimes the publicity of discussions about finances had always weakened public credit. "The secrecy of its deliberations has already guaranteed against the first inconvenience. It is up to the wisdom of the legislature to shield us from the second," the *Moniteur* concluded.[96] Here, the official newspaper of the government was casting the use of secrecy in the legislative process as a positive. Not only did it protect the economy from the vicissitudes occasioned by open discussions of state finances, but also, more significantly, it essentially bought time for representatives to reflect and deliberate. The use of secrecy in legislative deliberations led to wise and beneficial laws—a conviction that calls to mind James Madison's early writings in *The Federalist Papers*. This was a marked shift from the previous widespread championing of publicity as the only safeguard of the people.

Along these same lines, a tract published in the *Moniteur* on 4 Frimaire (late in November 1795) signed by "Trouvé" urged the people to have patience with the new government. Consider the dedication with which the legislature was meditating on the causes and remedies of the challenges facing the republic, the author urged. "Discussions of this importance, in which wisdom and secrecy presides, can only have happy results," he reassured readers. This kind of valorization of secrecy aligned with a revolutionary fatigue that was settling in after years of tumult. In a tract published in 1796, Benjamin Constant concluded that the greatest threat to the republic came not from external enemies but from "certain revolutionary habits, which reverse all principles, pervert all opinions, and weigh on the whole of society, and every individual, all the time and in all forms."[97] One of those habits was keeping what he called an excessive watch over government. While this may have been useful under despotic governments, it was too intense for a revolutionary or nascent government finding its footing.[98] Constant, a Swiss-French political writer and later opponent of the Napoleonic regime, urged readers to trust and be loyal to the representative government in place. In reasoning that carried strong echoes of Madison's writing on the idea of an extended republic in *The Federalist* No. 10, Constant praised the "sublime discovery of representative government." While maintaining a republican form, it could moderate its tendencies and possibly establish a just middle course.[99] Moreover, the vaster the republic the better, as "the scope of the topics make small passions disappear, exclude small media, and put between men a distance that allows them to limit their differences, their personal interests or jealousies."[100] Like Madison in the 1780s, Constant made the case for the value of distance and the insulation of representatives in order to stabilize government and ensure wise decisions. In short, insulated representation, rather than a reflective style, was what the French should aspire to; excessive publicity and surveillance had been detrimental.

But patience and trust proved elusive. Neither royalists nor a resurgent left-wing movement trusted the Directory. And their reasons were not unfounded. Concerned with the threat of being overthrown from either side of the political spectrum, the executive leadership of the Directory restricted popular influence. Repeatedly, the Directory emphasized that the people did not know what was best for themselves, as they invalidated election results and removed elected officials from office when they saw fit. Taking advantage of a constitutional provision allowing for the suspension of press freedom, the Directory also cracked down on publishing. It further built on a constitutional disavowal of popular societies to divest them of political power over the course of the regime's existence. By suppressing any belief that representation was a reflective process, the Directory divested itself of legitimacy based on this conception.[101] Some historians have pointed to a revolutionary fatigue as part of the reason why the Directory may have been able to advance this more insulated vision of representation that previous revolutionary regimes were unwilling to express and certainly unable to enact.[102]

In response to threats and instability—both perceived and sometimes real—the Directory invoked on more than one occasion a provision in the constitution allowing the government to abridge the freedom of the press for up to a year. Tellingly, those who argued for the abridgment focused on the danger of the press violating state secrets as the discretion that demanded restriction. Roland Gaspard Lemérer, who would later turn against the Directory, argued that even though suspending freedom of the press for a year appeared to be a violation of its constitutional guarantee, the possibility certainly implied that the government had the ability to punish abuses of press freedom. He defined such abuses as publications that advocated "pillage, massacre, or the dissolution of the government" but, curiously, added that "in this class, I would also include writings in which state secrets are divulged after being obtained."[103] Though he believed this act could be punished under the penal code against those who threatened the security of the state, it is also revealing that he classified it as among the worst possible abuses of the press.

Still, some deputies stood against abridgments of press freedom, pointing out its importance in a republic. As they discussed restricting the press in the spring of 1796, moderate deputy Emmanuel de Pastoret suggested that one either had to "maintain that heads of state were infallible, or permit them to be censored."[104] Without a free press, "who would publish their errors, their offenses, their crimes?" It was a defense of the importance of the press to representative government that harkened back to the early days of the Revolution. To support his point, he cited the American government. "Read the codes of all free peoples: It is above all against the government that the faculty of writing is guaranteed," he went on, citing the Pennsylvania state constitution and the American Bill of Rights. "Explaining frankly the acts of the government is a service to the country and its liberty," he concluded.[105] The next day, Cadroy bolstered Pastoret's argument, contending that "the press should keep up with the speed of events, it is the main method of abridging distance and rendering immediate all the thoughts within a large empire."[106] It was the press that made representative government possible across a vast territory, permitting an ongoing dialogue and development of ideas. Yet, despite proclaiming that "it is only for tyrants that this speed, publicity, and unity becomes terrible," Cadroy carved out an exception. If the press divulged state secrets and thereby compromised the outcome of a government plan, the freedom of printing could be justifiably diminished temporarily. "We would thereby justly stop a paper destined to publish a state secret lifted from the Directory's cabinet."[107]

Despite some scruples about suppressing the press, the Directory moved to do so, along with clamping down on the activity of popular societies. That these measures were aimed at establishing a version of insulated representation and rejecting reflective representation is clear in the context of their broader crackdowns. The Directory's efforts at repression were directed at suppressing both radicals on the left and royalists on the right. In the spring of 1797, after a long public trial, the leader of a left-wing movement in favor of the Constitution of 1793 was executed. After the Society of the Pantheon was dissolved in 1796, Babeuf went on to found a secret council to plan an uprising aimed at overthrowing the Directory and reinstating the Constitution of 1793, which the group considered the most legitimate constitution available because there had been a popular vote on it. Just days into planning, the leaders were arrested, and they were tried and convicted the next spring—a death knell to the left-wing movement. Later that fall of 1797, after elections put a large number of royalists and counter-revolutionaries in the legislature, the Directory launched a purge of 130 deputies, deporting them to Guiana. What came to be called the Coup of 18 Fructidor was a powerful and violent rejection of reflective representation. It was also a harbinger of things to come as the military was employed to essentially overturn the results of a popular election. In their efforts to end notions of reflective representation, the Directory normalized a state of exception, paving the way for an authoritarian takeover.[108]

The Directory ended with a whimper, as Napoleon Bonaparte seized power with the support of the Abbé Sieyès to establish the Consulate, a brief government preceding the general's crowning of himself as emperor in 1804. Viewing the popular general as a tool to establish the type of insulated representative government he had long advocated, Sieyès attempted to use Bonaparte only to be cast aside himself.[109] The consolidation of power at the conclusion of the French Revolution ultimately went far beyond the installation of an insulated representative regime. Bonaparte came to centralize and even personify power that was entirely directive, with no meaningful pretense of democracy.[110] David Bell has identified Bonaparte's style of rule as part of a pattern of charismatic leadership during the Age of Revolutions, unique in the extent to which it was personalized and failed to transfer to institutions.[111] Essentially, Bonaparte worked to establish a new type of representation, which was certainly insulated, but even more than that, personalized. Yet even as emperor, the general knew his power relied on popularity and, lacking any divine or hereditary sanction, he continued to hold plebiscites to at least gesture toward the continued presence of popular sovereignty.[112] Nonetheless, there was no talk of democracy. France needed not a democracy, but a savior. In the process of consolidating his power, Bonaparte relied on a particular form of publicity. Shutting the real work of government off from public view, he instead projected a calculated and controlled image of himself as unifying.[113]

This transformation began in the fall of 1799. On the 18th Brumaire, both houses of the legislature voted to convene the next day in Saint-Cloud, outside Paris, due to a supposed Jacobin threat. On the day of the coup that overthrew the Directory, the session of the Council of Ancients began with deputies demanding to know why the sessions had been moved from Paris. A back-and-forth ensued about whether they should go into secret session to discuss the move. Eventually Bonaparte appeared in the chamber. "Of course it is necessary to explain," he declared; "names must be named and I will do so."[114] He proceeded to declare that two of the Directors had proposed putting him at the head of a party that would be directed against men with liberal ideals. In response, a cry arose to close the doors and hear the speaker in secret session. This was met with requests to keep everything public. "Because General Bonaparte has come to denounce a conspiracy and conspirators, everything must be done in front of France," Pierre-Clément de Laussat, who would serve in the imperial government, declared. After Joseph Cornudet, who had collaborated with those executing the coup to move the meetings from Paris, stated that "there was nothing more to hide after what he had said," the chamber elected to keep its doors open.[115] Yet there was no one there to watch, since the session had been moved from the capital in anticipation of the regime's overthrow.

Sieyès, dating back to 1789, had a particular vision of insulated political representation that he was enforcing with this move as well. With the Constitution of 1799, the leaders of the Consulate declared the Revolution over. In some ways, it finally was. France entered a state of exception that lasted some sixteen years, which rendered it no longer exceptional.[116] The people were consigned to a passive role; surveillance became an activity of the state and publicity came to signify a broadcast of patriotic material rather than a dialogue. In this way, Napoleon would accomplish what many in 1789 had aimed to do themselves. In a proclamation issued by the incoming consuls on December 15, 1799, the constitution was deemed the end of the "in-certitudes" of what they referred to as the provisional government. "The Constitution is founded on the real principles of representative government," they declared, seeming to reject definitively any notion of reflective representation. Instead, the nation's representatives would lead from a distance with the strengthened power "necessary to guarantee the rights of citizens and the interests of the state." With their concluding line, the consuls pronounced on the values motivating the Revolution: "Citizens, the Revolution is fixed upon the principles that started it: it is finished."[117]

The Constitution of Year VIII, drafted at the end of 1799 and approved by plebiscite in the winter of 1800, did not appear on its face to limit publicity to a greater extent than before. In fact, it restricted the use of secrecy in the legislature to specific cases. In the upper house of the legislature, the Tribunat, discussions could take place in secret committee, when the government requested it, but only when they had to do with "declarations of war and treaties of peace, of alliance, or of comerce."[118] Otherwise, the "meetings of the Tribunat and those of the legislative body are public; the number of attendees in either cannot exceed two hundred."[119] Yet, in addition to restricting the number of people allowed to attend the deliberations, the constitution also established that the members of the lower house were to vote by secret ballot on all laws presented to them by the Tribunat and government, without discussion.[120] In short, there was not much need to maintain secrecy in the legislature because it did not do much. Meeting for only four months a year unless otherwise convened, the legislature was no longer the locus of political decision-making or governance. The Senate, which was a permanent body of appointed elders that served as a sort of constitutional arbitrator, met explicitly in secret.[121] And above that, the three consuls—referred to in the constitution as "the government"—were the source for all laws and no reference was made to them working in public or secret.

Bonaparte himself had become a master of a new type of publicity even before the coup that put him in power. From when he took over command of the army in Italy in 1796, the general diligently crafted his image as superhuman and therefore trustworthy.[122] The general availed himself of newspapers, paintings, and public performances surrounding him personally.[123] While in Italy, he apparently took to dining in front of an audience similarly to the French court at Versailles in the pre-revolutionary period.[124] When he returned from his ill-fated but ambitious campaign in Egypt just before the coup of 18 Brumaire in the fall of 1799, he was welcomed in Paris as a hero.[125] Once he came to political power, Bonaparte cracked down on the press with a strict censorship regime and his own propaganda efforts gained the force of the state.[126] Like Thomas Jefferson across the Atlantic, Bonaparte emphasized his connection with and affinity for the common people. But unlike Jefferson, Bonaparte made no show of being one of them. Instead, he portrayed himself, and was generally seen as, somehow perched above them: a genius leader, savior, and securer of glory for France.[127] When he returned from Egypt in 1799, one pamphlet described "all the citizens hurrying, rushing in tumultuous floods to see him as he passed, their eyes looking everywhere for him, gazing avidly at him."[128] The people were, finally and firmly, mere spectators.

Attitudes about secrecy in government had taken a curious path in the years after the Terror until the rise of Napoleon Bonaparte as emperor. Though initially deputies identified secrecy as part of the reason the Terror had been possible, it soon took on an important place in the Thermidorian government. As the deputies set up the government of the Directory, secrecy was even theorized as a positive tool to preserve representative government. Importantly, those who made the case for its utility were advancing an insulated style of representation, in contrast to the reflective representation that advocates of publicity had long desired. For the first time since 1789, revolutionaries were beginning to align their practices with the conception of political representation they aimed to establish. Insulated representation was all the more desirable after years of tumult and violence. Representatives were now simply telling the French people to trust them. And despite the uprisings led by those who clearly did not, eventually a majority were willing to take a gamble on a man who finally seemed trustworthy. Bonaparte's rise demonstrated the extreme of insulated representation—a complete vacating of democratic elements and personalization of representation in one individual.

Publicity, meanwhile, came to be cast as the cause of the worst excesses and abuses of the government led by Robespierre. This about-face was possible because Jacobins in leadership, like Robespierre, had never wavered in their rhetorical commitment to publicity, despite closing the doors and shutting down the press in an effort to establish insulated representation. Though the reintroduction of secrecy throughout many aspects of governance ultimately played an important role in the demise of representative democracy in France, the deputies who critiqued publicity did not entirely miss the mark. Ultimately, the Napoleonic regime—a decidedly anti-democratic one—relied on publicity to secure its legitimacy and perpetuate the emperor's personal power. Still, it was a new kind of publicity that enabled the general's rise, one less akin to transparency and more like propaganda. In this way, the end of the French Revolution marked the birth not so much of representative democracy, but of modern authoritarian government.[129]

Epilogue
Democracy Dies in Darkness?

As Jeremy Bentham sat writing instructions for the upcoming French Estates General in 1789, he saw few gray areas when it came to the imperative for transparency. Aside from three exceptions—in cases where it would help an enemy, unnecessarily injure innocent people, or inflict too severe a punishment on the guilty—publicity was always better than secrecy. There were six main reasons for this: first, to ensure members of an assembly did their jobs; second, to secure the confidence and assent of the people; third, to "enable the governors to know the wishes of the governed"; fourth, to "enable the electors to act from knowledge"; fifth, to allow the assembly members to benefit from "the information of the public"; and finally, for "the *amusement which results from it.*" Only three types of men, Bentham asserted, ever opposed publicity: "the malefactor," "the tyrant," and the "timid or indolent man."[1] Distilled in this one short section of his treatise were the most common arguments circulating during the late eighteenth century in favor of greater publicity in government, particularly in a representative democracy.

Bentham went on to address the most common objections to publicity—from the notion that the people were too ignorant to understand what they would see to the fear that elected officials would either face undeserved disdain or be reduced to constantly courting popularity. All such concerns would actually be allayed by more publicity, he proposed. Legislatures should take care to publish "the tenor of every motion," "the tenor of the speeches or the arguments for and against each motion," the issue of each, the number of votes on each side, the names of the voters, and the information upon which the decision was made.[2]

Little should be left to the imagination. Here, he turned his gaze across the Atlantic: "The American Congress, during the war of independence, was accustomed, if I am not deceived, to represent all its resolutions as unanimous."[3] Likely referring to the practices of deliberating behind closed doors and publishing limited journals, Bentham sought to disabuse American politicians, and others looking to their example, of the notion that withholding information accomplished their goals. "Its enemies saw in this precaution the necessity of hiding an habitual discord. This assembly, in other respects so wise, chose rather to expose itself to this suspicion, than to allow the degrees of dissent to the measures which it took, to be known."[4] Secrecy, although intended to bolster public confidence in the body's actions, would only tend to undermine it in the long term. The only problem for Bentham's theory was that, in this case, secrecy actually did appear to have more or less served its intended function. Still, he concluded, "though this trick might succeed in this particular case, this does not prove its general utility."[5]

Over the course of the late eighteenth century, state secrecy generated suspicion. Many British, American, and French thinkers valorized publicity in government, especially as a crucial component of representative politics. Once revolutions broke out aiming to establish political representation as a tool of popular sovereignty, the question of secrecy and publicity in government assumed central importance in the construction of new regimes. Thinking about these issues was muddled as secrecy and publicity became imbricated with theories and practices of representative politics. In the decisions revolutionaries made about the place of secrecy in government, and in the debates those decisions engendered, we can trace an underlying contest over the very function of political representation. Moreover, focusing on changing practices shows how the idea of representative democracy evolved and was shaped through the experience of its implementation.

In his conclusion about the American Continental Congress—which could be aptly applied to the Federal Convention of 1787 or the early national Senate or executive administration—Bentham was only half right. In some sense, the American, particularly Federalist, use of secrecy to shield much of the process of governing from public view was a trick, even if not a malicious one. Secrecy was considered useful for implementing the type of insulated representative government many of the Constitution's framers envisioned, wherein representatives were made legitimate by being elected and were thereafter to determine the best interest of the people without facing popular pressure. It was conceived of as one method, among others, of creating space between elected representatives and the public so that they would be able to make decisions for the common good of the nation without having to constantly reflect the shifting opinion of an ill-defined body of "the people." This use of secrecy also necessarily limited membership in "the people" being represented to those with a vote, which ended up excluding almost all Black men, all women, and even poorer white men.

Contrary to Bentham's assessment, the strategic use of secrecy did tend to cement the legitimacy of representative government more than undermine it. By employing secrecy—particularly in the form of closing doors, limiting reporting on deliberative bodies, and controlling the flow of political information to the public—early American politicians reinforced in practice a version of political representation that ultimately limited popular involvement in the day-to-day political decision-making process. Though the use of secrecy was justified during the war as primarily necessary due to the military and diplomatic exigencies of the situation, it was in fact employed in all realms of government work with the effect of empowering representatives to pursue policies without continually consulting public opinion. In framing the Federal Constitution, deputies—many of whom were concerned that the state legislatures of the 1780s were too responsive to popular pressure—again emphasized the utility of secrecy to insulating deliberations from undue external influence. And in the government they outlined and defended through the ratification debates, Federalists also guaranteed a capacious provision for the use of secrecy. The Washington administration, and its Federalist supporters in Congress, strategically shielded aspects of the political process from public view to aid in carrying out policy decisions that might not be popular but were, they believed, in the best interest of the country. The effect was to stabilize the representative government by removing the possibility of constantly exposing rifts between the decisions of elected officials and public opinion. The cost of this stability was exclusion—of those without the right to vote, including especially an entire segment of the population within the country that remained enslaved. And for some, like James Madison, who started out as a Federalist believer in the utility of secrecy to guaranteeing stable, insulated political representation, the political challenges of the early republic tested that view. Madison's shifting stance in the face of these developments is a reminder to look beyond government decisions at the debates to which they gave rise.

In fact, a Federalist vision of political representation based on a passive citizenry was not simply imposed or quickly entrenched. Rather, in debates over the proper use of secrecy and the definition of publicity in politics, we can see how the meaning of representative government was contested and continually reshaped through political practices. A persistent critique of the government's use of secrecy was embedded in challenges to the definition of representative institutions as tools of popular sovereignty in the early national United States. Starting during the War of Independence, a number of state constitutions guaranteed the publicity of legislative assembly meetings as a core component of their representative function, in the sense of guaranteeing ongoing accountability of elected officials to public wishes throughout the legislative process. During the ratification debates in 1787–88, Antifederalists criticized the Constitutional Convention for having met in secret and withheld records of its deliberations, suggesting these behaviors limited its ability to claim the people's voice. As proponents of a more reflective type of political representation, wherein elected officials were to mirror public opinion throughout the political decision-making process, Antifederalists identified secrecy as a tool used to undercut this relationship. In the 1790s, this critique was carried forward principally by Democratic-Republicans, who seized on the Washington administration's use of secrecy to challenge the implementation of policies with which they disagreed. Persistent efforts to open the deliberations of the Senate to a public audience and reporters, for example, led to a significant shift in 1795 that validated in practice a more responsive style of political representation in the new republic.

In France, though many deputies in the National Assembly subscribed to a conception of insulated representative politics similar to that of the Federalists in the United States, they adopted a much more comprehensive commitment to publicity, along the lines of what Bentham urged.[6] But this did not turn out as Bentham might have predicted it would. Rather than strengthen the legitimacy of the deputies as a voice of the people, publicity contributed to the erosion of their validity as representatives. By nurturing a competing conception of political representation as necessarily reflective of public opinion, publicity empowered the unelected to constantly question whether their elected officials were speaking on their behalf. How could it be so when they often seemed to disagree with what appeared to be public opinion? One major decision in particular—maintaining Louis XVI on the throne after his failed flight in 1791—seemed to show that the elected representatives were acting of their own accord, that they were not adhering to the expressed wishes of those on whose behalf they spoke. The ambiguity over what publicité meant in practice led the unelected to assert an active style of vigilance over representatives, which facilitated the vision of political representation as an ongoing dialogue between the elected and a potentially inclusive, but functionally limited, public. Ultimately, the deputies' commitment to working in view of the public invited ongoing oversight and undercut the implementation of the insulated type of political representation they had originally envisioned.

When secrecy was reintroduced in the French government during the Terror, it was part of an attempt to change the way political representation worked in practice. In doing so, Jacobin leaders were asserting in practice a theory of insulated political representation that had been articulated in the summer of 1789 and across the Atlantic by Federalists in the United States. If representatives were to be elected and then determine the best interest of the people without facing ongoing external influence, a certain degree of secrecy was necessary to insulate them and to set them apart from the people. By 1792, both Jacobin and Girondin leaders identified resistance from factions in the provinces and relentless popular pressure from Parisian radicals, respectively, as threats to their claims to speak on behalf of the people. As Jacobins seized power in 1793, they claimed that if public opinion was not aligned with their actions as representatives, it was merely because the public was not enlightened. As a representative government, it was their duty to lead the people, to guide the public in the nation's best interest, as determined by deputies in Paris. They affirmed a narrower definition of publicité as a strategic broadcast of information by the government to the public, and they began to deliberate in greater secrecy, most notably in the Committee of Public Safety. But employing secrecy and limiting the meaning of publicity after the legitimacy of political representation had been undermined by near constant claims that elected officials did not reflect the will of the people made the reintroduction of secrecy appear to be nothing more than a trick, as Bentham had labeled it.

While in France secrecy was reintegrated into the operations of the government over the course of the 1790s, across the ocean the balance of secrecy and publicity in government tended to tilt in the opposite direction. The American government gradually opened doors—from allowing public access in the House of Representatives in 1789 to the extension of this practice to the Senate in 1795 and the eventual rejection of press regulation going into the nineteenth century. Though the 1798 Sedition Act aimed to restrict speech critical of government, these last years of the eighteenth century in the United States are most accurately understood as final efforts to resist a swelling tide in favor of greater publicity in politics. With the election of 1800 that put Thomas Jefferson in office as president, a Democratic-Republican vision of reflective representative government came into power, even though the extent to which his administration lived up to this vision in practice is questionable. What is sure is that Jefferson's election, and the concurrent ushering in of a hefty Republican majority in Congress, signified a rejection of the Federalist vision of representative government as an enlightened group of men deliberating at a distance from popular influence.[7] The United States emerged into the nineteenth century as a representative republic that would undergo a fitful and uneven "rise of American democracy."[8] Still, Jefferson's continued rhetorical commitment to publicity, like his promotion of reflective representation, should not be taken at face value. In reality, the American democracy of the nineteenth century was one that had been voided of its more radical, participatory elements by 1800 and was based on a "people" that had been circumscribed to voters—a group functionally limited by race and gender. This was accomplished in no small part through the application of secrecy in government early on and the transformation of publicity into a passive, controlled broadcast of information as opposed to active vigilance.

France, on the other hand, emerged from the Terror to undergo a gradual erosion of representative government and an evolution into authoritarianism, abandoning any pretense to democracy altogether. The Directory, which arose after the fall of Robespierre, further restricted popular participation in government, emphasizing constitutionalism and rule of law over the ideal of popular sovereignty.[9] From there, French politics slipped into what some historians have called a liberal authoritarianism with the rise of Napoleon Bonaparte, who declared himself "consul for life" in 1802 and emperor in 1804.[10] Once again, the people were to be represented by one man. Yet, unlike the monarchs before him, Napoleon's legitimacy was ultimately dependent on his effective courting of popular support.[11] The emperor was a master of public relations from his earliest days as a general, and "without the explosion of the periodical press during the French Revolution, Napoleon's success would have been unimaginable," as David Bell put it.[12] The centrality of publicity to this regime cannot be underestimated, but it was certainly a crafted display of spectacle for passive public consumption. Thus France emerged into a century in which it would undergo a tumultuous series of regime changes and political experiments, which led François Furet to interpret much of it as a continued unfolding of the French Revolution begun in 1789.[13]

Bentham's work on deliberative assemblies, first printed in 1791 as a fragment of his larger work, and in small numbers, was not widely circulated until 1816, when his friend and Genevan political figure Etienne Dumont published a French translation and expansion of the treatise. Over the ensuing two decades, it was translated into German, Italian, Portuguese, and Spanish, and back into English, in which it was published in its definitive version in a compendium of Bentham's writings issued between 1838 and 1843. Bentham sent a copy of his original 1791 text to French interior minister Lazare Carnot during Napoleon's brief 100-day return in 1815 to pass on to the president of the newly formed Chamber of Deputies as a guide. And the reach of his work went well beyond Europe. Bernardino Rivadavia, who had taken part in negotiating Argentinian independence and later became president, wrote a letter of thanks to Bentham in 1824, informing him that the rules for the country's Chamber of Deputies were "entirely based on the incontestable and striking truths contained in your work."[14] Bentham's ode to publicity, as part of his guide to constructing effective deliberative assemblies, had traction among countries establishing representative institutions well into the nineteenth century.

Since the Age of Revolutions, we have come to associate representative democracy so firmly with publicity—or transparency—that secrecy is generally considered exceptional, problematic, even threatening.[15] This is certainly not to suggest that it was Bentham's ideas that led to this, but that his work and its reach is indicative of the trend. As state bureaucracies grew, the question of their compatibility with representative government was linked to the extent to which they inhibited publicity. Sociologist Max Weber wrote of modern bureaucracy's tendency to "exclude the public, to hide its knowledge and action from criticism as well as it can," and thus shift power away from parliaments and the public.[16] In the twentieth century, political theorists and philosophers asked whether democracy could survive the reliance on extensive uses of state secrecy during the Cold War.[17] As novel technologies have taken hold, new wars broken out, and cultural shifts unfolded, questions of secrecy and publicity have remained at the core of our evolving understandings of what it means to have a government by and for the people.

Our continued debate about the proper place of secrecy in a representative government remains in many ways strikingly similar to that of revolutionaries in the eighteenth century. One need only glance at recent headlines in the United States or France to note the extent to which we have yet to settle questions of when secrecy is, or is not, appropriate in government. Over the last few years, contests over the use of secrecy have come up repeatedly. As Congress launched an impeachment investigation of President Donald Trump in late 2019, critics seized on the fact that many of the hearings were held behind closed doors to try to discredit or at least question the legitimacy of the process.[18] As the impeachment went to the Senate for trial, op-eds mused on the potential benefits of holding the vote in secret.[19] In 2017, members of Congress faced criticism for the way they handled the formation of the bill to repeal and replace the Affordable Care Act. Republican leaders were accused of drafting legislation in a furtive manner and of holding floor votes late at night when public scrutiny could be minimized, accusations they had also made against Democrats when the original act was passed in 2010.[20] Almost identical claims were made from the inception of the U.S. Congress and the French National Assembly. The U.S. Supreme Court has also confronted criticism and breaches of its generally confidential processes. In the spring of 2022, a draft decision to overturn the 1973 *Roe v. Wade* ruling guaranteeing a constitutional right to abortion was leaked, prompting reflection on the changing nature of the court's relationship to the American people and its legitimacy.[21]

In the executive realm, despite his penchant for showmanship, Donald Trump tried to tightly control access to his administration, which was nonetheless plagued by leaks. The administration announced early on that it would no longer release White House visitor logs, prompting outcry that the move would diminish transparency and raise suspicion.[22] Trump also continued a business practice of his, requiring campaign, transition, and later White House staff to sign nondisclosure agreements to prevent them from speaking publicly about their time working with him.[23] When he left office in 2021, the former president took classified material with him and continued to ignore subpoenas from legal and congressional investigations.[24] Questions about the extent to which the public has a right to know who the elected executive meets and what they discuss go back to George Washington. Finally, apprehensions about the growth of the National Security Administration and its secret surveillance programs under the Bush and Obama administrations—programs which have spurred extensive public debate since Edward Snowden leaked details about them—have antecedents in the committees formed in both the United States and France during periods of revolutionary violence.[25] Though the growth of bureaucracy and advances in technology have greatly extended the scope, the link between a state's wish to discover secrets and its propensity to do so in secret goes back to the founding of modern representative government.

In other ways, as our political structures and communication methods have evolved, considerations of secrecy in politics have become more numerous. For example, the question of whether to require the public disclosure of donors to political campaigns has become especially vexing following the 2010 U.S. Supreme Court ruling that money can be equated to speech and therefore corporate or union spending on elections cannot be limited. The rise of political action committees (PACs) and money in politics is reshaping American politics, and determining the degree of secrecy and publicity in campaign finance has been central to that process.[26] Changes in communication technology have also led to debates about how we expect elected or appointed officials to work. The politically explosive issue of Hillary Clinton's use of a private email server and leaked emails of her campaign staff proved critical in the 2016 American presidential election. Months after Clinton campaign emails were hacked and published in 2016, in France a mass of hacked emails from the presidential campaign of Emmanuel Macron was also leaked just days before voting took place. Unlike news coverage in the United States, however, French media did not immediately report on the contents of the leak due to a law requiring a "media blackout" starting forty-four hours before an election.[27] How much does the public have a right to know about the daily interactions and work of government officials? Organizations ostensibly dedicated to promoting greater transparency by uncovering government secrets, even if it be illegally (most notably WikiLeaks), seem to answer: everything. Organizations that hack and leak the private correspondence of public figures feed into a suspicion of secrecy that dates back to the eighteenth century, and they justify the release of private correspondence as necessary information for voters. The line between public and private is continually being contested when it comes to elected officials, as citizens themselves open more of their own private lives to public view through social media.

Even though publicity—or transparency—tends to be valued as an essential component of representative government, tensions over its definition and application also remain. In some ways, transparency has been expanded as the means to implement it have evolved, first by mass printing, then by sound recording, television, and now the Internet. While in office, Trump sometimes seemed to provide a direct window into his mind through his tweets. The same can be said of members of Congress, who now communicate with constituents directly via social media platforms and give speeches captured live on C-SPAN. Yet with each new advance in methods of publicity come new realms of secrecy and redefinitions of what publicity itself means. Although we can claim to know what the former president may have been thinking on any given day at 5 a.m., for example, the public had no knowledge of his tax returns before the *New York Times* uncovered them in September 2020. In a message to the newspaper staff, publisher A. G. Sulzberger commended the reporters' efforts to "pierce the secrecy the president has maintained around his finances" and traced the work of exposure back to the founding: "Our nation's founders recognized that an informed public was essential to a strong and healthy democracy."[28]

Yet just like in the 1790s, what it means to render government work transparent and the implications of doing so are not entirely clear. As much as social media can be said to have increased direct communication between elected officials and constituents, it has also allowed for greater manipulation. An entire industry of public relations is built around strategically shaping the relationship between elected officials and public opinion through the media. The press, largely owned by profit-driven corporations, remains a crucial mechanism for ensuring government transparency, but its structure raises perennial questions about its motives. Social media companies present the same challenges, intensified by their power as aggregators of content undergirded by algorithms designed to capture attention. The modern connotation of the word "publicity" to mean advertising or promotion speaks to the blending of sales, spectacle, and political information.[29] The storming of the U.S. Capitol on January 6, 2021, fueled by Trump's unabashed and unabating lie that the election was stolen and, since then, the political battle to control the narrative of this event suggest some of the perils of publicity. Because Trump rarely hid his actions, no moment of revelation seemed to assume significance as evidence of criminality.[30] As it reported its findings, the congressional committee investigating events leading up to and on January 6 paid attention to presentation, emphasizing the importance of making facts compelling and accessible to the public.[31] And yet, going into the hearings, a widespread sentiment pervaded that they would likely amount to nothing: spectacle, yes, but accountability?[32] In such a circumstance, transparency may actually be incapacitating, a balm treating symptoms but allowing underlying illness to fester.[33] Maybe democracy does not die in darkness but in broad daylight.

Today, one must wonder if we are living with the consequences of treating politics as spectacle, contending with the logical conclusion of an excessive devotion of publicity of a particular kind. Though these are not new concerns, technology has further reduced temporal distance and disrupted hierarchies of authority to a degree that has rendered these questions ever more urgent. For Bentham, writing in the late eighteenth century, publicity was the antidote to demagoguery. "The publicity of debates has ruined more demagogues than it has made," he wrote. Once elected to an assembly, a demagogue "placed amid his equals or his superiors in talent . . . can assert nothing which will not be combated: his exaggerations will be reduced within the limits of truth, his presumption humiliated, his desire of momentary popularity ridiculed; and the flatterer of the people will finish by disgusting the people themselves."[34] Central to Bentham's confidence in this claim were the role of the press and the passage of time as mediating forces. "The speeches of the orators, which are known to [the people] only through the newspapers, have not the influence of the passionate harangues of a seditious demagogue," he wrote. "They do not read them till after they have passed through a medium which cools them; and besides, they are accompanied by the opposite arguments, which, according to the supposition, would have all the natural advantage of the true over the false."[35] Reading Bentham's words today is chilling; is it possible they no longer apply?

Arguably, yes. But it is also possible they did not apply even in his time; many people certainly did not think they did. The way publicity is talked about and implemented necessarily leads to further questions. Beyond what is secret and what is transparent, how do citizens determine what is true and what is false? If we accept that publicity is valuable in representative democracies and that public opinion is central to political decision-making, then how do we ensure that public opinion is based on truth? These questions feel urgent today, and they are. But they were just as urgent to revolutionaries in the eighteenth century. Understanding how such challenges were approached and addressed in the past is critical if we are to effectively confront them today. Representative democracy remains an experiment and how we practice it is crucial to shaping its very meaning.

Notes

Introduction

1. William Pierce, "Anecdote," undated, in *Records of the Federal Convention of 1787*, Vol. 3, ed. Max Farrand (New Haven: Yale University Press, 1911–1937), 3, 86–87.
2. *Archives Parlementaires, Tome VIII: Du 5 Mai au 15 Septembre, 1789* (Paris: Société d'Imprimerie et Libraire Administratives, 1884), 55, accessed September 21, 2020, Hathi Trust. De Volney may have been referring to the story of an ancient sage who reportedly declared that he wished his house was made of glass so that all his actions could be seen.
3. In taking on democracy as a subject of study, this book builds upon James Kloppenberg's approach of not studying democracy as a single concept but rather examining "the diverse meanings of terms used for multiple purposes, terms such as 'democracy,' 'self government,' and 'popular sovereignty,' to designate a variety of ideas with contested meanings not only across time but at every historical moment." However, while Kloppenberg defines democracy as "an ethical ideal, rather than merely a set of institutions," this study approaches the concept through a focus on institutional practices and procedures. Discourse, which was long the primary concern of historians on both sides of the Atlantic, is crucial to understanding the unfolding of revolutions and the evolution of political thought. But discourse attains meaning through praxis and vice versa. Procedural decisions and debates about them can illuminate the contested nature of ideas, particularly the way theories were translated into practice and changed in the process. See James T. Kloppenberg, *Toward Democracy: The Struggle for Self-Rule in European and American Thought* (Oxford: Oxford University Press, 2016), 3–4.
4. *Archives Parlementaires de 1787 à 1860*, Vol. 57: *du 12 janvier 1793 au 28 janvier, 1793* (Paris: Librairie administrative de P. Dupont, 1862–1913), 316.

5. Paul Friedland, *Political Actors: Representative Bodies and Theatricality in the Age of the French Revolution* (Ithaca: Cornell University Press, 2002), 11; Pierre Rosanvallon, "The History of the Word 'Democracy' in France," trans. Philip Constopoulos, *Journal of Democracy* 6, no. 4 (October 1995): 141–146; R. R. Palmer, "Notes on the Use of the Word 'Democracy,' 1789–1799," *Political Science Quarterly* 68, no. 2 (1953); Bernard Manin, *The Principles of Representative Government* (Cambridge: Cambridge University Press, 1997), 2–3. "Democracy" could also be used at the time to connote one segment of a mixed government that was characterized by popular participation and giving voice to the commons.
6. James Madison, *The Federalist* No. 10, in *The Federalist Papers*, ed. Cynthia Brantley Johnson (New York: Simon and Schuster, 2004), 65. Willi Paul Adams argued that Madison made the distinction for merely political purposes and that in fact the two terms were used interchangeably in early America. Even if this is so, the effect of making that distinction was significant for thinking going forward. Willi Paul Adams, *The First American Constitutions: Republican Ideology and the Making of the State Constitutions in the Revolutionary Era*, trans. Rita Kimber and Robert Kimber (Lanham, MD: Rowman and Littlefield, 2001), 110, 112. On the ancient origins of the distinction between a democracy and a republic, see Nadia Urbinati, "Competing for Liberty: The Republican Critique of Democracy," *American Political Science Review* 106, no. 3 (August 2012).
7. Maximilien Robespierre, "Sur les Principes de Morale Politique qui Doivent Guider la Convention Nationale dans l'Administration Intérieure de la République," in *Robespierre: Textes Choisis, Tome Troisième, aout 1793-juillet 1794*, ed. Jean Poperen (Paris: Editions Sociales, 1958), 112. This passage is also cited in the following: William Doyle, *The Oxford History of the French Revolution* (Oxford: Clarendon Press, 1989), 272; Ruth Scurr, "Varieties of Democracy in the French Revolution," in *Re-imagining Democracy in the Age of Revolutions: America, France, Britain, and Ireland, 1750–1850*, ed. Joanna Innes and Mark Philp (Oxford: Oxford University Press, 2013), 66–67; Palmer, "Notes on the Use of the Word 'Democracy,' 1789–1799," 214.
8. Mark Philp, "Talking about Democracy: Britain in the 1790s," in *Re-imagining Democracy in the Age of Revolutions;* Scurr, "Varieties of Democracy in the French Revolution"; Friedland, *Political Actors*, 11; Rosanvallon, "The History of the Word 'Democracy' in France," 147–153; Raymonde Monnier, " 'Démocratie Représentative' ou 'République Démocratique': De la Querelle des Mots (République) à la Querelle des Anciens et Modernes," *Annales historiques de la Révolution française*, No. 325 (2001); Katlyn Marie Carter, "The Invention of Representative Democracy," in *The Age of Revolutions* (July 23, 2018), accessed August 20, 2022, https://ageofrevolutions.com/2018/07/23/the-invention-of-representative-democracy/; Richard Tuck, *The Sleeping Sovereign: The Invention of Modern Democracy* (Cambridge: Cambridge University Press, 2016), 7. Tuck identifies a letter written by Alexander Hamilton in 1777

as the first use of the term "representative democracy" in English; he identifies the first printed use of the term in English in Noah Webster's 1785 *Sketches of American Policy.*

9. Identifying a common set of struggles against entrenched elites, R. R. Palmer made the case in 1959 that the last four decades of the eighteenth century witnessed a "single revolutionary movement" across what he identified as "Atlantic civilization." He deemed this movement essentially democratic in that there was a rising sentiment against rigid social hierarchy in favor of equality and the limited delegation of governmental authority. In 1965, French historian Jacques Godechot also argued that there was one "age of Atlantic Revolution," based on the conviction that the causes and objectives of each national movement were fundamentally the same. In the ensuing decades, the notion of a unitary "Age of Revolution" and its designation as democratic has been challenged by broadening the scope of analysis. See R. R. Palmer, *The Age of the Democratic Revolution: A Political History of Europe and America, 1760–1800*, 2 vols. (Princeton: Princeton University Press, 1969–1970); Jacques Godechot, *France and the Atlantic Revolution of the Eighteenth Century, 1770–1799*, trans. Herbert R. Rowen (New York: Free Press, 1965); Eric Hobsbawm, *The Age of Revolution, 1789–1848* (Weidenfeld and Nicholson, 1962); Jeremy Adelman, "An Age of Imperial Revolutions," *American Historical Review* 113 (2008); Wim Klooster, *Revolutions in the Atlantic World: A Comparative History* (New York: New York University Press, 2018); Julius S. Scott, *The Common Wind: Afro-American Currents in the Age of the Haitian Revolution* (London: Verso Books, 2018); David Brion Davis, *The Problem of Slavery in the Age of Revolution, 1770–1823* (Ithaca: Cornell University Press, 1975); Harriet B. Applewhite and Darline G. Levy, eds., *Women and Politics in the Age of the Democratic Revolution* (Ann Arbor: University of Michigan Press, 1990).

10. Legitimacy—a term used to denote the justification and validity of power—was defined variously depending on the theory of representation and vision of popular sovereignty to which one subscribed. Adopting a definition of legitimacy as a government "compatible with the value pattern of society" and "believed to be based on good title by most men subject to it," I use the term to refer to the widespread acceptance of the claim that representative regimes spoke on behalf of the people and were thus an organ of popular sovereignty. Legitimacy is intimately linked to trust and inherently contains an element of persuasion; in a representative government, unlike under a monarchy, it can be considered a measure of how effectively a population is convinced that their government represents them. This definition is an amalgamation of multiple definitions offered by political theorists: see Simone Goyard-Fabre, "Légitimité," in *Dictionnaire de culture juridique*, ed. D. Alland and S. Rials (Paris: Presses universitaires de France, 2003), 933; Peter G. Stillman, "The Concept of Legitimacy," *Polity* 7, no. 1 (1974): 39; Carl Joachim Friedrich, *Man and His Government: An Empirical Theory of Politics*

(New York: McGraw Hill, 1963), 234; Rhys Jones, "The Politics of Time During the Napoleonic Consulate, 1799–1804," *European Review of History: Revue européenne d'histoire* 28: 1, 75; Pierre Rosanvallon, *Democratic Legitimacy: Impartiality, Reflexivity, Proximity*, trans. Arthur Goldhammer (Princeton: Princeton University Press, 2011), 8–13.

11. Some political scientists and historians have explored temporality as an important part of democratic politics, including in some cases as a component of the deliberative process. See especially Jones, "The Politics of Time During the Napoleonic Consulate, 1799–1804"; Greg Weiner, *Madison's Metronome: The Constitution, Majority Rule, and the Tempo of American Politics* (Lawrence: University of Kansas Press, 2012); Elizabeth F. Cohen, *The Political Value of Time* (Cambridge: Cambridge University Press, 2018).

12. Hannah Pitkin, *The Concept of Representation* (Berkeley: University of California Press, 1967), 146; Manin, *The Principles of Representative Government*, 110. Manin identifies the real distinction between two types of representation as being between "likeness" and "distinction," where likeness is the idea that representative bodies are made representative by being a microcosm of society, and distinction is the notion that representatives are of superior capability to those who elect them. The terms I deploy group the "mandate" and "likeness" doctrines together under the term "reflective" and the "independence" and "distinction" doctrines together under the term "insulated." See also J. R. Pole, *Political Representation in England and the Origins of the American Republic* (Berkeley: University of California Press, 1971); Todd Estes, *The Jay Treaty Debate, Public Opinion, and the Evolution of Early American Political Culture* (Amherst: University of Massachusetts Press, 2006); John Phillip Reid, *The Concept of Representation in the Age of the American Revolution* (Chicago: University of Chicago Press, 1989); Eric Slauter, *The State as a Work of Art: The Cultural Origins of the Constitution* (Chicago: University of Chicago Press, 2009), 127–129.

13. John Parkinson, *Democracy and Public Space: The Physical Sites of Democratic Performance* (Oxford: Oxford University Press, 2012), 2, 15, 34; Bernard Manin, "On Legitimacy and Political Deliberation," *Political Theory* 15, no. 3 (August 1987): 359. On the other hand, it is possible that proponents of publicity failed to account for the possibility that transparency itself could undermine their theory of reflective representation by effectively rendering citizens passive spectators. Recently, political theorists have pointed to this as a threat to democracy, and work on women in politics in the eighteenth century has long pointed to this potential outcome. See especially Nadia Urbinati, *Democracy Disfigured: Opinion, Truth, and the People* (Cambridge, MA: Harvard University Press, 2014), 6, 171–227; Jan Lewis, "Politics and the Ambivalence of the Private Sphere: Women in Early Washington, D.C.," in *A Republic for the Ages: The United States Capitol and the Political Culture of the Early Republic*, ed. Donald R. Kennon (Charlottesville: University of Virginia Press, 1999), 122–151; Friedland, *Political Actors*, 300.

14. Jean-Jacques Rousseau, *Du Contrat Social* (Paris: Messidor/Editions sociales, 1987), 175.
15. Richard Tuck also identified this as the central problem Rousseau posed in his work. Although he was not an advocate of ancient democracy, Rousseau believed "merely electing representatives was not enough to count as the action of a democratic sovereign." See Tuck, *The Sleeping Sovereign*, x.
16. Edmund Morgan, *Inventing the People: The Rise of Popular Sovereignty in England and America* (New York: Norton, 1988), 13–15.
17. Thomas Paine, *Common Sense*, in *Thomas Paine: Rights of Man and Common Sense*, ed. Peter Linebaugh (London: Verso, 2009), 6.
18. Ibid., 7.
19. Pitkin, *The Concept of Representation*, 146; Manin, *The Principles of Representative Government*, 110.
20. On the effect of the Seven Years' War on imperial reforms, see especially Fred Anderson, *Crucible of War: The Seven Years' War and the Fate of Empire in British North America, 1754–1766* (New York: Alfred A. Knopf, 2000); Palmer, *The Age of Democratic Revolution*. On American and British criticisms of "virtual representation" and calls for reflective representation, see especially Reid, *The Concept of Representation in the Age of the American Revolution*, 51, 45, 58; Bernard Bailyn, *The Ideological Origins of the American Revolution* (Cambridge, MA: Belknap Press of Harvard University Press, 1967); Jack P. Greene, *Peripheries and Center: Constitutional Development in the Extended Polities of the British Empire and the United States, 1607–1789* (Athens: University of Georgia Press, 1986); Gordon Wood, *The Creation of the American Republic, 1776–1787* (Chapel Hill: University of North Carolina Press, 1969); J. G. A. Pocock, *The Machiavellian Moment: Florentine Political Thought and the Atlantic Republican Tradition* (Princeton: Princeton University Press, 1975); John Brewer, *Party Ideology and Popular Politics at the Accession of George III* (Cambridge: Cambridge University Press, 1976); John Brewer, *The Sinews of Power: War, Money, and the English State, 1688–1783* (Cambridge, MA: Harvard University Press, 1998); J. C. D. Clark, *English Society, 1688–1832: Ideology, Social Structure, and Political Practice During the Ancien Régime* (Cambridge: Cambridge University Press, 1985); Linda Colley, *Britons: Forging the Nation 1707–1837* (New Haven: Yale University Press, 1992); Lewis Namier, *England in the Age of the American Revolution* (New York: Saint Martin's Press, 1961); L. Namier and J. Brooke, eds., *The History of Parliament: The House of Commons, 1754–90* (New York: Oxford University Press, 1964); David Eastwood, *Government and Community in the English Provinces* (Basingstoke: Macmillan Press, 1997); J. M. Rosenheim, *The Emergence of a Ruling Order* (London: Longman, 1998); Paul Langford, *Public Life and the Propertied Englishman* (Oxford: Clarendon Press, 1991); Peter Jupp, *The Governing of Britain, 1688–1848* (New York: Routledge, 2006); Frank O'Gorman, *Voters, Patrons, and Parties: The Unreformed Electoral System* (Oxford: Clarendon Press, 1989); Tuck, *The Sleeping Sovereign*, 199.

21. Terry Bouton, *Taming Democracy: The People, the Founders, and the Troubled Ending of the American Revolution* (Oxford: Oxford University Press, 2007), 176–177; Woody Holton, *Unruly Americans and the Origins of the Constitution* (New York: Hill and Wang, 2007), 162–164; Jack Rakove, *Original Meanings: Politics and Ideas in the Making of the Constitution* (New York: Vintage Books, 1997), 48.
22. Rosemarie Zagarri, *The Politics of Size: Representation in the United States, 1776–1850* (Ithaca: Cornell University Press, 1987), 4–5, 18; Adams, *The First American Constitutions*, 231, 233; Rakove, *Original Meanings*, 203.
23. For more on notions of the king and representation in an absolutist model, see Friedland, *Political Actors*, 49–50; James B. Collins, *The State in Early Modern France* (Cambridge: Cambridge University Press, 2009), 80; Keith Michael Baker, *Inventing the French Revolution* (Cambridge: Cambridge University Press, 1990), 114.
24. Before Louis XVI agreed to call this meeting, there had been many other possible institutions floated as possible representative organs for a reformed French state. These ranged from the *Parlements*, which were legal courts, to provincial assemblies that were essentially miniature Estates General across the countryside, to the Assembly of Notables, which was convened in 1787 as a group of royally selected men deemed of importance. See Baker, *Inventing the French Revolution*, 225–251.
25. Adams, *The First American Constitutions*, 5–7. Adams points out that republicanism in North America was not set up in opposition to Parliament, but that Americans in fact built on existing institutions. This is in marked contrast to France, where republicanism was born of opposition to the absolutist regime that preceded it.
26. Madison, *The Federalist* No. 10, 66.
27. Ibid.
28. Pitkin, *The Concept of Representation*, 146; Manin, *The Principles of Representative Government*, 110.
29. Edmund Burke, *Speech to the Electors of Bristol*, November 3, 1774, accessed May 22, 2022, The Founders' Constitution.
30. Bouton, *Taming Democracy*, 171; Gordon Wood, *Revolutionary Characters: What Made the Founders Different* (New York: Penguin, 2007), 149; Holton, *Unruly Americans*, 5–7; Rakove, *Original Meanings*, 48; "Madison's Notes," Thursday, May 31, 1787, in Max Farrand, ed., *Records of the Federal Convention of 1787*, Vol. 1 (New Haven: Yale University Press, 1911–1937), 48.
31. Madison, *The Federalist* No. 10, 65–68.
32. Friedland, *Political Actors*, 160; François Furet, *Interpreting the French Revolution*, trans. Elborg Forster (Cambridge: Cambridge University Press, 1981).
33. In 1969, historian Gordon Wood called the American Constitution the final act of revolution, whereby a recently reviled virtual representation was essentially re-established using the same revolutionary rhetoric that had been used to decry it. Those who defended the Constitution, Wood asserted, were

disingenuous in their rhetorical emphasis on its democratic nature when in fact they were creating an essentially aristocratic structure that limited the exercise of power by the common people, even while rhetorically emphasizing its centrality. See Wood, *Creation of the American Republic*, 562–563. What Federalists were essentially trying to assert was that the state and the people were one, as historian David Waldstreicher put it. Edmund Morgan pointed to the precedent for such an assertion in English political thought, arguing that "the impossibility of empirical demonstration is a necessary characteristic of political fictions" and pointing to Parliament asserting back in the seventeenth century that it "was not simply the representative of the people, it was the people." See David Waldstreicher, *In the Midst of Perpetual Fêtes: The Making of American Nationalism, 1776–1820* (Chapel Hill: University of North Carolina Press, 1997), 140; Morgan, *Inventing the People*, 59, 64. In the French context, historian François Furet's landmark 1978 book examined the creation of what he called "democratic culture," wherein the vacuum of power created by the end of absolutism was filled by a language of "the people" and its "general will" as the sole foundation of political legitimacy. As a result, he suggested that power came to reside in whichever body could most convincingly claim the authority of "the people," rendering legitimacy something negotiated in the rhetorical realm without any foundation in reality. See Furet, *Interpreting the French Revolution*, 77, 51.

34. This book builds upon a thread of scholars who have called attention to political culture as a way of addressing such questions and pushing beyond the realms of rhetoric and ideology. In the French context, see especially Lynn Hunt, *Politics, Culture, and Class in the French Revolution* (Berkeley: University of California Press, 1988); Mona Ozouf, *Festivals and the French Revolution*, trans. Alan Sheridan (Cambridge, MA: Harvard University Press, 1988); Mona Ozouf, *L'Homme régénéré: essais sur la Révolution française* (Paris: Gallimard, 1989); Roger Chartier, *The Cultural Origins of the French Revolution* (Durham: Duke University Press, 1991). In the American context, see especially Waldstreicher, *In the Midst of Perpetual Fêtes;* Simon P. Newman, *Parades and the Politics of the Street: Festive Culture in the Early American Republic* (Philadelphia: University of Pennsylvania Press, 1997); Sean Wilentz, *Chants Democratic: New York City and the Rise of the American Working Class, 1788–1850* (New York: Oxford University Press, 1984); Catherine Allgor, *Parlor Politics: In Which the Ladies of Washington Help Build a City and a Government* (Charlottesville: University of Virginia Press, 2000); Jeffrey Pasley, *The Tyranny of Printers: Newspaper Politics in the Early American Republic* (Charlottesville: University of Virginia Press, 2001); Joanne Freeman, *Affairs of Honor: National Politics in the Early Republic* (New Haven: Yale University Press, 2011).

35. Scholars of both the United States and France have taken note of the centrality of publicity, which they have written about as such or as surveillance. See Seth Cotlar, *Tom Paine's America: The Rise and Fall of Transatlantic Radical-*

ism in the Early Republic (Charlottesville: University of Virginia Press, 2011), 162; Susan Maslan, *Revolutionary Acts: Theater, Democracy, and the French Revolution* (Baltimore: Johns Hopkins University Press, 2005), ix; Philippe Münch, "Révolution française, opinion publique et transparence: les fondements de la démocratie moderne," in *Appareil* 7 (2011): 5; Waldstreicher, *In the Midst of Perpetual Fêtes*, 131. In the eighteenth century, Rousseau also wrote about keeping watch over government as a way to ensure it did not become corrupted. See Tuck, *The Sleeping Sovereign*, 3.

36. This interpretation adopts Quentin Skinner's contention that even if actions are not originally motivated by principles, once justified in terms of principles, actions are constitutive of them. See Quentin Skinner, *Visions of Politics*, Vol. 1, *Regarding Method* (Cambridge: Cambridge University Press, 2002), 155. Jonathan Gienapp has also addressed this tension, concluding that "arguments and the mental images they form are consequential, even if uttered by the least sincere, least scrupulous actors." See Jonathan Gienapp, *The Second Creation: Fixing the American Constitution in the Founding Era* (Cambridge, MA: Harvard University Press, 2018), 17.
37. On the instability of the concept of "the people," "the public," and citizenship, see especially Carolyn Eastman, *A Nation of Speechifiers: Making an American Public After the Revolution* (Chicago: University of Chicago Press, 2009), 1–12; John M. Murrin, "A Roof Without Walls: The Dilemma of American National Identity," in *Beyond Confederation: Origins of the Constitution and American National Identity*, ed. Richard Beeman, Stephen Botein, and Edward Carter III (Chapel Hill: University of North Carolina Press, 1987), 333–347; Douglas Bradburn, *The Citizenship Revolution: Politics and the Creation of the American Union, 1774–1804* (Charlottesville: University of Virginia Press, 2009), 2–3; Jan Lewis, " 'Of Every Age Sex & Condition': The Representation of Women in the Constitution," *Journal of the Early Republic* 15, no. 3 (Autumn, 1995); Nathan Perl-Rosenthal, *Citizen Sailors: Becoming American in the Age of Revolutions* (Cambridge, MA: Harvard University Press, 2015). For more on public opinion in early America, see Jeffrey Smith, *Printers and Press Freedom* (Oxford: Oxford University Press, 1988); Michael Warner, *The Letters of the Republic* (Cambridge, MA: Harvard University Press, 1990); Mark Schmeller, *Invisible Sovereign: Imagining Public Opinion from the Revolution to Reconstruction* (Baltimore: Johns Hopkins University Press, 2016); Pasley, *The Tyranny of Printers*. On public opinion and the press in Britain proper, see especially Hannah Barker, *Newspapers, Politics, and Public Opinion in Late-Eighteenth Century England* (Oxford: Clarendon Press, 1998); Robert R. Rea, *The English Press in Politics 1760–1774* (Lincoln: University of Nebraska Press, 1963); Michael Harris, *A Patriot Press: National Politics and the London Press in the 1740s* (Oxford: Clarendon Press, 1993).
38. Cotlar, *Tom Paine's America*, 162.
39. Trish Loughran, *The Republic in Print: Print Culture in the Age of U.S. Nation Building, 1770–1870* (New York: Columbia University Press, 2007), 25.

Despite the rhetorical rejection of it, as Paul Downes suggested, democracy did not in fact do away with secrecy. Rather, its legitimacy depended on moments of secrecy, from the closed-door meeting of the Constitutional Convention to the secret ballot. See Paul Downes, *Democracy, Revolution, and Monarchism in Early American Literature* (Cambridge: Cambridge University Press, 2004). On the other hand, Kenneth Owen has suggested that in reality, "political legitimacy depended on being able to demonstrate popular support for representative institutions." See Kenneth Owen, "Legitimacy, Localism, and the First Party System," in *Practicing Democracy: Popular Politics in the United States from the Constitution to the Civil War,* ed. Daniel Peart and Adam I. P. Smith (Charlottesville: University of Virginia Press, 2015), 174.

40. This study builds upon Paul Friedland's work on laws and instances where elected officials attempted to silence the people or minimize their role in governance. I focus on decisions where they did the opposite (or at least had the effect of doing the opposite, sometimes despite their intentions). In highlighting procedural decisions and debates within the successive revolutionary legislatures, this argument deepens recent studies of the work and structures of the constituent and legislative assemblies, as well as of the convention and committees through the 1790s. See especially Friedland, *Political Actors,* 270–274; Timothy Tackett, *Becoming a Revolutionary: The Deputies of the French National Assembly and the Emergence of a Revolutionary Culture* (Princeton: Princeton University Press, 1996); André Castaldo, *Méthodes de Travail de la Constituante: les techniques délibératives de l'Assemblée nationale, 1789–1791* (Presses Universitaires de France, 1989); Armand Brette, *Histoire des édifices ou ont siégés les assemblées parlementaires de la révolution française et de la première république* (Paris: Imprimerie nationale, 1902); Edna Hindie Lemay, *Revolutionaries at Work: The Constituent Assembly, 1789–1791* (Oxford: Voltaire Foundation, 1996); Alain Cohen, *Le Comité des Inspecteurs de la Salle: Une Institution originale au service de la Convention nationale (1792–1795)* (Paris: L'Harmattan, 2011). It also builds on studies of the press and politics during the Revolution. See especially Jeremy Popkin, *Revolutionary News: The Press in France, 1789–1799* (Durham: Duke University Press, 1990); Hugh Gough, *The Newspaper Press in the French Revolution* (London: Routledge, 1988); Jack Censer, *Prelude to Power: The Parisian Radical Press, 1789–1791* (Baltimore: Johns Hopkins University Press, 1976); Charles Walton, *Policing Public Opinion in the French Revolution* (Oxford: Oxford University Press, 2009).

41. For examples of the way historians have equated these different types of representation as more or less democratic, see especially Dana Nelson, *Commons Democracy: Reading the Politics of Participation in the Early United States* (New York: Fordham University Press, 2015); Bouton, *Taming Democracy;* Holton, *Unruly Americans;* Wood, *The Creation of the American Republic,* 562, 546, 517; Friedland, *Political Actors,* 11; Yannicik Bosc, *Le Peuple Souverain et la Démocratie: Politique de Robespierre* (Paris: Editions Critiques, 2019), 14–15.

42. Manin, *The Principles of Representative Government*, 1. Nadia Urbinati articulates a similar claim: "Although we call contemporary Western governments democratic, their institutions were designed to contain rather than encourage democracy." See Nadia Urbinati, *Representative Democracy: Principles and Genealogy* (Chicago: University of Chicago Press, 2008), 1.
43. Morgan, *Inventing the People*, 13–15. Pierre Rosanvallon also suggests that democracy rests on a "fiction" of assimilating the majority to the whole. See Rosanvallon, *Democratic Legitimacy*, 13.
44. Rousseau's thinking about political representation encapsulates this dilemma. Though he warned against sovereignty being usurped by representatives, he also declared that the general will was something other than the sum of individual wills. To identify it, he turns to the ideal of an omniscient legislator—an impossibility in practice. Though he undermines the potential for representatives to be a legitimate voice of the people, his thinking could also justify the extensive power of representatives to claim to identify the general will. On Rousseau's thinking, see Rousseau, *Du Contrat Social*, 110, 121–122, 173–175; Bosc, *Le Peuple Souverain et la Démocratie*, 11; Tuck, *The Sleeping Sovereign*, 124, 134, 138; Furet, *Interpreting the French* Revolution, 51; Jean Roels, "J. J. Rousseau et les institutions representatives dans les Consideration sur le Gouvernement de Pologne," in *Parliaments, Estates, and Representations* 5, no. 1 (June 1985): 15, 16–18.
45. On women making claims to membership in "the people," despite not being classified as *active citizens* with the right to vote, see especially Katie Jarvis, *Politics of the Marketplace: Work, Gender, and Citizenship in Revolutionary France* (Oxford: Oxford University Press, 2019), 3, 32, 55, 59; Suzanne Desan, "Gender, Radicalization, and the October Days: Occupying the National Assembly," in *French Historical Studies* 43, no. 3 (August 2020). On *active* versus *passive* citizenship, see especially William Sewell, "Le citoyen/la citoyenne: Activity, Passivity, and the Revolutionary Concept of Citizenship," in *The French Revolution and the Creation of Modern Political Culture*, Vol. 1, *The Political Culture of the Old Régime*, ed. Keith Michael Baker (Oxford: Pergamon Press, 1987); Lewis, " 'Of Every Age Sex & Condition.' "
46. Madison, *The Federalist* No. 10.
47. Friedland, *Political Actors*, 291.
48. On the social/economic meaning of the term "democracy," see especially Matthew Rainbow Hale, "Regenerating the World: The French Revolution, Civic Festivals, and the Forging of Modern American Democracy, 1793–1795," *Journal of American History* 103 (March 2017); Rosanvallon, "The History of the Word 'Democracy' in France," 149–153; Palmer, "Notes on the Use of the Word 'Democracy,' 1789–1799," 212–215.
49. While the Haitian Revolution raises crucial questions about the meanings of democracy and limits of popular sovereignty, it does not speak directly to the origin of representative democracy and is thus not treated as a case study on its own in this book. As Laurent Dubois noted, "impulses toward democ-

racy would long run up against autocratic and militaristic political institutions" in Haiti. See Laurent Dubois, *Avengers of the New World: The Story of the Haitian Revolution* (Cambridge, MA: Belknap Press of Harvard University Press, 2004), 301.

50. See especially Steven Livitsky and Daniel Ziblatt, *How Democracies Die* (New York: Penguin Random House, 2018); *The 1619 Project: A New Origin Story*, ed. Nikole Hannah-Jones, Caitlin Roper, Ilena Silverman, and Jake Silverstein (New York: One World, 2021).

51. This book is picking up the call of recent scholarship focused on practice and culture as a way to usefully consider revolutions in tandem and as intertwined. More than a comparative work, this is a political history of Atlantic revolutions that draws on material from the United States and France to tell a story about the way in which politics develop when sovereign authority is held to inhere in the people See Nathan Perl-Rosenthal, "Atlantic Cultures and the Age of Revolution," *William and Mary Quarterly* 74, no. 4, *Writing To and From the Revolution: A Joint Issue with the Journal of the Early Republic* (October 2017); Sarah Knott, "Narrating the Age of Revolution," *William and Mary Quarterly* 73, no. 1 (January 2016): 24; Keith Michael Baker and Dan Edelstein, eds., *Scripting Revolution: A Historical Approach to the Comparative Study of Revolutions* (Stanford: Stanford University Press, 2015); Klooster, *Revolutions in the Atlantic World;* David Armitage and Sanjay Subrahmanyam, eds., *The Age of Revolutions in Global Context, c. 1760–1840* (London: Palgrave Macmillan, 2010); Jack R. Censer, *Debating Modern Revolution: The Evolution of Revolutionary Ideas* (London: Bloomsbury, 2016); Caitlin Fitz, *Our Sister Republics: The United States in the Age of American Revolutions* (New York: Norton, 2017); Suzanne Desan, Lynn Hunt, and William Max Nelson, eds., *The French Revolution in Global Perspective* (Ithaca: Cornell University Press, 2013); Janet Polasky, *Revolutions without Borders: The Call to Liberty in the Atlantic World* (New Haven: Yale University Press, 2015); Ashli White, *Encountering Revolution: Haiti and the Making of the Early Republic* (Baltimore: Johns Hopkins University Press, 2010); Philipp Ziesche, *Cosmopolitan Patriots: Americans in Paris in the Age of Revolution* (Charlottesville: University of Virginia Press, 2010). The book is also following a model of Atlantic intellectual and cultural history modeled in Sophia Rosenfeld, *Common Sense: A Political History* (Cambridge, MA: Harvard University Press, 2011).

52. Jeremy Bentham, *The Collected Works of Jeremy Bentham: Political Tactics*, ed. Michael James, Cyprian Blamires, and Catherine Pease-Watkin (Oxford: Clarendon Press, 1999), 31.

53. Daniel Jütte, *The Age of Secrecy: Jews, Christians, and the Economy of Secrets, 1400–1800*, trans. Jeremiah Riemer (New Haven: Yale University Press, 2015), 19; Filippo de Vivo, *Information and Communication in Venice: Rethinking Early Modern Politics* (Oxford: Oxford University Press, 2007); Jacob Soll, *The Information Master: Jean-Baptiste Colbert's Secret State Intelligence System*

(Cultures of Knowledge in the Early Modern World) (Ann Arbor: University of Michigan Press, 2011); Jon Snyder, *Dissimulation and the Culture of Secrecy in Early-Modern Europe* (Berkeley: University of California Press, 2009), xvi; Jürgen Habermas, *The Structural Transformation of the Public Sphere*, trans. Thomas Burger and Frederick Lawrence (Cambridge, MA: MIT University Press, 1989), 52; Dena Goodman, "Public Sphere and Private Life: Toward a Synthesis of Current Historiographical Approaches to the Old Regime," *History and Theory* 31, no. 1 (February 1992): 7; Ernst H. Kantorowicz, "Mysteries of State: An Absolutist Concept and Its Late Medieval Origins," *Harvard Theological Review* 48, no. 1 (January 1955); Lawrence Klein, "Gender and the Public/Private Distinction in the Eighteenth Century: Some Questions about Evidence and Analytic Procedure," *Eighteenth-Century Studies* 29, no. 1 (Fall 1995): 104. Political theorist Lawrence Quill traces a tradition of seeing utility for secrecy in government back to the ancient world, citing writings of Plato. However, he notes that it became even more normalized with the emergence of realpolitik in the sixteenth and seventeenth centuries. See Lawrence Quill, *Secrets and Democracy: From Arcana Imperii to WikiLeaks* (New York: Palgrave Macmillan, 2014), 19, 28.

54. Nicole Bauer has also noted this development in the French context. See Nicole Bauer, "Can You Keep a Secret? A Cultural and Historical Approach to the Issues of Secrecy and Transparency in Politics," *Berkeley Journal of Sociology* (Fall 2014); David Waldstreicher has likewise identified the association of secrecy with danger and monarchism among republicans in the American context. See Waldstreicher, *In the Midst of Perpetual Fêtes*, 131.

55. For more on the emergence of accountability as a concept, see especially Jacob Soll, *The Reckoning: Financial Accountability and the Rise and Fall of Nations* (New York: Basic Books, 2014), 139–141; Ronen Steinberg, *The Afterlives of the Terror: Facing the Legacies of Mass Violence in Postrevolutionary France* (Ithaca: Cornell University Press, 2019), 46.

56. For a discussion of the Enlightenment as an intellectual and social movement emphasizing the social applicability of knowledge, see Dan Edelstein, *The Enlightenment: A Genealogy* (Chicago: University of Chicago Press, 2011); Jonathan Israel, *A Revolution of the Mind: Radical Enlightenment and the Intellectual Origins of Modern Democracy* (Princeton: Princeton University Press, 2010); Robert Darnton, *The Literary Underground of the Old Regime* (Cambridge, MA: Harvard University Press, 1982); Darrin McMahon, *Enemies of the Enlightenment: The French Counter-Enlightenment and the Making of Modernity* (Oxford: Oxford University Press, 2001); Peter Gay, *The Enlightenment, an Interpretation: The Rise of Modern Paganism* (New York: Knopf, 1966); Peter Gay, *The Enlightenment: A Comprehensive Anthology* (New York: Simon and Schuster, 1973); Caroline Winterer, *American Enlightenments: Pursuing Happiness in the Age of Reason* (Stanford: Stanford University Press, 2016). For a more specific example of this kind of rhetoric and the increasing value placed on transparency and authenticity by philosophes, see Jean

Starobinski, *Jean-Jacques Rousseau: La transparence et l'obstacle* (Paris: Gallimard, 1971); Sarah Knott, *Sensibility and the American Revolution* (Chapel Hill: University of North Carolina Press, 2012).

57. On the expansion of the periodical press in England in the eighteenth century, see Jeremy Black, *The English Press in the Eighteenth Century* (London: Croom Helm, 1987), 12–14; Barker, *Newspapers, Politics, and Public Opinion in Late-Eighteenth Century England*, 23; Jeremy Popkin, *News and Politics in the Age of Revolution: Jean Luzac's Gazette de Leyde* (Ithaca: Cornell University Press, 1989), 2. On France, see Jack R. Censer, *The French Press in the Age of Enlightenment* (London: Routledge, 1994), 7. For a comparison of the growth of the press in England and France, see Stephen Botein, Jack R. Censer, and Harriet Ritvo, "The Periodical Press in English and French Society: A Cross-Cultural Approach," *Comparative Studies in Society and History* 23, no. 3 (1981). In terms of literacy rates, estimates place them in England at around 55 to 60 percent of adult males over the course of the century, whereas in France, estimates for the end of the century are around 40 percent for the same group, though the trend was positive in both countries. For more, see Botein, Censer, and Ritvo, "The Periodical Press in English and French Society: A Cross-Cultural Approach," 475.
58. For more on this topic, see especially Habermas, *The Structural Transformation of the Public Sphere*. On England, see Harris, *A Patriot Press;* Barker, *Newspapers, Politics, and Public Opinion in Late-Eighteenth Century England;* Rea, *The English Press in Politics 1760–1774*. On France see Mona Ozouf, "L'opinion publique," in Baker, *The French Revolution and the Creation of Modern Political Culture*, Vol. 1, 419–435; Baker, *Inventing the French Revolution*, 167–199; Chartier, *The Cultural Origins of the French Revolution;* Tabetha Ewing, "Invasion of Lorient: Rumor, Public Opinion, and Foreign Politics in 1740s Paris," in *Into Print: Limits and Legacies of the Enlightenment*, ed. Charles Walton (University Park: Pennsylvania State University Press, 2011), 101-112; Jon Cowans, *To Speak for the People: Public Opinion and the Problem of Legitimacy in the French Revolution* (New York: Routledge, 2001); Walton, *Policing Public Opinion in the French Revolution;* Sarah Maza, *Private Lives and Public Affairs: The Causes Célébres of Prerevolutionary France* (Berkeley: University of California Press, 1993); Antoine Lilti, *Figures Publiques: l'invention de la célébrité* (Paris: Fayard: 2014); Benjamin Nathans, "Habermas's 'Public Sphere' in the Era of the French Revolution," *French Historical Studies* 16 (1990); J. A. W. Gunn, *Queen of the World: Opinion in the Public Life of France from the Renaissance to the Revolution* (Oxford: Voltaire Foundation, 1995).
59. See Gordon Wood, "Conspiracy and the Paranoid Style: Causality and Deceit in the Eighteenth Century," *William and Mary Quarterly* 39, no. 3 (July 1982); Peter Campbell, "Perceptions of Conspiracy on the Eve of the French Revolution," in *Conspiracy in the French Revolution*, ed. Peter Campbell, Thomas Kaiser, and Marisa Linton (Manchester: Manchester University Press, 2007); Peter Campbell, "Conspiracy and Political Practice from

the Ancien Régime to the French Revolution," in Campbell, Kaiser, and Linton, *Conspiracy in the French Revolution*, 202; Steven Kaplan, *Bread, Politics, and Political Economy in the Reign of Louis XV*, 2nd ed. (London: Anthem Press, 2015).

60. Work on religion and the Catholic Church in the context of the Enlightenment and the eighteenth century more generally is extensive. For more on the role of the Church in intellectual and political debates in France, see especially McMahon, *Enemies of the Enlightenment;* Dale Van Kley, *The Religious Origins of the French Revolution: From Calvin to the Civil Constitution, 1560–1791* (New Haven: Yale University Press, 1996); Chartier, *The Cultural Origins of the French Revolution.* Anti-Catholicism in early America was pervasive and central to colonists' conceptions of their identity in contrast to the French, making the Quebec Act of 1765 very controversial. For more, see especially Colley, *Britons*, 18; Brendan McConville, *The King's Three Faces: The Rise and Fall of Royal America, 1688–1776* (Chapel Hill: University of North Carolina Press, 2006); Francis D. Cogliano, *No King, No Popery: Anti-Catholicism in Revolutionary New England* (Westport, CT: Greenwood Press, 1995).

61. Sissela Bok, *Secrets: On the Ethics of Concealment and Revelation* (New York: Pantheon Books, 1982), 6, 9. Bok also sets the term "secrecy" apart from its close relation "privacy" by pointing out that "privacy need not hide; and secrecy hides far more than what is private" (11). Furthermore, she insists on a rigorously neutral treatment of the term, which I also aim to maintain. See also Quill, *Secrets and Democracy*, 4.

62. Laura Mason, "The 'Bosom of Proof': Criminal Justice and the Renewal of Oral Culture During the French Revolution," *Journal of Modern History* 76 (March 2004); Katlyn Marie Carter, "The *Comités des Recherches:* Procedural Secrecy and the Origins of Revolutionary Surveillance," *French History* 32, no. 1 (March 2018): 55. In terms of criminal trial procedure, the American Constitution did ultimately guarantee a degree of publicity in the process with the Sixth Amendment, which states: "the accused shall enjoy the right to a speedy and public trial."

63. Rahul Sagar, *Secrets and Leaks: The Dilemma of State Secrecy* (Princeton: Princeton University Press, 2013), 7–8.

64. The term "transparency" took on its modern meaning and application relatively recently. See Jonathan Bruno, "Democracy Beyond Disclosure: Secrecy, Transparency, and the Logic of Self-Government" (PhD dissertation, Harvard University, 2017), 24; Christopher Hood, "Transparency in Historical Perspective," in *Transparency: The Key to Better Governance?* ed. Christopher Hood and David Heald (New York: Oxford University Press, 2006).

65. Lawrence Klein defines public in distinction to private: " 'Public' matters were those that were exposed to the perceptions of some others or of people in general, while 'private' matters were generally imperceptible or kept from the perception of others. The 'public' and the 'private' were, thus, aligned

with the difference between openness and secrecy, between transparency and opaqueness. The other specification of this sort of publicness was the question of accessibility. 'Public' referred to those matters that were open to participation by some others or by people in general, while 'private' matters were, in some respect, restricted or closed." See Klein, "Gender and the Public/Private Distinction in the Eighteenth Century," 104; Goodman, "Public Sphere and Private Life."

66. Académie française, *Dictionnaire critique de la langue française* (1762), accessed January 7, 2015, The ARTFL Project, University of Chicago.
67. Samuel Johnson, *A dictionary of the English language: in which the words are deduced from their originals, and illustrated in their different significations by examples from the best writers. To which are prefixed a history of the language, and an English grammar*, 2 volumes (London: W. Strahan, for J. and P. Knapton, 1755), accessed September 7, 2020, The Making of the Modern World.
68. Noah Webster, *American Dictionary of the English Language* (New York: N. and J. White, 1838), 653, accessed August 1, 2019, Hathi Trust.
69. The themes of deception and trickery pervaded literary work in both French and English in the eighteenth century. See especially Samuel Richardson, *Clarissa; or, the History of a Young Lady* (London: 1747–48); Wood, "Conspiracy and the Paranoid Style," 426; Maximillian E. Novak, "Introduction," in *English Literature in the Age of Disguise*, ed. Maximillian E. Novak (Berkeley: University of California Press, 1977), 1–14; Jean-Jacques Rousseau, *Confessions, Book II* (Geneva: 1782), 80. Jean Starobinski focuses on Rousseau's writings, particularly the *Confessions*, to highlight his attachment to the ideal of absolute transparency among people and the notion that society places a veil over nature and requires men to wear masks, which must be penetrated. See Starobinski, *Jean-Jacques Rousseau*. On the shift to seeing court politics as rotten due to its performative nature and requirement for self-fashioning and dissembling, see especially Campbell, "Conspiracy and Political Practice from the Ancien Régime to the French Revolution," 198, 206; Barry Coward and Julian Swann, eds., *Conspiracies and Conspiracy Theory in Early Modern Europe* (Burlington, VT: Ashgate, 2004), 5; Snyder, *Dissimulation and the Culture of Secrecy in Early-Modern Europe*, xvi; Wood, "Conspiracy and the Paranoid Style," 423.
70. The most lurid *libelles* in France claimed to expose the sex lives of courtiers and alleged the covert influence of women in particular on the monarchy; someone was always pulling the strings behind the curtain. For more, see especially Maza, *Private Lives and Public Affairs*, 180, 210; Robert Darnton, *The Corpus of Clandestine Literature in France, 1769–1789* (New York: W. W. Norton, 1995). Some examples include *Gazette du Cythère, ou, Histoire secrète de Madame la comtesse du Bary* (1775); *Memoire secret des amours de Louis XV ou anecdote curieuse de la vie de Madame de Pompadour avec luy* (1772); *Correspondance secrète, politique et littéraire, ou mémoires pour servir à l'histoire des cours, des sociétés et de la littérature en France, depuis la mort de Louis XV, Guillaume*

Imbert de Bourdeaux (1787–1790). In British popular thought throughout the eighteenth century, politics also "appeared to be little more than one intrigue and deception after another," as Wood put it. "Everywhere people sensed designs within designs, cabals within cabals" in Anglophone culture. See Wood, "Conspiracy and the Paranoid Style," 407. On the feminization of secrecy in the Anglo context, see especially Paula Baker, "The Domestication of Politics: Women and American Political Society, 1780–1920," *American Historical Review* 89, no. 3 (June 1984), 624.

71. Furet, *Interpreting the French Revolution*, 54; Hunt, *Politics, Culture, and Class in the French Revolution*, 43–44.
72. On the tension between authenticity and performance, see especially Rousseau, *Confessions, Book II*, 80; Starobinski, *Jean-Jacques Rousseau: La transparence et l'obstacle;* Mason, "The 'Bosom of Proof' "; Marisa Linton, "Robespierre et l'Authenticité Révolutionnaire," in *Annales historiques de la Révolution française*, no. 371 (Jan-Mars 2013), 154, 156; Goodman, "Public Sphere and Private Life," 5, 13.

Chapter One. Piercing the Impenetrable Darkness

1. Benjamin Franklin, "Tract," cited in Bernard Bailyn, *The Ordeal of Thomas Hutchinson* (Cambridge, MA: Belknap Press of Harvard University Press, 1974), 236. This account is drawn primarily from Bailyn's narrative.
2. Bailyn, *Ordeal of Thomas Hutchinson*, 221–238; Nathan Perl-Rosenthal, "Corresponding Republics: Letter Writing and Patriot Organizing in the Atlantic Revolutions, circa 1760–1792" (PhD dissertation, Columbia University, 2011), 99.
3. Bailyn, *Ordeal of Thomas Hutchinson*, 240.
4. Ibid., 242. Perl-Rosenthal, "Corresponding Republics," 102.
5. Rev. Samuel Cooper to Benjamin Franklin, June 14, 1773, cited in Bailyn, *Ordeal of Thomas Hutchinson*, 242.
6. Perl-Rosenthal, "Corresponding Republics," 102.
7. Nathan Perl-Rosenthal highlighted these debates as a clash over epistolary genres and expectations for privacy based on the writers and type of letters; Perl-Rosenthal, "Corresponding Republics," 105.
8. Russ Castronovo has recently written about the leaking of Hutchinson's letters, placing it in the context of a network disseminating private correspondence of colonial officials in the years leading up to the War of Independence. See Russ Castronovo, *Propaganda 1776: Secrets, Leaks, and Revolutionary Communications in Early America* (Oxford: Oxford University Press, 2014). On fears of miscommunication, see especially Gordon Wood, "Conspiracy and the Paranoid Style"; Jordan E. Taylor, "The Page of Revolutions: Information Politics and Atlantic Networks in Revolutionary America" (PhD dissertation, Indiana University, 2020).

9. The term "Americans" is used here in contrast to British subjects across the Atlantic. But two caveats are necessary. Firstly, this imposes an identity on colonists that did not exist at the time but emerged through the Revolution and even then remained nebulous. Secondly, it flattens the diversity among the many peoples that resided in the area claimed as part of the British Empire, many of whom would in fact side with the British in the revolutionary war and whom leaders of the Patriot movement did not consider part of the American people they were forging. For more on these points, see especially Murrin, "A Roof Without Walls," 334–340; Bradburn, *The Citizenship Revolution*, 8, 21, 57; Eastman, *A Nation of Speechifiers*, 1–6; Woody Holton, *Liberty Is Sweet: The Hidden History of the American Revolution* (New York: Simon and Schuster, 2021).
10. Literature on the causes and course of the American Revolution split between the ideological interpretation and economic or social interpretations. I argue that material concerns and ideological ones converged in the project of claiming popular sovereignty and establishing a representative government. On the ideological origins, see especially Bailyn, *Ideological Origins;* Greene, *Peripheries and Center;* Wood, *The Creation of the American Republic;* Pocock, *The Machiavellian Moment.* For work on social and economic causes of the Revolution, see especially Gary Nash, *The Urban Crucible: Social Change, Political Consciousness, and the Origins of the American Revolution* (Cambridge, MA: Harvard University Press, 1993); Benjamin Carp, *Rebels Rising: Cities and the American Revolution* (Oxford: Oxford University Press, 2007); Woody Holton, *Forced Founders: Indians, Debtors, Slaves, and the Making of the American Revolution in Virginia* (Chapel Hill: University of North Carolina Press, 1999); Eric Foner, *Tom Paine and Revolutionary America* (New York: Oxford University Press, 1976). On the relationship between ideology and material circumstances, see especially Wood, "Rhetoric and Reality in the American Revolution."
11. This approach builds on Kenneth Owen's in his study of Pennsylvania. See Kenneth Owen, *Political Community in Revolutionary Pennsylvania, 1774–1800* (Oxford: Oxford University Press, 2018), 17.
12. Carl Becker, *The History of Political Parties in the Province of New York, 1760–1776* (Madison: Bulletin of the University of Wisconsin, 1909).
13. On the ambiguity of "the people" or "the public," see especially Eastman, *A Nation of Speechifiers*, 1–6.
14. In taking on this topic, this chapter investigates a generally overlooked subject: the workings and culture of the Continental Congress and state governments during the Confederation. On the Continental Congress and Confederation, see Jennings Bryan Sanders, *Evolution of the Executive Departments of the Continental Congress* (Chapel Hill: University of North Carolina Press, 1935); Jennings Bryan Sanders, *The Presidency of the Continental Congress, 1774–89: A Study in American Institutional History* (Gloucester, MA: P. Smith, 1930); Lynn Montross, *Reluctant Rebels: The Story of the Continental*

Congress, 1774–1789 (New York: Harper, 1950); Merrill Jensen, *The Articles of Confederation: An Interpretation of the Social-Constitutional History of the American Revolution, 1774–1781* (Madison: University of Wisconsin Press, 1940); Merrill Jensen, *The New Nation: A History of the United States During the Confederation, 1781–1789* (New York: Alfred A. Knopf, 1950); Edmund Burnett, *The Continental Congress* (New York: Macmillan, 1941); Jack Rakove, *The Beginnings of National Politics: An Interpretive History of the Continental Congress* (New York: Knopf, 1979); Calvin Jillson and Rick K. Wilson, *Congressional Dynamics: Structure, Coordination, and Choice in the First American Congress, 1774–1789* (Stanford: Stanford University Press, 1994); Jerrilyn Greene Martson, *King and Congress: The Transfer of Political Legitimacy, 1774–1776* (Princeton: Princeton University Press, 1987); Peter Onuf, ed., *Congress and the Confederation* (New York: Garland, 1991); Benjamin Irvin, *Clothed in Robes of Sovereignty: The Continental Congress and the People Out of Doors* (New York: Oxford University Press, 2011). On the point that this period was crucial to the development of American politics, see Burnett, *The Continental Congress*, viii. On state governments, see Pauline Maier, *American Scripture: Making the Declaration of Independence* (New York: Knopf, Distributed by Random House, 1997); Gordon Wood, *The Creation of the American Republic;* Holton, *Unruly Americans;* Bouton, *Taming Democracy;* Jessica Choppin Roney, *Governed by a Spirit of Opposition: The Origins of American Political Practice in Colonial Philadelphia* (Baltimore: Johns Hopkins University Press, 2014); Owen, *Political Community in Revolutionary Pennsylvania;* Adams, *The First American Constitutions;* Tuck, *The Sleeping Sovereign.*

15. While I use the terms "England" and "Britain," "English" and "British," this is not to suggest they are interchangeable. "England" refers to the state before the Act of Union in 1707 united England, Scotland, and Wales, creating Great Britain. The term "British" encompasses these peoples united. By the time of the American Revolution, "Great Britain" best describes the state. However, many American colonists and French writers as well still used the terms "England" and "English" to talk about rights and political institutions that originated in this state. On British identity, see Linda Colley, *Britons: Forging the Nation 1707–1837.*
16. Brewer, *Party Ideology and Popular Politics at the Accession of George III*, 15, 42.
17. The initial rise of a reform movement from 1779 to 1785, historian Hannah Barker argues, serves as a crucial point for understanding the growing role of the press and public opinion in politics. See Barker, *Newspapers, Politics, and Public Opinion in Late-Eighteenth Century England.* Also focusing on the press, historian Robert Rea has identified the period from 1760 to 1774 as one in which "the English Constitution was in the process of reinterpretation before the bar of public opinion." See Rea, *The English Press in Politics 1760–1774.* Historian Peter Jupp has suggested a cohesive period from 1760 to 1848, characterized by the emergence of a genuine two-party system, a greater volume of activity in Parliament, and more engagement with the

public. See Peter Jupp, *The Governing of Britain, 1688–1848* (New York: Routledge, 2006), 185.

18. Brewer, *Party Ideology and Popular Politics at the Accession of George III*, 20.
19. Of note is that the debate over the Declaratory Act in the House of Commons was a secret session. See Edmund Morgan and Helen Morgan, *The Stamp Act Crisis: Prologue to Revolution* (Chapel Hill: University of North Carolina Press, 1995), 296.
20. Burke, *Speech to the Electors of Bristol.*
21. Brewer, *Party Ideology and Popular Politics at the Accession of George III*, 208.
22. David Lemmings, *Law and Government in England during the Long Eighteenth Century: From Consent to Command* (New York: Palgrave Macmillan, 2011), 138.
23. Brewer, *Party Ideology and Popular Politics at the Accession of George III*, 167; P. D. G. Thomas, *John Wilkes: A Friend to Liberty* (New York: Clarendon Press, 1996).
24. Brewer has noted that the Middlesex Election issue called into question the basis of parliamentary power, asserting that it was not located in the House itself but in the people. This, Brewer has rightly pointed out, was a challenge to the theory of virtual representation, and it opened the possibility of instruction from constituents. See Brewer, *Party Ideology and Popular Politics at the Accession of George III*, 165. Peter Jupp cites the Wilkes issue as one of the first where groups were not pushing for changes of particular policies but advocating for reform of the entire system. See Jupp, *The Governing of Great Britain*, 246.
25. While John Brewer has connected John Wilkes to this rethinking of political representation, so have historians of the American Revolution. In addition to noting the importance of the Stamp Act, Bernard Bailyn highlights Americans' awareness of John Wilkes and his case. See Bailyn, *Ideological Origins*, 110. See also Jack P. Greene, "Bridge to Revolution: The Wilkes Fund Controversy," *Journal of Southern History* 29, no. 1 (1963); Pauline Maier, "John Wilkes and American Disillusionment with Britain," *William and Mary Quarterly* 20, no. 3 (1963). There is also a case to be made that frustrated colonists were less motivated by political theory or ideas about representation and more concerned with the material ramifications of imperial policy—both in 1765 and the ensuing decade. While material interests were significant motivating factors, they were both perceived through the lens of, and led to real, concerns about political representation and how it functioned. For more on material causes of the American Revolution, see especially Holton, *Forced Founders;* Andrew David Edwards, "Grenville's Silver Hammer: The Problem of Money in the Stamp Act Crisis," *Journal of American History* 104, no. 2 (September 2017). On the relationship of ideology to material interests, see especially Wood, "Rhetoric and Reality."
26. Letter from the Boston Sons of Liberty to John Wilkes, November 4, 1769, in *General Correspondence of John Wilkes, with a few additions; 1739–1802*, Vol. 4, no. 222. British Library (BL): Add MS 30870 (1768–1769).

27. *General Correspondence of John Wilkes, with a few additions; 1739–1802*, Vol. 4. BL: Add MS 30870 (1768–1769).
28. "The sentiments of an English Freeholder, on the late decision of the Middlesex Election [i.e., the rejection of John Wilkes by the House of Commons]" (London: J. Dodsley, 1769), 18. British Library General Reference Collection T.920.
29. For more on the debates over the Stamp Act and how they led to theorizing about the nature of political representation, see Morgan and Morgan, *The Stamp Act Crisis*.
30. Bailyn, *Ideological Origins*, 47.
31. Ibid., 168.
32. Ibid., 173.
33. Paine, *Common Sense*, in *Thomas Paine: Rights of Man and Common Sense*, 7.
34. Bailyn, *Ideological Origins*, 164. For other work on colonial legislatures, see especially Alison G. Olson, "Eighteenth Century Colonial Legislatures and Their Constituents," *Journal of American History* 79, no. 2 (September 1992); Sister Joan de Lourdes Leonard, C.S.J., "The Organization and Procedure of the Pennsylvania Assembly, 1682–1776, I: Organization," *Pennsylvania Magazine of History and Biography* 72 (July 1948); Sister Joan de Lourdes Leonard, C.S.J., "The Organization and Procedure of the Pennsylvania Assembly, 1682–1776, II: The Legislative Process," *Pennsylvania Magazine of History and Biography* 72 (October 1948); Stanley M. Pargellis, "The Procedure of the Virginia House of Burgesses," *William and Mary Quarterly* 7 (April 1927); Elmer I. Miller, *The Legislature of the Province of Virginia: Its Internal Development* (New York: Columbia University Press, 1907); George Edward Frakes, *Laboratory for Liberty: The South Carolina Legislative Committee System, 1719–1776* (Lexington: University Press of Kentucky, 1970); Roger Ekirch, *"Poor Carolina": Politics and Society in Colonial North Carolina, 1729–1776* (Chapel Hill: University of North Carolina Press, 1981); Patricia U. Bonomi, *A Factious People: Politics and Society in Colonial New York* (New York: Columbia University Press, 1971); Raymond C. Bailey, *Popular Influence upon Public Policy: Petitioning in Eighteenth-Century Virginia* (Westport, CT: Greenwood Press, 1979); Robert Zemsky, *Merchants, Farmers, and River Gods: An Essay on Eighteenth Century American Politics* (Boston: Gambit, 1971); Michael Zuckerman, *Peaceable Kingdoms: New England Towns in the Eighteenth Century* (New York: Knopf, 1978); Michael Kammen, *Deputyes and Libertyes: The Origins of Representative Government in the American Colonies* (New York: Knopf, 1969); David Jordan, *Foundations of Representative Government in Maryland, 1632–1715* (Cambridge: Cambridge University Press, 1987); Alan Tully, *William Penn's Legacy: Politics and Social Structure in Provincial Pennsylvania, 1726–1755* (Baltimore: Johns Hopkins University Press, 1977); Thomas L. Purvis, *Proprietors, Patronage, and Paper Money: Legislative Politics in New Jersey, 1703–1755* (New Brunswick: Rutgers University Press, 1986); Mary P. Clarke, *Parliamentary Privilege in the American Colonies* (New Haven: Yale University Press, 1943).

35. Olson, "Eighteenth Century Colonial Legislatures and Their Constituents," 564.
36. Ibid. Eric Slauter has argued that before the 1780s most colonial newspapers still carried more reports on what happened in the House of Commons than in their colonial assemblies. See Slauter, *The State as a Work of Art*, 150.
37. Olson, "Eighteenth Century Colonial Legislatures and Their Constituents," 565. Olson points to evidence that in Virginia, by mid-century, the publication of these more robust journals was having an effect on how representation worked there.
38. Ibid., 554.
39. P. D. G. Thomas, "The Beginning of Parliamentary Reporting in Newspapers, 1768–1774," *English Historical Review* 74, no. 293 (October 1959); P. D. G. Thomas, *The House of Commons in the Eighteenth Century* (Oxford: Clarendon Press, 1971); Andrew Sparrow, *Obscure Scribblers: A History of Parliamentary Journalism* (London: Politico's, 2003); Rea, *The English Press in Politics, 1760–1774;* Dror Wahrman, "Virtual Representation: Parliamentary Reporting and Languages of Class in the 1790s," *Past & Present*, no. 136 (August 1992); Katlyn Marie Carter, "Practicing Politics in the Revolutionary Atlantic World: Secrecy, Publicity, and the Making of Modern Democracy" (PhD dissertation, Princeton University, 2017).
40. Neither Connecticut nor Rhode Island adopted state constitutions until the nineteenth century.
41. Rakove, *Beginnings of National Politics*, 30.
42. Agnes Hunt, *The Provincial Committees of Safety of the American Revolution* (Cleveland, OH: Press of Winn and Judson, 1904), 10, 11, 111, 118, 128, 130.
43. Ibid., 63, 68, 70, 76, 79, 82.
44. Ibid., 21, 30, 53. There is little scholarship on these quasi-executive bodies at the state level, though they are beginning to receive attention given their decidedly undemocratic structures and modes of operation. See Joshua P. Canale, *American Dictators: Committees for Public Safety During the American Revolution, 1775–1784* (PhD dissertation, State University of New York at Binghamton, 2014), 3.
45. The New York Provincial Congress, for example, explicitly voted on May 22, 1775, in its first meeting "That for the dispatch of business and to prevent interruptions, the doors at our meeting shall be shut and that none but members be permitted to take copies of our proceedings of this Congress." See *Journals of the Provincial Congress, Provincial Convention, Committee of Safety and Council of Safety of the State of New York*, Vol. II, *1775–1776–1777* (Albany: Printed by Thurlow Weed, Printer of the State, 1842), 8. On October 18, 1774, the Massachusetts Provincial Congress likewise "Ordered that the galleries be now cleared, and that the doors of the house be kept shut, during the debates of the Congress until further order thereof." See *The journals of each Provincial congress of Massachusetts in 1774 and 1775, and of the*

Committee of safety (Boston: Dutton and Wentworth, 1838), 22. See also Hunt, *Provincial Committees of Safety*, 17, 30, 69.

46. This summary description of the committees' composition and operations is drawn from the account of each state's committees in Hunt, *Provincial Committees of Safety*.
47. For more on these committees see Carter, "Practicing Politics in the Revolutionary Atlantic World."
48. Constitution of Maryland, Article XXVI (November 11, 1776), accessed May 25, 2017. The Avalon Project, Yale Law School.
49. Constitution of Virginia (June 29, 1776), accessed May 25, 2017. The Avalon Project, Yale Law School.
50. Constitution of Georgia (February 5, 1777), accessed May 25, 2017. The Avalon Project, Yale Law School.
51. Ibid.
52. Constitution of North Carolina (December 18, 1776), accessed May 25, 2017. The Avalon Project, Yale Law School.
53. Ibid.
54. Constitution of Massachusetts (1780), accessed May 25, 2017. National Humanities Institute.
55. Ibid., Part I, Article V.
56. Ibid., Part I, Article XVIII.
57. Constitution of New York, Article XV (April 27, 1777), accessed May 25, 2017. The Avalon Project, Yale Law School.
58. Thomas, *The House of Commons in the Eighteenth Century*, 138.
59. Benjamin Franklin's copy of one of these collections of state constitutions can be found in the Library Company of Philadelphia (LCP). See *Recueil des loix constitutives des colonies angloises: confédérées sous la dénomination d'Etats Unis de l'Amérique-Septentrionale* (Philadelphia [Paris], 1778). LCP, Am 1778 U.S. Cons Log 2771.D.
60. Constitution of New York, Article XV.
61. Ibid.
62. Constitution of the State of Pennsylvania (September 28, 1776), accessed May 25, 2017. The Avalon Project, Yale Law School.
63. Constitution of Vermont (July 8, 1777), accessed May 25, 2017. The Avalon Project, Yale Law School.
64. Constitution of Pennsylvania, Section 15.
65. Constitution of Pennsylvania, Section 35.
66. Kenneth Owen argues that Pennsylvanians "scrutinized the actions of their representatives in government and sought to develop means of ensuring that their voice could continue to have an impact on the governmental process." See Owen, *Political Community in Revolutionary Pennsylvania*, 13.
67. Ibid., 2.
68. Slauter, *The State as a Work of Art*, 150. Slauter notes that "the practice of transcribing the voices of representatives in the United States began in the

1780s, and was by no means uniform in 1787." In addition to this style of coverage emerging in Philadelphia, he points to South Carolina, where the *Charleston Evening Gazette* began printing proceedings of the state House of Representatives in 1785. Furthermore, most state legislatures published journals of their proceedings, which were "bare documents recording the presence of members and the outcomes of votes without dialogue."

69. Jillson and Wilson, *Congressional Dynamics*, 57. For more on the context of fears of British alliance with enslaved people and/or Native American peoples, see especially Holton, *Forced Founders*, 136–137; Alan Taylor, *The Internal Enemy: Slavery and War in Virginia, 1772–1832* (New York: Norton, 2013); Gregory Dowd, *Groundless: Rumors, Legends, and Hoaxes on the Early American Frontier* (Baltimore: Johns Hopkins University Press, 2015), 205.
70. Henry Laurens to William Livingston, April 23, 1779, *William Livingston Family Collection*, Vol. 2, *1775–1780*. Massachusetts Historical Society, Ms. N-1579.1.
71. Calvin Jillson and Rick Wilson argued that "most of the delegates felt that they had, at most, an advisory relationship to the formal and legal political institutions of their home colonies." See Jillson and Wilson, *Congressional Dynamics*, 2, 47.
72. Rakove, *Beginnings of National Politics*, 23; Jillson and Wilson, *Congressional Dynamics*, 43.
73. Rakove, *Beginnings of National Politics*, 22.
74. Ibid., 30–33.
75. Silas Deane to Mrs. Deane, in *Letters of members of the Continental congress*, Vol. 1, ed. Edmund C. Burnett (Washington, D.C.: Carnegie Institution of Washington Publication, 1963 reprint), 4.
76. Continental Congress, *Rough Journals*, Vol. 1, September 6, 1774, 16. U.S. National Archives, Fold3, NARA M247, Record Group: 360.
77. New Jersey delegate Joseph Galloway seems to have expected to regularly report back on what was happening to the governor of his home state. See Joseph Galloway to Governor of New Jersey (William Franklin), September 3, 1774, in *Letters of members of the Continental congress*, Vol. 1, 6.
78. John Adams to Abigail Adams, September 14, 1774, in *Letters of members of the Continental congress*, Vol. 1, 31.
79. Caesar Rodney to Thomas Rodney, September 12, 1774, in *Letters of members of the Continental congress*, Vol. 1, 30.
80. New York Delegates to Chairman and Freeholders of Dutchess County, November 7, 1774, in *Letters of members of the Continental congress*, Vol. 1, 84.
81. Ibid.
82. United States Congress, "Extracts from the votes and proceedings of the American Continental Congress, held at Philadelphia" (Philadelphia: William and Thomas Bradford, 1774), 17. LCP, 112586.0 (McNeil).
83. Samuel Seabury, *Free thoughts on the proceedings of the Continental Congress* (New York, 1774). LCP, Am 1774 Seabury 112614.O (McNeil). Another pamphlet, published in Boston early in 1775, also highlighted the fact that the published proceedings "cautiously omitted" at least one controversial

vote they had taken upon convening. See Harrison Gray, *A few remarks upon some of the votes and resolutions of the Continental Congress* (Boston, 1775). LCP, Am 1775, Gra Ar 75 G779.

84. Continental Congress, *Rough Journals*, Vol. 1, May 11, 1775, 59. U.S. National Archives, Fold3, NARA M247, Record Group: 360.
85. For more on the way the journals were composed, see Herbert Friedenwald, "The Journals and Papers of the Continental Congress," *Pennsylvania Magazine of History and Biography*, Vol. 21, no. 2 (1897).
86. Silas Deane to Mrs. Deane, undated, in *Letters of members of the Continental congress*, Vol. 1, 90.
87. These comments are taken from two separate letters: John Adams to James Warren, July 6, 1775, in *Letters of members of the Continental congress*, Vol. 1, 152; John Adams to James Warren, July 24, 1775, in *Letters of members of the Continental congress*, Vol. 1, 176.
88. John Adams to James Warren, October 2, 1775, in *Letters of members of the Continental congress*, Vol. 1, 213.
89. John Adams to Abigail Adams, October 10, 1775, in *Letters of members of the Continental congress*, Vol. 1, 225.
90. See, for example, William Williams to Joseph Trumbull, September 13, 1776, in *Letters of members of the Continental congress*, Vol. 2, ed. Edmund C. Burnett (Washington, D.C.: Carnegie Institution of Washington Publication, 1963 reprint), 87. The British postal system had a long history of using the post office to "assert control over the flow of politically sensitive information and to provide surveillance of groups and individuals who opposed the government." See Joseph Adelman, *Revolutionary Networks: The Business and Politics of Printing the News, 1763–1789* (Baltimore: Johns Hopkins University Press, 2019), 43.
91. Based on epistolary culture in the period, it could well be that Adams felt when he was writing in a private capacity to a friend or his wife that there was a reasonable expectation of confidentiality. See Perl-Rosenthal, "Corresponding Republics," 100.
92. Americans were also engaging in a certain degree of surveillance as they set up their own postal system in the 1770s. In October 1776, the Congress appointed an "inspector of dead letters" (dead letters being a term for undeliverable or unlabeled mail) who was to examine "dead letters; inform Congress of any that contained 'inimical schemes or intelligence'; and preserve money and other valuables found in the letters, keeping a record of such things as well as of all letters than came into his office." Furthermore, the inspector was "not to divulge their contents to any but the members of Congress or their agents." See Sanders, *Evolution of the Executive Departments*, 155. Ebenezer Hazard, when he became surveyor of Post Offices and Post Roads, also promised to fill the role of Inspector of Dead Letters in an oath taken in June 1778. *Oath taken by E. Hazard*, June 22, 1778, Ebenezer Hazard Papers, American Philosophical Society (APS), Mss.B.H338.

93. Continental Congress, *Transcript Journals*, Vol. 1, September 18, 1775, 11. U.S. National Archives, Fold3, NARA M247, Record Group: 360.
94. Continental Congress, *Transcript Journals*, Vol. 1, November 29, 1775, 144. U.S. National Archives, Fold3, NARA M247, Record Group: 360.
95. Samuel Adams to James Warren, November 23, 1778, in *Letters of members of the Continental congress*, Vol. 3, ed. Edmund C. Burnett (Washington, D.C.: Carnegie Institution of Washington Publication, 1963 reprint), 503.
96. Ibid. All these measures did not completely foreclose the possibility of espionage, which did happen. For example, Edward Bancroft, who worked as an assistant to Silas Deane and Benjamin Franklin in France, formally spied for the British government through the 1770s. Despite Congress's best efforts, leaks did occur.
97. Rakove, *Beginnings of National Politics*, 71; Adams, *The First American Constitutions*, 49.
98. Rakove, *Beginnings of National Politics*, 70.
99. John Adams to Moses Gill, June 10, 1775, in *Letters of members of the Continental congress*, Vol. 1, 117.
100. John Adams to Abigail Adams, June 10, 1775, in *Letters of members of the Continental congress*, Vol. 1, 117. See also John Adams to Abigail Adams, July 23, 1775, in *Letters of members of the Continental congress*, Vol. 1, 175.
101. Adelman, *Revolutionary Networks*, 83.
102. John Adams to James Warren, October 7, 1775, in *Letters of members of the Continental congress*, Vol. 1, 218. Adams was not alone among the delegates in desiring meaningful correspondence for the purpose of consultation in forming opinions. Samuel Adams expressed the same lamentations. See Samuel Adams to James Warren, November 4, 1775, in *Letters of members of the Continental congress*, Vol. 1, 249; Samuel Adams to William Heath, October 20, 1775, in *Letters of members of the Continental congress*, Vol. 1, 239.
103. Maier, *American Scripture*, 42.
104. Ibid., 30.
105. Benjamin Rush to Robert Morris, February 8, 1777, in *Letters of members of the Continental congress*, Vol. 2, 240.
106. Rakove also notes this breakdown in communication, stating that by 1777 "delegates found themselves struggling to maintain a barely adequate flow of information between Congress and their constituents." See Rakove, *Beginnings of National Politics*, 127.
107. Samuel Chase to Maryland Council of Safety, January 8, 1777, in *Letters of members of the Continental congress*, Vol. 2, 208.
108. Samuel Chase to Maryland Council of Safety, February 20, 1777, in *Letters of members of the Continental congress*, Vol. 2, 268.
109. Thomas Burke, Abstract of Debates, February 27, 1777, in *Letters of members of the Continental congress*, Vol. 2, 285. Jack Rakove suggested that this was proposed under pressure from the Maryland assembly. See Rakove, *Beginnings of National Politics*, 248.

110. Burke, Abstract of Debates, February 27, 1777, in *Letters of members of the Continental congress*, Vol. 2, 285.
111. Ibid.
112. Thomas Burke to the Governor of North Carolina (Richard Caswell), March 11, 1777, in *Letters of members of the Continental congress*, Vol. 2, 295.
113. The Virginia Delegates to the Speaker of the Virginia House of Delegates (George Wythe), May 20, 1777, in *Letters of members of the Continental congress*, Vol. 2, 366.
114. Ibid. Shortages of paper and ink also affected printers in the printing of newspapers and almanacs, as well as other printed material. On top of these shortages, networks of communication were also hampered, making the circulation of printed information challenging. For more, see Adelman, *Revolutionary Networks*, 169.
115. John Adams to Thomas Jefferson, May 26, 1777, in *Letters of members of the Continental congress*, Vol. 2, 375.
116. John Adams to James Warren, December 3, 1775, in *Letters of members of the Continental congress*, Vol. 1, 269.
117. Richard Smith Diary, December 14, 1775, in *Letters of members of the Continental congress*, Vol. 1, 275.
118. Friedenwald, "The Journals and Papers of the Continental Congress," 165.
119. Ibid., 167–168.
120. *Pennsylvania Packet* (December 8, 1778), accessed May 26, 2017. Readex: America's Historical Newspapers.
121. *Pennsylvania Packet* (December 15, 1779), accessed May 26, 2017. Readex: America's Historical Newspapers.
122. Ibid.
123. *Pennsylvania Packet* (December 29, 1779), accessed May 26, 2017. Readex: America's Historical Newspapers.
124. Henry Laurens, Notes of Debates, May 8, 1779, in *Letters of members of the Continental congress*, Vol. 4, ed. Edmund C. Burnett (Washington, D.C.: Carnegie Institution of Washington Publication, 1963 reprint), 201.
125. William Floyd to the Governor of New York (George Clinton), May 14, 1779, in *Letters of members of the Continental congress*, Vol. 4, 211.
126. Ibid.
127. James Lovell to Deputy Secretary of the Massachusetts Council (John Avery), May 17, 1779, in *Letters of members of the Continental congress*, Vol. 4, 217.
128. James Lovell to John Adams, June 13, 1779, in *Letters of members of the Continental congress*, Vol. 4, 262.
129. Henry Laurens, Notes of Proceedings, June 19, 1779, in *Letters of members of the Continental congress*, Vol. 4, 276.
130. Rakove, *Beginnings of National Politics*, 255.
131. Henry Laurens, Notes of Proceedings, June 19, 1779, in *Letters of members of the Continental congress*, Vol. 4, 276.

132. Rakove, *Beginnings of National Politics*, 256–257.
133. Letter from Americanus in the *Pennsylvania Gazette*, cited in *Letters of members of the Continental congress*, Vol. 4, 277.
134. Leonidas, *Pennsylvania Packet*, in *Letters of members of the Continental congress*, Vol. 4, 295.
135. "O Tempora! O Moses!" *Maryland Journal and Baltimore Advertiser*; in *Letters of members of the Continental congress*, Vol. 4, 307.
136. Henry Laurens, Notes of Proceedings, July 3, 1779, in *Letters of members of the Continental congress*, Vol. 4, 295. Gerry would change his tune on the issue of secrecy in 1787 as a delegate in the Federal Convention.
137. Henry Laurens to Richard Henry Lee, June 22, 1779, in *Richard Henry Lee Papers*. APS. Mss.B.L51.
138. Richard Henry Lee to Henry Laurens, July 10, 1779, in *Letters of members of the Continental congress*, Vol. 4, 308. Gouverneur Morris made a similar statement to Robert Livingston in a letter dated July 22, 1779. See *Letters of members of the Continental congress*, Vol. 4, 384.
139. Henry Laurens to William Livingston, July 5, 1779, in *Letters of members of the Continental congress*, Vol. 4, 299.
140. Articles of Confederation, Article IX (March 1, 1781), accessed May 25, 2017. The Avalon Project, Yale Law School. Rahul Sagar has cited this provision as precedent for what would be debates in the Federal Convention in 1787. See Sagar, *Secrets and Leaks*, 21.
141. The Pennsylvania Delegates to the Pennsylvania Council, December 30, 1783, in *Letters of members of the Continental congress*, Vol. 7, ed. Edmund C. Burnett (Washington, D.C.: Carnegie Institution of Washington Publication, 1963 reprint), 403.
142. Arthur Lee to George Washington, March 13, 1783, in *Letters of members of the Continental congress*, Vol. 7, 81.
143. Francis Dana to the Massachusetts Assembly, June 11, 1784, in *Letters of members of the Continental congress*, Vol. 7, 549.
144. Jack Rakove also notes this declining attention on Congress, citing its continuing to meet in secret and its limited capacity to act as reasons why little attention was paid to it. See Rakove, *Beginnings of National Politics*, 355.
145. Charles Thomson to Benjamin Brankson, August 31, 1784, in *Charles Thomson Papers*. Historical Society of Pennsylvania (HSP), #0658.
146. *The Papers of George Washington, Digital Edition*, Confederation Series, Vol. 5 (Charlottesville: University of Virginia Press, Rotunda, 2008), 9. Rahul Sagar identified this quotation as evidence that the framers were inclined to support the use of secrecy in government. See Sagar, *Secrets and Leaks*, 21. Of note also is that Washington skillfully developed spying methods and had a keen eye for propaganda during the war. Alexis Coe points out that Washington convinced the Congress to fund the *New Jersey Journal* and he proceeded to use the newspaper to spread stories of American success and British evil, such as cases of sexual assault committed by British

forces. On the other hand, Washington himself was personally involved in setting up and operating the Culper spy ring and other successful spying efforts. For more, see Alexis Coe, *You Never Forget Your First: A Biography of George Washington* (New York: Viking, 2020), 71–73, 81–86.

147. *The Papers of George Washington, Digital Edition*, Vol. 5, 9.

Chapter Two. Cracking the *Secret du Roi*

1. France, Contrôle General des Finances, *Compte Rendu au Roi par M. Necker, Directeur Général des Finances, Au Moi de janvier 1781* (Vienne: Chez J. Thomas, 1781), 1, accessed May 25, 2017. Eighteenth Century Collections Online.
2. Soll, *The Reckoning*, 140; Jean Egret, *The French Prerevolution, 1787–1788*, trans. Wesley D. Camp (Chicago: University of Chicago Press), 1977.
3. Jacques Necker, *Mémoire de M Necker, au Roi, sur l'établissement des Administrations Provinciales* (1785), 33, accessed May 25, 2017. The Making of the Modern World.
4. Soll, *The Reckoning*, xiii.
5. Ibid. See also Baker, *Inventing the French Revolution*, 192.
6. Soll, *The Reckoning*, xiii.
7. The "secret du Roi" referred specifically to the clandestine diplomatic dealings of Louis XV, which he ran through the Prince de Conti, the Compte de Broglie, and the Comte de Vergennes, and which, after 1756, increasingly had goals at odds with the official diplomacy of the French government. The phrase could also be used to refer more generally to a broader "art of politics" that was to be conducted privately rather than publicly. For more, see Gary Savage, "Favier's Heirs: The French Revolution and the Secret du Roi," *Historical Journal* 41, no. 1 (January 1998); Barker, *Inventing the French Revolution*, 116, 170.
8. Raymond Birn, "The Profit of Ideas: Privileges en Librairie in Eighteenth-Century France," *Eighteenth-Century Studies* 4, no. 2 (Winter 1970–1971), 139. There was an official newspaper of the French government, the *Gazette de France*, but its reporting was restricted mainly to ceremonial events and foreign affairs. While such a project was certainly aimed at promoting a public image of royal government, it was to be a carefully crafted ceremonial image as opposed to a detailed account of government operations or political decisions. Jürgen Habermas advances the notion that before the eighteenth century, there was a need for "representative publicness," which he describes as a display of status, as opposed to what would later become the "bourgeois public sphere," in which networks of communication emerged to create a realm of dialogue. While the situation of the French monarchy, particularly post-1750, cannot be fit into a sociological schema neatly, the concept is useful for thinking about the transformations taking place in the eighteenth century. For more on the type of publicity exercised under the

ancien régime, see Ralph E. Giesy, "The King Imagined," in Baker, *The French Revolution and the Creation of Modern Political Culture*, Vol. 1.

9. Jean-Marie Carbasse, "Lettres de Cachet," in *Dictionnaire du Grand Siècle*, ed. François Bluche (Paris: Fayard, 1990), 867.
10. Soll, *The Information Master*, 153–154. As Keith Baker put it: "The politics of absolutism was not a public politics." See Baker, *Inventing the French Revolution*, 170.
11. For more on the growth of the absolutist state, particularly the expansion of royal administration, see especially Michel Antoine, "La monarchie absolue," in Baker, *The French Revolution and the Creation of Modern Political Culture*, Vol. 1.
12. For more on notions of the king and representation in an absolutist model, see Friedland, *Political Actors*, 49–50; James B. Collins, *The State in Early Modern France* (Cambridge: Cambridge University Press, 2009), 80. On the way in which this was linked to the justification for secrecy, see especially Goodman, "Public Sphere and Private Life," 3; Kantorowicz, "Mysteries of State."
13. Baker, *Inventing the French Revolution*, 114. Baker writes: "It follows from this definition of absolutism that the king, and the king alone, is a public person. The king, alone among his subjects, sees the whole and can take counsel from the whole; his alone is a truly public will."
14. Censer, *The French Press in the Age of Enlightenment*, 15. For a study of one of the most influential of these periodicals, see Popkin, *News and Politics in the Age of Revolution*, and Popkin, *Revolutionary News*.
15. Tabetha Ewing, "Six Invasions of Lorient: Rumor, Public Opinion, and Foreign Politics in 1740s Paris," in *Into Print: Limits and Legacies of the Enlightenment; Essays in Honor of Robert Darnton*, ed. Charles Walton (University Park, PA: Penn State University Press, 2011), 108; Tabetha Leigh Ewing, *Rumor, Diplomacy, and War in Enlightenment Paris* (Liverpool: Liverpool University Press, 2014); Robert Darnton, *Poetry and the Police: Communication Networks in Eighteenth-Century Paris* (Cambridge, MA: Belknap Press of Harvard University Press, 2010); Robert Darnton, *The Devil in the Holy Water or the Art of Slander from Louis XIV to Napoleon* (Philadelphia: University of Pennsylvania Press, 2010). On the presence of rumors in pre-revolutionary Paris, see also Arlette Farge and Jacques Revel, *The Vanishing Children of Paris: Rumor and Politics before the French Revolution*, trans. Claudia Mieville (Cambridge, MA: Harvard University Press, 1993).
16. Ozouf, "L'opinion publique," 425–427; Ewing, "Invasion of Lorient: Rumor, Public Opinion, and Foreign Politics in 1740s Paris," 108; Jeffrey S. Ravel, *The Contested Parterre: Public Theater and French Political Culture, 1680–1791* (Ithaca: Cornell University Press, 1999); Sarah Maza, *Private Lives and Public Affairs*; Elizabeth Andrews Bond, *The Writing Public: Participatory Knowledge Production in Enlightenment and Revolutionary France* (Ithaca: Cornell University Press, 2021).

17. Baker, *Inventing the French Revolution*, 171–172. Contrary to Habermas's claim that the "public sphere" developed outside of government institutions, Baker suggests that it was in large part the monarchy itself that invented and appealed to "public opinion" as a principle of political legitimacy outside the state. Jeffrey Ravel also points to royal concern and appeals to public opinion in the form of the theater. See Ravel, *The Contested Parterre*, 9, 194, 196, 198. Dale Van Kley has also argued that in the 1750s, the crown began to appeal to "the public" in conflicts with the Paris Parlement over religious practice. See Van Kley, *Religious Origins of the French Revolution*, 194.
18. Baker, *Inventing the French Revolution*, 198.
19. Ibid., 199.
20. Jonathan Conlin, "Wilkes, the Chevalier D'Eon and 'The Dregs of Liberty': An Anglo-French Perspective on Ministerial Despotism, 1762–1771," *English Historical Review* 120, no. 489 (December 2005); Linda Colley, *Britons*, 5–6. A good example of how the English thought about France in comparison to their country can be found in a letter to John Wilkes, composed in 1764. Wilkes, who fled to Paris after being found guilty of seditious libel in 1763, was warned by a friend in London "how dangerous it is for a foreigner, especially one in your situation to interest himself in political cabals in the place of your present residence[;] should you unhappily embroil yourself in any difficulties of this nature, you would assuredly find that the gates of the Bastille at Paris were more strongly bolted than those of the Tower of London." See *General Correspondence of John Wilkes, with a few additions; 1739–1802*, Vol. 2. BL Add MS 30868: 1764–1765.
21. Darnton, *The Literary Underground of the Old Regime*, 204. See also Darnton, *The Forbidden Best-Sellers of Pre-Revolutionary France*. Darnton has argued that such material was more pervasive than the writings of the philosophes, suggesting it may have played a more central role in undercutting the monarchy's legitimacy.
22. Though Darnton's conclusion has been challenged, considering *libelles* in tandem with the contents of more intellectual tracts, as David Bell has suggested, can help to re-create the discursive context in which discussions were taking place. See David A. Bell, "Why Books Caused a Revolution: A Reading of Robert Darnton," in *The Darnton Debate: Books and Revolution in the Eighteenth Century*, ed. Haydn T. Mason (Oxford: Voltaire Foundation, 1998).
23. On this point, see also Nicole Bauer, "In the Kingdom of Shadows: Secrecy and Transparency in Eighteenth-Century France" (PhD dissertation, University of North Carolina at Chapel Hill, 2018). It bears mentioning that such characteristics were often gendered female. For more on the power of women under the monarchy and how it changed during the Revolution, see Joan Landes, *Women and the Public Sphere in the Age of the French Revolution* (Ithaca: Cornell University Press, 1988).

24. On the expanding role of the General Farm and perceptions of it, see Michael Kwass, *Contraband: Louis Mandrin and the Making of a Global Underground* (Cambridge, MA: Harvard University Press, 2014).
25. Montesquieu, *De l'Esprit des Lois*, Vol. 1 (Paris: Garnier Frères, 1973), 40, 67.
26. Thomas Kaiser, "The Evil Empire? The Debate on Turkish Despotism in Eighteenth-Century French Political Culture," *Journal of Modern History* 72, no. 1 (March 2000): 9. In the eighteenth century, many French writers, including Montesquieu in *De l'Esprit des Lois* and in *Lettres Persanes* (1721), would cite Muslims and/or "the East" as examples of despotism in contrast to English liberty on the opposite end of the spectrum. This did change by the outbreak of the Revolution. For more, see especially Ian Coller, *Muslims and Citizens: Islam, Politics, and the French Revolution* (New Haven: Yale University Press, 2020), 17–18.
27. Voltaire, *Lettres Philosophiques* (Paris: Garnier-Flammarion, 1964), 132.
28. Peter Robert Campbell, *The Ancien Régime in France* (Oxford: Basil Blackwell, 1988), 46.
29. See Van Kley, *The Religious Origins of the French Revolution;* Dale Van Kley, *The Damiens Affair and the Unraveling of the Ancien Régime, 1750–1770* (Princeton: Princeton University Press, 1984); Baker, *Inventing the French Revolution*, 32–58, 169.
30. David A. Bell, *Lawyers and Citizens: The Making of a Political Elite in Old Regime France* (New York: Oxford University Press, 1994), 25.
31. Campbell, *The Ancien Régime in France*, 48; Egret, *The French Pre-Revolution*, viii, ix; William Doyle, "The Parlements," in Baker, *The Political Culture of the Old Regimes*, Vol. 1.
32. Bell, *Lawyers and Citizens*, 5–6.
33. Ibid., 8.
34. Doyle, "The Parlements," 160–162.
35. Bell, *Lawyers and Citizens*, 10–11; Maza, *Private Lives and Public Affairs*, 5, 12; Doyle, "The Parlements," 162; Van Kley, *The Damiens Affair*, 112, 117.
36. Bell, *Lawyers and Citizens;* Van Kley, *The Religious Origins of the French Revolution;* Maza, *Private Lives and Public Affairs;* Jean-Luc Chartier, *Justice, une réforme manquée, 1771–1774: le chancelier Maupeou* (Paris: Fayard, 2009).
37. Bell, *Lawyers and Citizens*, 149; Doyle, "The Parlements," 164. Dale Van Kley explains how the emergence of the Parti Patriote following the Maupeou crisis united with Jansenist critics of the crown. See Van Kley, *Religious Origins of the French Revolution*, 13, 251.
38. "Le Chancelier Maupeou," detached from *Journal des gens du monde* (Paris, 1783). Firestone Library: (Ex)1509.171.624.251.
39. Van Kley, *The Religious Origins of the French Revolution*, 153; Van Kley, *The Damiens Affair*, 112–113. One of the bases advanced for the Parlement's role as a mediating body between king and people was the notion of the Parlement as a repository of fundamental laws that led it to serve "as the crucial institutional expression of the link between the monarch and his subjects,"

as argued by Louis Adrien Le Paige in *Lettres Historiques sur les fonctions essentielles du Parlement, sur le droit des pairs et sur les loix fondamentales du royaume* (1753–54). See Baker, *Inventing the French Revolution*, 42.

40. *Journal historique de la révolution opérée dans la Constitution de la Monarchie Françoise*, Vol. 1 (Amsterdam, 1774–1776), 9. Firestone Library: (Ex)1509.171.61.

41. *Correspondance· secrète et familière de M de Maupeou avec M. de Sor*** Conseiller du nouveau Parlement* (Pairs, 1771), 11. Firestone Library: (Ex) 1509.171.61.01.

42. The case was emblematic of the way Maupeou's supporters and later critics of the *parlements* would contest the courts' claims to be representative. In 1788 when the royal ministry established a new Plenary Court to bypass the Paris Parlement's authority to register edicts and taxes, supporters of the crown questioned whether an entity with such vested interest in tax policy, for example, could be representative. See Egret, *The French Prerevolution*, 159.

43. Keith Baker has also pointed to this trend. See Baker, *Inventing the French Revolution*, 116–127.

44. For more on the *secret du roi* and the effect of its revelation, see Savage, "Favier's Heirs"; Nicole Bauer, "The Fate of Secrets in a Public Sphere: The Comte de Broglie and the Demise of the Secret du roi," *Journal of the Western Society for French History* 43 (2015).

45. Brian E. Strayer, *Lettres de cachet and Social Control in the Ancien Régime, 1659–1789* (New York: Peter Lang, 1992).

46. Honoré-Gabriel de Riqueti Mirabeau, *Lettres de cachet et des prisons d'état: ouvrage posthume, composé en 1778* (Hambourg, 1782), 92. Firestone Library: (Ex) HV8203.M6.

47. Ibid., 106.

48. See *Recueil Fidèle de plusieurs manuscrits trouves a la Bastille, dont on concerne spécialement l'homme au Masque de Fer, le tout pour servir de supplément aux trois livraisons de la Bastille Dévoilée* (Paris, 1789), 4. BNF: FRBNF33571900; *Les Révolutions de Paris, no.* 2, 9.

49. "Etat de ceux des papiers de la Bastille concernant les prisonniers renfermées dans cette forteresse qui ont été mise en ordre jusqu'à présent pour être communiquée au Public," Administration de la Bastille: Classement des Archives de la B. postérieur à 1789. BNF Arsenal Ms. 12725; "Municipalité de Paris: Par le Maire et les Officiers Municipaux. Extrait du Régistre des Déliberations du Corps Municipal. Du Vendredi 11 novembre, 1791," Administration de la Bastille: Classement des Archives de la B. postérieur à 1789. BNF Arsenal Ms. 12725.

50. Hans-Jurgen Lusebrink and Rolf Reichardt, *The Bastille: A History of a Symbol of Despotism and Freedom* (Durham: Duke University Press, 1997), 15.

51. Ibid.

52. For more on fear of prisons and what they contained in the eighteenth century, see Jeffrey Freedman, "The Dangers Within: Fears of Imprisonment in Enlightenment France," *Modern Intellectual History* (January 2016).

53. Chrétien Guillaume de Lamoignon Malesherbes, "Remonstrances de 1775" in *Les Remonstrances de Malesherbes, 1771–1775*, ed. Elisabeth Badinter (Paris: Union générale d'éditions, 1978), 206. Baker has also analyzed this tract and its promotion of publicity. See Baker, *Inventing the French Revolution*, 117–119.
54. Malesherbes, "Remonstrances de 1775," 211.
55. Ibid., 213.
56. Ibid., 260.
57. Ibid., 266.
58. Ibid., 272.
59. Ibid., 265.
60. *Œuvres Posthumes de M Turgot; ou Mémoire de M Turgot, sur les administrations provinciales, mis en parallèle avec celui de M Necker, suivi d'une Lettre sur ce plan et des Observations d'un républicain sur ces mémoires* (Lausanne: Du Point de Nemours, Pierre Samuel, 1787), 11, accessed May 25, 2017. The Making of the Modern World.
61. Cited in Egret, *The French Prerevolution*, 22.
62. Ibid, 23.
63. Ibid., 100, 114–115.
64. Ibid., 145–148, 150–153.
65. Ibid., 158–159.
66. Filippo Mazzei, *Recherches historiques et politiques sur les Etats-Unis de l'Amérique Septentrionale, Tome I* (Paris, 1788), 334, accessed February 2, 2018. Hathi Trust.
67. Ibid., 335
68. Ibid., 341.
69. Mazzei, *Recherches historiques et politiques, Tome II*, 55.
70. Mazzei, *Recherches historiques et politiques, Tome IV*, 251.
71. Importantly, there was very little talk of ending the monarchy at this point. Rather, republican government was considered compatible with monarchy as it connoted less a form of government without a monarch, but a mode of government guided by liberty and the common good. See Bosc, *Le Peuple Souverain et la Démocratie*, 48–50; Dan Edelstein, *The Terror of Natural Right: Republicanism, the Cult of Nature, and the French Revolution* (Chicago: University of Chicago Press, 2009), 10.
72. This was widely taken as a declaration of press freedom. See Egret, *The French Prerevolution*, 190.
73. Gough, *The Newspaper Press in the French Revolution*, 16.
74. Malesherbes, "Mémoire sur la liberté de la presse," in *Mémoires sur la Librairie et sur La Liberté de la Presse*, ed. Graham E. Rodmell (Chapel Hill: University of North Carolina Press, 1979), 232.
75. Ibid.
76. Letter dated April 3, 1789, Archives Nationalles (AN) /V/1/549.
77. Letter signed by Abbé Barret, dated March 13, 1789, AN/V/1/550.

78. For examples of historians who cite the American Revolution as a guiding example for the French, see especially Jon Butler, *Becoming America: The Revolution Before 1776* (Cambridge, MA: Harvard University Press, 2000); Joyce Appleby, "America as a Model for the Radical French Reformers of 1789," *William and Mary Quarterly* 28, no. 2 (April 1971), pp. 267–286.
79. Jacques-Pierre Brissot de Warville, *Le Patriote françois: journal libre, impartial et national* (Paris: Buisson, March 16, 1789), 2. BNF: FRBNF32834106.
80. Shortly after returning to France, Brissot would publish a reflection on his travels in the United States: *Nouveau voyage dans les États-Unis d'Amérique septentrionale, fait en 1788*, 3 vols. (Paris, 1791).

Chapter Three. Behind the Veil of Secrecy

1. James Madison to Thomas Jefferson, September 6, 1787, in *The Papers of James Madison*, Congressional Series, Vol. 10, 27 *May 1787–3 March* 1788, ed. J. C. A. Stagg (Charlottesville: University of Virginia Press, Rotunda, 2010), 164. Numerous publications throughout the summer and once the Constitution was published noted the secrecy of the convention's proceedings. See, for example, "Extract of a Letter from Philadelphia, 21 July Charleston Columbian Herald," August 9, 1787, in *The Documentary History of the Ratification of the Constitution, Digital Edition*, Vol. 13, *Commentaries on the Constitution*, no. 1, ed. John P. Kaminski, Gaspare J. Saladino, Richard Leffler, Charles H. Schoenleber, and Margaret A. Hogan (Charlottesville: University of Virginia Press, 2009), 124; Roger Alden, "*Memorandum New York*," September 21, 1787, in *Documentary History of the Ratification of the Constitution*, Vol. 13, 220. Portions of this chapter originally appeared in Katlyn Marie Carter, "Denouncing Secrecy and Defining Democracy in the Early American Republic," *Journal of the Early Republic* 40, no. 3 (Fall 2020).
2. Historians have ventured some reasons to explain why the framers met behind closed doors, ranging from a strategic desire to avoid the prying eyes of foreign governments to a propensity to protect their reputations and avoid misunderstandings back in their home states. Determining the effect of meeting in secret has been the focus of most scholars who have addressed the secrecy rule at any length. See Carol Berkin, *A Brilliant Solution: Inventing the American Constitution* (New York: Harcourt, 2002), 64–65; John P. Kaminski, *Secrecy and the Constitutional Convention* (Madison, WI: Center for the Study of the American Constitution, 2005); David O. Stewart, *The Summer of 1787: The Men Who Invented the Constitution* (New York: Simon and Schuster, 2007), 51; Richard Beeman, *Plain, Honest Men: The Making of the American Constitution* (New York: Random House, 2009), 83; Michael Klarman, *The Framers' Coup: The Making of the United States Constitution* (Oxford: Oxford University Press, 2016), 252–253; Loughran, *The Republic in Print*, 142–143; Linda Colley, *The Gun, the Ship, and the Pen: Warfare, Constitutions, and the Making of the Modern World* (New York: Norton, 2021), 107, 122;

Downes, *Democracy, Revolution, and Monarchism in Early American Literature*, 118.

3. While decisions about whether to deliberate in secret or public were discussed more directly as related to different conceptions of how representation should work, these decisions also carried implications for who exactly was to be represented. For more on the confusions and contestation over the meaning of, and membership in, "the people," or "the public," see especially Eastman, *A Nation of Speechifiers*, 1–12; Murrin, "A Roof Without Walls," 333–347; Bradburn, *The Citizenship Revolution*, 2–3; Lewis, " 'Of Every Age Sex & Condition.' "
4. While Michael Klarman made a similar point about the limited consideration given to public opinion in the convention, the assertion runs counter to Jürgen Heideking's and Alfred Young's conclusion that the sense of public opinion played a crucial limiting function. See Klarman, *The Framers' Coup*, 3; Jürgen Heideking, *The Constitution Before the Judgment Seat: The Prehistory and Ratification of the American Constitution, 1787–1791* (Charlottesville: University of Virginia Press, 2012), 25; Alfred Young, *Liberty Tree: Ordinary People and the American Revolution*, 185, 195–202. There are indeed points in the notes from that summer when delegates reportedly referred to "the people" and what they would accept. See especially William Patterson saying on June 9: "We must follow the people; the people will not follow us." Or Elbridge Gerry on June 12 saying "that it was necessary to consider what the people would approve." See Farrand, *Records of the Federal Convention of 1787*, Vol. 1, 178, 215.
5. Gordon Wood, "Conspiracy and the Paranoid Style," 429.
6. For more on the thinking and demands of Antifederalists, see Herbert Storing, *What the Antifederalists Were For* (Chicago: University of Chicago Press, 1981), 17; Jack Rakove, *Original Meanings*, 229; Jürgen Heideking, *The Constitution Before the Judgment Seat*, 120, 149; Saul Cornell, *The Other Founders: Anti-Federalism and the Dissenting Tradition in America, 1788–1828* (Chapel Hill: University of North Carolina Press, 1999); Slauter, *The State as a Work of Art*, 127, 133, 135; Carol Berkin, *The Bill of Rights: The Fight to Secure America's Liberties* (New York: Simon and Schuster, 2015), 22; Carter, "Denouncing Secrecy and Defining Democracy in the Early American Republic."
7. On this method, see Skinner, *Visions of Politics*, 155; Gienapp, *The Second Creation*, 17.
8. Wood, *Creation of the American Republic*, 562, 546, 517. Paul Downes makes a similar observation, arguing that American revolutionaries removed the people entirely from government, despite framing the Constitution in the name of the people. Instead, the government was to be run entirely by representatives. See Downes, *Democracy, Revolution, and Monarchism*, 29.
9. This perspective further advances work that examines challenges to the framing of the federal government as democratic. See especially Nelson, *Commons Democracy*, and Bouton, *Taming Democracy*.

10. Klarman, *The Framers' Coup*, 263.
11. Ibid., 248–252.
12. The rules adopted on May 29 stated: "That no copy be taken of any entry on the journal during the sitting of the House without the leave of the House. That members only be permitted to inspect the journal. That nothing spoken in the House be printed, or otherwise published, or communicated without leave." See "Journal," Tuesday, May 29, 1787, in Farrand, *Records of the Federal Convention of 1787*, Vol. 1, 15.
13. "Manasseh Cutler: Journal," July 13, 1787, in Max Farrand, *Records of the Federal Convention of 1787*, Vol. 3, 58. There were two formal efforts recorded over the summer to lift or alter the secrecy rule. Both were defeated. See "Madison's Notes," Monday, July 16, 1787, and Thursday, July 25, 1787, in Farrand, *Records of the Federal Convention of 1787*, Vol. 2, 18, 115.
14. John K. Alexander, *The Selling of the Constitutional Convention: A History of News Coverage* (Madison: Madison House, 1990), 88; John P. Kaminski, Gaspare J. Saladino, eds., *Documentary History of the Ratification of the Constitution*, Vol. 13, *Commentaries on the Constitution* (Madison: State Historical Society of Wisconsin, 1981), 120–122.
15. An early June report in the *Pennsylvania Herald* emphasized the strict nature of the secrecy, claiming that "all debate is suspended upon the entrance of their own inferior officers." The author went on to note the "anxiety of the people" being heightened with the mystery surrounding the convention and urged speed in the delegates' work. At least one report, in the *Boston America Herald* suggested that "The profound secrecy hitherto observed by this august body, we cannot help considering as a happy omen; as it demonstrates, that the spirit of party, on any great and essential point, cannot have arisen to any height." See "*Pennsylvania Herald*," June 2, 1787, in *Documentary History of the Ratification of the Constitution*, Vol. 13, 122; "*Boston American Herald*," August 6, 1787, ibid., 185.
16. Mary Sarah Bilder, "How Bad Were the Official Records of the Federal Convention?" *George Washington Law Review* 80, no. 6 (2012): 1636.
17. Article I, Section 5 states: "Each House shall keep a Journal of its Proceedings, and from time to time publish the same, excepting such Parts as may in their Judgment require Secrecy." Article I, Section 9 states: "No Money shall be drawn from the Treasury, but in Consequence of Appropriations made by Law; and a regular Statement and Account of the Receipts and Expenditures of all public Money shall be published from time to time."
18. Berkin, *A Brilliant Solution*, 64–65; Colley, *The Gun, the Ship, and the Pen*, 115.
19. The delegates rarely directly stated whom they considered themselves to be representing, though the use of "We the People of the United States" to open the Constitution casts the document as written in the name of the American people, which itself was ill-defined. A rare occasion of direct reflection on this question in the convention arose on July 5, when Gouver-

neur Morris reportedly stated that "He came here as a representative of America; he flattered himself he came here in some degree as a Representative of the whole human race; for the whole human race will be affected by the proceedings of this Convention." See "Madison's Notes," Thursday, July 5, 1787, in Farrand, *Records of the Federal Convention of 1787*, Vol. 1, 529.

20. Alexander Martin to Richard Caswell, July 27, 1787, in Farrand, *Records of the Federal Convention of 1787*, Vol. 3, 64.

21. George Mason to George Mason, Jr., May 27, 1787, in Farrand, *Records of the Federal Convention of 1787*, Vol. 3, 28.

22. James Madison to Thomas Jefferson, June 6, 1787, *The Papers of James Madison*, Vol. 10, 29.

23. "Madison's Notes," Tuesday, June 12, 1787, in Farrand, *Records of the Federal Convention of 1787*, Vol. 1, 215.

24. For more on this, see especially Holton, *Unruly Americans*, 5–8. The phrase "excess of democracy" was used by Elbridge Gerry on May 31 when he declared that "The evils we experience flow from the excess of democracy." See "Madison's Notes," Thursday, May 31, 1787, in Farrand, *Records of the Federal Convention of 1787*, Vol. 1, 48. For more on Madison's thinking about the problems and pitfalls of the state governments, see James Madison, "Vices of the Political System of the United States," April 1787, in *Madison: Writings*, ed. Jack Rakove (New York: Library of America, Penguin Putnam, 1999), 69–80.

25. Bouton, *Taming Democracy*, 171. See also Wood, *Revolutionary Characters*, 149; Alan Taylor, *American Republics: A Continental History of the United States, 1783–1850* (New York: Norton, 2021), 37.

26. Lance Banning, *The Sacred Fire of Liberty: James Madison and the Founding of the Federal Republic* (Ithaca: Cornell University Press, 1995); Colleen Sheehan, *James Madison and the Spirit of Republican Self-Government* (Cambridge: Cambridge University Press, 2009); Weiner, *Madison's Metronome;* Tuck, *The Sleeping Sovereign*, 230; Alan Gibson, "Madison's Republican Remedy: The Tenth *Federalist* and the Creation of an Impartial Republic," in *The Cambridge Companion to the Federalist*, ed. Jack Rakove and Colleen Sheehan (Cambridge: Cambridge University Press, 2020), 263–301; Colleen Sheehan, "The Republicanism of Publius: The American Way of Life," in Rakove and Sheehan, *The Cambridge Companion to the Federalist*, 302–329; Larry Kramer, " 'The Interest of Man': James Madison's Constitutional Politics," in *The Cambridge Companion to the Federalist*, 330–369; Jack Rakove, "Politics Indoors and Out-of-Doors: A Fault Line in Madison's Thinking," in *The Cambridge Companion to the Federalist*, 370–399; Greg Weiner, " 'The Cool and Deliberate Sense of the Community': *The Federalist* on Congress," in *The Cambridge Companion to the Federalist*, 400–425.

27. Weiner, *Madison's Metronome*, 1, 49; Weiner, " 'The Cool and Deliberate Sense of the Community,' " 400–425.

28. Willi Paul Adams suggested this was one of the earliest distinctions made between these two types, which had before been treated as interchangeable.

See Adams, *The First Constitutions*, 112. Akhil Reed Amar agrees with Adams, calling the notion that the word "democracy" was "anathema to the Founding generation" a "prominent modern canard." See Akhil Reed Amar, *America's Constitution: A Biography* (New York: Random House, 2006), 14.

29. Madison, *The Federalist* No. 10, 65–68.
30. Other elements of the Constitution that can and have been interpreted as undemocratic are the Electoral College, the structure of the Senate, and life tenure for judges. See Klarman, *The Framers' Coup*, 626–627.
31. In declining to sign, Mason said: "This Constitution had been formed without the knowledge or idea of the people. A second convention will know more of the sense of the people, and be able to provide a system more consonant to it." See "Madison's Notes," Saturday, September 15, 1787, in Farrand, *Records of the Federal Convention of 1787*, Vol. 2, 632.
32. James Madison, "Public Opinion," *The National Gazette*, December 19, 1791, accessed September 7, 2020. NewsBank: Readex: America's Historical Newspapers.
33. Wood, *Revolutionary Characters*, 155.
34. Banning, *Sacred Fire of Liberty*, 9; Sheehan, *James Madison and the Spirit of Republican Self-Government*, 9.
35. Alan Gibson, "Veneration and Vigilance: James Madison and Public Opinion, 1785–1800," *Review of Politics* 67, no. 1 (2005): 9; Wood, *Revolutionary Characters*, 152; David Siemers, *Ratifying the Republic: Antifederalists and Federalists in Constitutional Time* (Stanford: Stanford University Press, 2002), 105; Andrew Shankman, *Original Intents: Hamilton, Jefferson, Madison, and the American Founding* (Oxford: Oxford University Press, 2017), 111; Douglas Bradburn, " 'Parties Are Unavoidable': Path Dependence and the Origins of Party Politics in the United States," in Peart and Smith, *Practicing Democracy*, 28, 31.
36. Jeremy Bailey, *James Madison and Constitutional Imperfection* (Cambridge: Cambridge University Press, 2015), 18; Siemers, *Ratifying the Republic*, 120; Jack Rakove, *A Politician Thinking: The Creative Mind of James Madison* (Norman: University of Oklahoma Press, 2017).
37. "Madison's Notes," Friday, August 10, 1787, in Farrand, *Records of the Federal Convention of 1787*, Vol. 2, 256.
38. "Madison's Notes," Saturday, August 11, 1787, in ibid., 259.
39. Ibid., 260.
40. Ibid. Of note is that this proposed wording matches, almost exactly, the wording in the Articles of Confederation, wherein Article IX stated that Congress "shall publish the journal of their proceedings monthly, except such parts thereof relating to treaties, alliances or military operations, as in their judgement require secrecy." See Articles of Confederation, March 1, 1781, accessed May 26, 2017. The Avalon Project, Yale Law School. Rahul Sagar also highlights this passage as precedent for authorizing secrecy in American government. See Sagar, *Secrets and Leaks*, 21.

41. "Madison's Notes," Saturday, August 11, 1787, in Farrand, *Records of the Federal Convention of 1787*, Vol. 2, 260.
42. Ibid.
43. "Madison's Notes," Friday, September 14, 1787, in ibid., 613.
44. Ibid.
45. Ibid., 619.
46. Ibid.
47. Sagar, *Secrets and Leaks*, 25–30. Sagar points to *The Federalist* Nos. 53, 64, and 75 as examples of an assumed ability of the executive to keep secrets and of the Senate, in particular, to act as a check against abuses of this power. Lindsay Chervinsky has argued that the refusal to create an executive council was actually rooted in the delegates' distaste for the secrecy of the British cabinet. See Lindsay Chervinsky, *The Cabinet: George Washington and the Creation of an American Institution* (Cambridge, MA: Harvard University Press, 2020), 112–115.
48. John Jay, *The Federalist* No. 64, in *The Federalist Papers*, ed. Cynthia Brantley Johnson (New York: Simon and Schuster, 2004). Sagar also highlights this reference to make the case that the framers had an expectation that the executive would be able to keep secrets, which was often cited as a benefit of executive power over legislative. See Sagar, *Secrets and Leaks*, 29.
49. Article II, Section 2 of the Constitution states that the president "may require the Opinion, in writing, of the principal Officer in each of the executive Departments, upon any Subject relating to the Duties of their respective Offices." Lindsay Chervinsky has suggested this was an effort to "ensure that communication between the president and his advisors would be transparent." See Chervinsky, *The Cabinet*, 116.
50. Neither oral arguments before the Supreme Court or the reading of opinions are open to television cameras. In 2020 during the Coronavirus pandemic the court did release live audio of arguments, which opened further discussion about whether more transparency should be introduced into the process. See "How the Court Works," accessed July 8, 2020, The Supreme Court Historical Society; Erik Wemple, "Supreme Court Gives in on Live Audio of Oral Arguments," *Washington Post*, accessed April 14, 2020, www.washingtonpost.com/opinions/2020/04/14/supreme-court-gives-live-audio-oral-arguments/. It should also be noted that in terms of criminal trial procedure, the Constitution did ultimately also guarantee a degree of publicity in the process with the Sixth Amendment, which states "the accused shall enjoy the right to a speedy and public trial."
51. Downes, *Democracy, Revolution, and Monarchism*, 118; Colley, *The Gun, the Ship, and the Pen*, 122.
52. James Madison to George Washington, September 30, 1787, *The Papers of James Madison*, Vol. 10, 180.
53. Richard Henry Lee to George Mason, October 1, 1787, in *Documentary History of the Ratification of the Constitution*, Vol. 18, *Ratification of the Constitution*

by the States: Virginia, ed. John P. Kaminski and Gaspare Saladino (Madison: Wisconsin Historical Society, 1988), 281–282.

54. George Washington to James Madison, October 10, 1787, *The Papers of James Madison*, Congressional Series, Vol. 10, 189. Trish Loughran has also identified this quotation from Washington and cited it as evidence that Federalist figures saw value in maintaining and exploiting distance between elected officials and their constituents. Loughran, *The Republic in Print*, 144.
55. "Madison's Notes," Monday, September 17, 1787, in Farrand, *Records of the Federal Convention of 1787*, Vol. 2, 643.
56. "Madison's Notes," Monday, September 17, 1787, in Farrand, *Records of the Federal Convention of 1787*, Vol. 2, 645, 647.
57. "Madison's Notes," Saturday, September 15, 1787, in Farrand, *Records of the Federal Convention of 1787*, Vol. 2, 632.
58. William Jackson to George Washington, September 17, 1787, in *The Papers of George Washington, Digital Edition*, Confederation Series, Vol. 5, 329.
59. James H. Hutson, "The Creation of the Constitution and the Integrity of the Documentary Record," in *Interpreting the Constitution: The Debate over Original Intent*, ed. Jack Rakove (Boston: Northeastern University Press, 1990), 155.
60. James Hutson notes that it was French envoy Edmond Genêt who edited a transcript of Yates's notes that had been previously transcribed by John Lansing from the original after Yates's death in 1801. Genêt, who was a French agent and partisan figure in the 1790s, openly admitted he edited and published the notes for political purposes and, in the process, altered them significantly. See Hutson, "The Creation of the Constitution and the Integrity of the Documentary Record," 156–158.
61. James Madison to Thomas Ritchie, September 15, 1821, in Farrand, *Records of the Federal Convention of 1787*, Vol. 3, 447.
62. Farrand, *Records of the Federal Convention of 1787*, Vol. 1, xiv. On Madison editing his notes, see Bilder, "How Bad Were the Official Records of the Federal Convention?" 1667; Mary Sarah Bilder, *Madison's Hand: Revising the Constitutional Convention* (Cambridge, MA: Harvard University Press, 2015).
63. Bilder, *Madison's Hand*, 15. Even if Madison's notes were faithful to what he recorded, Hutson raises the point that they would likely not be faithful to reality just given how short they are relative to the amount of time spent in deliberation, a result of the technical limitations in recording speech and the interpretive decisions required in the process. See Hutson, "The Creation of the Constitution and the Integrity of the Documentary Record," 166–167.
64. James Madison, *The Writing of James Madison*, Vol. 6 (New York: G. P. Putnam's Sons, 1906), 272. Jonathan Gienapp points to Madison's frustration in the debate over whether Congress had the authority to request papers from the executive related to the negotiation of the Jay Treaty as the reason he identified the ratifying conventions as the source of original meaning of the Constitution. After Washington cited the records of the Federal Convention

as the source of meaning, Madison sought to turn attention to the ratifying conventions as a source of authority. See Gienapp, *The Second Creation*, 317–319. James Hutson suggests that the framers initially expected judges to get at the intent of the Constitution from the text itself and suggests that before the 1840s, the Supreme Court did not tend to refer to records from the Federal Convention. See Hutson, "The Creation of the Constitution and the Integrity of the Documentary Record," 152–153.

65. David Waldstreicher, *Slavery's Constitution: From Revolution to Ratification* (New York: Hill and Wang, 2009), 103.
66. Klarman, *The Framers' Coup*, 297; Waldstreicher, *Slavery's Constitution*, 133.
67. Waldstreicher, *Slavery's Constitution*, 115, 133–134.
68. Ibid., 133–141.
69. Ibid., 16, 19.
70. Paul Finkelman, *Slavery and the Founders: Race and Liberty in the Age of Jefferson* (New York: M. E. Sharpe, 2001), 3, 5.
71. Sean Wilentz, *No Property in Man: Slavery and the Antislavery at the Nation's Founding* (Cambridge, MA: Harvard University Press, 2018), 6–7.
72. Ibid., 7.
73. Ibid., 11.
74. For an articulation of this argument, see Klarman, *The Framers' Coup*, 624–625. In the context of the Reconstruction Amendments, Eric Foner has also made the point that ambiguity in constitutional language has the potential to lead to limitations of rights, but also to opening possibilities. See Eric Foner, *The Second Founding: How the Civil War and Reconstruction Remade the Constitution* (New York: Norton, 2019), xxvi.
75. On the treatment of women in the Constitution, specifically the potential for both inclusion and exclusion inherent in the gender-neutral language, see especially Lewis, " 'Of Every Age Sex & Condition' "; Linda Kerber, *No Constitutional Right to Be Ladies: Women and the Obligations of Citizenship* (New York: Hill and Wang, 1998); Rosemarie Zagarri, "The Rights of Man and Woman in Post-Revolutionary America," *William and Mary Quarterly* 55, no. 2 (April 1998). Similar dynamics were at play in France during the same period. For more on the exclusionary effect of universalism, see especially Joan Wallach Scott, *Only Paradoxes to Offer: French Feminists and the Rights of Man* (Cambridge, MA: Harvard University Press, 1997). On the broader point that the Constitution used the term "citizen" without defining it and the way in which this drove many of the struggles of the nineteenth century, see especially Bradburn, *The Citizenship Revolution*, 17; Foner, *The Second Founding*, 3: Eastman, *A Nation of Speechifiers*, 6, 11.
76. Gregory Ablavsky, "The Savage Constitution," *Duke Law Journal* 63, no. 5 (February 2014): 999–1089.
77. Linda Colley suggests that "One of the consequences of the spread of these instruments [constitutions] was that women's pre-existing exclusion from much formal political activity was increasingly codified and therefore made

harder to change." See Linda Colley, "Writing Constitutions and Writing World History," in *The Prospect of Global History*, ed. James Belich, John Darwin, Margret Frenz, and Chris Wickham (Oxford: Oxford University Press, 2016), 167.

78. On the challenges for an originalist approach to interpreting the Constitution, see especially Hutson, "The Creation of the Constitution and the Integrity of the Documentary Record," 153, and Rakove, *Original Meanings*, 4–20.
79. Critics pointed both to specific clauses and the entire document as ambiguous with the effect of concealing true meaning, See, for example, "Speech by Benjamin Gale," November 12, 1787, in *The Documentary History of the Ratification of the Constitution, Digital Edition*, Vol. 3, *Delaware, New Jersey, Georgia, and Connecticut*, ed. John P. Kaminski, Gaspare J. Saladino, Richard Leffler, Charles H. Schoenleber, and Margaret A. Hogan (Charlottesville: University of Virginia Press, 2009), 424–425; "Brutus III," *New York Journal*, November 15, 1787, in *The Documentary History of the Ratification of the Constitution, Digital Edition*, Vol. 19, *New York*, 253; "A Farmer, *Philadelphia Freeman's Journal*," April 23, 1788, in *The Documentary History of the Ratification of the Constitution, Digital Edition*, Vol. 17, *Commentaries on the Constitution*, no. 5, ed. John P. Kaminski, Gaspare J. Saladino, Richard Leffler, Charles H. Schoenleber, and Margaret A. Hogan (Charlottesville: University of Virginia Press, 2009), 145; Aratus, "To the People of Maryland," November 2, 1787, in *The Documentary History of the Ratification of the Constitution, Digital Edition*, Vol. 11, *Maryland*, no. 1, ed. John P. Kaminski, Gaspare J. Saladino, Richard Leffler, Charles H. Schoenleber, and Margaret A. Hogan (Charlottesville: University of Virginia Press, 2009), 38.
80. Thomas Jefferson to John Adams, August 30, 1787, in *The Papers of Thomas Jefferson, Digital Edition*, Main Series, Vol. 12, ed. James P. McClure and J. Jefferson Looney (Charlottesville: University of Virginia Press, Rotunda, 2008–2022), 69.
81. Saul Cornell has emphasized that even though Antifederalists shared common critiques of the Constitution, this did not mean they shared common ideals. Nonetheless, they broadly seemed to agree on the need to resist centralization and believed in federalism, Constitutional textualism, and the need for a robust public sphere. I argue that they shared a common understanding of political representation. See Cornell, *The Other Founders*, 11.
82. "An officer of the Late Continental Army, *Independent Gazetteer*," November 6, 1787, in *The Documentary History of the Ratification of the Constitution*, Vol. 2, *Ratification of the Constitution by States: Pennsylvania*, ed. Merrill Jensen (Madison: State Historical Society of Wisconsin, 1976), 215.
83. Numerous publications made this point. See especially A Federal Republican, "A Review of the Constitution," November 28, 1787, in *The Documentary History of the Ratification of the Constitution, Digital Edition*, Vol. 14, *Commentaries on the Constitution*, no. 2, ed. John P. Kaminski, Gaspare J. Sal-

adino, Richard Leffler, Charles H. Schoenleber, and Margaret A. Hogan (Charlottesville: University of Virginia Press, 2009), 259; "A Dialogue Between Mr. Schism and Mr. Cutbrush, *Boston Gazette*," October 29, 1787, in *The Documentary History of the Ratification of the Constitution, Digital Edition*, Vol. 4, Massachusetts, no. 1, ed. John P. Kaminski, Gaspare J. Saladino, Richard Leffler, Charles H. Schoenleber, and Margaret A. Hogan (Charlottesville: University of Virginia Press, 2009), 164; "Curtiopolis," *New York Daily Advertiser*, January 18, 1788, in *The Documentary History of the Ratification of the Constitution, Digital Edition*, Vol. 15, Commentaries on the Constitution, no. 3, ed. John P. Kaminski, Gaspare J. Saladino, Richard Leffler, Charles H. Schoenleber, and Margaret A. Hogan (Charlottesville: University of Virginia Press, 2009), 400.

84. Max Edling, *A Revolution in Favor of Government: Origins of the U.S. Constitution and the Making of the American State* (Oxford: Oxford University Press, 2003), 22.
85. Cornell, *The Other Founders*, 37.
86. Columbus, *Pennsylvania Herald*, December 8, 1787, *Documentary History of the Ratification of the Constitution*, Vol. 2, *Ratification of the Constitution by States: Pennsylvania*, 314.
87. On anti-Catholic sentiment in America see McConville, *The King's Three Faces;* Cogliano, *No King, No Popery*. This was not the only time the convention was referred to as a conclave. See, for example, "Spurious Luther Martin: Address No. V," Philadelphia Federal Gazette, April 10, 1788, in *The Documentary History of the Ratification of the Constitution, Digital Edition*, Vol. 12, *Maryland*, no. 2, ed. John P. Kaminski, Gaspare J. Saladino, Richard Leffler, Charles H. Schoenleber, and Margaret A. Hogan (Charlottesville: University of Virginia Press, 2009), 500.
88. The Republican Federalist, *Massachusetts Centinel*, January 2, 1788, in *The Documentary History of the Ratification of the Constitution by States*, Vol. 5, *Massachusetts*, ed. John P. Kaminski and Gaspare J. Saladino (Madison: Wisconsin Historical Society Press, 1997), 591.
89. A Plebian, *An Address to the People of the State of New York*, April 17, 1788, in *The Documentary History of the Ratification of the Constitution by States*, Vol. 20, *New York*, ed. John P. Kaminski and Gaspare J. Saladino (Madison: Wisconsin Historical Society Press, 2004), 951.
90. Philip S. Foner, ed., *The Democratic Republican Societies, 1790–1800* (Westport, CT: Greenwood Press, 1976); Cotlar, *Tom Paine's America*.
91. "Cato" was suspected at the time and by some historians since to be New York governor George Clinton, though more recently Linda Grant DePauw has suggested he was more likely New York Antifederalist Abraham Yates. The question of Cato's identity remains open. "Caesar" was long rumored to be Alexander Hamilton, but this theory has largely been abandoned. See *Documentary History of the Ratification of the Constitution*, Vol. 19, *New York*, 58–59, 69.

92. Cato, *New York Journal*, September 27, 1787, *Documentary History of the Ratification of the Constitution*, Vol. 19, *New York*, 60.
93. Caesar, *New York Daily Advertiser*, October 1, 1787, *Documentary History of the Ratification of the Constitution*, Vol. 19, *New York*, 70.
94. Cato, *New York Journal*, October 11, 1787, *Documentary History of the Ratification of the Constitution*, Vol. 19, *New York*, 81.
95. Curtius, *New York Daily Advertiser*, October 18, 1787, *Documentary History of the Ratification of the Constitution*, Vol. 19, *New York*, 99.
96. A Country Federalist, *Poughkeepsie Country Journal*, December 19, 1787, *Documentary History of the Ratification of the Constitution*, Vol. 19, *New York*, 431. Many defenders of the convention made a similar allegation—both in published pieces and private correspondence—that the focus on secrecy was merely a strategic calculation to try to discredit the Constitution. See, for example, "Letter from New York," October 31, 1787, *Documentary History of the Ratification of the Constitution*, Vol. 3, *Delaware, New Jersey, Georgia, and Connecticut*, 391; "A. B. to Elbridge Gerry, *Massachusetts Centinel*," November 14, 1787, *Documentary History of the Ratification of the Constitution*, Vol. 4, *Massachusetts*, 229; Alexander Contee Hanson to James Madison, June 2 1788, *Documentary History of the Ratification of the Constitution*, Vol. 12, *Maryland*, 672.
97. Honorious, *Independent Chronicle*, January 3, 1788, *Documentary History of the Ratification of the Constitution*, Vol. 5, *Massachusetts*, 604–605. The point that, while once concealed, the result of the convention's work was now available for all to see was made by others as well. For example, see "Gazette of the State of Georgia," March 20, 1788, *Documentary History of the Ratification of the Constitution, Digital Edition*, Vol. 16, *Commentaries on the Constitution*, no. 4, ed. John P. Kaminski, Gaspare J. Saladino, Richard Leffler, Charles H. Schoenleber, and Margaret A. Hogan (Charlottesville: University of Virginia Press, 2009), 442. Only twelve states sent delegates to the Federal Convention; Rhode Island did not have a delegation.
98. Some states held less formal ratification conventions, including Delaware, where delegates met over just four days and ratified unanimously, New Jersey where just 38 people met in a Trenton tavern, and Georgia where just 26 delegates discussed the framework very briefly. See Pauline Maier, *Ratification: The People Debate the Constitution, 1787–1788* (New York: Simon and Schuster, 2000), 122.
99. Maier, *Ratification*, ix; Edling, *A Revolution in Favor of Government*, 19, 28; Heideking, *Constitution Before the Judgment Seat*, 261.
100. *Pennsylvania Herald*, November 21, 1787, *Documentary History of the Ratification of the Constitution*, Vol. 2, *Pennsylvania*, 331.
101. For an overview of the processes of publishing state convention records, and their limitations, see Hutson, "The Creation of the Constitution: The Integrity of the Documentary Record," 158–161. Eric Slauter has also made the point that despite a culture of publicity, the notes of ratifying conventions are not transparent. See Slauter, *The State as a Work of Art*, 22.

102. *The Address and reasons of dissent of the minority of the Convention of the States of Pennsylvania* (1787). LCP, #1787 Pen Con 8706.F (Chew).
103. Hampden, *Pittsburgh Gazette*, February 16, 1788, *Documentary History of the Ratification of the Constitution*, Vol. 2, *Pennsylvania*, 664–665.
104. This point was made on multiple occasions throughout 1788. See also "A Farmer, *Philadelphia Freeman's Journal*," April 23, 1788, *Documentary History of the Ratification of the Constitution, Digital Edition*, Vol. 17, *Commentaries on the Constitution*, 145; *Newport Herald*, November 6, 1788, *Documentary History of the Ratification of the Constitution, Digital Edition*, Vol. 25, *Rhode Island*, no. 2, ed. John P. Kaminski, Gaspare J. Saladino, Richard Leffler, Charles H. Schoenleber, and Margaret A. Hogan (Charlottesville: University of Virginia Press, 2009), 431.
105. Luther Martin, *The genuine information: delivered to the legislature of the State of Maryland, relative to the proceedings of the general convention, lately held at Philadelphia* (Philadelphia, 1788), 2. LCP, Aa.788 P64.
106. "A Citizen, *New York Journal*," November 24, 1787, *Documentary History of the Ratification of the Constitution*, Vol. 19, *New York*, 305. Max Edling has also pointed out that Antifederalist critiques of the convention's secrecy were due in part to a belief that this prevented "delegates from entering into dialogue with informed public opinion." See Edling, *A Revolution in Favor of Government*, 24.
107. Convention Debates, June 9, 1788, in *Documentary History of the Ratification of the Constitution by States*, Vol. 9, *Virginia*, ed. John P. Kaminski and Gaspare J. Saladino (Madison: Wisconsin Historical Society Press, 1990), 1066. A similar argument about the danger of permitting Congress to use secrecy at its discretion was made in a published piece that appeared in February of that year in New Hampshire, in which the author suggested: "It is easy for men to believe secrecy, when it is for their own interest, how much soever it may be against the publick." See "A Friend to the Rights of the People: Anti-Federalist, No. I," *Exeter Freeman's Oracle*, February 8, 1788, *Documentary History of the Ratification of the Constitution, Digital Edition*, Vol. 28, *New Hampshire*, ed. John P. Kaminski, Gaspare J. Saladino, Richard Leffler, Charles H. Schoenleber, and Margaret A. Hogan (Charlottesville: University of Virginia Press, 2009), 113.
108. Convention Debates, July 19, 1788, in *Documentary History of the Ratification of the Constitution by States*, Vol. 23, *New York*, ed. John P. Kaminski, Gaspare J. Saladino, Richard Lefler, and Charles H. Schoenleber (Madison: Wisconsin Historical Society Press, 2009), 2239.
109. Convention Debates, June 14, 1788, in *Documentary History of the Ratification of the Constitution by States*, Vol. 10, *Virginia*, ed. John P. Kaminski and Gaspare J. Saladino (Madison: Wisconsin Historical Society Press, 1993), 1296.

Chapter Four. Building a House of Glass

1. Prospectus included with a letter signed by the Abbé Ducros, addressed to the officials of the Librairie on May 22, 1789, AN/V/1/551.
2. On the theory of political representation as it was elaborated through the debates surrounding the founding of the National Assembly, see Friedland, *Political Actors*, 140–152. Friedland's work builds directly on that of Keith Michael Baker in the essay "Representation," in Baker, *The French Revolution and the Creation of Modern Political Culture*, Vol. 1.
3. Friedland, *Political Actors*, 11.
4. Yannick Bosc has also made the point that the conflict was not between direct democracy and representative government, but between two styles of representation, one of which was democratic in the sense of being participatory and the other that was akin to a trustee theory. See Bosc, *Le Peuple Souverain et la Démcoratie*, 15, 51.
5. Historians have often treated revolutionary radicalism through a Marxist lens of social conflict and largely in the period from 1793–94. Debates about radicalism in the French Revolution stem back to the event itself. Most early scholarship treats popular politics as linked to social goals and circumstances. See Albert Soboul, *The Sans-Culottes: The Popular Movement and Revolutionary Government, 1793–1794*, trans. Rémy Inglis Hall (Garden City, NY: Anchor Books, 1972); R. B. Rose, *The Making of the Sans-Culottes: Democratic Ideas and Institutions in Paris, 1789–92* (Manchester: Manchester University Press, 1983); George Rudé, *In the Crowd in the French Revolution* (Oxford: Clarendon Press, 1959); Isabelle Bourdin, *Les Sociétés Populaires à Paris pendant la Révolution* (Paris: Recueil Sirey, 1937). There have also been studies that aim to illuminate the political aspects of radical activity; see Michael Kennedy, *The Jacobins in the French Revolution* (Princeton: Princeton University Press, 1982); Leigh Whaley, *Radicals: Politics and Republicanism in the French Revolution* (Thrupp, Stroud, Gloucestershire: Sutton Publishing Limited, 2000).
6. The focus on violence and conflict between the revolutionary elite and popular crowds has been similarly overwrought, as Micah Alpaugh recently suggested. See Micah Alpaugh, *Non-Violence and the French Revolution: Political Demonstration in Paris, 1787–1795* (Cambridge: Cambridge University Press, 2015).
7. By looking at how concerns about state secrecy were carried into the revolutionary context, I am building upon Keith Baker's notion that "the Old Regime invented, structured, and limited the Revolution." See Baker, *Inventing the French Revolution*, 11. In focusing on practices, the present study builds upon a strain of scholarship, in the vein of Roger Chartier's insistence on the importance of social practices, aimed at elucidating aspects of Revolutionary ideology and discourse by connecting them to measures and experiences of revolutionaries. See Chartier, *Cultural Origins of the French*

Revolution; Hunt, *Politics, Culture, and Class in the French Revolution;* Ozouf, *Festivals and the French Revolution;* Tackett, *Becoming a Revolutionary;* Sophia Rosenfeld, *A Revolution in Language: The Problem of Signs in Late Eighteenth-century France* (Stanford: Stanford University Press, 2001); Edelstein, *The Terror of Natural Right.*

8. We cannot know what secrecy or *publicité* meant, or how they related to understandings of representative politics, without examining the practices and procedures put in place either to combat or to assure them. Existing examinations of the quotidian activity of the National Assembly, however, have tended to neglect ideology. Treating behavior and thought in tandem, starting from the moment the Estates General convened in Versailles, shows how they were in fact co-constitutive. Taking this approach also puts the study in dialogue with the abundant scholarship that has examined the meaning and influence of public opinion and the press on the political culture of the Revolution, which has largely aimed to integrate the study of discourse and that of social practice. On the daily work of the National Assembly, see Castaldo, *Méthodes de Travail de la Constituante;* Brette, *Histoire des édifices ou ont siégés les assemblées parlementaires de la révolution française et de la première république;* Lemay, *Revolutionari es at work*; Tackett, *Becoming a Revolutionary.* On the press, see Censer, "La Presse vue par elle-même. Le prospectus et le lecteur révolutionnaire"; Jack R. Censer, *Prelude to Power: The Parisian Radical Press 1789–1791* (Baltimore: Johns Hopkins University Press, 1976); Censer, *The French Press in the Age of Enlightenment;* Gough, *The Newspaper Press in the French Revolution;* Jeremy Popkin, "Journals: The News Face of News," in *Revolution in Print,* ed. Robert Darnton and Daniel Roche (Berkeley: University of California Press, 1989); Popkin, *Revolutionary News.* On public opinion see Chartier, *The Cultural Origins of the French Revolution;* Cowans, *To Speak for the People;* Walton, *Policing Public Opinion in the French Revolution.* Recently, Antoine Lilti has contended that the birth of democratic politics was inextricably bound up with the birth of modern media and the possibility of publicité, which led to the fusion of celebrity and politics; see Lilti, *Figures Publiques,* 16–17.

9. Castaldo, *Les Méthodes de Travail de la Constituante,* 305. Castaldo references Jules Michelet for the upper number and the correspondence of deputy Jean-François Gaultier de Biauzat for the 2,000 number reported on June 9, 1789. Once the Assembly moved to Paris, there was much less space in the chamber. Castaldo cites the number of non-deputies in the room as closer to 300 or 400. This was in the meetings of the Third Estate; as Bailly noted in his memoires, the rooms where the nobility and clergy met were barely big enough to hold the deputies and did not have space for an audience. See Lynn Hunt, "The National Assembly," in Baker, *The French Revolution and the Creation of Modern Political Culture,* Vol. 1, 412.

10. Tackett, *Becoming a Revolutionary,* 20. In his regular correspondence with his wife, deputy François René Pierre Ménard de La Groye estimated that

more than 1,000 people came daily to listen to them deliberate and "among them are seigneurs and ladies of the highest rank." See François Réné Pierre Ménard de La Groye, *Correspondance publiée et annotée par F. Mirouse, François Ménard de la Groye, correspondance, 1789–1791, Conseil General de la Sarthe, 1989* (La Mans: Conseil générale de la Sarthe, 1989), 38. BNF: FRBNF36637964.

11. Etienne Dumont, *Souvenirs sur Mirabeau et sur les deux premières assemblées législatives* (Paris 1932), 43–44, cited in Castaldo, *Les Méthodes de Travail de la Constituante*, 101.
12. *Archives Parlementaires, Tome VIII*, 55.
13. Tackett, *Becoming a Revolutionary*, 141.
14. Edna Hindie Lemay, *Dictionnaire des constituants, 1789–1791*, Vol. 2 (Paris: Universitas, 1991), 942.
15. *Archives Parlementaires, Tome VIII*, 55. Volney may have been referring to the story of an ancient sage who reportedly declared that he wished his house was made of glass so that all his actions could be seen. Many accounts of this exchange exist in the memoires of deputies. See also Jean Sylvain Bailly, *Mémoires d'un témoin de la Révolution, ou Journal des faits qui se sont passés sous ses yeux et qui ont préparé et fixe la Constitution française, tome 1* (Paris: Levrault, Schoell et Cie, an XII-1804), 82. BNF: FRB NF30048105; M. Mounier, *Recherches sur les causes qui ont empéché les François de devenir libres* (Paris: Chez Gattey, 1792).
16. Emmanuel Joseph Sieyès, *Qu'est-ce-que le Tiers état?* (Paris: Editions de Boucher, 2002), 1.
17. *Archives Parlementaires, Tome VIII*, 109.
18. Peter Campbell, *French Electoral Systems and Elections since 1789* (Hamden, CT: Archon Books, 1965), 47–48.
19. Ibid. In Paris, the qualification to select electors was more restricted: men had to pay at least six *livres* in direct taxes and belong to certain occupational groups in order to select electors.
20. *Lettre du comte de Mirabeau à ses commettans*, Lettre XI des 13, 14, 15, 16, et 17 juin (1789), 216. BNF: FRBNF32806045; *Archives Parlementaires, Tome VIII*, 113, 119, 244, 250, 237. Lynn Hunt has pointed out that starting in late 1788, pamphlets appeared advancing the notion that the Third Estate was the nation and should be represented as such. By May 1789, she suggests, many deputies for the Third Estate had adopted this view and come to see the other two orders as exceptions. See Hunt, "The National Assembly," 408–409.
21. One especially notable example of the potentially expansive nature of this conception of whom they were representing is that women, while not formally participating as electors (and defined as passive citizens in the Constitution of 1791), did often figure in conceptions and manifestations of the French people. As Katie Jarvis has argued, the *Dames des Halles*, or market women of Paris, "more than any other group—represented 'the people' at

the outset of the Revolution." See Jarvis, *Politics of the Marketplace*, 3, 32, 55, 59. On active versus passive citizenship in the Constitution of 1791, see Sewell, "Le citoyen/la citoyenne: Activity, Passivity, and the Revolutionary Concept of Citizenship." On the other hand, many scholars have long pointed to the exclusionary effect of universalism, suggesting that the public sphere and ideal citizen were gendered male and women were thereby excluded from what was defined as universal but was in actuality gendered male. See Scott, *Only Paradoxes to Offer*, 8, 20; Landes, *Women and the Public Sphere in the Age of the French Revolution*, 3, 7, 45. Landes suggests that in 1789 women asserted their rights to be represented as part of the people through crowd action, but she says this was ultimately dismissed as more akin to a history of "bread riots."

22. Friedland, *Political Actors*, 93.
23. Ibid., 160.
24. Bailly, *Mémoires d'un témoin de la Révolution*, 188.
25. Ibid., 199.
26. *Archives Parlementaires, Tome VIII*, 142.
27. Ibid., 144.
28. Bailly, *Mémoires d'un témoin de la Révolution*, 225.
29. Friedland, *Political Actors*, 11. When he does talk about a wall between the deputies and the public in his analysis, Friedland discusses the idea of a "fourth wall" in theater, which unlike a brick wall would be transparent but was not supposed to be breached. One of the primary ways in which the deputies attempted to construct this wall was by making the distinction between active and passive citizens in the Constitution of 1791, wherein active citizens were defined as males over age 25 who paid taxes and could thus vote, while passive citizens were theoretically represented in "the people" but did not have a right to vote. See Sewell, "Le citoyen/la citoyenne: Activity, Passivity, and the Revolutionary Concept of Citizenship"; Bosc, *Le Peuple Souverain et la Démocratie*, 29.
30. *Archives Parlementaires, Tome VIII*, 155.
31. Friedland writes about the creation of political spectators as a passive audience to the representative process; see *Political Actors*, 300.
32. *Archives Parlementaires, Tome VIII*, 155. This incident is also reported in Mirabeau's *Lettres à ses Commettans* and in a periodical devoted to accounts of the assembly proceedings called *Journal de Versailles, ou affiches, announces, et avis divers*, no. 44, June 27, 1789. BNF: FRBNF32799019.
33. *Archives Parlementaires, Tome VIII*, 155.
34. Thomas Jefferson to John Jay, June 24, 1789, *The Papers of Thomas Jefferson, Digital Edition*, Vol. 15, ed. James P. McClure and J. Jefferson Looney (Charlottesville: University of Virginia Press, Rotunda, 2008–2017), 208.
35. Chapter III, Section II, Article I of the Constitution of 1791 states: "Les délibérations du Corps législatif seront publiques, et les procès-verbaux de ses séances seront imprimés." However, the next article does allow the assem-

bly to enter in *Comité général* with the approval of fifty members, which would require removal of attendees. See Constitution de 1791, accessed September 14, 2021, Conseil Constitutionnel.

36. Castaldo, *Méthodes de Travail de la Constituante*, 362. The text of the July 29 regulations can be found in the *Archives Parlementaires, Tome VIII*, 300–303.
37. Desan, "Gender, Radicalization, and the October Days: Occupying the National Assembly," 381, 383.
38. Jarvis, *Politics in the Marketplace*, 54–61; Landes, *Women and the Public Sphere in the Age of the French Revolution*, 109; Desan, "Gender, Radicalization, and the October Days," 360.
39. Suzanne Desan has suggested that "the gender dynamics of the event in essence enabled a largely female crowd to smuggle the expansion of popular sovereignty in through the back door." She argues that in this case, women diplayed a central role in establishing the precedent of crowd action and "direct popular pressure on the nation's representatives" as a way of claiming "popular sovereignty in action rather than words." See Desan, "Gender, Radicalization, and the October Days," 362, 384. For more on the October Days and their significance, see also Barry Shapiro, *Revolutionary Justice in Paris, 1789–1790* (Cambridge: Cambridge University Press, 1993).
40. Makeshift galleries were constructed and collapsed at one point. See La Groye, *Correspondance publiée et annotée par F. Mirouse*, 132.
41. Letter signed by Guillotin, undated, AN/C/31, doss. 260.
42. AN/C/132.
43. David Bell, *The First Total War: Napoleon's Europe and the Birth of Warfare as We Know It* (Boston: Houghton Mifflin, 2007), 90.
44. Letter, December 18, 1789., AN/C/33, doss. 286.
45. AN/C/133, doss. 471, doc. 1.
46. Lilti, *Figures Publiques*, 225; Patrick Brasart, *Paroles de la Révolution: Les Assemblées parlementaires, 1789–1794* (Paris: Minerve, 1988); J. C. Bonnet, " 'La sainte-masure,' sanctuaire de la parole fondatrice," in *La Carmagnole des Muses: L'homme de lettres et l'artiste dans la Révolution*, ed. Armand Colin (Paris: A. Colin, 1988), 185–222; Angelica Goodden, "The Dramatising of Political Theatricality and the Revolutionary Assemblies," *Forum for Modern Language Studies* 20 (1984): 193–212; Pierre Frantz, "Pas d'entracte pour la Révolution," in *La Carmagnole des Muses*, 381–399.
47. Friedland, *Political Actors*, 2.
48. AN/DXXIXbis/32/II, doss. 325, doc. 22. A letter filed in the Comité des Recherches' "Notes et renseignemens considérés comme pièces secrètes et remis au Comité des Recherches," dated September 10, 1790, reports an investigation by the Sixéme Bataillon into three members who were reportedly paid to attend the National Assembly meetings and applaud particular speeches.
49. Castaldo, *Méthodes de Travail*, 298–299. In legislation reforming the judicial system in 1791, deputies similarly focused on opening the courtroom to a public

audience as a way to "transform an abstract and textual public into one of flesh and blood," as Laura Mason put it. As she argues, revolutionaries believed not only that publicity of trials would be crucial to guaranteeing justice but that jurors needed to "experience the totality of performances by defenders, accusers, and other interested parties" in order to render judgments. This thinking about the importance of witnessing speech in person to making determinations is aligned with the enduring commitment to keeping doors to the legislature open to a public audience. See Laura Mason, "The 'Bosom of Proof,' " 37, 39. This conviction in the ability for an audience to form judgments also had roots in thinking about the parterre—whether it should be seated, silenced, or crowded—in theaters. See Ravel, *The Contested Parterre*, 210–222.

50. *Mémoire des huissiers à la Constituante*, AN/C/132, doss. 471.
51. Castaldo, *Méthodes de Travail*, 302. Castaldo cites a fixed number of occasions upon which there were efforts made to remove all but deputies from the chamber, totaling six: two were in 1789, three in 1790, and one in 1791. Following the discovery of the missing king in June 1791, there was an effort to remove all but deputies from the room.
52. Dubois, *Avengers of the New World*, 76. Dubois cites a printing of these letters: *Lettres des députés de Saint-Domingue à leurs comettants en date du 12 août 1789* (Paris, 1790).
53. Dubois, *Avengers of the New World*, 77.
54. Ibid.
55. Ibid.
56. Tackett, *Becoming Revolutionaries*, 219–220.
57. Ibid., 221.
58. Castaldo, *Méthodes de Travail*, 206.
59. Committee records held in the *Archives Nationales* suggest that neither guaranteeing transparency via public accessibility nor maintaining secrecy by closing doors was directly discussed by the deputies forming these groups at first. The notes from the first meeting of the Finance Committee, held on July 20, contain no discussion of procedural points regarding who could enter the meetings or what could be communicated. Only gradually, into the fall of 1789, did the committee's notes indicate that certain reports were "not to be communicated before the National Assembly, until the committee had decided the form in which it was to be presented" and the point where "its publicity would not make the political interests of the kingdom susceptible to any danger." AN/D/VI/17, doss. 1, doc. 183; AN/D/VI/17, doss. 1, Notes, September 2, 1789.
60. AN/C/132, doss. 474. There are many examples in this folder of requests for tickets to be issued to particular individuals to enter committee meetings, as employees of the committee, experts offering testimony on a topic, or messengers carrying correspondence among committees. For more on the debates over the *Comité des Recherches* meeting in secret, see Carter, "The *Comités des Recherches*."

61. Tackett, *Becoming Revolutionaries*, 236.
62. Ibid., 235.
63. *Archives Parlementaires, Tome VIII*, 512.
64. Ibid. Charles Walton also treated this letter in his examination of press law during the early Revolution. See Walton, *Policing Public Opinion in the French Revolution*, 97.
65. Walton, *Policing Public Opinion in the French Revolution*, 98.
66. Camille Desmoulins, *Réclamation en faveur du marquis de Saint-Huruge* (sans lieu, 1789), 8. BNF: FRBNF36003709.
67. Ibid., 8.
68. "L'Assemblée des représentans de la Commune de Paris, séance du Soir, Mardi 28 juillet, 1789," in *Les Cordeliers dans la Revolution française; textes et documents*, ed. Jacques De Cock (Lyon: Fantasques edition), 56. For more on how these entities viewed and practiced democracy, see especially Maurice Genty, "Pratiques et Théorie de la Démocra tie Directe: L'exemple des districts parisiens (1789–1790)," *Annales historiques de la revolution française* 57, no. 259 (Janvier-Mars 1985).
69. For example, see "Opinion de M Loyseau, membre de la Société des Amis de la Constitution, sur le mode de responsabilité des ministres et des autres agents du pouvoir exécutive, lue le 29 mai, 1790," in *La Société des Jacobins: Recueil des Documents pour l'Histoire du Club des Jacobins de Paris*, ed. A. F. Aulard (Paris: AMS Press, 1889), 116. See also Micah Alpaugh, "The British Origins of the French Jacobins: Radical Sociability and the Development of Political Club Networks, 1787–1793," *European History Quarterly* 44, no. 4 (2014): 604.
70. Kennedy, *The Jacobin Clubs in the French Revolution*, 10.
71. Alpaugh, "The British Origins of the French Jacobins," 604–605.
72. Susan Branson, *These Fiery Frenchified Dames* (Philadelphia: University of Pennsylvania Press, 2001), 58. Branson cites letters Marianna Williams received from her sister Bethia Alexander who was in Paris saying she attended the National Assembly and Jacobin Club, writing in one letter in July 1791: "you must know that I sometimes assist at their meetings, in a little private corner destined for the ladies."
73. "Loustalot: Suite de l'affaire des representans de la commune, avec le district des Cordeliers, & autres districts adherans a son arrete, Samedi 28 Novembre 1789," in De Cock, *Les Cordeliers dans la Revolution francaise*, 223.
74. "Lettre du Club des Capucins aux représentans de la Commune contre le District des Cordeliers, suivi d'un arrêté de ce district, rédigé par M de Chenier, Mardi 11 mai, 1790," in De Cock, *Les Cordeliers dans la Revolution francaise*, 543; "Extrait du Registre des deliberations du District des Cordeliers, du 9 juin, 1790," ibid., 562.
75. "Ruteledge: A mes frères les amis des droits de l'homme et du Citoyen, séants aux Cordeliers, Lundi 28 mars, 1791," ibid., 715.

76. "Avis divers Invitation a tous les citoyens Extrait des registres du club des Droits de l'Homme, Mardi 27 avril, 1790," ibid., 631. It is important to note that in deploying this rhetoric and defining this role for themselves, these clubs were also laying claim to the identity and voice of "the people," which in turn made it more challenging for women, for example, to claim this mantle. Deputies also soon viewed the potential for a rival voice of the public as potentially problematic, outlawing the expression of collective opinions from corporate groups in the spring of 1791. See Friedland, *Political Actors*, 271–274; Jarvis, *Politics in the Marketplace*, 53; Landes, *Women and the Public Sphere in the Age of the French Revolution*, 123.
77. Gough, *The Newspaper Press in the French Revolution*, 26.
78. Ibid.
79. Ibid., 44.
80. Popkin, *Revolutionary News*, 2.
81. AN/V/1/550, Letter signed by Abbé Ducros, undated, but replied to in a missive dated January 26, 1789.
82. Walton, *Policing Public Opinion*, 75.
83. Jacques-Pierre Brissot de Warville, *Le Patriote françois: journal libre, impartial et national* (Paris: Buisson, May 6, 1789), 1. BNF: FRBNF32834106.
84. Brissot, *Le Patriote françois: journal libre, impartial et national*, 5.
85. Ibid.
86. Jacques Pierre Brissot de Warville, *Plan de Conduite pour les députés du peuple aux états-Généraux de 1789* (Paris, 1789), 67, accessed May 9, 2022. The Making of the Modern World.
87. Darnton, *The Literary Underground of the Old Regime*, 41. See also Elizabeth Eisenstein, *Grub Street Abroad: Aspects of the French Cosmopolitan Press from the Age of Louis XIV to the French Revolution* (Oxford: Clarendon Press, 1992).
88. *Lettres du Comte de Mirabeau à ses commettans, pendant la tenue des Etats-Generaux de 1789, et suivantes* (May 2, 1789), vii. BNF FRBNF32806045. This periodical ran in a series of 19 letters under this title from May 10 through July 25, 1789, after which point it was renamed the *Courier de Provence*. Claude Bellanger notes that the periodical was not just composed by Mirabeau, but contributed to by a number of deputies. For more, see Claude Bellanger, *Histoire générale de la presse française, tome I* (Paris: Presse Universitaires de France, 1969).
89. Mirabeau was not the only deputy to found a newspaper. Another Third Estate deputy, Dominique-Joseph Garat from the Pays Basques, became the correspondent to the *Journal de Paris*, providing accounts of the meetings to the established newspaper. By mid-June, yet another periodical had been launched by Bertrand Barère—Third Estate deputy from the Pays de Bigorre, who would radicalize over the course of the Revolution, later becoming a member of the Committee of Public Safety—and a team of deputies to provide a daily account of "all that happened the previous day in the National Assembly." See *Point du Jour, ou Résultat de ce qui s'est passé la veille à l'Assemblée Nationale* (June 18, 1789). Firestone Library: 1509.178.728.

90. Censer, "La Presse vue par elle-même," 123.
91. *Révolutions de France et de Brabant*, No. 1, 12. Firestone Library: 1509.178.75243.
92. *Révolutions de France et de Brabant*, No. 2, 46.
93. *Le Publiciste Parisien, Journal Politique, Libre et Impartial, par une société des patriotes, et rédigé par M Marat, Auteur de l'Offrande a la Patrie, du Moniteur et du Plan de la Constitution, etc.*, No. 1, 10. Firestone Library: 1509.178.7374.
94. *Annales patriotiques et littéraires de la France, et Affaires politiques de l'Europe, Journal Libre, par une société d'écrivains patriots, et dirigé par M Mercier*, Prospectus, 3. Firestone Library: MICROFILM S01030.
95. This style of reporting held the promise of providing a definitive account of what transpired in the assembly and was related to early efforts to develop stenography. However, the limitations of the method meant even what purported to be verbatim were only reconstructions, often with errors. See Sophia Rosenfeld, *Democracy and Truth: A Short History* (Philadelphia: University of Pennsylvania Press, 2018), 59; Rosenfeld, *A Revolution in Language*, 204; Slauter, *The State as a Work of Art*, 149, 155, 160–161.
96. AN/AA40, doc. 80.
97. Walton, *Policing Public Opinion in the French Revolution*, 116. A survey of the "Régistres d'Audience du Conseil au Criminel" (AN/Y/10546) gives brief entries summarizing the cases and judgments rendered. These cases tended to be brought by individuals or small groups against the authors or printers of periodicals or pamphlets that they argued had damaged their reputations. Among the cases tried in the regular criminal court were charges against Louis Sebastien Mercier for contents in his *Annales patriotiques*, which a group of National Guardsmen successfully proved to have been redefamatory (AN/Y/10546): the case against Mercier is entered into the record on August 6, 1790. A couple of cases against Camille Desmoulins also pop up in this record, deeming him guilty of having portrayed a marquis as guilty of efforts to distract the National Assembly from its work or of generally libeling at least two other individuals (AN Y/10546): the case against Desmoulins on behalf of the Marquis de Crilon was entered on June 8, 1790. Two cases against Desmoulins on behalf of a M. Talon are entered on July 6, 1790, and again on August 6, 1790. Another case against him on behalf of M. De Dorlay was entered on October 16, 1790.
98. Walton, *Policing Public Opinion in the French Revolution*, 116. A general survey of the register shows that these were the most commonly issued punishments in cases involving libel or calumny in printed material.
99. Shapiro, *Revolutionary Justice in Paris, 1789–1790*, 14; G. A. Kelly, "From Lèse-Majesté to Lèse-Nation: Treason in Eighteenth-Century France," *Journal of the History of Ideas* 42, no. 2 (1981).
100. Walton, *Policing Public Opinion in the French Revolution*, 183. Walton notes that when the Haute-Court sought to obtain the list of open *lèse-nation* cases to be transferred from the Châtelet in April 1791, prosecutors were

unsure what to ask for and classify as *lèse-nation*, to which the Minister of Justice responded that only the National Assembly could define what *lèse-nation* meant and it was unfortunate that the deputies had not yet done so. When the minister presented the National Assembly with a list of 23 open cases at that point, he advised the deputies to drop all having to do with speech as he believed these cases diminished the intended severity of the accusation of *lèse-nation*. They dropped all but one case.

101. See Walton, *Policing Public Opinion in the French Revolution*, 178–185; "Inventaire de procédures de crimes de lèse nation," AN/Y/10509; AN/Y/10506.
102. Munro Price, *The Fall of the French Monarchy* (London: Macmillan, 2002), 170.
103. Ibid.
104. "*Détail Exact De Tout ce qui s'est passé hier a L'arrivée du Roi, avec le nom de ceux qui ont trempé dans le complot, et qui l'ont aide dans sa fuite*" (Paris: L'imprimerie Patriotique, June 26, 1791), 3.
105. On the Flight to Varennes and its impact on the course of the Revolution, see Price, *The Fall of the French Monarchy;* Timothy Tackett, *When The King Took Flight* (Cambridge, MA: Harvard University Press, 2003); Mona Ozouf, *Varennes: La Mort de La Royauté* (Paris: Gallimard, 2005); Michel Winock, *L'Echec au roi: 1791–1792* (Paris: Olivier Orban, 1991). On republicanism before the Flight to Varennes, see especially Bosc, *Le Peuple Souverain et la Démocratie*, 48–51.
106. *Archives Parlementaires, Tome XXVII, du 6 juin 1791 au 5 juillet 1791* (Paris: Société d'Imprimerie et Libraire Administratives, 1862–1913), 359.
107. Ibid., 362.
108. Ibid., 375.
109. Ozouf, *Varennes: La Mort de La Royauté*, 81; Winock, *L'Echec au roi: 1791–1792*, 76.
110. *Archives Parlementaires, Tome XXVII*, 378.
111. Ibid., 381.
112. For examples, see *Patriote françois*, No. 683 (June 22, 1791); *L'Ami du Peuple*, No. 497 (June 22, 1791).
113. Ozouf, *Varennes: La Mort de La Royauté*, 81; Winock, *L'Echec au roi: 1791–1792*, 76.
114. *Archives Parlementaires, Tome XXVII*, 420.
115. Ibid.
116. *Annales patriotiques et littéraires*, No. DCXXX (June 24, 1791).
117. "Decree of the Position of the King, 15 July," in *French Revolutionary Documents*, Vol. 1, ed. J. M. Roberts and R. C. Cobb (Oxford: Basil Blackwell, 1966), 325.
118. *Archives Parlementaires, Tome XXVIII* (Paris: Société d'Imprimerie et Libraire Administratives, 1862–1913), 331.
119. Ibid., 323–324, 331.

120. For more on notions of the king and representation in an absolutist model, see Friedland, *Political Actors*, 49–50; Collins, *The State in Early Modern France*, 80; Baker, *Inventing the French Revolution*, 114.
121. Kelly, "From Lèse-Majesté to Lèse-Nation," 279–280; Jarvis, *Politics in the Marketplace*, 52; Hunt, "The National Assembly," 403; Bosc, *Le Peuple Souverain et la Démocratie*, 45.
122. Price, *The Fall of the French Monarchy*, 207; "Petition to the National Assembly, July 17," in *The Old Regime and the French Revolution*, ed. Keith Michael Baker (Oxford: Pergamon Press, 1987), 275.
123. Price, *The Fall of the French Monarchy*, 207.
124. Ibid., 208.
125. David Andress, *Massacre at the Champ De Mars* (Suffolk: Royal Historical Society and Boydell Press, 2000), 157.
126. Ibid., 160, 176.
127. Bellanger, *Histoire générale de la presse française, tome I*, 433. The law targeted all people "qui auront provoqué le meurtre, le pillage, l'incendie ou conseillée formellement la désobéissance de la loi, soit par des placards et affichés, soit par des écrits publiés ou colportés."
128. Ibid., 433–434.
129. AN/AA40, docs. 28, 49, 85, 87, 95, 96, 97, 98, 100. There are numerous examples of such conditioned approvals for access to the chamber. On June 9, 1791, Guillotin issued a permission to the editor of the *Journal de l'Assemblée nationale et commune de Paris* to sit in the tribune of the *Journal des Débats et Derêts*, on condition that he not bring any strangers to the space. On June 15, 1791, a journalist was granted an "enclosed chair" in a corner of the chamber "to take notes on each session" (AA40, doc. 85). This journalist was the son of a *huissier* of the assembly, who was launching a *Journal National et Etranger* (doc. 87).
130. AN/AA40, doc. 58.
131. AN/AA40, doc. 59.
132. AN/AA40, doc. 52.
133. AN/AA40, doc. 53.
134. Règlement sur le service des huissiers de l'Assemblée Nationale, le 5 mai, 1792, AN/C/177, doss. 2.

Chapter Five. Mere Spectators of Events

1. On the malleability of Jacobin conceptions of representation, see Lucien Jaume, "La Representation: Une fiction malmenée," *Pouvoirs: Voter*, no. 120 (2007): 11; Friedland, *Political Actors*, 288. Others maintain that Robespierre and the Montagnard deputies were committed to a reflective style of representation. See Bosc, *Le Peuple Souverain et la Démocratie*, 14–15; Rosanvallon, "The History of the Word 'Democracy' in France," 147. Michel Vovelle has pointed to the critical need to differentiate between (and among) Jacobins

within the National Convention and in the Jacobin Club, let alone the wider population of Parisian radicals. See Michel Vovelle, *Les Jacobins: De Robespierre à Chevènement* (Paris: La Découverte/Poche, 2001), 26.

2. Scholars point to Robespierre's and other Jacobin leaders' constant calls for vigilance, surveillance, and publicity as evidence of their commitment to a reflective style of representation in the spirit of democracy. See especially Maslan, *Revolutionary Acts*, 3, 146; Bosc, *Le Peuple Souverain et la Démocratie*, 132–133.

3. An older generation of historians maintained that the measures of the Terror were necessary responses to the circumstances in which the revolutionary government found itself: at war with its neighbors and much of its own population. This view has also been recently revived, perhaps most notably by David Andress, who has argued that "The Terror was above all the consequence in real civil war of a failure of consensus that had edged steadily closer to complete collapse for over three years." See David Andress, *The Terror: Civil War in the French Revolution* (London: Little Brown, 2005), 5. The revisionist school initiated by François Furet in the late 1970s dismissed this argument, asserting instead that the Terror was inherent in the discourse of equality, that 1794 was not only the logical outcome but the fulfillment of 1789's ideology. See Furet, *Interpreting the French Revolution*, 62, 70. At the dawn of the twenty-first century, a number of historians argued that the Terror was comprehensible only within revolutionary political culture and discourse but it was also a response to events in 1793–94. See especially Patrice Gueniffey, "La Terreur: circonstances exceptionnelles, idéologie et dynamique révolutionnaire," *Historical Reflections/Réflexions Historiques* 29, no. 3, *Violence and the French Revolution* (Fall 2003); Patrice Higonnet, "Terror, Trauma, and the 'Young Marx' Explanation of Jacobin Politics," *Past & Present*, no. 191 (May 2006). More recently, historians who have taken up the task of explaining, in the words of Timothy Tackett, "how revolutionaries became terrorists," have turned their attention to psychology and the emotional factors compelling revolutionaries to adopt repressive measures and deploy violence. See especially Timothy Tackett, *The Coming of the Terror in the French Revolution* (Cambridge, MA: Belknap Press of Harvard University Press, 2015); Marisa Linton, *Choosing Terror: Virtue, Friendship, and Authenticity in the French Revolution* (Oxford: Oxford University Press, 2013). Furthermore, historians are recently urging a reconsideration of using the term "Terror" to characterize this period, pointing out that it was a label constructed afterward and imposed retroactively. See Colin Jones, *The Fall of Robespierre* (Oxford: Oxford University Press, 2021), 434; Michel Biard and Marisa Linton, *Terror: The French Revolution and Its Demons* (Cambridge, U.K.: Polity Press, 2021), 1–24; Bosc, *Le Peuple Souverain et la Démocratie*, 180; Jean-Clément Martin, *Violence et Révolution. Essai sur la naissance d'un mythe national* (Paris: Seuil, 2006). While recognizing this is important, I adopt David Bell's contention: "However one understands the

Terror, though, it is important to recognize that something horrific took place in France in the year before 9 Thermidor and came to an end as a result of it." See David Bell, "The End of the Terror," in *New York Review* (March 10, 2022).

4. This chapter builds upon Hesse's work on trial procedure in the revolutionary tribunals to further advance our understanding of Jacobin ideology read out from government practices. See Carla Hesse, "La preuve par la lettre: Pratique juridique au tribunal révolutionnaire de Paris (1793–1794)," *Annales. Histoire, Sciences Sociales*, 51e Année, no. 3 (May–June 1996): 630. In a slightly different vein, this approach also builds upon Dan Edelstein's work exploring the relationship between the creative and repressive aspects of Jacobinism. Arguing that it was legal and political thought, rather than emotional or social circumstances, that played a more important role in leading to the Terror, Edelstein asserts that "what Jacobin leaders projected to create, as difficult as it may be to determine, is a central piece in the puzzle of the Terror." Edelstein, *The Terror of Natural Right*, 4, 22. Unlike Edelstein, Sophie Wahnich retains the centrality of emotions in explaining the Terror and articulates an explicitly redemptive purpose; she also has called for a focus on the generative aspects of the Jacobin-led Terror. See Sophie Wahnich, *In Defence of the Terror: Liberty or Death in the French Revolution*, trans. David Fernbach (New York: Verso Books, 2012).
5. Though I acknowledge that it was in response to crisis, I argue that the structure of the Committee of Public Safety involved deliberate thinking rather than a haphazard, ad hoc response to circumstances. This is contrary to the interpretation posed by Timothy Tackett, who argues that there was no systematic plan to the Terror and that its institutions were cobbled together as improvisations in response to various dangers, in an atmosphere of passion and mistrust. See Tackett, *The Coming of the Terror*, 277.
6. On the notion of regeneration and the creation of a new people and nation, see especially Mona Ozouf, *L'Homme régénéré: essais sur la Révolution française* (Paris: Gallimard, 1989); David A. Bell, *The Cult of the Nation in France: Inventing Nationalism, 1680–1800* (Cambridge, MA: Harvard University Press, 2001).
7. *Archives Parlementaires de 1787 à 1860*, Vol. 52 (Paris: Librairie administrative de Paul Dupont, 1862–1913), 493.
8. Andrew Freeman, *The Compromising of Louis XVI: The Armoire de Fer and the French Revolution* (Exeter: University of Exeter Press, 1989), 1–2, 48–49.
9. Freeman, *The Compromising of Louis XVI*, 7.
10. *Annales Patriotiques et Littéraires, No. CCXXVI* (November 21, 1792). Firestone Library, MICROFILM S01030.
11. For more on the narrative of *dévoilement* constructed in 1789, see Carter, "The *Comités des Recherches*."
12. *Le Patriote François*, no. 1214 (December 7, 1792). Firestone Library: MICROFILM S00170.

13. Ibid.
14. Tackett, *The Coming of the Terror*, 234.
15. *Archives Parlementaires de 1787 à 1860*, Vol. 54 (Paris: Librairie administrative de Paul Dupont, 1862–1913), 363.
16. Ibid., 364–367.
17. Ibid., 373.
18. *Archives Parlementaires de 1787 à 1860*, Vol. 53 (Paris: Librairie administrative de Paul Dupont, 1862–1913), 652.
19. Ibid.
20. *Archives Parlementaires de 1787 à 1860*, Vol. 54, 66.
21. There is some debate as to whether these factions really existed in 1792 and early 1793, but based on the instances of recorded votes during the National Convention, I am confident the divide is noteworthy. See Michael Lewis-Beck, Anne Hildreth, and Alan B. Spitzer, "Was There a Girondist Faction in the National Convention, 1792–1793?" *French Historical Studies* 15, no. 3 (1988).
22. *Archives Parlementaires de 1787 à 1860*, Vol. 53, 494.
23. *Patriote françois*, no. 1199 (November 21, 1792).
24. *Journal de la République Française*, no. 54 (November 23, 1792). Firestone Library: (Ex) 1509.178.7375.
25. *Journal de la République Française*, no. 5145 (November 26, 1792).
26. Ibid.
27. *Archives Parlementaires de 1787 à 1860*, Vol. 53, 512.
28. Ibid.
29. Freeman, *The Compromising of Louis XVI*, 25.
30. The king's trial has been examined for what it shows about the ideology of the Jacobins, the effect it had on the birth of the republic, and the pattern it set for judicial practices during the Terror. See especially David P. Jordan, *The King's Trial: Louis XVI vs the French Revolution* (Berkeley: University of California Press, 1978), 73; Price, *The Fall of the French Monarchy;* Edelstein, *The Terror of Natural Right;* Soboul, *Le Procès de Louis XVI* (Paris: Gallimard, 1989); Pierrette Girault de Coursac, *Enquête sur le Procès du Roi* (Paris: François-Xavier de Guibert, 1992); Susan Dunn, *The Deaths of Louis XVI: Regicide and the French Political Imagination* (Princeton: Princeton University Press, 1994); Clizia Mayoni, "La référence à l'Angleterre et au républicanisme anglais pendant le procès de Louis XVI," in *La Révolution française*, Vo l. 5 (2013); Michael Walzer, ed., *Regicide and Revolution: Speeches at the Trial of Louis XVI*, trans. Marian Rothstein (Cambridge: Cambridge University Press, 1974). The contention that the trial of the king marked a pivotal point in the Revolution was also recently made in Jean Clément Martin, *L'exécution du roi: 21 janvier, 1793* (Paris: Perrin, 2021), 9.
31. Of note is that an *appel au peuple* essentially precluded an insulated style of political representation because it presumed that both representatives and "the people" could act. See Jean-Marie Picard, "L'Appel au Peuple," in *Revue*

Française d'Histoire des Idées Politiques 2, no. 38 (2013): 294. An unsuccessful proposal to include a mechanism of popular appeal in the constitution as counter-balance to a royal veto was proposed in 1789 by deputies who later became Girondins. Reilly, "Ideology on Trial," 31; Richard Tuck, *The Sleeping Sovereign: The Invention of Modern Democracy* (Cambridge: Cambridge University Press, 2016), 151. After the Flight to Varennes, Parisian clubs had called for a referendum to gather the public's opinion before making a decision on the king, yet deputies rejected the idea. Reilly, "Ideology on Trial," 31. There were some calls for an appeal in the fall of 1792 after royalty had been abolished and the constitution the National Convention was drafting was to be sent to the primary assemblies for ratification upon its completion. Reilly, "Ideology on Trial," 31; *Archives Parlementaires*, Vol. 56, 461, 502.

32. Jordan, *The King's Trial*, 143; Tackett, *The Coming of the Terror*, 228–232, 237. Jordan calls this one of the most significant conflicts between the Girondins and Montagnards, and Tackett suggests Girondins proposed the *appel* to "portray themselves as the true supporters of popular sovereignty, and in this way to retake the initiative from the Mountain."
33. On the efforts of Girondins to operationalize popular sovereignty through institutions, see especially Lisa Disch, "How could Hannah Arendt glorify the American Revolution and revile the French? Placing *On Revolution* in the historiography of the French and American Revolutions," in the *European Journal of Political Theory*, Vol. 10, No. 3 (2011), 362; Gary Kates, *The Cercle Social, the Girondins and the French Revolution* (Princeton: Princeton University Press, 1985).
34. See especially Tackett, *The Coming of the Terror*, 7; Linton, *Choosing Terror*, 22; Martin, *L'exécution du roi*, 14.
35. Tackett, *The Coming of the Terror*, 193–216; Martin, *L'exécution du roi*, 14.
36. Jordan, *The King's Trial*, 174.
37. On the tension between authenticity and performance, see especially Jean-Jacques Rousseau, *Confessions, Book II* (Geneva: 1782), 80; Jean Starobinski, *Jean-Jacques Rousseau: La transparence et l'obstacle* (Paris: Gallimard, 1971); Laura Mason, "The 'Bosom of Proof' "; Marisa Linton, "Robespierre et l'Authenticité Révolutionnaire," *Annales historiques de la Révolution française*, no. 371 (Jan-Mars 2013): 154, 156.
38. *Archives Parlementaires de 1787 à 1860*, Vol. 56 (Paris: Librairie administrative de Paul Dupont, 1862–1913), 9.
39. Ibid., 149. Many deputies, mostly Girondins, similarly pointed to the separation between the general will and representations of it and argued that representatives could only carry out the expressed will of the sovereign people. Elected officials under this model had limited leeway to act without consulting the population. Some cited Rousseau's contention that the general will could never be represented to bolster their points. These deputies were indeed building on Rousseau's notion of a distinction between the sovereign and government. In the *Social Contract*, Rousseau did make the point that the

general will could not be represented and that elected deputies were thus not representatives, but merely *commissaires* of the people who could not rule definitively on anything. As Richard Tuck has argued, Rousseau did not disavow the possibility of representative government entirely; rather, he believed it had a limited executive function and saw plebiscites as a necessary check when it came to fundamental laws. It was the Girondins, as Tuck suggests, who were the real heirs of Rousseau in their insistence that a separate sovereign will existed outside the legislature and that it should be consulted. See Jean-Jacques Rousseau, *Du Contrat Social* (Paris: Messidor/Editions sociales, 1987), 175; Bosc, *Le Peuple Souverain et la Démocratie*, 11; Tuck, *The Sleeping Sovereign*, 124, 134, 138, 153. See also Jean Roels, "J. J. Rousseau et les institutions representatives dans les Consideration sur le Gouvernement de Pologne," *Parliaments, Estates, and Representations* 5, no. 1 (June 1985): 15, 17–18.

40. *Archives Parlementaires de 1787 à 1860*, Vol. 56, 13.
41. Ibid., 15.
42. This line of argument echoed those made in the judicial reform of 1791, which placed value on the jury hearing and seeing oral testimony directly. Mason, "The 'Bosom of Proof,' " 39.
43. *Archives Parlementaires de 1787 à 1860*, Vol. 56, 157.
44. Ibid., 96. Like their opponents, deputies attempting to drive home the people's inability to make such a weighty decision cited Rousseau. Moreau's assertion echoed Rosseau's vision for the purpose of a "legislator" to enlighten the people in determining the general will. He and others also built upon Rousseau's conception of the general will as more than the sum of individual wills and thus the possibility he saw for the people's discernment of the general will to be wrong. The way these deputies used Rousseau highlights the fundamentally anti-democratic potential in the philosopher's notion of the general will; if the general will is not the sum of individual wills, a minority can simply claim to identify it. See Rousseau, *Du Contrat Social*, 121–122; Roels, "J. J. Rousseau et les institutions representatives dans les Considerations sur le Governement de Pologne," 16.
45. Ibid., 18.
46. Ibid., 210.
47. Ibid., 202.
48. Ibid.
49. "Le séance extraordinaire du 10 Xembre, 1792," AN/C/361, doss. 1.
50. *Archives Parlementaires de 1787 à 1860*, Vol. 57 (Paris: Librairie administrative de Paul Dupont, 1862–1913), 63.
51. Ibid., 600.
52. Ibid., 601.
53. The shift in thinking about political representation from being reflective to being directive aligns with the Jacobin desire to create the people anew by

changing religious rituals, the calendar, units of measurement, etc. For more on this, see especially Ozouf, *L'homme régénère.*

54. Timothy Tackett also notes the significance of seventeen Parisian journalists being elected to the Convention. See Tackett, *The Coming of the Terror*, 224.
55. Maximilien Robespierre, "Lettres à ses commettants: Exposé des principes et but de cette publication," in *Oeuvres*, Tome V, ed. M. Bouloiseau, G. Lefebvre, and A. Soboul (Paris: 1910–1967), 15.
56. Ibid.
57. Ibid. Yannick Bosc has pointed to this kind of rhetoric as evidence that Robespierre remained steadfast in his commitment to a reflective style of representation and to surveillance as a tool to enforce it. He cites a speech Robespierre gave on May 10, 1793, in which he declared: "The entire nation has the right to know the conduct of its proxies (*mandataires*). If it were possible, the assembly of proxies should deliberate in the presence of all French people. The meetings of the legislature should be held in a lavish and majestic edifice, open to twelve thousand spectators. Before the eyes of such a large number of witnesses, neither corruption, intrigue, nor perfidy would dare show themselves; the general will alone would be consulted, the voice of reason and the public interest alone would be heard." However, the fact that he, as a deputy, launched a periodical to enact this kind of publicity is significant when reflecting on how he intended publicity to function and who was to enact it. See Bosc, *Le Peuple Souverain et la Démocratie*, 131–133.
58. This is something Desmoulins reportedly reflected on when Brissot and his political allies were executed in October 1793. He felt that his publications dedicated to unmasking Brissot and the Girondins had played a role in their death. See Linton, *Choosing Terror*, 184.
59. Cohen, *Le Comité des Inspecteurs de la Salle*, 86.
60. Ibid.
61. "Procès verbal du 5 janvier, 1793," AN/C/161, doss. 2.
62. Cohen, *Le Comité des Inspecteurs de la Salle*, 86.
63. Lettre sans-date, AN/C/161, doss. 3.
64. Lettre sans-date, AN/C/161, doss. 3.
65. *Archives Parlementaires de 1787 à 1860*, Vol. 55 (Paris: Librairie administrative de Paul Dupont, 1862–1913), 40.
66. Ibid.
67. Ibid., 47.
68. Ibid., 48.
69. Lettre du 18 janvier, 1793, AN/C/361, doss. 2.
70. Tackett, *The Coming of the Terror*, 255.
71. Ibid.
72. Paul Friedland discusses this effort to make spectators passive as a central component of the establishment of representative government and new styles of theater in the eighteenth century. For more, see Friedland, *Political Actors.*

73. AN/C/161, doss. 3, "Procès verbal, 28 mars, 1793."
74. Cohen, *Le Comité des Inspecteurs de la Salle*, 87.
75. Ibid.
76. Tackett, *The Coming of the Terror*, 264.
77. *Archives Parlementaires de 1787 à 1860*, Vol. 61 (Paris: Librairie administrative de Paul Dupont, 1862–1913), 105–106.
78. Ibid., 128.
79. Ibid.
80. Ibid.
81. Ibid.
82. Ibid., 373.
83. Ibid., 374.
84. "Procés verbal, 6 avril, 1793," AN/AF/II*/45.
85. "Procés verbal, 9 avril, 1793," AN/C/161, doss. 3.
86. "Procés verbal, 7 avril, 1793," AN/AF/II*/45.
87. AN/AF/II/23, doss. 180, 21 septembre, 1793.
88. AN/AF/II/31.
89. AN/AF/II/23, doss. 188, undated document.
90. Ibid.
91. AN/AF/II*/284.
92. Over the spring and summer of 1793, the Committee of Public Safety, along with the Comité de Sureté Générale, set up an office to systematically open and record the contents of all mail coming from or going to territories not controlled by the French army. See AN/AF/II*/45, "Procés verbal, 16 avril, 1793."
93. For more on the "state of exception" and the idea of the Revolution itself as a source of legitimacy, see especially Dan Edelstein, "Do We Want a Revolution without Revolution? Reflections on Political Authority," *French Historical Studies* 25, no. 2 (March 2012).
94. AN/D/XL/30, doss. 5.
95. AN/C/360, doss. 1.
96. AN/D/XL/30, doss. 5.
97. "Procés verbal, 15 avril, 1793," AN/AF/II*/45.
98. For more on the deputies sent to the provinces, see especially R. R. Palmer, *Twelve Who Ruled: The Year of the Terror in the French Revolution* (Princeton: Princeton University Press, 1941).
99. Friedland, *Political Actors*, 288. Tackett also points to the expulsion of the Girondin and another invasion of the assembly chamber on September 5, 1793, as moments sparking concern among Jacobin deputies. Rather than arguing that it was due to a divergent conception of what was to make them legitimate as representative, Tackett instead discusses the incidents as simply spurring concern that they were losing legitimacy. See Tackett, *The Coming of the Terror*, 286–300.

100. Ibid., 290. On recognizing the divisions among Jacobins, see Vovelle, *Les Jacobins: De Robespierre à Chevènement*, 26.
101. Friedland, *Political Actors*, 291.
102. *Archives Parlementaires de 1787 à 1860*, Vol. 68 (Paris: Librairie administrative de Paul Dupont, 1862–1913), 513.
103. Ibid.
104. Ibid.
105. The number of committee members was later increased to twelve. See R. R. Palmer, *Twelve Who Ruled: The Year of the Terror in the French Revolution* (Princeton: Princeton University Press, 1989), 4.
106. "Le Journal des Débats et correspondance," Société des Jacobins, no. 435, in Bouloiseau et al., *Oeuvres, Tome IX: Discours*, 572.
107. *Constitution du 24 juin 1793*, accessed March 3, 2019, Conseil Constitutionnel.
108. *Archives Parlementaires de 1787 à 1860*, Vol. 76 (Paris: Librairie administrative de Paul Dupont, 1862–1913), 313.
109. Ibid., 316.
110. Ibid., 315.
111. Colin Jones, "The Overthrow of Maximilien Robespierre and the 'Indifference' of the People," *American Historical Review* 119, no. 3 (June 2014); Colin Jones, "9 Thermidor: Cinderella Among Revolutionary *Journées*," *French Historical Studies* 38, no. 1 (February 2015); Jones, *The Fall of Robespierre*, 433.
112. Jones, *The Fall of Robespierre*, 455.
113. Jones, "The Overthrow of Maximilien Robespierre," 707.
114. Jones, "The Overthrow of Maximilien Robespierre," 711.

Chapter Six. Politics Behind the Curtain

1. "Toasts Drunk at the Eighteenth-anniversary celebration of American Independence, July 4, 1794," *American Daily Advertiser*, July 7, 1794, in Foner, *The Democratic Republican Societies*, 107. Portions of this chapter originally appeared in Carter, "Denouncing Secrecy and Defining Democracy in the Early American Republic."
2. A great deal of scholarship on the early national period has been essentially directed at explaining how the new federal government was made legitimate and determining what type of government it was. A lot of this work is broadly focused on explaining the rise of national identity and practices of popular politics. See Waldstreicher, *In the Midst of Perpetual Fêtes;* Newman, *Parades and the Politics of the Street;* Wilentz, *Chants Democratic;* Jeffrey Pasley, Andrew Robertson, and David Waldstreicher, eds., *Beyond the Founders: New Approaches to the Political History of the Early American Republic* (Chapel Hill: University of North Carolina Press, 2004); Bradburn, *The Citizenship Revolution.* A particular focus among historians has been to determine whether

the newly created federal government was "democratic" or whether it was actually undemocratic by design. See Bouton, *Taming Democracy;* Barbara Clark Smith, *The Freedoms We Lost: Consent and Resistance in Revolutionary America* (New York: New Press, 2010), 206; Nelson, *Commons Democracy*, 7; Sandra Gustafson, *Imagining Deliberative Democracy in the Early American Republic* (Chicago: University of Chicago Press, 2011); Banning, *The Sacred Fire of Liberty;* Sheehan, *James Madison and the Spirit of Republican Self-Government.*

3. There is less discussion of publicity and secrecy in the judicial branch. The Supreme Court was not made up of elected officials, but appointed judges. There is evidence that by the time the court sat in Washington, D.C., arguments were open to an audience. See Lewis, "Politics and the Ambivalence of the Private Sphere," 140–141.
4. For more on the incident of the Jay Treaty and how it ties into debates about secrecy dating back to the ratification debates, see Carter, "Denouncing Secrecy and Defining Democracy in the Early American Republic."
5. Washington to John Jay, Philadelphia, December 18, 1794, in *The Papers of George Washington*, Presidential Series, Vol. 17 (Charlottesville: University of Virginia Press, Rotunda, 2008), 287.
6. Republican Society of Lancaster, "Constitution and Address" (January 3, 1795), in Foner, *The Democratic-Republican Societies*, 120.
7. Democratic Society of the City of New York, "Address to the Republican Citizens of the United States" (May 28, 1794), in Foner, *The Democratic-Republican Societies*, 176.
8. Republican Society of the Town of Newark, "Cato to the Newark Gazette" (March 12, 1794), in Foner, *The Democratic-Republican Societies*, 144.
9. Jerald Combs, *The Jay Treaty: Political Battleground of the Founding Fathers* (Berkeley: University of California Press, 1970), 160.
10. Immediately after the president presented the treaty to the Senate, it was ordered that "the Senators be under an injunction of secrecy on the communication this day received from the President of the United States, until the further order of the Senate," and "That the secretary procure, printed under an injunction of secrecy, thirty-one copies only of the Treaty referred to in this Message of the President of the United States, of this day, for the use of the Senate." See *Annals of Congress*, Vol. 4, *Third Congress*, 855. On June 13, the Senate revisited this injunction but voted 20–9 to maintain it. See *Annals of Congress*, Vol. 4, *Third Congress*, 858. Combs reports that this was done at the urging of Federalist members. Combs, *The Jay Treaty*, 161.
11. Lindsay Chervinsky has also made the point that the development of the presidential cabinet and the way it worked over 1793–94 re-enforced executive authority over diplomatic affairs. See Chervinsky, *The Cabinet*, 195.
12. *Treaty of amity, commerce, and navigation, between his Britannick Majesty, and the United States of America. By their president, with the advice and consent of their Senate* (Printed by Benjamin Franklin Bache, Philadelphia, 1795).

13. *Annals of Congress, Special Session, June 8–June 26, 1795*, 867.
14. Combs, *Jay Treaty*, 162. This belief that the secrecy surrounding the treaty was doing more harm than good for the Federalist case has also been cited by Stanley Elkins and Eric McKitrick in *The Age of Federalistm: The Early American Republic, 1788–1800* (Oxford: Oxford University Press, 1993), 420.
15. Pasley, *The Tyranny of Printers*, 91–92. Pasley documented Bache's journey to spread the text of the treaty in his account of the politicization of printers in the early republic.
16. "Resolutions Adopted on Jay's Treaty, Sept. 28, 1795," *City Gazette*, Charleston, October 28, 1795, in Foner, *The Democratic Republican Societies, 1790–1800*, 403–408.
17. William Maclay to Benjamin Rush, March 19, 1789, in *Documentary History of the First Federal Congress of the United States of America*, Vol. 15, *Correspondence, first session: March–May 1789*, ed. Linda Grant DePauw (Baltimore: Johns Hopkins University Press, 2004), 78.
18. George Washington to David Stuart, July 26, 1789, in *The Papers of George Washington*, Presidential Series, Vol. 3, *June–Sept, 1789*, ed. W. W. Abbot (Charlottesville: University of Virginia Press, 1989), 321.
19. George Washington to Catherine Macaulay, January 9, 1790, in *The Papers of George Washington*, Presidential Series, Vol. 4, *September 1789–January 1790*, ed. Dorothy Twohig (Charlottesville: University of Virginia Press, 1993), 552.
20. *New York Daily Gazette*, April 9, 1789, in *Documentary History of the First Federal Congress of the United States of America*, Vol. 10, ed. Charlene Bangs Bickford, Kenneth R. Bowling, and Helen Veit (Baltimore: Johns Hopkins University Press, 1992), xi.
21. Comte de Moustier to Comte de Montmorin, June 9, 1789, in *Documentary History of the First Federal Congress of the United States of America*, Vol. 16, *Correspondence, first session: June–August 1789*, ed. Linda Grant DePauw (Baltimore: Johns Hopkins University Press, 2004), 730.
22. Jack Rakove, "The Structure of Politics at the Accession of George Washington," in Beeman et al., *Beyond Confederation: Origins of the Constitution and American National Identity*, 292. Editors of the documentary collection of the First Congress also assert that the opening of the doors to the House was inevitable. See Charlene Bangs Bickford, Kenneth Bowling, and Helen Veit, eds., *Documentary History of the First Federal Congress*, Vol. 10, xvi; Berkin, *The Bill of Rights*, 51.
23. Abigail Adams to John Adams, May 1, 1789, in *Documentary History of the First Federal Congress*, Vol. 15, ed. Charlene Bangs Bickford, Kenneth R. Bowling, Helen E. Veit, and William C. diGiacomantonio (Baltimore: John Hopkins University Press, 2004), 422.
24. Comte de Moustier to Comte de Montmorin, June 9, 1789, in *Documentary History of the First Federal Congress*, Vol. 16, 730.
25. *Gazette of the United States* (New York: John Fenno, April 15, 1789), accessed January 25, 2016, Readex: America's Historic Newspapers.

26. John Adams to Benjamin Rush, April 18, 1790, in *Documentary History of the First Federal Congress*, Vol. 19, *Correspondence, 15 March–June 1790*, ed. Charlene Bangs Bickford, Kenneth Bowling, Helen Veit, and William Charles di-Giacomantonio (Baltimore: Johns Hopkins University Press, 2012), 1261. For more on the mindsets of these first printers of congressional proceedings, see Pasley, *The Tyranny of Printers*. For a detailed explanation of Lloyd's shorthand notes, see Marion Tinling, "Thomas Lloyd's Reports of the First Federal Congress," *William and Mary Quarterly* 18, no. 4 (October 1961).
27. Marcus Daniel, *Scandal and Civility: Journalism and the Birth of American Democracy* (Oxford: Oxford University Press, 2010), 20, 27.
28. John Fenno to John Ward Fenno, August 5, 1789, in "Letters of John Fenno and John Ward Fenno," in *Proceedings of the American Antiquarian Society*, ed. John B. Hench (Worcester, MA: American Antiquarian Society, 1980), 334.
29. John Carey, *The system of short-hand practiced by Mr. Thomas Lloyd, in taking down the debates of Congress: and now (with his permission) published for general use* (Philadelphia, 1793), 16. LCP: Wxz.1. For more on the notion of shorthand as a way to synchronize speech and writing and to promote truth and accountability, see especially Slauter, *The State as a Work of Art*, 149; Rosenfeld, *Democracy and Truth: A Short History*, 59; Rosenfeld, *A Revolution in Language*, 204.
30. Mildred Amer, *The Congressional Record* (Washington, D.C.: Congressional Research Service, October 21, 1986), 2.
31. "A Bill Entitled 'An act to provide for the safe keeping of the Acts, Records, and Seal of the United States,' signed into law on September 15, 1789," accessed May 18, 2022, U.S. Capitol Visitor Center.
32. Amer, *The Congressional Record*, 7.
33. Hutson, "The Creation of the Constitution and the Integrity of the Documentary Record," 169; Slauter, *The State as a Work of Art*, 160–161.
34. Hutson, "The Creation of the Constitution and the Integrity of the Documentary Record," 168.
35. Of note is that the copyright for a recorded speech was ultimately held by the reporter who had taken it down, highlighting the role of the transcriber in the production of the record. See Slauter, *The State as a Work of Art*, 155.
36. Daniel, *Scandal and Civility*, 29.
37. Ibid., 30.
38. Governor John Pickering to John Langdon, April 17, 1789, in *Documentary History of the First Federal Congress*, Vol. 15, 277.
39. William Bradford to Elias Boudinot, April 20, 1789, in *Documentary History of the First Federal Congress*, Vol. 15, 294; William Bradford to Elias Boudinot, May 3, 1789, in *Documentary History of the First Federal Congress*, Vol. 15, 439.
40. Thomas B. Wait to George Thatcher, April 15, 1789, in *Documentary History of the First Federal Congress*, Vol. 15, 271.
41. Richard R. John, *Spreading the News: The American Postal System from Franklin to Morse* (Cambridge, MA: Harvard University Press, 1995), 31–36. As

the Post Office Act of 1792 was debated, there was disagreement as to whether there should be no fee or simply a reduced fee for sending newspapers through the mail. Printer Benjamin Franklin Bache and Representative Elbridge Gerry argued that there should be no fee based on the important role of the press in a republic, while James Madison urged the need for some fee. Ultimately, newspapers could be sent through the mail at a modest fee, and the result was an increased volume of newspapers circulating. By the 1830s, newspapers made up one-third to one-half of the mail by weight.

42. *From John Steele*, January 15, 1792, in *Circular Letters of Congressmen to Their Constituents, 1789–1829*, Vol. 1, *First Congress–Ninth Congress*, ed. Noble E. Cunningham, Jr. (Chapel Hill: University of North Carolina Press, 1978), 9.
43. Kenneth Bowling, "A Capital Before a Capitol: Republican Visions," in Kennon, *A Republic for the Ages*, 41.
44. Scholars have noted the persistent importance of orality in this period and the way in which oratory could either be seen as promoting transparency in the sense of authenticity by stirring emotions and passions, and thus leading to sound judgments, or stymieing reason. For more, see especially Eastman, *A Nation of Speechifiers;* Carolyn Eastman, *The Strange Genius of Mr. O: The World of the United States' First Forgotten Celebrity* (Chapel Hill: University of North Carolina Press, 2021), 6; Jay Fliegelman, *Declaring Independence: Jefferson, Natural Language and the Culture of Performance* (Stanford: Stanford University Press, 1993); Mason, " 'The Bosom of Proof' "; Ravel, *The Contested Parterre*, 215–216.
45. Quoted in Jan Lewis, "Politics and the Ambivalence of the Private Sphere: Women in Early Washington, D.C.," in Kennon, *A Republic for the Ages*, 136. Lewis notes that Lee represented the view of an older generation at the time that "men cannot help responding to women in a sexualized way, even when they should be debating political issues rationally."
46. See especially Rosemarie Zagarri, *Revolutionary Backlash: Women and Politics in the Early American Republic* (Philadelphia: University of Pennsylvania Press, 2007); Linda Kerber, Nancy Cott, Robert Gross, Lynn Hunt, Carroll Smith-Rosenberg, and Christine Stansell, "Beyond Roles, Beyond Spheres: Thinking about Gender in the Early Republic," *William and Mary Quarterly* 46, no. 3 (July 1989); Branson, *These Fiery Frenchified Dames;* Allgor, *Parlor Politics;* Mary Kelley, *Learning to Stand and Speak: Women, Education, and Public Life in America's Republic* (Chapel Hill: University of North Carolina Press, 2006); Lewis, "Politics and the Ambivalence of the Private Sphere"; Padraig Riley, "The Lonely Congressmen: Gender and Politics in Early Washington, D.C.," *Journal of the Early Republic* 34 (Summer 2014); Eastman, *A Nation of Speechifiers*, 54–55.
47. Branson, *These Fiery Frenchified Dames*, 131; Berkin, *The Bill of Rights*, 51; Allgor, *Parlor Politics*, 9.
48. Lewis, "Politics and the Ambivalence of the Private Sphere," 136.
49. Ibid., 130–132; Riley, "The Lonely Congressmen," 155.

50. Lewis, "Politics and the Ambivalence of the Private Sphere," 124.
51. Ibid., 132; Branson, *These Fiery Frenchified Dames*, 122–126, 130–134. Allgor, *Parlor Politics*, 1, 9.
52. Lewis, "Politics and the Ambivalence of the Private Sphere," 130; Branson, *These Fiery Frenchified Dames*, 125.
53. Lewis, "Politics and the Ambivalence of the Private Sphere," 127, 133. For more on the possibility for publicity to render citizens passive and deprive them of power in a representative democracy, see especially Urbinati, *Democracy Disfigured*, 14–15.
54. Lewis, "Politics and the Ambivalence of the Private Sphere," 137. This "gendered division between the floor of Congress, where men orated, and the galleries where women listened" was also noted by Padraig Riley. See Riley, "The Lonely Congressmen," 262.
55. Edmund Pendleton to James Madison, May 3, 1789, in *Documentary History of the First Federal Congress*, Vol. 15, 446.
56. William Ellery to Benjamin Huntington, July 21, 1789, in *Documentary History of the First Federal Congress*, Vol. 16, 1096.
57. William Wetmore to Benjamin Goodhue, February 14, 1790, cited in Bowling, "A Capital Before a Capitol," 48. Bowling also cites an editorial that appeared in the *Federal Gazette* on September 28, 1789, arguing in favor of placing the capital in a big city because "rulers require to be watched, and the more people surround them, the more they will be enlightened and checked." The editorial named the French National Assembly located in Paris as an example.
58. Jan Lewis suggested that "The public was expected to come to Washington, but it was not supposed to engage in the sorts of activities that would create interests antagonistic to, nor were they supposed to make any claim upon, the public good. The public was supposed to attend the government, then, as spectator." See Lewis, "Politics and the Ambivalence of the Private Sphere," 123.
59. William Maclay to Benjamin Rush, March 6, 1789, in *Documentary History of the First Federal Congress*, Vol. 15, 41; Thomas Hartley to Tench Coxe, March 30, 1789, in *Documentary History of the First Federal Congress*, Vol. 15, 157.
60. Alexander White to Horatio Gates, April 27, 1789, in *Documentary History of the First Federal Congress*, Vol. 15, 371.
61. Benjamin Goodhue to Richard Ward, April 22, 1789, in *Documentary History of the First Federal Congress*, Vol. 15, 316.
62. For more on Maclay's fear of politics unfolding in private, see Freeman, *Affairs of Honor*, 49–52.
63. Bickford, Bowling, and Veit, *Documentary History of the First Federal Congress*, Vol. 10, xxiii.
64. John James Beckley, "Inventory of Furnishings," *John James Beckley Papers* (November 17, 1790). Virginia Historical Society: Mss1 B3886a, Folder 2.
65. Peter Muhlenberg to John Hubley, April 4, 1789, in *Documentary History of the First Federal Congress*, Vol. 15, 197.

66. Peter Muhlenberg to Benjamin Rush, June 25, 1789, in *Documentary History of the First Federal Congress*, Vol. 16, 855.
67. Berkin, *The Bill of Rights*, 88. Berkin suggests the rejection of the right of instruction cemented a particular style of representative politics.
68. *Annals of Congress*, Vol. 2, *First Congress, Second Session*, 1186.
69. Ibid., 1187.
70. Ibid., 1189.
71. *Annals of Congress*, Vol. 1, *First Congress, First Session*, 687–688; *Annals of Congress*, Vol. 1, 1055–1056.
72. *Annals of Congress*, Vol. 3, *Second Congress*, 414. Closed sessions continued to happen throughout the early 1790s to discuss a range of topics, from the South Sea Company in 1790 to ongoing warfare with Native Americans on the western edges of the country to negotiations with Algiers regarding piracy off the coast of North Africa.
73. *Annals of Congress*, Vol. 4, *Third Congress*, 149–150.
74. Ibid., 151, 152.
75. *Annals of Congress*, Vol. 4, *Third Congress*, 522.
76. Governor Charles Pinckney to James Madison, March 28, 1789, in *Documentary History of the First Federal Congress*, Vol. 15, 140.
77. David Stuart to George Washington, July 14, 1789, in *The Papers of George Washington*, Presidential Series, Vol. 3, 199.
78. George Washington to David Stuart, July 26, 1789, in *The Papers of George Washington*, Presidential Series, Vol. 3, 324.
79. Paine Wingate to Timothy Pickering, April 29, 1789, in *Documentary History of the First Federal Congress*, Vol. 15, 391.
80. There was a great deal of concern in the young republic about where to locate the capital and the problem of corruption seeping into political institutions if it were in particular cities as well as the potential for mob violence or pressure. For more on these discussions, see Elkins and McKitrick, *The Age of Federalistm*, 164; Freeman, *Affairs of Honor*, 8; Bowling, "A Capital Before a Capitol," 39–40.
81. Richard Peters to John Adams, May 28, 1789, in *Documentary History of the First Federal Congress*, Vol. 15, 645.
82. *Annals of Congress*, Vol. 2, *First Congress, Second Session*, 135.
83. *Annals of Congress*, Vol. 2, *First Congress, Second Session, 1766–1768*.
84. *Annals of Congress*, Vol. 3, *Second Congress*, 637–638.
85. *Annals of Congress*, Vol. 4, *Third Congress*, 45–46.
86. John Adams to Abigail Adams, February 23, 1794, in *Adams Family Correspondence*, Vol. 10, *January 1794–June 1795*, *Digital Edition*, ed. Margaret A. Hogan, C. James Taylor, Sara Martin, Hobson Woodward, Sara B. Sikes, Gregg L. Lint, and Sara Georgini (Cambridge, MA: Belknap Press, 2011), 87.
87. Charles Adams to John Adams, January 8, 1794, in *Adams Family Correspondence*, Vol. 10, *January 1794-June 1795*, 34.

88. For more on the cabinet's work, see Chervinsky, *The Cabinet*, 142–143.
89. George Washington to John Adams, May 10, 1789, in *The Papers of George Washington*, Presidential Series, Vol. 2, *April–June 1789*, ed. W. W. Abbot (Charlottesville: University of Virginia Press, 1987), 245–246.
90. George Washington to James Madison, May 12, 1789, in *The Papers of George Washington*, Presidential Series, Vol. 2, 282.
91. Alexander Hamilton to George Washington, May 5, 1789, in *The Papers of George Washington*, Presidential Series, Vol. 2, 213.
92. T. H. Breen, *George Washington's Journey: The President Forges a Nation* (New York: Simon and Schuster, 2016), 46.
93. Ibid., 5. See also Susan Dunn, *Jefferson's Second Revolution: The Election Crisis of 1800 and the Triumph of Republicanism* (Boston: Houghton Mifflin, 2004), 16.
94. On "representative publicness," see: Habermas, *The Structural Transformation of the Public Sphere*, 11, 21.
95. For more on the use of codes and cyphers during the Revolutionary period, see John A. Nagy, *Invisible Ink: Spycraft of the American Revolution* (Yardley, PA: Westholme, 2010).
96. George Washington to Benjamin Harrison, March 9, 1789, in *The Papers of George Washington*, Presidential Series, Vol. 1, *September 1788–March 1789*, ed. W. W. Abbot (Charlottesville: University of Virginia Press, 1987), 376.
97. Benjamin Harrison to George Washington, April 3, 1789, in *The Papers of George Washington*, Presidential Series, Vol. 2, 14. One of the instances that plagued Washington was regarding letters he had in fact never written but which had been attributed to him and printed as propaganda during the war. These "spurious letters" continued to haunt Washington through his term as president. For more on the practice of leaking and counterfeiting letters, see Castronovo, *Propaganda 1776*, 117.
98. For more on the importance of sentimentalist discourse to American politics, see Sarah Knott, *Sensibility and the American Revolution* (Chapel Hill: University of North Carolina Press, 2009). For more on the importance of epistolary practices, see Perl-Rosenthal, *Corresponding Republics*.
99. Alexander Hamilton to William Seton, December 3, 1790, in *The Papers of Alexander Hamilton*, Vol. 7, *September 1790–January 1791*, ed. Harold C. Syrett (New York: Columbia University Press, Rotunda, 2011), 190.
100. George Washington to Timothy Pickering, February 15, 1799, in *The Papers of George Washington*, Retirement Series, Vol. 3 (Charlottesville: University of Virginia Press, Rotunda, 2008), 381.
101. For more, see Pasley, *Tyranny of Printers*, 60–65; Elkins and McKitrick, *Age of Federalism*, 282.
102. Chervinsky, *The Cabinet*, 182–183.
103. Marcus Daniel suggests Freneau began the paper as a cautiously balanced outlet in order to legitimate later opposition; however, I would argue its ultimate aims were implied in its earliest content. Daniel, *Scandal and Civility*, 83.

104. Gibson, "Veneration and Vigilance: James Madison and Public Opinion, 1785–1800," 9.
105. Siemers, *Ratifying the Republic*, 105; Shankman, *Original Intents*, 111; Wood, *Revolutionary Characters*, 152.
106. *National Gazette*, December 19, 1791 (Philadelphia: Philip Freneau). APS: 071 N21, vol. 1, no. 1–104.
107. Shankman, *Original Intents*, 113, 115, 122.
108. Colleen Sheehan, *The Mind of James Madison: The Legacy of Classical Republicanism* (Cambridge: Cambridge University Press, 2017), 12, 15.
109. Shankman, *Original Intents*, 123; Bailey, *James Madison and Constitutional Imperfection*, 102; Wood, *Revolutionary Characters*, 165; Siemers, *Ratifying the Republic*, 92.
110. For more on Madison as theorist grounded in experience, see Rakove, *A Politician Thinking*.
111. "Memoranda of Consultations with the President, March 11–April 9, 1792," in *The Papers of Thomas Jefferson, Digital Edition*, Vol. 23, *January 1 to 31 May, 1792*, ed. Barbara B. Oberg and J. Jefferson Looney (Charlottesville: University of Virginia Press, Rotunda, 2008–2016), 261.
112. Ibid., 262.
113. Ibid.
114. Ibid.
115. Ibid. A similar situation unfolded in January 1794, when the Senate requested all correspondence between Gouverneur Morris, the American envoy to France, and the French Republic, as well as that of the office of the Secretary of State. Under the advisement of Attorney General William Bradford that "it is the duty of the Executive to withhold such parts of the said correspondence as in their judgment of the executive shall be deemed unsafe and improper to be disclosed," Washington transmitted redacted copies of the letters on February 26. See William Bradford to George Washington, January 1794, in *The Papers of George Washington*, Presidential Series, Vol. 17, *Oct. 1, 1794–31 March, 1795*, ed. David R. Hoth, Carol S. Ebel, and Edward G. Lengel (Charlottesville: University of Virginia Press, 2013), 166; Letter to the United States Senate, February 26, 1794, in *The Papers of George Washington*, Vol. 17, 284.
116. John Jay to George Washington, September 23, 1791, in *The Papers of George Washington, Digital Edition*, Vol. 9, ed. Theodore J. Crackle (Charlottesville: University of Virginia Press, Rotunda, 2008), 2.
117. *The Diaries of George Washington: 1784–1799*, Vol. 4, *1789–1799*, ed. John C. Fitzpatrick (Boston: Houghton Mifflin, 1925), 69.
118. Another early, and repeated, instance of this practice was with all information regarding the negotiation over Americans held captive in Algiers. Transmitting details of the negotiation to Congress on December 16, 1793, Washington noted: "While it proper our citizens should know that subjects which so much concern their interests and feelings have duly en-

gaged the attention of their legislature and executive, it would still be improper that some of the particulars of this communication should be made known." Letter to the United States Senate and House of Representatives, December 16, 1793, in *The Papers of George Washington*, Presidential Series, Vol. 16 (Charlottesville: University of Virginia Press, Rotunda, 2008), 534.

119. Waldstreicher, *In the Midst of Perpetual Fêtes*, 134. This report written by Genêt to the French Minister of Foreign Affairs on May 31, 1793, is quoted and used as the inspiration for the title of Waldstreicher's book. Waldstreicher makes the Citizen Genêt Affair a central point of analysis in his study of popular politics and the formation of nationalism in the early republic, arguing that Federalists faced criticism for their style of politics being secretive and anti-republican in contrast to Genêt's close relationship to the public.

120. *National Gazette* (Philadelphia: Philip Freneau, June 1, 1793), accessed May 28, 2017, Readex: America's Historic Newspapers.

121. German Republican Society of Philadelphia, "To Friends and Fellow Citizens" (April 11, 1793), in Foner, *The Democratic Republican Societies*, 54; Democratic Society of Pennsylvania, "Principles, Articles and Regulations, Agreed upon, Drawn, and Adopted, May 30, 1793" (May 30, 1793), in *Democratic Republican Societies*, 64; Republican Society of Norfolk and Portsmouth, "Declaration of Sentiments and Principles" (June 3, 1793), in *Democratic Republican Societies*, 345.

122. Seth Cotlar has argued these societies envisioned and fashioned themselves in relation to contemporaneous European popular societies, although older scholarship argued they were revivals of American Revolutionary society movements. See Seth Cotlar, "Reading the Foreign News: Imagining an American Public Sphere: Radical and Conservative Visions of 'The Public' in Mid-1790s Newspapers," in *Periodical Literature in Eighteenth-Century America*, ed. Mark Kamrath (Knoxville: University of Tennessee Press, 2005), 315–317; Albert Koschnik, "The Democratic Societies of Philadelphia and the Limits of the American Public Sphere, circa 1793–1795," *William and Mary Quarterly* 58, no. 3 (2001): 618; Matthew Shoenbachler, "Republicanism in the Age of Democratic Revolution: The Democratic-Republican Societies of the 1790s," *Journal of the Early Republic* 18, no. 2 (1998), 238; Estes, *The Jay Treaty Debate*, 53.

123. Democratic Society of Pennsylvania, "Principles, Articles and Regulations, Agreed upon, Drawn, and Adopted, May 30, 1793" (May 30, 1793), in Foner, *The Democratic Republican Societies*, 64.

124. Facing criticism for using secrecy, Federalists turned this rhetoric on the popular societies, alleging that they could not speak for the people since they were secretive and mysterious entities themselves. See Robert Martin, *Government by Dissent: Protest, Resistance, and Radical Democratic Thought in the Early American Republic* (New York: New York University Press, 2013), 99; Koschnik, "The Democratic Societies of Philadelphia," 633; Estes, *The Jay Treaty Debate*, 65.

125. Elkins and McKitrick, *Age of Federalism*, 345.
126. Edmond Charles Genêt to Thomas Jefferson, December 20, 1793, in *The Papers of Thomas Jefferson, Digital Edition*, Vol. 27, ed. James P. McClure and Jefferson Looney (Charlottesville: University of Virginia Press, Rotunda, 2008–2020), 593.
127. Notes of a cabinet meeting on the president's address and messages to Congress, November 28, 1793, in *The Papers of Thomas Jefferson*, Vol. 27, 453. See also Chervinsky, *The Cabinet*, 223.
128. George Washington to Thomas Jefferson, December 1, 1793, in *The Papers of George Washington*, Presidential Series, Vol. 14 (Charlottesville: University of Virginia Press, Rotunda, 2008), 449.
129. Thomas Jefferson to George Washington, December 2, 1793, in *The Papers of Thomas Jefferson*, Vol. 27, 472.
130. Ibid.
131. *Letters of Franklin, on the Conduct of the Executive, Letter XI, May 18, 1795* (Philadelphia: Oswald, 1795), accessed May 28, 2017, Sabin Americana.
132. William Cobbett, *A Little Plain English, by Peter Porcupine* (Philadelphia: Bradford, 1795), 83, accessed May 28, 2017, Evans Early American Imprints.
133. Cobbett, *A Little Plain English*, 88.
134. "Address by a Member to the Democratic Society on Jay's Treaty, Sept. 3, 1795," *New York Journal, New York*, October 14, 1795, in Foner, *The Democratic Republican Societies, 1790–1800*, 247.
135. Estes, *The Jay Treaty Debate*, 6.
136. Ibid., 133.
137. Ibid., 153.
138. Notably, among these people were women; Jan Lewis has pointed out that women were present "virtually every time a debate of any significance was held in Congress." This was particularly true during the Antebellum period. See Lewis, "Politics and the Ambivalence of the Private Sphere," 134–135.
139. Loughran, *The Republic in Print*, 212.

Chapter Seven. Surrounded by Spectators

1. *Annals of Congress*, Vol. 5, *Fourth Congress, First Session*, 435.
2. *Annals of Congress*, Vol. 7, *Fifth Congress*, 238.
3. *Annals of Congress*, Vol. 6, *Fourth Congress, Second Session*, 1538.
4. For others who have made a similar point, see Estes, *The Jay Treaty Debate*, 9; Wood, *Revolutionary Characters*, 28; Gordon Wood, *The Radicalism of the American Revolution* (New York: Vintage Books, 1993), 294; Waldstreicher, *In the Midst of Perpetual Fêtes*, 86.
5. Elkins and McKintrick, *The Age of Federalism*, 691; John Ferling, *Adams vs. Jefferson: The Tumultuous Election of 1800* (Oxford: Oxford University Press,

2005); Dunn, *Jefferson's Second Revolution;* James Roger Sharp, *The Deadlocked Election of 1800: Jefferson, Burr, and the Union in the Balance* (Lawrence: University Press of Kansas, 2010); James Horn, Jan Ellen Lewis, and Peter Onuf, eds., *The Revolution of 1800: Democracy, Race, and the New Republic* (Charlottesville: University of Virginia Press, 2002).

6. For more on Thomas Jefferson as a contradictory figure, see especially Annette Gordon-Reed, *The Hemingses of Monticello: An American Family* (New York: W. W. Norton, 2009); Peter Onuf, *Jefferson and the Virginians: Democracy, Constitutions, and Empire* (Baton Rouge: Louisiana State University Press, 2018); Sean Wilentz, *The Rise of American Democracy: Jefferson to Lincoln* (New York: Norton, 2009), 52; Peter S. Onuf, *Jefferson's Empire: The Language of American Nationhood* (Charlottesville: University Press of Virginia, 2000).
7. For notable examples see Wilentz, *The Rise of American Democracy;* Pasley, *Tyranny of Printers*. On the other hand, Reeve Huston has suggested that, partly due to a lack of clarity on what is meant by the term "democracy" (whether it is defined by electoral practices, the franchise, style, or procedures of governance), democratization was uneven over the course of the early nineteenth century. See Reeve Huston, "Rethinking the Origins of Partisan Democracy in the United States, 1795–1840," in Peart and Smith, *Practicing Democracy*, 54–55; Reeve Huston, "What We Talk About When We Talk About Democracy," *Common Place*, no. 9.1 (October 2008). Focusing specifically on enfranchisement, Alan Taylor suggests that "after 1815, politics became more democratic" as most states eliminated property qualifications to vote, with the major caveat that "democratization flowed within limits of gender and race." In fact, avenues for women and Black men to participate formally in government contracted in the Antebellum period and not until Reconstruction was there another expansion of enfranchisement, which still excluded women and was arguably not realized for Black citizens until the Voting Rights Act of 1965. For more, see especially Taylor, *American* Republics, 205; Zagarri, *Revolutionary Backlash*, 149; Lewis, " 'Of Every Age Sex & Condition,' " 382–387; Foner, *The Second Founding*, 93–123; Hannah-Jones et al., *The 1619 Project*, xxxii.
8. Cotlar, *Tom Paine's America*, 162; Loughran, *The Republic in Print*, 212.
9. This interpretation builds upon that of Barbara Clark Smith, who argues: "When government originated in the people and fully assumed that mantle, there was less space for people to act as 'the people.' Representation became the heart of political life and the focus of political contest. The people would be present less often, represented far more. Their ideals and their views would be filtered and mediated. Vox populi would be replaced by public opinion, formulated at the polls and the press." See Smith, *The Freedoms We Lost*, 206. The contention that the use of secrecy was central to establishing the legitimacy of the federal government also supports recent scholarship pointing to the strength of the state in the early republic, despite

common conceptions that it was weak, particularly in realms where it was least visible. For more, see especially Brian Balogh, *A Government Out of Sight: The Mystery of National Authority in Nineteenth-Century America* (Cambridge: Cambridge University Press, 2012); Gautham Rao, *National Duties: Customs Houses and the Making of the American State* (Chicago: University of Chicago Press, 2016); Max Edling, *A Hercules in the Cradle: War, Money, and the American States, 1783–1867* (Chicago: University of Chicago Press, 2014).

10. *Annals of Congress*, Vol. 5, *Fourth Congress, First Session*, 400.
11. Ibid., 427.
12. Ibid., 444.
13. Ibid., 429.
14. Ibid., 436.
15. Ibid., 428.
16. Ibid., 448.
17. Ibid.
18. Ibid., 453.
19. Ibid., 460.
20. Ibid., 430.
21. Ibid., 437.
22. Ibid., 430.
23. Ibid., 461.
24. Ibid., 612.
25. Ibid., 642.
26. Alexander Hamilton to George Washington, March 7, 1796, in *The Papers of George Washington*, Vol. 19 (Charlottesville: University of Virginia Press, Rotunda, 2008), 537.
27. George Washington to Alexander Hamilton, March 31, 1796, ibid., 640.
28. Charles Lee to George Washington, March 26, 1796, ibid., 592–593.
29. Oliver Wolcott to George Washington, March 26, 1796, ibid., 610.
30. Ibid., 611.
31. Ibid., 612.
32. George Washington to the U.S. House of Representatives (March 30, 1796), ibid., 635.
33. Gienapp, *The Second Creation*, 312–313.
34. George Washington, *Farewell Address* (1796), accessed September 10, 2020. The Avalon Project, Yale Law School.
35. On the XYZ Affair, see Elkins and McKintrick, *The Age of Federalism*, 549–578; Nathan Perl-Rosenthal, "Private Letters and Public Diplomacy: The Adams Network and the Quasi-War, 1797–1798," *Journal of the Early Republic* 31, no. 2 (Summer 2011); Eugene F. Kramer, "New Light on the XYZ Affair: Elbridge Gerry's Reasons for Opposing War with France," *New England Quarterly* 29, no. 4 (December 1956).
36. Sharp, *The Deadlocked Election of 1800*, 37.

37. Alexander White to George Washington, March 17, 1798, in *The Papers of George Washington*, Vol. 2 (Charlottesville: University of Virginia Press, 2008), 146–147.
38. *Annals of Congress*, Vol. 8, *Fifth Congress, Second Session*, 1349.
39. Ibid., 1357.
40. Ibid., 1359–1360.
41. Ibid., 1361.
42. Ibid., 1363.
43. Ibid., 1365.
44. Ibid., 1375.
45. Ibid., 1380.
46. Joseph Hopkinson, *What is our situation? And what are our prospects? A few pages for Americans* (Philadelphia: 1798), 8. Clements Library, University of Michigan: C2 1798 Ho.
47. Cotton Tufts to John Adams, May 2, 1798, *The Adams Papers, Digital Edition*, Vol. 13 (Charlottesville: University of Virginia Press, 2008–2020), 6.
48. Ronald Angelo Johnson, "A Revolutionary Dinner: U.S. Diplomacy toward Saint Domingue, 1798–1801," *Early American Studies: An Interdisciplinary Journal* 9, no. 1 (Winter 2011): 127–128; Ronald Angelo Johnson, *Diplomacy in Black and White: John Adams, Toussaint Louverture, and Their Atlantic World Alliance* (Athens: University of Georgia Press, 2014), 3, 5.
49. Johnson, "A Revolutionary Dinner," 129.
50. Ibid., 115.
51. Ibid., 123.
52. *Aurora General Advertiser* (June 16, 1798), accessed July 15, 2020, Readex: America's Historic Newspapers.
53. *Aurora General Advertiser* (June 21, 1798).
54. *Annals of Congress*, Vol. 8, *5th Congress, Second Session*, 1972.
55. Abigail Adams to Mary Smith Cranch, June 19, 1798, in *The Adams Papers, Digital Edition*, Vol. 13, 135.
56. Abigail Adams to William Smith, June 19, 1798, ibid., 137.
57. Abigail Adams to Mary Smith Cranch, June 19, 1798, ibid., 135–136.
58. Abigail Adams to Cotton Tufts, June 29, 1798, ibid., 165.
59. Ibid.
60. Abigail Adams to Mary Smith Cranch, May 26, 1798, ibid., 55.
61. *An Act in Addition to the Act, Entitled "An Act for the Punishment of Certain Crimes Against the United States"* (1798), accessed September 10, 2020. The Avalon Project, Yale Law School.
62. On the Sedition Act, see especially James P. Martin, "When Repression Is Democratic and Constitutional: The Federalist Theory of Representation and the Sedition Act of 1798," *University of Chicago Law Review* 66, no. 1 (Winter 1799); David Jenkins, "The Sedition Act of 1798 and the Incorporation of Seditious Libel into First Amendment Jurisprudence," in *American Journal of Legal History* 45, no. 2 (April 2001); James Morton Smith, *Free-*

dom's Fetters: The Alien and Sedition Laws and American Civil Liberties (Ithaca: Cornell University Press), 1956; Wendell Bird, *Press and Speech Under Assault: The Early Supreme Court Justices, the Sedition Act of 1798, and the Campaign Against Dissent* (Oxford: Oxford University Press, 2016); Joanne Freeman, "Explaining the Unexplainable: The Cultural Context of the Sedition Act," in *The Democratic Experiment: New Directions in American Political History*, ed. Meg Jacobs, William Novak, and Julian Zelizer (Princeton: Princeton University Press, 2003); Marc Lendler, " 'Equally Proper and at All Times Necessary': Civility, Bad Tendency, and the Sedition Act," *Journal of the Early Republic* 24, no. 3 (Autumn, 2004).

63. As historian James Morton Smith suggested, the effort was intended "to cut republican members off from any public audience by restricting what they could communicate." See Smith, *Freedom's Fetters*, 120.
64. Ibid., 122.
65. *Annals of Congress*, Vol. 8, *Fifth Congress, Second Session*, 2104.
66. *Circular Letters of Congressmen to Their Constituents, 1789–1829*, Vol. 1, xxxxix.
67. Ibid., xxxv.
68. *"From Samuel J. Cabell"* (March 7, 1796), in *Letters of Congressmen to Their Constituents, 1789–1829*, Vol. 1, 42–43.
69. Cunningham, *Letters of Congressmen to Their Constituents, 1789–1829*, Vol. 1, xxxviii. Cabell's letter, dated May 31, 1797, appeared in the June 6, 1797, issue of the *Aurora* in Philadelphia.
70. "From John Clopton" (June 19, 1797), in *Letters of Congressmen to Their Constituents, 1789–1829*, Vol. 1, 95.
71. *Annals of Congress*, Vol. 8, *Fifth Congress, Second Session*, 2140.
72. Ibid., 2110.
73. Ibid.
74. Ibid., 2144.
75. Ibid.
76. Ibid., 2149.
77. Ibid., 2150.
78. Ibid., 2149.
79. Ibid., 2150.
80. For more on resistance to the Sedition Act, see Douglas Bradburn, "A Clamor in the Public Mind: Opposition to the Alien and Sedition Acts," *William and Mary Quarterly* 65, no. 3 (July 2008); Wendell Bird, "Reassessing Responses to the Virginia and Kentucky Resolutions: New Evidence from the Tennessee and Georgia Resolution and from Other States," *Journal of the Early Republic* 35, no. 4 (Winter 2015).
81. *The Virginia Resolution* (1798), accessed September 10, 2020. The Avalon Project, Yale Law School.
82. Ibid.
83. Bird, *Press and Speech under Assault*, 7, 385.
84. Smith, *Freedom's Fetters*, 182.

85. *The Lyon's Case*, 15FED.CAS-75, Case No. 8,646, 3, accessed September 10, 2020, YesWeScan: The Federal Cases.
86. Ibid., 4.
87. Ibid.
88. For a thorough account of Duane's life and career, see Daniel, *Scandal and Civility*, 234–257.
89. *Adams Family Papers, The Adams Papers, Digital Edition*, Vol. 13, 534.
90. Ibid.
91. Ibid.
92. James Lewis, "What Is to Become of Our Government?" in Horn et al, *The Revolution of 1800*, 12.
93. Quoted in *Annals of Congress*, Vol. 10, *Sixth Congress*, 114.
94. Ibid., 115.
95. Ibid., 114.
96. Ibid., 85.
97. Ibid., 113.
98. Ibid. 115.
99. Ibid.
100. Sharp, *The Deadlocked Election of 1800*, 106; Elaine Everly and Howard Wehmann, "Then Let Us to the Woods Repair," in *Establishing Congress: The Removal to Washington, D.C. and the Election of 1800*, ed. Kenneth Bowling and Donald Kennon (Columbus: Ohio University Press, 2005), 56.
101. Sharp, *The Deadlocked Election of 1800*, 130.
102. Ibid., 132.
103. Joanne B. Freeman, "The Election of 1800: A Study in the Logic of Political Change," *Yale Law Journal* 108, no. 8, *Symposium: Moments of Change: Transformation in American Constitutionalism* (June 1999): 1979–80.
104. Joanne Freeman, "Corruption and Compromise in the Election of 1800," in Horn et al., *The Revolution of 1800*, 91.
105. Sharp, *The Deadlocked Election of 1800*, 125.
106. Sharp, *The Deadlocked Election of 1800*, 127; Lewis, "What Is to Become of Our Government?" 11.
107. Sharp, *The Deadlocked Election of 1800*, 149.
108. Lewis, "What Is to Become of Our Government?" 14, 18.
109. Michael Bellesiles, "The Soil Will Be Soaked with Blood," in Horn et al., *The Revolution of 1800*, 60.
110. Freeman, "Corruption and Compromise in the Election of 1800," 102; Freeman, "The Election of 1800: A Study in the Logic of Political Change," 1970.
111. Thomas Jefferson to Matthew Carey, November 10, 1796, in *The Papers of Thomas Jefferson, Digital Edition*, Vol. 29, ed. James P. McClure and J. Jefferson Looney (Charlottesville: University of Virginia Press, Rotunda, 2008–2020), 205.

112. Thomas Jefferson to James Madison, August 23, 1799, in *The Papers of Thomas Jefferson, Digital Edition*, Vol. 31, ed. James P. McClure and J. Jefferson Looney (Charlottesville: University of Virginia Press, Rotunda, 2008–2020), 174.
113. Wilbur Samuel Howell, *Jefferson's Parliamentary Writings* (Princeton: Princeton University Press, 2014).
114. Thomas Jefferson, *A manual of parliamentary practice, composed originally for the use of the Senate of the United States* (Philadelphia: Hogan and Thompson, 1840), viii, accessed September 10, 2020, Haithi Trust.
115. C. M. Harris, "Jefferson, the Concept of the Modern Capitol, and Republican Nation-Building," in Bowling and Kennon, *Establishing Congress*, 88.
116. Thomas Jefferson to Elbridge Gerry, January 26, 1799, in *The Papers of Thomas Jefferson, Digital Edition*, Vol. 30, ed. James P. McClure and J. Jefferson Looney (Charlottesville: University of Virginia Press, Rotunda, 2008–2020), 650.
117. Thomas Jefferson to Philip Norborne Nicholas, April 7, 1800, in *The Papers of Thomas Jefferson*, Vol. 31, 485.
118. Ibid.
119. Thomas Jefferson, *First Inaugural Address* (March 4, 1801), accessed September 10, 2020. The Avalon Project, Yale Law School.
120. James Hopkins to Thomas Jefferson, July 16, 1801, in *The Papers of Thomas Jefferson, Digital Edition*, Vol. 34, ed. James P. McClure and J. Jefferson Looney (Charlottesville: University of Virginia Press, Rotunda, 2008–2020), 576.
121. Ibid.
122. Stephanie Newbold, *All But Forgotten: Thomas Jefferson and the Development of Public Administration* (Albany: State University of New York Press, 2011), 11.
123. Ibid., 22, 25.
124. Ibid., 12; Allgor, *Parlor Politics*, 19.
125. Allgor, *Parlor Politics*, 21–22.
126. Ibid., 23.
127. Gordon-Reed, *The Hemingses of Monticello*, 565. G. S. Wilson, *Jefferson on Display: Attire, Etiquette, and the Art of Presentation* (Charlottesville: University of Virginia Press, 2018).
128. Allgor, *Parlor Politics*, 34.
129. Ibid., 27.
130. Ibid., 24.
131. Ibid.
132. Lindsay Chervinsky, " 'Having been a member of the first administration under Genl. Washington': Thomas Jefferson, George Washington, and the Development of the President's Cabinet," *Journal of the Early Republic* 40, no. 4 (Winter 2020), 637.
133. Gordon-Reed, *The Hemingses of Monticello*, 583–585.

134. Ibid., 570.
135. Ibid., 613–614.
136. Ibid., 616. The propensity to relegate slavery to the "private sphere" was a common tendency among Southern planters who insisted it was a "domestic institution." As Stephanie McCurry has demonstrated in the case of South Carolina, this notion was central to the reluctance of state officials to regulate domestic relations or interfere with private property. See Stephanie McCurry, *Masters of Small Worlds: Yeoman Households, Gender Relations, and the Political Culture of the South Carolina Low Country* (Oxford: Oxford University Press, 1995).

Chapter Eight. The Disastrous Effects of Publicity

1. See especially Jones, "The Overthrow of Maximilien Robespierre and the 'Indifference' of the People"; Jones, "9 Thermidor: Cinderella Among Revolutionary *Journées*"; Mette Harder, "A Second Terror: The Purges of French Revolutionary Legislators After Thermidor," *French Historical Studies* 38, no. 1 (February 2015); François Gendron, *The Gilded Youth of Thermidor* (Montreal: McGill-Queens University Press, 1993); Laura Mason, "The Culture of Reaction: Demobilizing the People After Thermidor," *French Historical Studies* 39, no. 3 (August 2016).
2. On the challenges Thermidorian deputies faced, see especially Bronislaw Baczko, *Ending the Terror: The French Revolution After Robespierre*, trans. Michel Petheram (Cambridge: Cambridge University Press, 1994); Andrew Jainchill, *Reimagining Politics After the Terror: The Republican Origins of French Liberalism* (Ithaca: Cornell University Press, 2008); Howard Brown, "Robespierre's Tail: The Possibilities of Justice After the Terror," *Canadian Journal of History* 45 (Winter 2010); Steinberg, *The Afterlives of the Terror;* George Lefebvre, *The Thermidorians and the Directory: Two Phases of the French Revolutions*, trans. Robert Baldick (New York: Random House, 1964).
3. For more on the Directory, see especially Howard Brown, *Ending the French Revolution: Violence, Justice, and Repression from the Terror to Napoleon* (Charlottesville: University of Virginia Press, 2007); Martyn Lyons, *France Under the Directory* (Cambridge: Cambridge University Press, 1975).
4. David A. Bell, *Men on Horseback: The Power of Charisma in the Age of Revolution* (New York: Farrar, Straus, and Giroux, 2020); Bell, *The First Total War;* Howard Brown, "Napoleon Bonaparte, Political Prodigy," *History Compass* 5, no. 4 (2007).
5. Stanislas Fréron, *Opinion sur la liberté de la presse et sur d'autres objets de legislation: suivi d'un projet de décret* (Paris: Imprimerie nationale, 1794), 5–6.
6. Ibid., 11.
7. Ibid., 12.
8. Ibid.
9. Ibid.

10. Ibid.
11. Robespierre, "Lettres à ses commettants: Exposé des principes et but de cette publication," in Bouloiseau et al., *Oeuvres*, Tome V, 15.
12. Mason, "The Culture of Reaction: Demobilizing the People After Thermidor," 447.
13. Ibid., 452, 460.
14. Ibid., 460.
15. Louis-Marie Prudhomme, *Dictionnaire des individus envoys à la mort judiciairement* (Paris, 1796–97), 6. BNF No. 8-LA32–46.
16. Ibid., 5.
17. Ibid., 6.
18. Ibid.
19. Steinberg, *The Afterlives of the Terror*, 36.
20. Ibid.
21. Brown, "Robespierre's Tail: The Possibilities of Justice After the Terror," 509.
22. Ibid., 510.
23. Ronen Steinberg, "Accountability, Transitional Justice, and the Affaire Le Bon in Thermidorian France," *French Historical Studies* 39, no. 3 (August 2016), 433.
24. Ibid., 433–435.
25. Ibid., 420.
26. Quoted in Brown, "Robespierre's Tail: The Possibilities of Justice After the Terror," 511.
27. Baczko, *Ending the Terror*, 145.
28. Brown, "Robespierre's Tail: The Possibilities of Justice After the Terror," 511–512.
29. *Réimpression de l'ancien Moniteur, Tome 21* (Paris: Henri Plon, Imprimeur-Editeur, 1861), 688, accessed September 10, 2020, Haithi Trust.
30. *Réimpression de l'ancien Moniteur, Tome 23* (Paris: Henri Plon, Imprimeur-Editeur, 1861), 660, accessed September 10, 2020, Haithi Trust.
31. Ibid.
32. *Réimpression de l'ancien Moniteur, Tome 21*, 606.
33. Ibid., 607.
34. Ibid.
35. Ibid, 614.
36. Ibid., 657.
37. Ibid., 660.
38. *Réimpression de l'ancien Moniteur, Tome 22* (Paris: Henri Plon, Imprimeur-Editeur, 1861), 500, accessed September 10, 2020, Haithi Trust.
39. *Réimpression de l'ancien Moniteur, Tome 21*, 661.
40. *Réimpression de l'ancien Moniteur, Tome 22, 508.*
41. *Réimpression de l'ancien Moniteur, Tome 23*, 682.
42. Ibid., 683.

43. Ibid., 676.
44. Ibid., 715.
45. Ibid., 682.
46. Ibid., 711.
47. Ibid., 677.
48. *Réimpression de l'ancien Moniteur, Tome* 24, 320.
49. Ibid.
50. Ibid., 389.
51. Ibid.
52. Ibid., 427.
53. *Journal de la liberté de la press*, no. 1 (Paris: 17 Fructidor, an II), 5, accessed September 10, 2010, BNF Gallica.
54. Ibid.
55. *Journal de la liberté de la press*, no. 6 (Paris: 27 Fructidor, an II), 6, accessed September 10, 2010, BNF Gallica.
56. Ibid.
57. Baczko, *Ending the Terror*, 234.
58. Ibid., 239; Harder, "A Second Terror: The Purges of French Revolutionary Legislators After Thermidor," 50.
59. Baczko, *Ending the Terror*, 241.
60. *Réimpression de l'ancien Moniteur, Tome* 24, 117.
61. Ibid., 501.
62. Gendron, *The Gilded Youth of Thermidor*, 186.
63. *Réimpression de l'ancien Moniteur, Tome* 25 (Paris: Henri Plon, Imprimeur-Editeur, 1861), 299, accessed September 10, 2020, Haithi Trust.
64. Ibid.
65. Ibid.
66. Ibid.
67. Ibid.
68. Ibid.
69. Ibid.
70. Ibid.
71. Ibid.
72. Constitution du 5 Fructidor An III, Titre V, Article 64, accessed September 10, 2020, Conseil Constitutionnel.
73. Constitution du 5 Fructidor An III, Titre V, Article 65.
74. Constitution du 5 Fructidor An III, Titre V, Article 122.
75. Constitution du 5 Fructidor An III, Titre V, Article 72. Lynn Hunt has also pointed to the uniforms adopted under this government as a way of reinforcing respect and creating a "circumscribed political arena." See Hunt, *Politics, Culture, and Class in the French Revolution*, 85.
76. Constitution du 5 Fructidor An III, Titre VI, Article 143.
77. Constitution du 5 Fructidor An III, Titre VI, Articles 165 and 168.
78. Constitution du 5 Fructidor An III, Titre VI, Article 166.

79. Constitution du 5 Fructidor An III, Titre XII, Articles 330 and 333.
80. AN/C/412, doss. 482.
81. AN/C/435, doss. 2.
82. AN/C/507, doss. 399.
83. AN/C/507, doss. 398.
84. AN/C/507, doss. 398.
85. AN/C/508, doss. 400.
86. AN/C/508, doss. 400.
87. AN/C/528.
88. The distance between France and its Caribbean colonies—particularly Saint-Domingue where enslaved people had thrown off their regime and the French battled the English for control of the island—led to suspicions. As a result, throughout the life of the Thermidorian National Convention and the subsequent years of the Directory, though much was discussed behind closed doors there was also a culture of revelation around events across the Atlantic. For example, after the return of Léger-Félicité Sonthonax, who had issued a proclamation freeing enslaved people in 1794, his behavior drew scrutiny. Sonthonax was eventually cleared of suspicions, but investigation into what had happened in Saint-Domingue was ongoing. See *Réimpression de l'ancien Moniteur, Tome* 27, 91.
89. *Réimpression de l'ancien Moniteur, Tome* 27, 311.
90. Ibid.
91. For more on "stockjobbing," see especially Will Slauter, "Forward-Looking Statements: News and Speculation in the Age of the American Revolution," *Journal of Modern History* 81, no. 4 (December 2009).
92. *Réimpression de l'ancien Moniteur, Tome* 26, 476.
93. Ibid.
94. Ibid., 534.
95. Ibid., 654.
96. Ibid., 508.
97. Benjamin Constant, *De la force du Gouvernement actuel et de la nécessité de s'y rallier* (Paris: 1796).
98. Ibid., 8.
99. Ibid., 82.
100. Ibid.
101. Howard Brown has described the Directory as a regime that attempted to obtain stability through adopting the rule of law but then continually skirted the law with "exceptional measures" in the name of protecting that law and thus undermining its legitimacy. See Brown, *Ending the French Revolution*, 11.
102. Lyons, *France Under the Directory*, 159; Louis Bergeron, *France Under Napoleon*, trans. R. R. Palmer (Princeton: Princeton University Press, 1981), 100.
103. *Réimpression de l'ancien Moniteur, Tome* 28, 19.

104. *Réimpression de l'ancien Moniteur, Tome 27*, 699.
105. Ibid.
106. Ibid., 711.
107. Ibid.
108. Brown, *Ending the French Revolution*, 352.
109. J. B. Morton, *Brumaire: The Rise of Bonaparte* (Plainview, NY: Books for Libraries, 1976), 207; Bell, *Men on Horseback*, 123.
110. For more on this rejection of political representation, see especially Louis Bergeron, "Napoleon ou l'état post-révolutionnaire," in *The French Revolution and the Creation of Modern Political Culture*, Vol. 2, ed. Colin Lucas (Oxford: Pergamon Press, 1988), 437; Bergeron, *France Under Napoleon*, 5.
111. Bell, *Men on Horseback*, 131.
112. Ibid., 130. Louis Bergeron has also made this point, highlighting the existence of legislative institutions as a way of camouflaging the true nature of the regime, while Alan Forrest has pointed to his reliance on propaganda to establish his legitimacy. See Bergeron, "Napoleon ou l'état post-révolutionnaire," 437; Alan Forrest, "Propaganda and the Legitimation of Power in Napoleonic France," *French History* 18, no. 4 (2004): 430.
113. While Bonaparte relied on publicity, he also constructed an elaborate and effective censorship apparatus through which "he showed an inflexible instinct to regulate publication and to censor any expression of opposition." See Forrest, "Propaganda and the Legitimation of Power in Napoleonic France," 427–428.
114. *Réimpression de l'ancien Moniteur, Tome 29*, 892.
115. Ibid., 892.
116. Howard Brown has noted the way in which, even under the Directory, a "state of exception" was normalized. See Brown, *Ending the French Revolution*, 352.
117. *Proclamation des Consuls de la République du 24 frimaire an VIII* (15 décembre 1799), accessed September 10, 2020, Conseil Constitutionnel.
118. *Constitution du 22 Frimaire An VIII, Titre IV, Article 50*, accessed September 10, 2020, Conseil Constitutionnel.
119. *Constitution du 22 Frimaire An VIII, Titre III, Article 35*.
120. *Constitution du 22 Frimaire An VIII, Titre IV, Article 34*.
121. *Constitution du 22 Frimaire An VIII, Titre IV, Article 23*.
122. Bell, *Men on Horseback*, 119. Alan Forrest notes how the general would place letters in the Parisian press through the late 1790s to "parade his successes before the French people." See Forrest, "Propaganda and the Legitimation of Power in Napoleonic France," 432.
123. Bell, *Men on Horseback*, 120.
124. Ibid., 119.
125. Ibid., 123.
126. Ibid., 124–125. As Louis Bergeron put it, "the press existed in his eyes only for service to the state and as an instrument of propaganda." See Bergeron,

France Under Napoleon, 8; Forrest, "Propaganda and the Legitimation of Power in Napoleonic France," 427–428.

127. Bell, *Men on Horseback*, 127–128.
128. Ibid., 126.
129. This point has also been made, in a different context, by Howard Brown. See Brown, *Ending the French Revolution*, 16.

Epilogue

1. Bentham, *The Collected Works of Jeremy Bentham: Political Tactics*, ed. Michael James, Cyprian Blamires, and Catherine Pease-Watkin (Oxford: Clarendon Press, 1999), 29–34.
2. Ibid., 38.
3. Ibid., 39.
4. Ibid.
5. Ibid.
6. The deputies were not, however, following Bentham's advice. Despite his efforts to get his work translated into French before the Estates General convened in the spring of 1789, he did not succeed. English versions were circulated, however, to prominent figures involved in the Estates General, including Jacques Necker, the Duc de la Rochefoucauld and the Marquis de la Fayette. Bentham had also sent at least a sketch of the contents to his correspondent Etienne Dumont, a Genevan who was friends with the Comte de Mirabeau and helped edit his periodical. Dumont, finding the National Assembly to be chaotic in the fall of 1789, encouraged Bentham to pick the work back up. Yet the first printed version of "Essay on Political Tactics" did not appear until January 1791. Later that year, deputy Jean Philippe Garran de Coulon referenced another of Bentham's works on judicial reform in France during a deliberation in the Legislative Assembly. He began a correspondence with Bentham, who sent him a copy of "Essay on Political Tactics." Though Garran de Coulon reported sharing it with the *comité de legislation*, he lamented in a letter to Bentham that they had not had time to read it. See "Editorial Introduction," in Bentham, *Political Tactics*.
7. Sean Wilentz notes that during Jefferson's presidency, popular participation in politics grew in most parts of the country, such that "the filters on democracy created by the Framers were proving porous, while the suppression of democracy sought by the Federalists in the 1790s was thoroughly discredited." See Wilentz, *The Rise of American Democracy*, 66.
8. Wilentz, *The Rise of American Democracy*. On the limitations and concurrent restrictions of democracy, see especially Huston, "What We Talk About When We Talk About Democracy"; Taylor, *American Republics*, 205; Zagarri, *Revolutionary Backlash*, 149; Lewis, " 'Of Every Age Sex & Condition,' " 382–387; Foner, *The Second Founding*, 93–123; Hannah-Jones et al., *The 1619 Project*, xxxii.

9. Brown, *Ending the French Revolution*, 23.
10. Bell, *The First Total War*, 228–229, 244. Bell characterizes Napoleon Bonaparte's empire as a regime based on military victory, wherein the military was elevated above civil society, even though government was not run by the military. Brown called it a liberal authoritarian regime, wherein legitimacy came from restoring and maintaining order. See Brown, *Ending the French Revolution*, 16.
11. Bell, *The First Total War*, 228.
12. Ibid., 206.
13. François Furet, *Revolutionary France, 1770–1880*, trans. Antonia Nevill (Oxford: Blackwell, 1992).
14. "Editorial Introduction," in Bentham, *Political Tactics*, xxxvii. The account of how Bentham's work evolved and spread is based on the account given in the editorial introduction.
15. Of course, a need for some degree of secrecy is assumed in modern democracies, particularly in the realm of security, military, and diplomatic affairs. But most modern work of political scientists, sociologists, and philosophers assumes a negative view of state secrecy and proceeds to either challenge the assumption or propose possible solutions to limit the threat of secrecy to democratic government. See Bok, *Secrets;* Quill, *Secrets and Democracy;* Sagar, *Secrets and Leaks;* K. G. Robertson, *Secrecy and Open Government: Why Governments Want You to Know* (London: Macmillan Press, 1999).
16. Max Weber, *Economy and Society: An Outline of Interpretive Sociology*, Vol. 3, ed. Guenther Roth and Claus Wittich (New York: Bedminster Press, 1968), 992.
17. For example, see Francis E. Rourke, *Secrecy and Publicity: Dilemmas of Democracy* (Baltimore: Johns Hopkins Press, 1961).
18. Laurie Kellman, "Hot, Crowded, and Secret Room Now Part of Impeachment Lore," *Associated Press* (November 8, 2019), accessed September 14, 2020, https://apnews.com/c9aa24db2ceb40ed9f89fefabb721806; Editorial Board, "Impeachment in Secret," *Wall Street Journal* (October 8, 2019), accessed September 14, 2020, www.wsj.com/articles/impeachment-in-secret-11570576668.
19. Jonathan S. Gould and David Pozen, "The Senate Impeachment Trial Could Use a Little Secrecy," in *The Atlantic* (December 16, 2019), accessed September 14, 2020, www.theatlantic.com/ideas/archive/2019/12/senate-impeachment-trial-transparency/603463/.
20. For examples of how this has been covered in the media, see Jeffrey Young, "Republicans Are Rushing to Pass the Health Care Bill Before You Find Out What's In It," *Huffpost*, May 3, 2017, accessed May 11, 2017, www.huffingtonpost.com/entry/republicans-rush-obamacare-repeal-reasons_us_590a114be4b05c39768588e3; Alana Abramson, "5 Quotes Haunting Republicans as They Vote on Health Care," *Time*, May 4, 2017, accessed May 11, 2017, http://time.com/4766895/health-care-vote-republicans-process-quotes/.

21. Adam Liptak, “A Leaky Supreme Court Starts to Resemble the Other Branches,” *New York Times*, May 11, 2022, accessed June 23, 2022, www.nytimes.com/2022/05/11/us/supreme-court-leak-roe-wade.html.
22. Merrit Kennedy, “White House Says It Will No Longer Release Visitor Logs to the Public,” *National Public Radio*, April 14, 2017, accessed May 11, 2017, www.npr.org/sections/thetwo-way/2017/04/14/523968950/white-house-says-it-will-no-longer-release-visitor-logs-to-the-public.
23. Scott Horsley, “Sworn to Secrecy: Trump’s History of Using Nondisclosure Agreements,” *National Public Radio*, March 19, 2018, accessed June 23, 2022, www.npr.org/2018/03/19/595025070/sworn-to-secrecy-trumps-history-of-using-nondisclosure-agreements.
24. Patricia Zengerle, “Trump Took Classified Material from White House to Florida, National Archives Says,” *Reuters*, February 22, 2022, accessed June 23, 2022, www.reuters.com/world/us/trump-took-classified-material-white-house-florida-national-archives-says-2022–02–18/; Ilya Marritz, “Trump Is Being Held in Contempt for Failing to Comply with Subpoena,” *National Public Radio*, April 25, 2022, accessed June 23, 2022, www.npr.org/2022/04/25/1094680401/trump-is-being-held-in-contempt-of-court-for-failing-to-comply-with-subpoena; Betsy Woodruff Swan, “Trump Tells 4 Former Aides to Defy Jan. 6 Committee Subpoena,” *Politico*, October 7, 2021, accessed June 23, 2022, www.politico.com/news/2021/10/07/trump-jan-6-committees-subpoena-515593.
25. For more on the Snowden incident, see David P. Fidler, ed., *The Snowden Reader* (Bloomington: Indiana University Press, 2015).
26. For more, see “From Citizens United to Super PACs: A Campaign Finance Reading Guide,” *Pro Publica*, February 21, 2013, accessed May 11, 2017, www.propublica.org/article/from-citizens-united-to-super-pacs-a-campaign-finance-reading-guide.
27. Amanda Erickson, “Macron’s Emails Got Hacked. Here’s Why French Voters Won’t Hear Much about Them before Sunday’s Election,” *Washington Post*, May 6, 2017, accessed May 11, 2017, www.washingtonpost.com/news/worldviews/wp/2017/05/06/macrons-emails-got-hacked-heres-why-french-voters-wont-hear-much-about-them-before-sundays-election/?utm_term=.f613696583777.
28. Cliff Levy (@cliffordlevy, Sept. 27, 2020): https://twitter.com/cliffordlevy/status/1310397555319156736.
29. On the blending of entertainment and politics, see Kathryn Cramer Brownell, *Showbiz Politics: Hollywood in American Political Life* (Chapel Hill: University of North Carolina Press, 2014).
30. Max Boot, “Why Trump So Often Says the Quiet Part Out Loud,” *Washington Post*, August 24, 2020, accessed June 25, 2022, www.washingtonpost.com/opinions/2020/08/24/why-trump-so-often-says-quiet-part-out-loud/; Ewan Palmer, “Donald Trump Just Said the Quiet Part Out Loud,” *Newsweek*, January 31, 2022, accessed June 25, 2022, www.newsweek.com/trump-overturn-election-mike-pence-1674436.

31. Annie Karni, "The Committee Hired a TV Executive to Produce the Hearings for Maximum Impact," *New York Times*, June 9, 2022, accessed June 23, 2022, www.nytimes.com/2022/06/09/us/the-committee-hired-a-tv-executive-to-produce-the-hearings-for-maximum-impact.html.
32. Jamelle Bouie, "Why It Matters That the Jan. 6 Hearings Put 'a War Scene' on Display," *New York Times*, June 10, 2022, accessed June 25, 2022, www.nytimes.com/2022/06/10/opinion/jan-6-hearings-trump.html. Bouie makes the distinction between congressional oversight and "overspeech" as an attempt to sway public opinion, identifying spectacle as potentially powerful. "The Jan. 6 hearings should be about more than the facts of the investigation. They should be about the performance of those facts," he wrote. "Spectacle is what we need, and judging from the first night of televised hearings on Thursday, spectacle is what we're going to get."
33. Urbinati, *Democracy Disfigured*, 171–227; Friedland, *Political Actors*, 300.
34. Bentham, *Political Tactics*, 36.
35. Ibid.

Index

absolutism, 307nn11–12
Adams, Abigail, 42, 45–46, 173, 220–21
Adams, Charles, 186
Adams, John, 19, 40–48, 87, 175, 186–88, 207–20, 228–33, 302n91, 303n102
Adams, Samuel, 24, 303n102
Adams, Willi Paul, 280n6
Adet, Pierre-Auguste, 171
Affordable Care Act, 274
Age of Revolutions, 4–6, 13, 20, 281n9, 325n8
Alien and Sedition Act, 19, 221–22. *See also* Sedition Act
Allen, John, 216, 222
Allgor, Catherine, 235
Almon, John, 227
American War of Independence, 17–18, 39. *See also* Revolution (American)
Andress, David, 335n3
Annales patriotiques et littéraires de la France (Mercier & Carra), 126, 139, 153
Antifederalists, 76–77, 81–83, 91–98, 102–3, 160, 180, 270, 320n81, 323n106
"Apparition de l'ombre de Mirabeau," 142
appel au peuple, 145, 148
Archives Nationales, 329n59
armoire de fer, 139–45, 150. *See also* Louis XVI, King
Articles of Confederation, 53–55
Assemblée nationale (Borel & Ponce), 109
Assembly of Notables, 68
Aurora General Advertiser, 171, 227

Babeuf, Gracchus, 251, 262. See also *Journal of Press Freedom*
Bache, Benjamin Franklin, 171, 177, 200, 219–21, 227, 346n41
Bailly, Jean-Sylvain, 111–13, 325n9
Baker, Keith Michael, 59, 308n17, 324n7
Baldwin, Abraham, 205, 217
Barère, Montagnard Bertrand, 141–45, 148–49, 331n89
Barker, Hannah, 296n17
Barlow, Joel, 226
Barnave, Antoine, 114, 129
the Bastille prison, 66
Bayard, James, 216–17
Beaumarchais, Pierre August Caron de, 50
Beckley, John James, 181
Bell, David, 263, 272
Bellanger, Claude, 331n88
Bentabole, Pierre-Louis, 245, 268
Bentham, Jeremy, 14, 267–73, 277, 364n6
Berlier, Théophile, 255
Bilder, Mary Sarah, 88

Bill of Rights, 182
Boissy d'Anglas, François Antoine de, 244, 248
Bonaparte, Napoleon, 11, 19–20, 229, 237–39, 252, 263–66, 272, 363n113
Bosc, Yannick, 324n4
Boston Sons of Liberty, 28
Bouillé, Françoi Claude Amour, marquis de, 128
Bourbon monarchy, 18, 58
Boyer-Fonfrède, Jean-Baptiste, 157
Breen, T.H., 188
Brewer, John, 297n25
Brienne, Loménie de, 68
Brissot, Jacques Pierre, de Warville Brissot de, 71–72, 124–25, 140, 143, 153, 240, 340n58
Broglie, Comte de, 306n7
Brown, Howard, 242, 362n101
Buck, Daniel, 210
Bunel, Joseph, 219
Burke, Edmund, 8, 27, 182
Burke, Thomas, 47, 52
Burr, Aaron, 230
Bush, George W., 274
Buzot, Girondin François, 147, 150, 158

Cabell, Samuel, 223
Cadroy, Paul, 247, 262
Calonne, Charles Alexandre de, 68
Cambon, Pierre-Joseph, 157
Camus, Armand-Gaston, 129
Carey, John, 175
Carey, Mathew, 37
Carnot, Lazare, 273
Carra, Jean-Louis, 139, 148, 153
Carroll, Charles, 178
carte de civisme, 156
Catholic Church, 15, 292n60
certificats de civisme, 159
Champlin, Christopher, 217
Chapelières, Jacques Defermon des, 144
Charlier, Louis-Jospeh, 253
Chartier, Roger, 324n7
Chase, Samuel, 46–47
The Châtelet, 127
Chervinsky, Lindsay, 343n11
citizen. *See* citizenship
citizenry. *See* citizenship
citizenship, 5, 221
Clermont-Tonnerre, Stanislas-Marie-Adelaide, comte de, 119
Clinton, Hillary, 275
Clopton, John, 223–24
Cobbett, William, 198–99
Coe, Alex, 305n146
Coercive Acts, 39
Cohen, Alain, 156
Colbert, Jean Baptiste, 58
colonialism (French), 118, 218–19, 362n88
Comité de pétitions dépêches et correspondances, 161
Comité des Inspecteurs de la salle, 151–55, 158
Comité des Recherches, 120
Comité de sûreté générale, 156, 159, 166, 341n92
Committee of Correspondence, 44–45
Committee of Public Safety, 158–63, 166, 241, 246–50, 271, 336n5, 341n92
Common Sense (Paine), 6, 72
Commune of Paris, 126, 164–66
communication technology, 275, 277. *See also* social media
Comte Rendu au Roi (Necker), 57–58
Congress (American), 18, 40–55, 80, 168–88, 197, 205–12, 268, 318n64, 323n107
Conseils Supérieurs, 62–64
Constant, Benjamin, 260–61
Constitution, French, 2, 163–64, 210, 238, 254–55, 327n21, 327n29
Constitution, United States, 18, 37, 56, 75–78, 83–103, 212–13, 284n33, 292n62, 312n1, 317n50. *See also* First Amendment; Sixth Amendment

Constitutional Convention, 1–2, 8–9, 75–81, 86–89, 91–102, 270, 287n40, 313n4, 323n106
the Consulate (French), 263–64
Continental Congress, 17, 25, 31, 34, 38–39, 42–43, 185, 295n14
Cooper, Samuel, 24
Cornell, Sue, 320n81
Cornudet, Joseph, 264
Cotlar, Seth, 351n122
Council of Five-Hundred, 258–59
Council of the Ancients, 258, 264
Council of the Governor, 32
Coup of 18 Fructidor, 263–64
Coxe, Tench, 228
Crassous, Jean-François, 249, 259
Creuzé-Latouche, Jacques Antoine, 25

Daunou, Pierre-Claude-François, 250, 254
David, Jacques-Louis, 111–13
Deane, Silas, 39, 42, 48–52
Declaration of Independence, 231
Declaration of the Rights of Man and of the Citizen, 116, 119, 163
Delacroix, Charles François, 141
Delacroix, Eugène, 141
De l'Esprit des Lois (Montesquieu), 61, 309n26
democracy: definition of, 3, 13, 279n3, 280n5, 288n48, 353n7; deliberative, 2–3, 27; direct, 8, 324n4; representative, 3–4, 11, 16–20, 82, 106, 166, 237, 266, 273, 280n6; and secrecy, 20, 249, 287n39, 365n15
Democratic-Republicans, 11, 19, 83, 101, 160, 169, 194–96, 217–18, 270–72
Democratic Society of Pennsylvania, 168, 195
Desan Suzanne, 328n39
Des lettres de cachet et des prisons d'êtat (Riquetti), 65
Desmoulins, Camille, 121, 126, 143, 153, 162, 240, 332n97, 340n58
despotism, 61, 64–67, 72, 98, 125, 144
Dictionnaire des individus envoyés à la mort judiciairement (Prudhomme), 241
diplomacy, 169, 196, 201, 246–48, 259
the Directory, 166, 256, 258–59, 261–63, 272, 362n101
Downes, Paul, 287n39
Duane, William, 227–30
Dubois, Laurent, 119, 288n49
Ducros, Abbé, 104, 123
Dumont, Etienne, 108, 273
Duroy, Jean-Michel, 245

Edling, Max, 323n106
Electoral College, 3
Ellery, William, 180
Ellsworth, Oliver, 84
Encyclopédie (Malesherbes), 66
Enlightenment, 14, 17, 290n56
Estates General, 2, 7–9, 14, 35, 69–72, 104–7, 124, 134, 364n6. *See also* National Assembly
Estes, Todd, 198
executive branch, 33, 86, 170–71, 187–88, 192–94, 209–14, 235, 317n48

Federal Convention, 18, 37, 56, 168
Federalist Papers, 82, 85, 191, 213, 260
Federalists, 18–19, 77–83, 101–6, 168–72, 184, 195–206, 216–36, 269–71, 285n33, 351n124
Fenno, John, 174–77, 190
Findley, William, 92, 99
First Amendment, 226. *See also* Constitution, United States
Flight to Varennes, 139
Floyd, William, 50
Foner, Eric, 319n74
foreign affairs. *See* diplomacy
foreign relations. *See* diplomacy
Fouquier-Tinville, Antoine-Quentin, 242
Fox, Charles, 49

Franklin, Benjamin, 23–24, 35, 86, 198, 346n41
Freeman, Joanne, 230
French dispatches, 214–20. *See also* XYZ affair
French Monarchy, 7, 58–62, 67, 306n8, 311n71
French National Convention, 19
Freneau, Philip, 177, 190–91. See also *National Gazette*
Fréron, Louis-Marie Stanislas, 239–41, 251
Friedland, Paul, 287n40, 327n29
Furet, François, 273, 285n33, 335n3

Gallatin, Albert, 208, 217, 224
Garat, Dominique-Joseph, 331n89
Garrison, William Lloyd, 89
Gates, Horatio, 181
gender, 16, 90, 180, 272. *See also* women
Genêt, Edmond-Charles, 193–97, 248, 318n60
Gensonné, Girondin Armand, 147
Gerry, Elbridge, 52, 83, 87, 215, 315n24, 346n41
Gienapp, Jonathan, 213
Gilbert, Ezekiel, 210
Giles, William, 208, 216
Girondins, 145, 151–53, 162, 245, 271, 338n31–338n33, 341n99
Godechot, Jacques, 281n9
Goodhue, Benjamin, 181
Gordon-Reed, Annette, 236
government: insulated, 214, 261–66, 270–71; reflective, 7, 147, 194–206, 214, 224–40, 250–51, 335n2, 340n57; representative, 5–17, 27–39, 54–56, 69–83, 91–125, 134–71, 194–206, 224–41, 250–55, 266–75; republican, 31, 82, 183, 311n71; transparency of, 190, 197–99
Grenville, George, 27
Griswold, Roger, 226
Guillotin, Joseph Ignace, 116–17, 127, 133, 334n129

Habermas, Jürgen, 306n8
Haitian Revolution, 13, 219, 288n49
Hamilton, Alexander, 85, 187–92, 196–97, 211, 236
Hancock, John, 47
Harper, Robert Goodloe, 209–10, 220–23
Harrison, Benjamin, 189
Heath, John, 209
Heideking, Jürgen, 313n4
Hemmings, Sally, 231, 236
Henry, Patrick, 100
A History of the United States of America (Goodrich), 79
Hopkins, James, 234
Hopkinson, Joseph, 218
House of Commons, 27, 30, 35, 39
House of Representatives, 171–74, 183, 188, 205, 230, 271
Hunt, Lynn, 326n20
Huston, Reeve, 353n7
Hutchinson, Thomas, 23–24, 294n8

Independent Gazetteer, 198. *See also* Oswald, Eleazer

Jackson, James, 182
Jacobin Club. *See* Jacobins
Jacobins, 12–18, 136–38, 145–53, 160–68, 238–41, 250–51, 271, 334n1, 335n2, 336n4
Jay, John, 85, 169, 192, 206–9, 318n64, 343n4
Jay Treaty, 172, 198–200, 206–9, 318n64, 343n4
Jefferson, Thomas, 19, 48, 90–91, 115, 188–97, 206–7, 219–37, 272, 353n6
Johnson, Ronald Angelo, 219
Jones, Colin, 165–66
Journal of Press Freedom, 251. *See also* Babeuf, Gracchus

Journals of Congress, 34, 48, 50–51, 80, 84, 186, 314n12, 316n40
Jupp, Peter, 296n17

Kent, James, 96
Klarman, Michael, 313n4
Klein, Lawrence, 292n65
Kloppenberg, James, 279n3
Knox, Henry, 197

LaFayette, Marquis de, 132
Laignelot, Joseph François, 248
L'Ami du Peuple, 126
Lanjuinais, Jean Denis, comte, 254
La Porte, Arnaud II de, 140–41
La Révellière-Lépeaux, Louis-Marie de, 248
Laurens, Henry, 38, 50–53
Laussat, Pierre-Clément de, 264
Le Bon, Joseph, 242–43
Lee, Arthur, 44, 49–54
Lee, Charles, 212
Lee, Richard Henry, 52–53, 86, 179
Legendre, Louis, 254
Legislative Assembly (French), 135
legislative branch, 33, 86, 171, 187, 209, 254–55, 260, 265
Lemérer, Roland Gaspard, 261
L'Enfant, Pierre Charles, 174
Le Patriote françois, 124
Le Publiciste parisien, 126
lettres de cachets, 58, 65–66
Lettres Philosophiques (Voltaire), 61
Lewis, Jan, 179
libelles, 293n70, 308n22
Librairie, 66, 71, 123–24
Livingston, Edward, 207–8, 211, 217, 223
Lloyd, Thomas, 37, 174–76, 190
Loughran, Trish, 200
Louisiana Territory, 231, 270
Louis XVI, King, 2, 18, 58–70, 111–16, 128–32, 139–51, 188. See also *armoire de fer*
Loustalot, Elysée, 122
Louverture, Toussaint, 219
Louvet, Pierre-Florent, 243
Lovell, James, 50
Lyon, Matthew, 226–27

Macaulay, Catharine, 173
Maclay, William, 172, 181
Macron, Emmanuel, 275
Madison, James, 3–12, 75–90, 101, 176–82, 191, 225, 260, 269, 280n6, 318n64–319n64
Mailhe, Jean-Baptiste, 254, 259
Malesherbes, Chrétien Guillaume de Lamoignon de, 66–67, 70–71
Mallarmé, François René, 245
Manin, Bernard, 11
Manuel, Louis Pierre, 154–55
Marat, Jean-Paul, 126, 143–44, 153, 157, 240
Marie Antoinette, Queen, 116
Martin, Alexander, 80–81, 100
Martin, Luther, 99
Maryland Journal and Baltimore Advertiser, 52–53
Mason, George, 80–84, 87
Mason, Laura, 241, 329n49
Mason, Steven, 171
Maupeou, René Nicolas Charles Augustin de, 62–64, 310n42
Maupeou Revolution (1771–74), 62
Mazzei, Philip, 69–70
McKean, Thomas, 51
Mercer, John, 84
Mercier, Louis-Sébastien, 139, 153, 332n97
Mirabeau, Honoré Ganriel Riquetti, the Comte de, 65, 124–25, 141–42, 145, 177, 331n88–331n89
Mitchell, Catharine, 179
Monroe, James, 185
Montagnards, 137, 145–47, 151–52
Moreau, Marie-François, 148
Morgan, Edmund, 285n33

Morris, Gouverneur, 51, 89, 350n115
Morrison, Charles François-Gabriel, 259
Mounier, Jean-Joseph, 119
Moustier, Comte de, 173–74
Muhlenberg, Peter, 182
Murray, William Vans, 210

National Assembly, 18, 72, 105–23, 126–32, 270, 325n8, 333n100, 364n6. *See also* Estates General
National Convention, 19, 136–45, 149–52, 156, 243–46, 250–54
National Gazette, 190–91. *See also* Freneau, Philip
National Security Administration, 274
Native Americans, 90, 192–93
Naturalization Act, 221
Necker, Jacques, 57–58, 67
Neutrality Proclamation (1793), 194–97
Nicholas, John, 208, 224
Nicholas, Philip Norborne, 233
"Notes of Government" (Madison), 191

Obama, Barack, 274
Oswald, Eleazer, 198. See also *Independent Gazetteer*
Ottis, Harrison Gray, 225
Ottoman Empire, 61

Paine, Thomas, 6, 29, 49–50, 72
Palmer, R. R., 281n9
parlement, 59, 62–64, 68, 310n42
Parlement of Paris, 59, 62–63, 68
Parliament (British), 26–30
Parti Patriote, 63
Pastoret, Emmanuel de Pastoret, 262
Paterson, John, 227
Patriote françois, 153, 240
Patriots (party), 7, 25
Pendleton, Edmund, 180
Pennsylvania Assembly, 29, 174
Pennsylvania Convention, 97–98
Pennsylvania Packet, 49–53
Peters, Richard, 185
Pickering, Timothy, 184, 219, 226
Pinckney, Charles Cotesworth, 88
Pinckney, Thomas, 228
Pitt, William, 248
political action committees (PACs), 275
political clubs, 194–96, 201, 331n76
Popkin, Jeremy, 123
popular sovereignty, 6–14, 25, 82, 106–7, 148, 183, 238–41, 281n10, 338n33
Post Office Act (1792), 178, 302n90–302n92, 346n41
the press, 14–15, 28–37, 58–60, 69–72, 123–33, 151–56, 166–81, 224–26, 239–40, 250–51
Prudhomme, Louis-Marie, 241
publicité. *See* publicity
publicity, 11–39, 53–72, 104–61, 173–83, 206–16, 224–54, 261–77, 282n13, 285n35, 306n8
public opinion, 5–15, 59–60, 69–72, 115–21, 146–47, 156–60, 232–38, 241, 296n17, 308n17

Quakers, 182
Quirot, Jean-Baptiste, 255

race, 13, 272. *See also* slavery
Rakove, Jack, 45–46
Randolph, Edmund, 87, 170, 197
ratification, 19, 37, 54, 76–77, 86–103, 150, 171–72, 198–200, 208, 214
ratifying conventions. *See* ratification
Ravel, Jeffrey, 308n17
Rea, Robert, 296n17
Remonstrances des Cour des aides (Malesherbes), 66
Report on Manufactures (Hamilton), 191
republic, 3, 9–19, 26–38, 54–58, 69–103, 128–46, 154–72, 179–249, 260–62, 269–74
Revolution (American), 6, 25, 69, 295n10, 297n25. *See also* American War of Independence

Revolution (French), 6, 11, 58, 60, 106, 237, 266, 273, 324n5
Revolution of 1800, 206, 230
Révolutions de France et de Brabant (Desmoulins), 126
Rewbell, Jean-François, 246
Rivadavia, Benardino, 273
Robespierre, Maximillian, 3, 138, 148, 163–66, 237–53, 266, 335n2, 340n57
Rodney, Caesar, 40
Roe v. Wade, 274
Roland, Jean-Marie, 138–39, 142–44, 150
Rough Journals (Continental Congress), 43, 48
Rousseau, Jean-Jacques, 6, 14, 288n44, 338n39, 339n39, 339n44
Rush, Benjamin, 46
Rutledge, James, 123
Rutledge, John, 83

Saint André, Jean Bon, 162
Saint-Domingue, 218–19, 362n88
Saint-Etiénne, Jean-Paul Rabaut de, 146
Saint-Fargeau, Louis-Michel Lepeletier, marquis de, 155
Saint-Just, Louis de, 164
salon culture, 59
Sans-Culottes, 250, 252
Seabury, Samuel, 41
secrecy: in congress, 15–19, 38–47, 54, 80–85, 169, 197, 317n47, 323n107; as conspiracy, 16, 52–55, 91–96, 119, 171, 198, 216, 244–50, 266; and the constitution, 53–56, 76–78, 89–103, 172, 212–13, 231, 312n1, 322n96, 323n106; and democracy, 20, 83, 183, 249, 271, 287n39, 365n15; and the executive branch, 33, 86, 170–71, 187–94, 209, 214, 235, 317n48; in foreign affairs, 210–11, 219; and the legislative branch, 151, 170–71, 187, 254–55, 260, 265; and the monarchy, 58–67, 105–7; and publicity, 17, 50, 168, 173, 267, 270, 273, 325n8; and representative government, 4–31, 128–39, 160–61, 199–201, 231–37, 250–55, 266–74, 290n53, 305n146, 313n3; state, 33, 165, 171, 268; in war time, 18, 44, 158, 324n7
secret du Roi, 58, 65, 306n7
"Secret Journals," 42, 48
Sedition Act, 207, 223–27, 234, 272, 355n62, 356n80. *See also* Alien and Sedition Act
the Senate, 171–73, 184–86, 200, 206, 265, 271
Sergent, Antoine-Louis François, 252
"*Serment du Jeu de Paume, le 20 juin 1789*," 113
Seven Years' War, 7, 283n20
Sewall, Samuel, 206
Sherman, Gerry, 84
Sherman, Roger, 84
Sieyès, Emmanuel-Joseph, Abbé, 9, 106, 110–11, 263–64
Sixth Amendment, 317n50. *See also* Constitution, United States
Skinner, Quentin, 286n36
slavery, 6, 88–90, 118–19, 182, 219, 362n88. *See also* race
Smith, Barbara Clark, 353n9
Smith, Nathaniel, 209
Smith, Richard, 48
Snowden, Edward, 275
social media, 276. *See also* communication technology
Société des Amis de la Constitution, 122
Société des Amis des Droits de l'Homme et du Citoyen, 123
Society of the Pantheon, 251
Stamp Act (1765), 27–28, 297n25
state constitutions, 31–37, 55
Steele, John, 178
Steinberg, Ronen, 242
Stone, Michael J., 182
Sulzberger, A. G., 276

surveillance, 55, 239–40, 261, 264, 285n35, 302n92, 335n2, 340n57

Talleyrand, Charles, 219
Tallien, Jean-Lambert, 246
the Terror, 19, 137–38, 149, 165–66, 237–54, 266, 271, 335n3
Thatcher, George, 220
Thermidorian movement, 166, 238, 241–44, 250, 253, 266, 359n2
Thibaudeau, Antoine Claire, 249
Third Estate, 105–8, 111, 325n9, 326n20
Thomson, Charles, 48
Thuriot, Jacques-Alexis, 154, 245–46
Tracy, Uriah, 210, 229
transparency (in government), 4–7, 11–19, 190, 197–99, 242, 273–77, 282n13, 292n64
Trump, Donald, 274–76
Tufts, Cotton, 218
Turgot, Anne-Roberts-Jacques, 67

"*The United States Capitol*" (Latrobe), 233
U.S. Supreme Court, 274, 343n3

Vergennes, Comte de, 306n7
Victor, Pierre, 110
vigilance, 10–11, 28–32, 38, 55, 105–7, 115, 121–31, 135–39, 271
Villetard, Alexandre Edmé Pierre, 248, 259
Virginia Resolution, 226
Volney, Constantin-François Chasseboeuf de, 2–3, 11, 110, 143
Voltaire, 61, 66

Wait, Thomas B., 177
Waldstreicher, David, 89, 285n33, 351n119
Warren, James, 42
Washington, George, 1–3, 10, 55–56, 86–87, 168–73, 183–217, 269, 274, 305n146, 318n64
Weber, Max, 273
Weiner, Greg, 82
Whately, Thomas, 23
Whig (party), 7, 25
White, Alexander, 181, 215–16
WikiLeaks, 275
Wilentz, Sean, 89
Wilkes, John, 27–28, 297n25, 308n20
Williams, John, 210
Wilson, James, 84
Wingate, Paine, 184
Wolcott, Oliver, 212–13
women, 12, 45, 90, 116, 179–80, 235, 245, 288n45, 308n23, 319n75–319n77. *See also* gender
Wood, Gordon, 78, 83, 284n33

XYZ affair, 215, 219–20, 354n35. *See also* French dispatches

Yates, Robert, 87
Young, Alfred, 313n4